THE GENERAL ASSEMBLY
OF
THE UNITED NATIONS

A Study of Procedure and Practice

AUSTRALIA
The Law Book Co. of Australasia Pty Ltd.
Sydney : Melbourne : Brisbane

INDIA
N. M. Tripathi Private Ltd.
Bombay

NEW ZEALAND
Sweet & Maxwell (N.Z.) Ltd.
Wellington

PAKISTAN
Pakistan Law House
Karachi

U.S.A. AND CANADA
Frederick A. Praeger Inc.
New York

THE
GENERAL ASSEMBLY
OF THE
UNITED NATIONS

A Study of Procedure and Practice

By

SYDNEY D. BAILEY

Published under the auspices of
THE CARNEGIE ENDOWMENT FOR INTERNATIONAL PEACE

FREDERICK A. PRAEGER, *Publishers*
NEW YORK

BOOKS THAT MATTER

*First published in 1960
by Stevens & Sons Limited
of 11 New Fetter Lane
in the City of London
and printed in Great Britain
by Wembley Press Ltd.,
Perivale, Middlesex*

*Published in the United
States of America in 1961
by Frederick A. Praeger,
Inc., Publishers, 64 University Place, New York 3, N.Y.*

©

Stevens & Sons Limited, London
1960

CONTENTS

page

TABLES

vii

CHARTS

PREFACE

TO THE READER—I have undertaken a subject that I am very sensible requires one of more sufficiency than I am master of to treat it as, in truth, it deserves . . . but since bunglers may stumble upon the game as well as masters, though it belongs to the skilful to hunt and catch it, I hope this essay . . . may provoke abler pens to improve and perform the design with better judgment and success.[1]

WILLIAM PENN

Whenever a new institution of social and political co-operation is born, there are those who are sceptical. I have no doubt that some medieval Englishmen complained that Parliament was the fad of a few muddle-headed idealists. It had no real power to enforce its decisions; members talked too much; it wasted the tax-payers' money; it interfered in matters which were essentially within the jurisdiction of the counties; it was hamstrung by the royal veto.

I expect there were also a few enthusiastic supporters of Parliament, who would have killed it with kindness. They had infinite faith in its ability to solve problems, and when it was by-passed they did the medieval equivalent of writing to the newspapers.

Parliament was able to survive the scorn of the doubters and the zeal of the supporters for two main reasons. First, it was a necessary institution in the sense that if it had not evolved fortuitously, it would have been necessary to invent it. Secondly, it had the capacity to change.

The United Nations is a necessary institution, and it has managed to survive in our tumultuous world because it has been able to change. Its usefulness depends to a considerable extent on its capacity to change still further.

In the introduction to his annual report in 1959, Secretary-General Dag Hammarskjold insists that an organization for international co-operation on the basis of universality is essential, and he adds that the only practical question is whether an evolution of procedures should be envisaged in order to adapt the United Nations more adequately to the needs as experienced. The United Nations, he writes, is a living organism and has the necessary scope for continuous adaptation.[2]

---

[1] This quotation and those at the head of each Chapter are taken from *An Essay Towards the Present and Future Peace of Europe by the Establishment of an European Diet, Parliament, or Estates,* by William Penn, first published in 1693.
[2] General Assembly Official Records (G.A.O.R.): 14th Sess., 1959, Suppl. No. 1A (A/4132/Add.1), p. 2.

In this book I examine the working of the only principal organ of the United Nations of which all Member States of the Organization are permanent members. This organ—the General Assembly—has been growing in importance and changing in function. Many of the merits of contemporary diplomatic processes, and also some of the disadvantages, can be seen in exaggerated form in the General Assembly.

I am concerned primarily with procedure rather than with politics. Although good results cannot be guaranteed by good procedure, they can certainly be prevented by bad procedure. Good procedure is a lubricant rather than a fuel; it does not drive the machine, but its absence soon brings the machine to a halt, and in extreme cases can cause irreparable damage. I remember hearing Mrs. Eleanor Roosevelt, at a dinner to celebrate the tenth anniversary of the Universal Declaration of Human Rights, express the opinion that most people in public life underestimate the importance of good procedure. Recalling her experience as a delegate to the United Nations, Mrs. Roosevelt said that there had been occasions when good procedure " meant the difference between success and failure."

Procedure should be a servant and not a master. One of the requirements of a good chairman is that he has one blind eye, and knows when not to see. There are occasions in the history of any living organization when the formal procedure should be forgotten.

In order to forget the formal procedure, however, one must first know what it is. In the case of the General Assembly of the United Nations, the formal procedure is derived from three main sources. There is, in the first place, the United Nations Charter itself, which cannot easily be amended. Certain provisions of the Charter, such as Article 9 relating to the composition of the Assembly and Article 18 relating to voting, determine part of the procedure of the Assembly.

Secondly, there are the Rules of Procedure, including annexes; these Rules correspond to the standing orders or rules of order of parliamentary bodies.[3] The first annex to the Rules of Procedure consists of " Recommendations and Suggestions " of a committee on procedure, which were approved by the General Assembly in 1949. The second annex consists of " Recommendations " of the Assembly

---

[3] The Rules of Procedure now in force are based on a draft prepared by the Executive Committee of the Preparatory Commission of the United Nations in 1945. This draft was revised by the Preparatory Commission and approved by the Assembly during the first part of the first session (1946) on a provisional basis. The Provisional Rules were amended by General Assembly resolutions 2, 15, 17, 73, 77, 87 and 88 of the first session. They were amended during the second session by resolutions 116 and 173, and the word " Provisional " was dropped from the title. The Rules have been amended since the second session by resolutions 262 (III), 362 (IV), 377A (V), 475 (V), 689B (VII), 791 (VIII), 844 (IX), 1104 (XI) and 1192 (XII). See Appendix C.

on certain legal and drafting questions, together with excerpts from the report of a special committee of the Assembly which had considered such questions. The third annex consists of six Special Rules, approved by the Assembly in 1954, on the procedure for the examination of reports and petitions relating to the territory of South West Africa. These Special Rules have a particular importance since Special Rule F of Annex III represents the only explicit determination by the Assembly that a particular category of question is " important," within the meaning of Article 18 (2) of the Charter, and should therefore be among the matters decided by a two-thirds majority of the Members present and voting.

Certain resolutions of the Assembly itself form a third source of procedure. Resolution 264 (III), for example, determined the conditions under which a State which is a party to the Statute of the International Court but is not a Member of the United Nations may participate in the election of judges of the Court. Resolution 1192 (XII) confirmed what was already the practice regarding the regional distribution of chairmanships of Main Committees of the Assembly, and an annex to the same resolution set forth a pattern of representation of Vice-Presidents of the Assembly.

Supplementing the formal and written procedure are the accepted practices and precedents. These may be usages which are now generally observed in intergovernmental assemblies, or which have been implicitly accepted by the General Assembly, or which have become established as a result of express decision or presidential ruling. Examples of usages which are now accepted in the United Nations Assembly are:

Representatives of States which are permanent members of the Security Council are not elected to the presidency of the Assembly.

At the beginning of each session of the Assembly, there takes place in plenary meeting a General Debate in which heads of delegations express the views of their countries on matters of common concern to the United Nations.

Representatives in plenary meetings of the Assembly speak from the rostrum, while in committees they speak from their places.

Delegations sit in the English alphabetical order of the names of Member States.

The Main Committee of the Assembly concerned with administrative and budgetary matters considers the budget estimates by means of two consecutive " readings."

Sometimes the Assembly codifies practices and incorporates them in the Rules of Procedure. During the second session, for example, the following practices were formally codified:

> The phrase "Members present and voting," which is used in Article 18 of the Charter, means Members casting an affirmative or negative vote; Members abstaining are considered as not voting (now Rules 88 and 127).
>
> During the course of a debate, the presiding officer may announce the list of speakers and, with the consent of the Assembly or committee, declare the list closed (now part of Rules 75 and 116).
>
> If a Vice-President of the Assembly finds it necessary to be absent during a meeting of the General Committee, he may designate a member of his delegation as his substitute; a Chairman of a Main Committee shall, in case of absence, designate the Vice-Chairman of the Committee as his substitute (now part of Rule 39).

The relation of procedure to practice is analogous to that between statute law and common law. However, since reports of procedural discussions are often not included in the official records of the Assembly, knowledge of what really is the practice or what really are the precedents depends to a considerable extent on oral tradition. It is here that the role of the Secretariat is important. Sir Alfred Zimmern, writing of the League, commented that a major source of the power of the League Secretariat was in the domain of procedure.

> . . . knowledge of "the tricks of the trade" is particularly formidable in the international sphere where the members of the Committee or larger body concerned are none of them doing their work according to familiar rules and are for the most part labouring under a certain sense of helplessness. Moreover there is always a proportion of new-comers who are particularly susceptible to the spell of the habitué.[4]

Chapters 1 and 2 of this book deal with the political background against which the General Assembly operates. Chapters 3, 4 and 5 examine the opening of the Assembly, the appointment of the Credentials Committee, the election of officers, the General Debate, and the responsibilities of the Assembly in connection with items proposed for inclusion in the agenda. Chapters 6 and 7 describe two phases of "parliamentary diplomacy," public debate and the means by which the Assembly reaches conclusions; as will be made clear

---

[4] *The League of Nations and the Rule of Law, 1918–1935* (London: Macmillan, 1936), p. 473.

later, these overt processes are accompanied by private negotiations. Chapters 8 and 9 are concerned with certain of the electoral responsibilities of the Assembly. Chapter 10 comprises a case study of a particular question with which the Assembly has dealt. The final Chapter represents certain tentative conclusions and suggestions.

Before I began to write this book, I had decided that I would not examine possible amendments to the Charter. In part this was because it seemed necessary to limit the subject-matter of the book; it also arose from my conviction that difficulties the United Nations has encountered are not primarily caused by defects in the Charter. My conviction in this respect has become stronger while I have been writing the book. It is easy to create an alibi by blaming the Charter for the follies of one's own or some other government. I have been impressed not only by the flexibility of action that is possible within the present Charter, but also by the further evolution that can take place.

Charters are worked by people, and I have been struck by the decisive importance in United Nations affairs of such personal qualities as honour, probity, integrity, tolerance and fair-mindedness. The role a Member State plays in the United Nations is determined to a considerable extent by the quality of its representatives. Although problems in international relations may be aggravated by the intrusion of moral considerations where they do not belong, it can hardly be denied that such problems are often eased by the personal moral qualities of those who must deal with them.

In writing of the activities of Member States, it is tempting to use certain shorthand expressions such as " Afghanistan proposed that . . . ," " Bulgaria took the same view . . . ," or " Colombia greatly regretted . . . ." It would, admittedly, be more exact to write " the representative of Afghanistan proposed that . . . ," " the Chairman of the Bulgarian delegation took the same view . . . ," or " the Colombian Minister for External Relations expressed great regret . . . ." To have adopted this practice throughout the book would have cluttered up the text for the sake of unnecessary exactitude, and I have therefore not hesitated to use briefer if less accurate expressions.

SYDNEY D. BAILEY,
February 1960

ACKNOWLEDGMENTS

A BOOK of this kind is a collective effort, though I am responsible for the present version. Most of the cost of the study was met by a grant from the Rockefeller Foundation. Dean Rusk, President of the Foundation, and Kenneth W. Thompson, Director of the Social Sciences Division, took a personal as well as an official interest in the study. To them, and to the trustees of the Foundation, I wish to express my deep gratitude.

The research and writing was done under the auspices of the Carnegie Endowment for International Peace, and the Endowment also made a financial contribution to the project. I can think of no institution which would have provided a more congenial setting for the study. To the trustees and officers of the Endowment, and to all my colleagues on the staff, I express my appreciation. I am particularly grateful for the guidance and help I received from James T. Shotwell, President Emeritus of the Endowment; Joseph E. Johnson, President; Lawrence S. Finkelstein, Vice-President; and to Charles Burton Marshall, Anne P. Simons, and Anne Winslow.

During the course of the study I was able to obtain factual information regarding the procedure and practice of the General Assembly from members of the Secretariat of the United Nations. The fact that I have not expressed my appreciation to these persons by name does not mean that I am not grateful for their help. The Secretariat always wears a cloak of anonymity.

At an early stage in the study, two informal meetings were held at the Carnegie Endowment International Center to discuss a paper which I had prepared on the role of the General Assembly in contemporary diplomacy. These off-the-record discussions were of great help in identifying fruitful lines of inquiry, and I would like to thank the following who were among those who took part in one or both of these meetings: Harold Beeley, C.M.G., C.B.E., Frederick H. Boland, Charles D. Cook, Sir Claude Corea, K.B.E., H. Field Haviland, Jr., James N. Hyde, Philip C. Jessup, Per Naevdal, O. Frederick Nolde, C. S. A. Ritchie, and Mrs. Agda Rössel.

Many of the matters of procedure and practice with which this book deals are discussed and decided in private conversations outside the formal United Nations meetings. These discussions do not form part of the public record, but some knowledge of them is essential to an understanding of the way the General Assembly works. I could not have completed this study had I not been the recipient of much useful information and good advice. I wish to thank all those who helped me in this way, and I trust that my discretion has matched their candour. To some who do not wish to be mentioned by name, and to the following, I record my great appreciation: U. A. Ansari, F. S. Arkhurst, P. W. J. Buxton, Jorge Castañeda, Dário Castro Alves, Sir Andrew Cohen, K.C.M.G., K.C.V.O., C.B.E., Mohamed Fathalla El-Khatib, W. V. J. Evans, C.M.G., M.B.E., W. D. Forsyth, O.B.E., Benjamin Gerig, John G. Hadwen, John W. Holmes, J. D. L. Hood, C.B.E., Masayoshi Kakitsubo, Johan Kaufmann, K. T. Kelly, M. R. Kidron, Charles T. O. King, Manfred Lachs, Arthur S. Lall, Omar Loutfi, Jacek Machowski, Charles Mâlik, Mircea Malitza, Jerzy Michalowski, Abdel Karim Mirghani, A. K. Mitra, A. R. Moore, Geoffrey S. Murray, Djura Nincic, Conor Cruise O'Brien, Richard F. Pedersen, A. B. Perera, R. Q. Quentin-Baxter, Shabtai Rosenne, Aleksander W. Rudzinski, Carlos Salamanca, E. L. C. Schiff, Joseph J. Sisco, Luc Smolderen and Bredo Stabell.

I wish to thank the Board of Editors of *International Organization* for permission to reprint certain paragraphs of an article on the future composition of the Trusteeship Council, which was published in that journal (Vol. XIII, No. 3).

S. D. B.

A NOTE ON UNITED NATIONS DOCUMENTS

I ONCE submitted an article to a scholarly quarterly published in a country which it is not necessary to mention here. The editor accepted the article, but asked me to " insert a few footnotes." I re-read the article several times, but for the life of me I was unable to see where footnotes were needed. I wrote to the editor asking if he would indicate where footnotes would improve the article. He replied that this was my responsibility, not his. The policy of the journal was to publish articles with footnotes, and he hoped I would co-operate by adapting my article to conform with editorial policy.

On the day I received this letter, I came across a reference in a book to the creation of the world. The author, as if to cite additional evidence that the world did in fact exist, had inserted as a footnote " *Genesis* 1:1."

Footnotes can be pretentious and distracting, and I wish there were fewer in this book. I have, however, accepted the advice of those who know more about the matter than I do and given in foot-notes the United Nations documents I have quoted or referred to in the text.

A brief explanation is needed about the symbols used. Verbatim or summary records of meetings of the General Assembly, the Main Committees, and the General Committee are referred to as G.A.O.R. (General Assembly Official Records), followed by the number of the session (whether a regular session, a special session, or an emergency special session); a note as to whether it was a plenary or committee meeting and, if a committee, its name or number; the number and date of the meeting; and the page or paragraph number.

With regard to the fourteenth session (15 September - 13 December 1959), all of the final printed records had not been issued when this book went to press. I have, accordingly, referred in a number of cases to the provisional mimeographed records. The symbols of the provisional records are as follows, in each case followed by the number and date of the meeting:

General Committee — A/BUR/SR . . .
Plenary Meetings of the Assembly — A/PV . . .
First Committee — A/C.1/PV . . .
Special Political Committee — A/SPC/SR . . .
Committees Two to Six — A/C. (number of Committee) /SR . . .

The resolutions of the General Assembly have been numbered consecutively and are cited as General Assembly Res., followed by the number of the resolution, with the number of the session given in parenthesis in roman numerals.

Most of the documents issued in connection with the Assembly have as a symbol A/ and a number; some of these documents are issued as supplements or annexes to the official records of the General Assembly.

The draft Rules of Procedure recommended by the Preparatory Commission of the United Nations (PC/20, pp. 8–18; A/4) and adopted on a provisional basis during the first session of the General Assembly are referred to in this book as the Provisional Rules of Procedure. The Rules of Procedure now in force are issued under symbol A/3660 and Corr. 1 (see Appendix C).

In cases other than those already mentioned, I have given the title as well as the symbol of any United Nations document cited, either in the text or in a footnote.

The Rules of Procedure provide that representatives may vote " yes," " no," or " abstention." There is no proxy voting, so that Members who are absent cannot participate in the voting; Members who are absent are permitted to indicate at a later stage how they would have voted had they been present when the vote was taken, although such indication does not alter the result of the vote. Sometimes the records of the Assembly indicate that a Member was present but did not vote. Throughout this book, the result of a vote, other than a ballot, is given by means of three figures separated by dashes; those in favour (voting " yes "), those against (voting " no "), and those abstaining. A draft resolution on the financing of the United Nations Emergency Force was approved by the Assembly on 5 December 1959, by 49 in favour, 9 against, with 21 abstentions; the result of this vote would be given as 49–9–21, it being implied that three Members were either absent or were present but did not participate in the voting.

CHAPTER 1

CONTEMPORARY DIPLOMACY AND THE UNITED NATIONS

> The advantage that justice has upon war is seen by the success of embassies, that so often prevent war by hearing the pleas and memorials of justice in the hands and mouths of the wronged party. . . . [But] men seek their wills by war rather than peace. . . . Though I must needs say the remedy is almost ever worse than the disease: the aggressors seldom getting what they seek, or performing, if they prevail, what they promised. . . . For that which prevents a civil war in a nation is that which may prevent it abroad, *viz.*, justice. . . . Now if the sovereign princes . . . would . . . agree to meet by their stated deputies in a . . . parliament, and there establish rules of justice for sovereign princes to observe one to another; and thus to meet yearly. . . . For it saves the great expense that frequent and splendid embassies require, and all their appendages of spies and intelligence, which in the most prudent governments have devoured mighty sums of money; and that not without some immoral practices also; such as corrupting of servants to betray their masters, by revealing their secrets.
>
> WILLIAM PENN

IT is often said, and rightly, that the United Nations supplements the traditional processes of diplomacy. The present Secretary-General of the United Nations has described the Organization as " an admittedly imperfect but indispensable instrument of nations in working for a peaceful evolution toward a more just and secure world order." [1] This instrument, while indispensable, differs greatly from the traditional diplomacy it supplements, and to some extent replaces. Traditional diplomacy, during the three centuries ending in 1919, was predicated on the assumption that everything important happened in Europe or was done by Europeans; it was based on the principle of the inequality of States; and it assumed that all negotiation, whether regarding the matrimonial affairs of sovereigns or the annexation of territory, should be conducted in private.

I cannot examine here all the factors that have contributed to the growth of new diplomatic institutions and methods. I will, however, refer briefly to those factors that have a particular relevance for the United Nations.

---

[1] Dag Hammarskjold, " The Vital Role of the United Nations in a Diplomacy of Reconciliation," *United Nations Review*, Vol. IV, No. 11 (May 1958), p. 7.

The rapid development of science and technology has had important effects on diplomacy. The ease of communication in the modern world has enabled governments to learn almost instantly of troublesome incidents abroad which, in former times, would have cleared themselves up before all but a few could do anything about it. " So much becomes unimportant," Dean Acheson has written, " if one does not know about it for months or years." [2] Moreover, it is not only information that can be transmitted rapidly to any part of the globe; foreign ministers and heads of government can travel almost as fast. John Foster Dulles, during his six years as United States Secretary of State, travelled half a million miles abroad and visited my own country a dozen times. The speed of travel, which makes possible the high-level diplomacy of political leaders, has changed the role of professional diplomats.

It is often said that the world has shrunk and history has been accelerated. These phenomena have undoubtedly occurred, but a distinguished French writer has suggested that a different process was at work in Europe during the first decade of the atomic age. History was retarded, leading to " diplomatic immobilism."

How are problems to be settled when neither force nor the threat of force is used? Time is needed, more time than in any other periods of history when there was no hesitation about coercing the weak, when the fragmentation of the diplomatic field allowed the full exploitation of a local superiority.[3]

There is another respect in which scientific and technological development has added to the difficulty of dealing with diplomatic problems. Every generation tends to consider that the problems it faces are uniquely grave; ours is no exception. No doubt there have been other times in history when wise men considered that civilization was at stake, but the undeniable fact about the contemporary international situation is that mistakes are more costly than they were. Since the dawn of history, men have fought for the things they valued and have progressively become more efficient at fighting, but a stage of diminishing returns has now been reached. As weapons have become more destructive, their use has become more risky. Until our day, it was possible to assume that if the diplomats failed, the generals could take over; to regard war as a political instrument, a continuation of diplomacy by other means. Today war is anachronistic and self-defeating. Some of today's difficulties, to be sure, are the

[2] *Power and Diplomacy* (Cambridge: Harvard Univ. Press, London: Oxford Univ. Press, Toronto: Saunders, 1958), p. 126.

[3] Raymond Aron, *On War*, translated by Terence Kilmartin (Copyright 1958 by Martin Secker and Warburg, Ltd. Reprinted by permission of Doubleday & Co., Inc.), p. 20.

consequence of yesterday's mistakes; others are the consequence of today's successes.

It is difficult for the layman to understand the scale or implications of contemporary scientific development. The number of scientists in the United States doubled between 1950 and 1956. Men have great faith in the ability of science to solve our problems. Yet the desert, which could blossom as the rose, has been a place for testing devilish weapons. " We prepare for war like precocious giants," said Lester B. Pearson in his Nobel Peace Prize lecture, " and for peace like retarded pygmies." [4]

Political changes throughout the world have affected the environment in which diplomacy operates. Europe's long-standing claim to centricity has been challenged. The Bolshevik Revolution in Russia in 1917, and the more recent extension of the Soviet system in Eastern Europe and Asia, have brought to power in a large and populous mass of territory people who are sharply opposed to the aristocratic Europe of yesterday. The peoples of the newly independent and still-emerging countries of Asia and Africa are no less opposed to European imperialism. The United States was largely peopled by refugees from European oppression. Europe is not now the political centre of the world.

The two colossi of today's bipolarized world, the United States and the Soviet Union, have been in rebellion against the wickedness of old-fashioned diplomacy. Wilson and Lenin, with equal fervour, denounced secret covenants, asserted the principle of self-determination, and appealed to the peoples of Europe over the heads of governments.

Ideology has intruded into diplomacy, so that our age is comparable to the period of the Crusades or the religious struggles of Europe. We are constantly asked to choose sides, to declare ourselves for or against communism, colonialism or constitutional democracy. These are important questions, but in international affairs they often cloak the real issues. Though the conflicts of the cold war have been aggravated by ideological differences, many of these conflicts would have been there to plague us if ideology had not entered the picture. George Bernard Shaw, writing when Russia was still governed by Tsar Nicholas II, based his case for an international organization to prevent war on the assumption (which at the time was regarded as slightly subversive) that international problems after the First World War would not differ essentially from those that had existed before, and indeed had caused, that war.

[4] *Diplomacy in the Nuclear Age* (Cambridge: Harvard Univ. Press, 1959), p. 106.

Russia will still burn to protect the Balkans . . . to cling to Poland like a big brother, and to pick up more of the White Man's Burden in Asia than the other Powers may think healthy for her, or than India, for instance, may be disposed to cast on any shoulders but her own.[5]

Russia's strategic interests are affected but little by the ideology of her rulers. Raymond Aron has insisted that

Whatever her regime, whether Communist or Czarist, Russia was bound to find herself one of the two great world powers after the defeat of Germany and she was bound to regard the United States as a rival. The incompatibility of the Russian and American ideologies reinforced an opposition that was implicit in the classic game of diplomacy.[6]

Yet States of differing ideologies can enjoy friendly relations. Since breaking with the Cominform, Yugoslavia has developed normal relations with the capitalist and semi-capitalist States of the Western camp, though Tito remains a Communist and Milovan Djilas is in prison.

The strongly ideological character of the contemporary world has retarded the progress towards reliance on the rule of law in international affairs. The present Secretary-General of the United Nations has drawn attention to this matter on several occasions, especially in the introductions to his annual reports. He has pointed out that nations have, for the most part, been slow to submit their juridical disputes to the International Court of Justice; and that fewer than half of the parties to the Statute of the Court have accepted the Court's compulsory jurisdiction. Mr. Hammarskjold has repeatedly pleaded for the greatest possible restriction of the sphere where sheer strength is an argument and for the extension of the area ruled by considerations of law and justice.[7] Although there is some evidence of renewed interest in the role of law in international affairs, one cannot dissent from the conclusions of Lincoln Bloomfield that

One of the most curious and depressing features of modern international society has been the steady decline in the role played by law and legal method in the settlement of disputes among nations. It is curious because this decline has taken place in a period of unparalleled construction of international institutions and frameworks within which law was expected to play an increasingly dominant part.[8]

But although international law has not played as significant a role as the founders of the League of Nations and the United Nations had

---

[5] Bernard Shaw in L. S. Woolf, *International Government* (New York: Brentano, 1916), pp. xi–xii.   [6] *Op. cit.*, pp. 121–122.

[7] *The Annual Report of the Secretary-General on the Work of the Organization*, in G.A.O.R.: 8th Sess., 1953, Suppl. No. 1 (A/2404), pp. xi–xii; G.A.O.R.: 10th Sess., 1955, Suppl. No. 1 (A/2911), p. xii; and *Introduction to the Annual Report of the Secretary-General on the Work of the Organization*, G.A.O.R.: 12th Sess., 1957, Suppl. No. 1 (A/3594/Add. 1), pp. 4–5.

[8] "Law, Politics and International Disputes," *International Conciliation*, No. 516 (Jan. 1958), p. 257.

hoped, there has been a remarkable proliferation of organs for international co-operation, particularly to help the less privileged people
of the world; slaves, refugees, victims of war or natural disaster,
the homeless and the hungry, the ignorant and the diseased. Such
humanitarian action is not wholly disinterested; governments may
act from moral principles, but they are rarely moved by compassion.
It is realized, however, that bad economic and social conditions breed
the instability and discontent which so often lead to international
tension and trouble. The urge to save succeeding generations from
the scourge of war requires not only the concept of the fire brigade,
by which the flames of conflict are extinguished; it requires also
vigilant efforts to remove the causes of fire.

The contraction of the world and the rise of democracy during
the past century and a half has meant that every crisis is now everybody's crisis. It is not only that foreign offices know and respond
to each development in the international situation; public opinion,
too, knows much of what is happening.

Foreign relations are no longer, as in earlier times, an esoteric business
involving communication among small professional groups in the various
foreign offices expert in the peripheral relations of sovereigns. They
involve assemblies and populaces. Their communications consist no
longer mainly of stately messages addressed from governments to other
governments. They involve torrents of words addressed by governments
to their own populations and to the populations of foreign nations and
designed for the eyes and ears not merely of a few professionals but of
masses of people.

A pronouncement made in one major capital may reverberate
throughout the world in a day. A crisis of government in any quarter
may become a matter of instant knowledge everywhere.[9]

There may be millions of people who do not know the difference
between ECOSOC and UNESCO, between the European Common
Market and the European Free Trade Association, between the United
Arab Republic and the League of Arab States; and yet these same
millions may have strong, if vague, convictions about such questions
as the status of Berlin, the border dispute between India and China,
or whether the people of some African territory are ready for
independence.

Moreover, parliaments in the democratic countries participate in
the formulation of foreign policy. Wilson's experience in connection
with the League of Nations, the opposition in Britain to the Hoare–
Laval Pact, and (to come to a contemporary question) the widespread
anxiety expressed in the parliaments of many countries about the
effects of testing nuclear weapons, are examples of the influence of

9 Charles Burton Marshall, *The Limits of Foreign Policy* (New York: Henry Holt,
1954), p. 64.

public and parliamentary opinion on the emphasis or direction of foreign policy.

Public opinion is not easily evaluated. Those who are most vociferous in any country are not necessarily most wise or most representative. Foreign policy (including its military aspects) is the one subject on which governments often reach decisions on the basis of information that is not available to the general public. Because the public does not have information which a government may regard as decisive, and because laymen are necessarily given to over-simplification, public opinion is sometimes little more than a collection of slogans.

John Foster Dulles was once asked at a Press conference how much weight should be given to public opinion in connection with United States policy in the Far East, and his comments revealed the predicament in which many foreign ministers must find themselves.

> You see, this isn't a normal situation. We are having a very critical negotiation with the Chinese Communists. They are pushing and probing to find out whether we are weak or whether we are strong. . . . The letters that have come in [to the State Department] are interesting and useful but also difficult to evaluate. . . . I think public opinion is always important because obviously you cannot carry out effectively a public policy without the support of public opinion. . . . Most of the letters are written by people who don't want to have a war, that say, " Let's not get into a war." Well, I can assure you that there is nobody that is less anxious to have a war than President Eisenhower is. The question of how to keep out of war is a much more complicated question. . . .[10]

Alexis de Tocqueville, in an oft-quoted passage, maintained that it was especially in the conduct of foreign relations that democracies were decidedly inferior to other forms of government.

> Foreign politics demand scarcely any of those qualities which are peculiar to a democracy; they require, on the contrary, the perfect use of almost all those in which it is deficient. . . . [A] democracy can only with great difficulty regulate the details of an important undertaking, persevere in a fixed design, and work out its execution in spite of serious obstacles. It cannot combine its measures with secrecy or await their consequences with patience.[11]

These reflections have surely been echoed by many foreign ministers.

Public opinion tends to reduce international problems to the simplest terms: to be for or against appeasement, unconditional surrender or the liberation of colonial peoples. And the public in the democratic West seems on the whole to prefer the known hazards

10 U.S. Department of State *Bulletin*, Vol. XXXIX, No. 1008 (20 Oct. 1958), p. 598.
11 *Democracy in America.* English translation ed. Phillips Bradley (New York: Knopf, 1954), Vol. I, p. 243; abridgment ed. Henry Steele Commager (London: Oxford Univ. Press, 1946), p. 161.

of the *status quo* to the unknown hazards of change. It is usually easy to demonstrate that to change a policy is dangerous, but it is sometimes equally or more dangerous not to change a policy. In an imperfect world, there is no policy that has no risks.

Foreign policy partakes of the imperfections of all politics. Though a government may willingly affirm its support for certain general principles of international conduct, its foreign policy consists in large measure of improvised responses to external events which in some degree affect the national interest. These responses may be based in part on consistent standards, but perhaps the outstanding fact about them is that they are almost always compromises; compromises between conflicting principles, compromises between different political and social pressures within a country, compromises between various departmental interests within a government, compromises between the need to avoid injuring too severely the interest of hostile or potentially hostile States on the one hand and the need to placate friendly or potentially friendly States on the other hand. In this sense, foreign policies tend to be impure, questions are rarely decided on their intrinsic merits, and few public statements of foreign policy can be taken entirely at face value.

Diplomacy has been described as a process of seeking international compromises out of national compromises. A communiqué from a diplomatic conference or a resolution from an intergovernmental agency may often seem vague, platitudinous and evasive, but this is inevitable. What is left out is often more important than what is put in. Moreover, the words that are public may represent only the visible part of an iceberg, of which the larger and more significant part is hidden from view. A resolution of the General Assembly may be much less important than the fact that an issue has been publicly debated; and the public debate may have been much less important than the fact that the issue was privately discussed.

It was never intended that the United Nations should disavow the principle of privacy in negotiation, nor was it intended that its own procedures for public debate should be a substitute for negotiation. The insidious lure of public debate, with the temptation to establish before the world the guilt of others, with the tendency to dramatization and exaggeration, is not wholly harmful. It may, on occasion, release tension by enabling States to verbalize their anxieties. But public debate is no substitute for negotiation and is sometimes a bad prelude to it. Lester B. Pearson, a former President of the United Nations General Assembly, put the matter this way:

The United Nations is a place where we can meet either to settle problems or to make settlement more difficult. It is a place where we can try to find collective solutions, or one which we can use to get support and publicity for purely national solutions. It is a place where we can talk to each other with a view to securing general agreement, or to television and radio audiences in order to explain that disagreement is the fault of somebody else. In any event, whatever face the United Nations now presents to the public is enlarged to alarming proportions by all the media of information which now carry our words, our attitudes, even our appearances, to the ends of the earth.

But the United Nations has, or it should have, a private as well as a public face. There should be opportunities here for other than public appearances. . . .

It is, of course, essential that all free peoples should know and understand the great issues of policy which may mean life or death to them. But it is not essential, as I see it—indeed it is often harmful—for the negotiation of policy always to be conducted in glass houses. . . .[12]

" PARLIAMENTARY DIPLOMACY "

There was no moment in time when traditional diplomacy was dramatically cast aside and something new put in its place. Many of the methods of traditional diplomacy are still used. But within the past fifty years new institutional methods have been developed to help in managing the relations among nations. The League of Nations and the United Nations, and the related technical agencies, have performed mainly new tasks in mainly new ways.

In point of time, the first important change in diplomatic method was the wide acceptance of the idea of public debate of diplomatic questions. Arthur H. Vandenberg called the General Assembly " truly the town meeting of tomorrow's world." [13] The same idea had been expressed more eloquently by another great American.

The real underlying conception of the assembly . . . is that it is the forum of opinion. . . . It is the debating body; it is the body where the thought of the little nation along with the thought of the big nation is brought to bear upon . . . those matters which affect the good understanding between nations upon which the peace of the world depends; where the stifled voice of humanity is at last to be heard, where nations that have borne the unspeakable sufferings of the ages that must have seemed to them like aeons will find voice and expression, where the moral judgment of mankind can sway the opinion of the world.

The assembly was created in order that anybody that purposed anything wrong should be subjected to the awkward circumstance that everybody could talk about it.[14]

This was how Woodrow Wilson described the League Assembly.

12 G.A.O.R.: 8th Sess., 441st Plenary Mtg., 23 Sept. 1953, paras. 16–18.
13 *The Private Papers of Senator Vandenberg*, ed. Arthur H. Vandenberg, Jr., with collaboration of Joe Alex Morris (Boston: Houghton Mifflin, London: Gollancz, Toronto: Allen, 1952), p. 190.
14 *The Messages and Papers of Woodrow Wilson* (New York: The Review of Reviews Corp., 1924), Vol. II, pp. 985, 1118–1119.

It is relatively easy to pass from the idea of public debate to the idea that the debate should be terminated by voting on a draft resolution. The use of voting in the United Nations symbolizes the principle of the juridical equality of States, though this principle is not consistently applied. Whatever view one may take of the rule of unanimity of the five Great Powers in the Security Council, it is clearly a discriminatory rule. If States were really equal, all or none would have the veto.

In the General Assembly of the United Nations, however, the formal principle of equality is applied. All Member States have one vote.[15] If two States are created where one existed before, as happened in the case of India and Pakistan, the successor States have one vote each. If two States merge, as when Egypt and Syria joined to form the United Arab Republic, the new State has one vote.

Though all nations of the world have an equal stake in the maintenance of international peace, all nations do not have an equal interest in every particular question that arises.

Equality is all very well [H. A. L. Fisher wrote of the League in 1921] so long as it is accompanied by an equal sense of responsibility—but it is just this equal sense of responsibility which it is difficult if not impossible to ensure. . . . Let us assume that the question to be decided is whether or no Georgia [now a constituent republic of the U.S.S.R.] should be admitted to the League. However seriously minded Uruguay may be, she can hardly be expected to approach the consideration of the problem as seriously as Great Britain, for Uruguay is well aware that the admission of Georgia cannot conceivably involve her in practical responsibilities, whereas Great Britain knows that a vote for the admission of Georgia might in certain contingencies very well entail a British naval expedition to Batum.[16]

The achievement of sovereignty and United Nations membership by a score of countries in Asia and Africa which were formerly under colonial rule, and the crystallization of regional or ideological *blocs* and groups, have had important effects on voting. A group's voting power in the General Assembly may bear little relation to its military strength, economic resources or population. Table 1 shows the percentage of seats (and thus of votes) in the General Assembly, the percentage of the regular budget of the United Nations, and the percentage of population, of various regional groups.[17] It is interesting to note that only one regional group—Western Europe—has approximately the same percentage in each column.

---

[15] The Soviet Union is in an exceptional situation in that the Byelorussian and Ukrainian Soviet Socialist Republics have separate membership in the Organization.

[16] *An International Experiment* (Oxford: Clarendon Press, 1921), p. 28.

[17] I have classified Member States in accordance with the method explained in Chap. 2.

TABLE 1

Regional Distribution of Member States

	Percentage of		
	Seats in General Assembly	Regular U.N. Budget*	Population**
Latin America	24·39	4·89	6·68
Asia and Africa, excluding China, Israel, South Africa and Turkey	34·15	7·95	32·09
Eastern Europe, including Yugoslavia	12·20	19·44	10·78†
Western Europe, including Turkey	20·73	24·22	20·44
Older Commonwealth countries	4·88	5·88	·16
Israel	1·22	·14	·07
China	1·22	5·01	23·57††
United States	1·22	32·51	6·21

* This totals 100·04 per cent. as Guinea's assessment is in addition to the scale of assessments of 100 per cent. authorized during the thirteenth session of the General Assembly.

** Excluding overseas dependencies and States not Members of the United Nations.

† The population of the Soviet Union includes Byelorussian S.S.R. and Ukrainian S.S.R.

†† Continental China and Taiwan (Formosa).

The only alternative to equality of voting is inequality of voting, which would require that each State should be given a number of votes determined by such factors as population, area and financial contribution to the budget of the United Nations. It is not difficult to devise systems of weighted voting (such systems are, in fact, used in some intergovernmental organizations), but I question whether any of them are practicable at the present time.

It is sometimes said that the system of one vote for one nation . . . and the consequent preponderance of votes by the middle and smaller powers, damages the usefulness of the United Nations. . . . It is certainly not a perfect system, but is there any proposal for weighted voting that would not have even greater defects?[18]

It should, in any case, be emphasized that a sense of international responsibility is not a monopoly of powerful, rich or large countries. Time and again in the affairs of the United Nations, medium and small Powers have played a decisive role in efforts to preserve or restore peace.

I do not believe that the small nations have less of an understanding of central political problems of concern to the whole world than those who are more closely related to them and who traditionally wield greater

[18] Dag Hammarskjold, " The Vital Role of the United Nations in a Diplomacy of Reconciliation," *United Nations Review*, Vol. IV, No. 11 (May 1958), p. 7. For further discussion of the question of weighted voting, *cf.* John Foster Dulles, *War or Peace* (New York: Macmillan, 1957), pp. 191–194; *Strengthening the United Nations*, Report of the Commission to Study the Organization of Peace (New York: Harper, 1957), pp. 227–232.

power in the international councils. For that reason, I cannot . . . share the view of those who regard the possible influence of smaller Powers as a danger. . . .[19]

It is the practice of public debate, followed by voting, which has given to so much of contemporary multilateral diplomacy its " parliamentary " character, yet the General Assembly is not a parliament. In the parliaments of those countries where the democratic tradition is firmly entrenched, sharp differences of opinion can safely be revealed and even exaggerated because the parties tacitly accept that politics is a game which should be played according to certain rules; the issues may be important, but disagreement is unlikely to lead to mortal danger. The situation is different in international politics: the rules themselves are often in question, and disagreement can be disastrous. Most national legislatures operate within precisely defined limits, geographical and constitutional; the limits within which the General Assembly operates are blurred and, to some extent, changing. Most national legislatures function in relation to a known political executive which exercises leadership; the leadership in the General Assembly changes from issue to issue, and there is no political executive comparable to a national cabinet. When national legislatures resort to voting, it is normally to resolve a difference of opinion; a vote in the General Assembly on a contentious political question often reveals and emphasizes, rather than resolves, a difference of opinion.

Sir Harold Nicolson has suggested that these new methods of diplomacy, which are symbolized by public debate and voting, developed from the belief that what had worked well in internal affairs ought to work well in external affairs.

It was not the telephone that, from 1919 onwards, brought about the transition from the old diplomacy to the new. It was the belief that it was possible to apply to the conduct of *external* affairs, the ideas and practices which, in the conduct of *internal* affairs, had for generations been regarded as the essentials of liberal democracy.[20]

Whether or not one accepts this as the sole explanation of a complex development, it is surely significant that increasingly there have come into use in international affairs a number of expressions derived from domestic politics, such as " a democratic foreign policy," " the legislative power of the General Assembly " and " parliamentary diplomacy."

The term " parliamentary diplomacy " was coined by Dean Rusk, President of the Rockefeller Foundation and formerly a high official

---

[19] Press Conference by the Secretary-General at U.N. headquarters. Note to Correspondents, No. 1983, 30 Apr. 1959.
[20] *The Evolution of the Diplomatic Method* (New York: Macmillan, London: Constable, Toronto: Longmans, 1954), p. 84.

of the United States State Department, to describe a form of multi-lateral negotiation involving the following factors:

First, a continuing organization with interest and responsibilities which are broader than the specific items that happen to appear upon the agenda at any particular time—in other words, more than a traditional international conference called to cover specific agenda. Second, regular public debate exposed to the media of mass communication and in touch, therefore, with public opinions around the globe. Third, rules of procedure which govern the process of debate and which are themselves subject to tactical manipulation to advance or oppose a point of view. And lastly, formal conclusions, ordinarily expressed in resolution, which are reached by majority votes of some description, on a simple or two-thirds majority or based upon a financial contribution or economic stake —some with and some without a veto. Typically, we are talking about the United Nations and its related organizations, although not exclusively so, because the same type of organization is growing up in other parts of the international scene.[21]

The process described by Mr. Rusk is in some respects akin to the procedures of a democratic legislature of the Western type. In its original form, derived from the French *parler* and retained in the English " parley," the word " parliamentary " conveys the idea of discussion and is apt, but more should not be read into the expression than Mr. Rusk intended.

The practice of " parliamentary diplomacy " brings with it the practice of " diplomatic oratory." It has been said that speeches may change opinions, but they never change votes. The fact is that in many cases nowadays, speeches are not meant primarily for the ears of the diplomats who hear them.

We addressed our speeches [wrote Trotsky of the Brest-Litovsk negotiations] to the war-weary workers of all countries. . . . When speaking to Kühlmann and Czernin, we all the time had in our mind's eye our friends and comrades, Karl Liebknecht and Fritz Adler. [22]

We made it the task of our diplomacy to enlighten the masses of the peoples, to open their eyes to the real meaning of the policy of their governments, in order to weld them together in a common struggle.[23]

Forty years later, this is a commonplace of the diplomatic process. Speeches and votes are directed not only to other delegations and governments but to the unseen millions.

There is another factor that encourages diplomatic oratory. A study of the United Nations prepared for the Canadian Institute of

---

21 " Parliamentary Diplomacy—Debate vs. Negotiation," *World Affairs Interpreter*, Vol. XXVI, No. 2 (Summer 1955), pp. 121–122. See also Philip C. Jessup, *Parliamentary Diplomacy* (Leyden: A. W. Sijthoff, 1956).

22 Leon Trotsky, *The History of the Russian Revolution to Brest-Litovsk* (London: Allen & Unwin, 1919), p. 5.

23 Trotsky, *From October to Brest-Litovsk* (Brooklyn, N.Y.: Socialist Publication Society, 1919), p. 84.

International Affairs and the Carnegie Endowment for International Peace makes this comment.

The delegates of the Member States are appointed by their governments, and whether or not they wish to be reappointed, many of them aspire to a public career of some kind which may well be furthered by their performance at the Assembly. A politician or official . . ., presented with a chance to appear on a world stage, naturally strives to make the most of it in the interest of increasing his reputation in his own country. . . . Opportunities for such indulgence are all too plentiful.[24]

It has been an outstanding contribution of Dag Hammarskjold to insist that " parliamentary diplomacy " should not exclude quiet diplomacy.

We find introduced in conference diplomacy an aspect of propaganda and an element of rigidity which may be harmful to sound negotiation. . . . It is my feeling that there now is a broader recognition than before of the value of quiet diplomacy within the framework of the Organization as a complement to the conference diplomacy of the public debates.[25]

The [United Nations] Organization should be more than an instrument of what may be described as conference diplomacy. This new diplomacy . . . is not . . . sufficient for the efforts towards understanding and reconciliation which are of such importance now. . . . Conference diplomacy may usefully be supplemented by more quiet diplomacy within the United Nations. . . .[26]

The legislative process in the United Nations is not a substitute for diplomacy. It serves its purpose only when it helps diplomacy to arrive at agreements. . . . It is diplomacy, not speeches and votes, that continues to have the last word in the process of peace-making.[27]

Mr. Hammarskjold does not underestimate the usefulness of public debate, provided it is carried on in the right way and at the right time. Public debate can sometimes play a vital role in promoting conciliation; in the last resort, however, the reconciliation of differences which leads to a meeting of minds, or at least an accommodation of interests, usually takes place in an atmosphere of quiet, where there is no gallery to play to. The drama of disputes publicly discussed, the clashes of temperament and tradition, the cut and thrust of debate—these may provide exciting copy for the journalists, but they can frustrate the adjustments of view and the compromises which are, after all, the final purposes of diplomacy.

[24] F. H. Soward and Edgar McInnis, with assistance of Walter O'Hearn, *Canada and the United Nations* (New York: Manhattan Publishing, 1956), pp. 220–221.

[25] Address at the University of California. United Nations Doc. SG/428, 25 June 1955.

[26] *Annual Report of the Secretary-General* . . . , G.A.O.R.: 10th Sess., 1955, *op. cit.*, pp. xi–xii.

[27] Address at Ohio University. United Nations Doc. SG/656, 3 Feb. 1958, p. 3.

ELEMENTS OF CONTINUITY
IN "PARLIAMENTARY DIPLOMACY"

Mr. Rusk gives as the first essential feature of "parliamentary diplomacy" the idea of a continuing organization with broader interests and responsibilities than the specific items of the agenda at any particular time. This element of continuity is facilitated by two new diplomatic institutions: permanent diplomatic missions accredited to intergovernmental agencies, and international secretariats to service those agencies.

The Secretariat of the League of Nations was concerned that there should be orderly means for communicating with governments, and members of the League were encouraged to establish special sections on League affairs within their foreign ministries. This system, while useful, did not entirely meet the need, and in consequence governments began the practice of designating diplomatic representatives stationed in or near Geneva to act in a liaison capacity with the League. Poland was the first member of the League to establish a permanent liaison office in Geneva (1920). By 1922, ten League members had established offices in Geneva, and fifteen others had designated diplomatic representatives in other cities to maintain contact with League affairs.[28] States which were not members of the League, such as Germany (before 1926) and the United States, often designated the Consul or Consul-General in Geneva as having special duties regarding liaison with the League. Delegations to maintain contact with the League were occasionally maintained in Geneva or Paris by governments in exile (for example, Armenia and the Ukraine).

There was no uniformity of title or method of appointment of these "permanent delegations," as they were usually termed. Some were accredited to the Secretary-General and some to the Secretariat, while others were not "accredited" to the League in any formal sense. The Secretary-General was often, but not invariably, informed of their appointment, either by the government or by the person appointed. Those diplomatic representatives who were stationed permanently in Geneva enjoyed diplomatic privileges and immunities. They were often referred to as the *corps diplomatique*, but it was not until the early 1930s that they were constituted as a formal *corps diplomatique*, with a *doyen*, and were received as a corporate body by the Secretary-General.

The most important function of the permanent delegations was to act as a channel of communication between the League Secretariat and the governments. In a few cases, they also acted as national

[28] Four in Berne, ten in Paris and one in Monaco.

representatives to organs of the League. Some of the permanent delegates acquired considerable expertise regarding the inner workings of the League. They maintained close contact with officials of the Secretariat, particularly with officials of the same nationality as their own, but Francis P. Walters comments in his history of the League that " the system of Permanent Delegations was of no serious significance in League history." [29] This judgment could not be applied to the permanent diplomatic missions at United Nations headquarters.

The Charter of the United Nations made no provision for permanent diplomatic representation of Member States, but the fact that the Security Council " shall be so organized as to be able to function continuously " (Article 28) meant that at least eleven of the original fifty-one Member States had to maintain continuous representation at the seat of the Organization. Members of the other two Councils and of various subsidiary organs soon established similar forms of permanent representation. By May 1948, forty-one Member States had submitted to the Secretary-General lists of persons who were members of permanent delegations to the United Nations. In September 1949, all Member States except Burma, El Salvador, Ethiopia, Honduras, Lebanon, Luxembourg, Paraguay and Yemen had Permanent Missions at United Nations headquarters, and fifteen Member States had Permanent Missions attached to the European Office of the United Nations in Geneva.

At the present time, all Member States have appointed Permanent Representatives and have transmitted credentials to the Secretary-General; the Permanent Missions of Laos and Morocco are represented by chargés d'affaires.[30] The Byelorussian S.S.R. and Ukrainian S.S.R. have a joint office in New York with the Soviet Union. Iceland, Libya and Nepal handle relations with the United Nations through their embassies in Washington, but establish offices in New York during sessions of the General Assembly. The Federal Republic of Germany, the Republic of Korea, Monaco, Switzerland and the Republic of Viet-Nam, though not Members of the United Nations, maintain permanent observers in New York to keep in touch with United Nations affairs. The status of these representatives is imprecise, but they are granted facilities to carry on their function of observation.

It is the normal diplomatic practice for a State to obtain the *agréation*, or prior agreement, that any diplomatic agent to be

---

[29] *A History of the League of Nations* (London: Oxford Univ. Press, 1952), Vol. I, p. 199. See also Pitman B. Potter, *Permanent Delegations to the League of Nations* (Geneva: League of Nations Association of the U.S., 1930).
[30] United Nations Doc. A/4347, 10 Dec. 1959, paras. 2, 3.

appointed is acceptable to the State to which he will be accredited. In the case of the United Nations, no such practice is followed. In 1949 the Secretary-General suggested a standard form of credentials,[31] but there is no question of the Secretary-General granting or withholding recognition to the Permanent Representative of a Member State. Questions relating to the credentials of representatives are decided by United Nations organs, on the basis of a report from a credentials committee or the Secretary-General.

A regular nomenclature has now been established. Diplomatic missions of Member States attached to the United Nations are known as " Permanent Missions," and the head of each Mission is known as " Permanent Representative to the United Nations." The " Permanent Representative " usually has the rank of Ambassador Extraordinary and Plenipotentiary, though in a few cases " Permanent Representatives " have the rank of Envoy Extraordinary and Minister Plenipotentiary or simply Minister Plenipotentiary.[32] The representatives of a Member State to the General Assembly comprise its delegation. A delegation normally includes the staff of the Permanent Mission, together with a number of foreign service officers and other civil servants. More than half of the delegations to the General Assembly are headed by foreign ministers during the first month or more of the session. Some Members, such as Canada, Sweden and the United States, include members of the legislature as full delegates or observers. Many delegations include distinguished scholars or representatives of non-governmental organizations.

There has taken place a steady development of the functions of the Permanent Missions. Some of the newer nations, which do not yet have fully developed diplomatic services and are perhaps represented in a dozen or even fewer foreign capitals, can keep in touch with eighty governments or more through their Permanent Missions at United Nations headquarters. In cases where diplomatic relations have been severed, representatives in New York can engage in informal discussions. The Secretary-General can readily communicate, either formally or informally, with Members of the United Nations through the Permanent Representatives. National representatives at United Nations headquarters are often able to find out from members of the Secretariat the general trend of thinking on international questions. There are permanently in New York

---

[31] G.A.O.R.: 4th Sess., 6th Committee, Annex, 1949, Agenda item 50 (A/939/Rev. 1 and Rev. 1/Add. 1, Annex), p. 17.

[32] I am told that there has occasionally been confusion between Permanent Missions and Visiting Missions of the Trusteeship Council, and a Trusteeship Council Visiting Mission recently reported that in one Trust Territory " the name ' Visiting Mission ' is often confused with religious missions." United Nations Doc. T/1451, 8 June 1959, para. 204.

some 600 members of the diplomatic corps, constituting what Mr. Hammarskjold has called " a standing diplomatic conference." [33] Personal intimacy and understanding often develop among the staffs of these Permanent Missions, even across the most substantial political barriers. " Perhaps the most important result of conducting diplomacy by conference," wrote Lord Hankey, " is the knowledge responsible statesmen acquire of one another." [34]

The existence of Permanent Missions at United Nations headquarters makes possible continuous negotiation on a variety of questions and can facilitate the informal preparation for meetings of the General Assembly and other United Nations bodies. Informal discussions can take place between delegations, within groups of delegations, and between delegations and the Secretariat, on such matters as the choice of officers and the planning of the agenda. In 1956, for example, following the admission of sixteen new Member States, consultations were held between the Secretariat and Permanent Representatives regarding the work of the eleventh Assembly and the steps that might be taken to assure the efficient operation of the Assembly and keep its duration within reasonable limits. This consultation served a useful purpose, though the eruption of crises regarding Hungary and Suez just before the eleventh session was due to open showed how easily the best laid schemes " gang aft a-gley."

The presence at United Nations headquarters of representatives of Member States has facilitated the development of *blocs* and groups. The United Nations now has so many Members that some form of informal organization of States with similar interests facilitates the smooth operation of the Organization. Proposals for United Nations action are often given " trial runs " in the groups, and are later presented to an organ of the United Nations in an amended and more widely acceptable form.

The advantages of having Permanent Missions attached to the United Nations are obvious, but two potential drawbacks should be mentioned. When expert or technical bodies are created by one or another of the principal organs of the United Nations, it is desirable that the members of such bodies should have a special competence in the field in which work is to be done. Since almost all governments have too few officials chasing too much work, however, it is tempting to designate as a representative on a United Nations body a diplomatic officer who happens to be stationed wherever the body will meet. Thus a member of a Permanent Mission may find himself

[33] Address before the Norwegian Association for the United Nations. United Nations Press Release SG/683, 2 June 1958, p. 4.
[34] Maurice Hankey, *Baron Hankey. Diplomacy by Conference* (New York: Putnam, London: Benn, 1947), p. 35.

an expert on sovereignty over natural resources in February, international commodity trade in April, and outer space in June. All matters dealt with by the United Nations bear some relation to all other matters dealt with by the Organization, and diplomatic versatility is to be welcomed; all the same, in certain highly technical matters, expertise is more important than versatility.

A second potential drawback of Permanent Missions arises from the fact that in some foreign services advancement may be hastened by having served with distinction on some organ of the United Nations. It would be a distortion to say that members of Permanent Missions consciously and deliberately strive to create United Nations bodies so that they may be worthily employed between sessions of the Assembly. Most Permanent Missions are, in fact, overwhelmed with the pressure of business and feel that they are inadequately staffed to discharge their responsibilities; yet diplomats are not immune to human frailty, and are rarely free from personal ambition.

A second element of continuity in parliamentary diplomacy is provided by the secretariats of intergovernmental agencies. The Charter of the United Nations is not very explicit about the functions and role of the Secretariat. The Secretary-General is described as the chief administrative officer of the Organization, and he is to appoint the staff in accordance with principles stated in the Charter and under regulations established by the General Assembly. The Secretary-General and the staff are neither to seek nor receive instructions from any government, and Member States undertake not to seek to influence the staff in the discharge of their responsibilities. The Secretary-General may draw the attention of the Security Council to threats to the peace, and the Secretariat as a whole is designated a principal organ of the United Nations.

The Secretary-General is, of course, more than an administrator. Walter Bagehot wrote nearly a century ago that a British monarch of great sense and sagacity would want only three rights: the right to be consulted, the right to encourage, and the right to warn. These are rights which the Secretary-General of the United Nations should have; and they are rights which are usually best exercised in private. The present Secretary-General has stated that the holder of the office " has a clear duty to offer advice and to express opinions when he deems it helpful and pertinent to do so." [35]

The morale and quality of work of the United Nations Secretariat depend very greatly on the leadership and versatility of the

[35] *Annual Report of the Secretary-General . . . , 1 July 1953—30 June 1954*, G.A.O.R.: 9th Sess., 1954, Suppl. No. 1 (A/2663), p. xiv.

Secretary-General. He appoints and directs a large multilingual staff and co-ordinates the activities of the departments and offices in the Secretariat. He must evoke the loyalty of his subordinates. If they make mistakes, he takes the blame; if they do good work, he deflects the credit. He keeps in contact with other intergovernmental organizations, and he presides over a co-ordinating committee of the executive heads of technical agencies.

He is the recipient of much information, and must distinguish between what is confidential and what is intended for the ears of others. If he is not given information to which he feels he is entitled, he must restrain his annoyance. He must always tell the truth, but rarely the whole truth. He must speak and write with caution but without ambiguity.

He takes political initiatives, either because he considers that in so doing he has the support of a sufficient number of governments or because it is a matter of deep personal conviction. In the latter event, he must be prepared to resign his office if his initiative does not carry substantial support. In any case, it is in the nature of things that some initiatives will fail.

His work will never be finished, yet he must find time for relaxation and time for contemplation. He will have many acquaintances but few friends. He must divest himself of national or ideological prejudices. He must be agile in mind, robust in body, equable and serene in spirit. His only ambition must be to serve the Organization.

A continuing problem for the Secretary-General, and for the Secretariat as a whole, arises from the fact that the Secretariat does not correspond exactly to a national civil service which, under the direction of the executive branch of government, and within constitutional limits established by the judiciary, administers the laws passed by the legislature. The General Assembly and the Councils of the United Nations, and their subsidiary organs, may be akin to parliamentary bodies and their decisions may have some of the attributes of legislation, but where is the executive branch of government or a continuing focus of leadership and initiative?

This problem becomes especially acute in connection with the larger organs, and particularly the General Assembly. Even before the League of Nations had been established, James T. Shotwell foresaw that the League Assembly would suffer from "the greatest element of weakness in all legislative bodies, namely, heterogeneity." [36] The founding fathers of the United Nations intended that the three Councils should provide a focus of leadership and

---

[36] *At the Paris Peace Conference* (New York: Macmillan, 1937), p. 232.

initiative. It is true that the Economic and Social Council and the Trusteeship Council were to operate " under the authority of the General Assembly " (Articles 60 and 85), but they were given quite specific and important functions and powers. On the other hand, it was never intended that the Security Council should operate under the authority of the Assembly.

The Assembly has, in practice, assumed a predominant role in the United Nations system and has interpreted broadly its powers under the Charter. Because the conflict among the permanent members of the Security Council has reduced the importance of an organ which depends for its effectiveness on their unanimity, and also because some countries find the Assembly a more advantageous forum than the Security Council, the Assembly has assumed responsibilities which—on a strict interpretation of the Charter—belong to the Council. The Charter was drafted with the intention of preventing the Assembly and the Security Council from dealing concurrently with the same question. It was assumed that the Security Council, by a vote of any seven of its members and without veto, would be able to prevent the Assembly from making any recommendations with regard to a dispute or situation simply by putting the matter on its agenda. In practice, these provisions have been circumvented, and the Assembly has on several occasions adopted resolutions concerning certain aspects of disputes and situations which were on the agenda of the Council. During its third and fourth sessions, for example, the Assembly discussed the question of Indonesia even though the Council was actively considering the matter, and on both occasions the Assembly adopted resolutions (though not recommendations).

In view of the difficulties encountered in the Security Council, various procedures have been followed for transferring questions from the Council's jurisdiction to that of the Assembly. Proposals that the Council specifically refer a question to the Assembly have generally run into a veto. Prior to 1950 the usual procedure was for one or more Members to ask the Assembly to consider a question and then for the Security Council to remove the matter from its agenda, a decision taken by a procedural vote. The Spanish question and the question of the Greek frontier incidents were handled in this way. A similar procedure was used to enable the Assembly to consider Chinese Communist intervention in Korea. The " Uniting for Peace " resolution provided a means by which, should the Council be unable to act because of the lack of unanimity among the Permanent Members, emergency special sessions of the Assembly may be called. This procedure was invoked in connection with the Suez and Hungarian questions in 1956, and the complaints by Lebanon and Jordan of interference by the United Arab Republic in 1958.

The Assembly has increasingly taken the lead in economic, social and trusteeship questions. It is true that the two Councils concerned, and their subsidiary organs, have often prepared the ground for the initiatives which the Assembly has taken, but the fact remains that the questions discussed and decided by the Assembly have steadily increased in number, importance and complexity.

At one time it seemed possible that the Assembly's General Committee might become a real steering committee and thus provide a focus of authority for the Assembly. The General Committee has, however, declined in political importance as its size has increased.

In the absence of a continuing centre of leadership, a number of informal arrangements have developed which meet part of the need. The President of the Assembly and the Chairmen of Main Committees can provide leadership in matters of procedure. The organization of *blocs* and groups has given to the Assembly some of the characteristics of a national legislature of the multiparty type. If the trend towards a more formal organization of *blocs* and groups continues, it may be that there will be more contact between the chairmen of these groups and *blocs* on matters concerning the organization of the business of the Assembly.

The leadership of delegations in the Assembly is necessarily diffused and erratic. It normally cannot come from the chief protagonists, and in practice there has emerged a nucleus of countries, reputed for their moderation and prudence, and somewhat detached from the more pressing exigencies of the power struggles, which has provided leadership. The nucleus varies from issue to issue and from period to period, but countries like Brazil, Canada, India, Ireland, Mexico, Norway, Sweden and Yugoslavia have provided a focus of leadership on some of the more difficult issues. One delegate commented to me recently that he did not mind being in the minority on a question so long as these eight States were in the minority with him.

This moderate leadership has not, however, entirely filled the gap. It has, at times, been vital; but it has inevitably been sporadic. The only continuing source of leadership has been the Secretariat. The Secretary-General, members of the Secretariat of under-secretary or equivalent rank, and the Executive Office of the Secretary-General can provide a continuing focus of leadership and initiative for the Assembly.

The proper role of the Secretariat is not easily defined. It is proper for the Secretariat to supply information on matters of United

Nations concern which are on the public record, such as past decisions of a United Nations organ on some question. It is proper for the Secretariat to state informally but objectively the arguments likely to be advanced by governments for or against a particular policy. The Secretariat thus plays a vital role in preparations for and the organization of United Nations bodies. The Secretary-General has pointed out that the method of his appointment is intended to ensure that he shall, as far as possible, be placed outside or lifted above conflicts which may split United Nations organs. This means that the Secretary-General should " have the opportunity of functioning as the spokesman of the Organization in its capacity as an independent opinion factor." He may accord himself the right to take a stand in emerging conflicts " to the extent that such stands can be firmly based on the Charter and its principles and thus express what may be called the independent judgment of the Organization." This can be done successfully, Mr. Hammarskjold has said, on two conditions. First, Member States must have the full confidence that the Secretary-General is independent and free from personal motives. Secondly, the Secretary-General " must accept the limitation of acting mainly on inner lines without publicity." In the rare cases in which he feels that the situation requires that he publicly appeal to opinion over the heads of governments, " he must be prepared to see his future value as a negotiator endangered or even lost. In the latter case, he ought, naturally, to resign from his post." [37]

The Secretary-General has, in conformity with these principles, made statements or taken initiatives on controversial questions. Let me cite some examples.

(*a*) At a Press conference on 8 April 1958, Mr. Hammarskjold welcomed the Soviet suspension of nuclear tests, adding that he was also in favour of proper inspection of the cessation of tests and of the stopping of production of nuclear weapons.[38]

(*b*) On 29 April 1958, Mr. Hammarskjold welcomed the United States initiative in the Security Council in proposing consideration of methods to guard against surprise attack.[39]

(*c*) Following the failure of the Security Council to take action in July 1958 in connection with the crisis in the Middle East, Mr. Hammarskjold stated that, " acting in accordance with the wishes of the members of the Council," he would proceed with " the further development of the United Nations

37 Address in Copenhagen. United Nations Doc. SG/812, 1 May 1959, p. 9.
38 Note to Correspondents No. 1779.
39 United Nations Doc. S/PV. 815, pp. 61–65 and SG/675.

Observation Group " which had been set up to prevent illegal infiltration into Lebanon.[40]

(*d*) At the meeting on 8 August 1958 of the emergency special session of the Assembly called to consider the situation in Lebanon and Jordan, Mr. Hammarskjold made an important statement on " some of the basic needs for action in the region, which, in view of the experience of the Secretariat, require urgent attention." [41]

(*e*) On 30 September 1958, Mr. Hammarskjold took the initiative in proposing that the General Assembly, at its thirteenth session, consider the question of disarmament. On 11 September 1959, Mr. Hammarskjold proposed that the Assembly, at its fourteenth session, include in the agenda the report of the Disarmament Commission.[42]

(*f*) Following the receipt of a request from the Government of Laos for an emergency force to halt aggression in September 1959, Mr. Hammarskjold requested the President of the Security Council to convene the Council urgently.[43] Mr. Hammarskjold later emphasized that he was not, by this action, invoking Article 99 of the Charter, which empowers the Secretary-General to bring to the attention of the Security Council any matter which in his opinion threatens the maintenance of international peace and security. Following a personal visit to Laos in November, Mr. Hammarskjold made practical arrangements for reviewing the economic situation in that country, in particular the role of economic and technical assistance for the furtherance of economic growth and stability.

It is a mark of the confidence in Mr. Hammarskjold's determination to uphold the principles of the Charter that these statements and actions were widely regarded as being constructive contributions to highly difficult situations; indeed, their timing was in many ways as important as their content.

The Secretary-General has from time to time been entrusted with important diplomatic tasks in which he has acted, in a sense, as " the spokesman of the Organization." Mr. Hammarskjold has insisted that resolutions of United Nations organs requesting him to act in

[40] United Nations Doc. S/PV. 837, 22 July 1958, pp. 11–12 and United Nations Doc. SG/708, 22 July 1958.

[41] G.A.O.R.: 3rd Emergency Special Sess., 732nd Plenary Mtg., paras. 34–44 and United Nations Doc. SG/714.

[42] G.A.O.R.: 13th Sess., 1958, Annexes, Agenda items 64, 70 and 72 (A/3936), p. 18; United Nations Doc. A/4209.

[43] United Nations Docs. S/4212, 5 Sept. 1959, S/4213, 6 Sept. 1959, S/PV. 847, 7 Sept. 1959, p. 6.

this capacity neither detract from nor add to the authority of the Secretary-General under the Charter.[44]

Resolutions of the Assembly requesting the Secretary-General to undertake some task have, in several cases, been couched in the most general terms. One resolution asked the Secretary-General " to take any initiative that he deems helpful . . . in conformity with the principles of the Charter and the resolutions of the General Assembly " ; another requested him " to make forthwith, in consultation with the Governments concerned and in accordance with the Charter . . . such practical arrangements as would adequately help in upholding the purposes and principles of the Charter. . . ." [45] It may be assumed that, in light of the prevailing circumstances and as part of the duties of his office, the Secretary-General has been content to assume the additional heavy responsibilities placed on him by such requests. On one occasion, when it seemed possible that he might be asked to undertake certain duties, he let it be known that " in view of the many pressing and onerous tasks now entrusted to him . . . he felt that he would not be able to do full justice to such an important request." [46]

In a recent case, two Member States requested the Secretary-General to send a special representative to assist them to overcome certain border difficulties that had arisen and had led to a suspension of diplomatic relations between the two countries. After consultation with the members of the Security Council, the Secretary-General acted in accordance with the request. With the help of the good offices thus provided, diplomatic relations between the two States were resumed.[47] This was a novel procedure, as one of the foreign ministers concerned emphasized later. The representative of the Secretary-General

was neither an observer responsible for reporting the facts, nor an arbiter whose task was to induce the parties to accept a given solution. . . . [He] was simply an intermediary who placed himself at the disposal of the two Governments in order to facilitate the restoration of diplomatic relations between them and pave the way for improved relations between the two countries.

We believe that this new course followed by the Secretary-General is a most promising one. It made prompt intervention possible without involving the prestige of the Organization in case of failure. This is a tactful and ingenious procedure. . . .[48]

---

44 Security Council Official Records (S.C.O.R.): 11th Yr., 722nd Mtg., 4 Apr. 1956, para. 51.
45 General Assembly Res. 1131(XI), 12 Dec. 1956 and Res. 1237(ES-III), 21 Aug. 1958.
46 G.A.O.R.: 11th Sess., 4th Committee, 579th Mtg., 20 Dec. 1956, para. 33.
47 *Introduction to the Annual Report of the Secretary-General* . . . , G.A.O.R.: 14th Sess., 1959, Suppl. No. 1 (A/4132/Add. 1), p. 4.
48 G.A.O.R.: 14th Sess., 798th Plenary Mtg., 17 Sept. 1959, paras. 115–116.

A few days later, the other foreign minister concerned repeated the tribute which had been paid to the Secretary-General.[49]

In two important matters the Assembly has created advisory committees, consisting of representatives of Member States, which meet under the chairmanship of the Secretary-General.[50] This is an interesting development, of which the Secretary-General has spoken with appreciation. Both committees meet in private, and no vote is taken. The Secretary-General sums up his conclusions, and any member of the committee is free to place on the record any objection to the summary. In practice, no member of either committee has ever found it necessary to record any objection to the Secretary-General's summing-up.[51]

These diplomatic responsibilities of the Secretary-General have arisen in part from the inability of the Security Council to exercise primary responsibility for maintaining peace; and also from the fact that in a number of important matters it has been impossible to mobilize a two-thirds vote in the Assembly for a precise and definite decision of substance. "The new eminence of the Secretary-General," Hans Morgenthau has written, "is but a function of the General Assembly's embarrassment at being called upon to act without being able to."[52] This, to be sure, is correct as far as it goes. All the same, it may be that the Assembly had been attempting tasks for which it is not well fitted. The diplomatic functions of the Secretary-General, though often exercised for reasons which were not fully foreseen when the Charter was drafted, may be a vital means of quiet diplomacy.

It is, I think, clear that there are many ways in which quiet diplomacy, either within or outside the United Nations framework, can help to achieve the lofty purposes of the Charter. Quiet diplomacy and "parliamentary diplomacy" are not alternatives; each has its own role to play.

---

[49] *Ibid.*, 806th Plenary Mtg., 24 Sept. 1959, para. 143.

[50] The Advisory Committee on the U.N. Emergency Force and the Scientific Advisory Committee.

[51] See the following speeches of the Secretary-General: "The Element of Privacy in Peace-making," United Nations Doc. SG/656, 3 Feb. 1958; "The Vital Role of the United Nations in a Diplomacy of Reconciliation," *op. cit.*, pp. 6–10.

[52] "The New United Nations," *Commentary*, Nov. 1958, copyright American Jewish Committee, p. 379.

CHAPTER 2

COALITIONS, GROUPS AND *BLOCS* IN THE ASSEMBLY

Nor is it said the lamb shall lie down with the lion, but the lion shall lie down with the lamb.

WILLIAM PENN

ONE of the reasons why the General Assembly of the United Nations bears some resemblances to a parliamentary body is that there operates within it an embryonic party system. And just as political parties were once regarded as disreputable instruments for the suppression of individual liberty, so the activities of *blocs* and groups of States at the United Nations have sometimes been condemned on the ground that moral principle is cynically sacrificed for some selfish sectional interest. It is said, for example, that no question is ever decided on its merits; there is always a *quid pro quo*.

Many of the complaints about the embryonic party system at the United Nations seem to me exaggerated. It is part of the political process, national or international, governmental or non-governmental, that few disputed questions can be settled on their intrinsic merits. Indeed, it has long been a recognized diplomatic practice to link a number of questions together in order to achieve an overall settlement based on mutual compromise, and one of the constant problems of public diplomacy by conference is that questions have to be placed on an agenda and dealt with seriatim and seemingly in isolation.

Ordinarily, issues in diplomacy may be joined together, and in resolving problems with your friends you can give a little on one and take a little on the other. Perhaps, since many of them involve disagreeable choices, you can put a bundle of them together and get a result where you will like one part and your friends will like another part, but you find some basis on which to work it out.[1]

What Mr. Rusk says about resolving problems " with your friends " applies with equal force to negotiations with unfriendly States.

It is a normal part of diplomacy for States to consult each other on matters of common interest, and perhaps one of the chief reasons why this happens rather often at United Nations headquarters is that it is rather easy. Representatives of Member States constantly meet each other, not necessarily by careful prearrangement but rather

[1] Dean Rusk, " Parliamentary Diplomacy—Debate *vs*. Negotiation," *World Affairs Interpreter*, Vol. XXVI, No. 2 (Summer 1955), pp. 129–130.

because they so often have business to discharge in the same building, eat in the same dining room, use the same elevators, patronize the same barber. There takes place a continual process of consultation, arranged and casual, both among friends and across barriers. Much of this consultation is not directly related to the immediate and current problems of world politics. It is a normal diplomatic attempt to increase mutual understanding, to win friends and influence people, to acquire or give information.

This diplomatic consultation ought not to give rise to criticism. Nevertheless, some of the most zealous supporters of the United Nations have the idea that the crystallization of coalitions, groups and *blocs* deprives the Assembly of the possibility of reaching an objective and unbiased judgment. To a certain extent, this charge is true—though the situation could hardly be otherwise. The Assembly is not a body of scientists or philosophers engaged in an academic search for ultimate truth; it is not even a judicial body, pursuing justice; it is a political body, searching for the solutions which are often compromises and have merit only because the alternatives are even more disagreeable.

States associate with each other to achieve the common ends which seem to them desirable. In this complex process of association, each may sacrifice something, not through any cynical disregard of principle, but because States know that their national interests can be promoted only by taking account of the national interests of others. This recognition of an international interest which transcends the interests of each nation is at the basis of the United Nations Charter.

Bargaining in the lobbies of the Assembly and the capitals is, perhaps, most frequent in connection with elections. Most Assembly elections are based, explicitly or implicitly, on the representative principle. It is, of course, impossible to constitute every United Nations organ so that it is an exact representation in miniature of the whole; the whole is too variegated. Since it would be impracticable to have every organ composed of all Member States, bodies of limited membership are set up, usually in such a way as to be broadly representative of the whole.

It has been the general experience in many realms of social and political organization that once the membership of an executive or deliberative organ exceeds about fifteen, the character of the organ begins to change. Intimacy and cohesion fade; there is a temptation to establish sub-committees; instead of discussing the business in hand, members start reading speeches. If the effective operation of organs of limited membership were the sole factor of which account should be taken, such organs would no doubt usually be kept small. There is, however, another factor that is often of equal if not greater importance. An organ of limited membership can be successful only if it enjoys a high degree of confidence of the whole, and in practice this usually means that it should contain within itself representatives of the main streams of thought of the larger body.

In the political life of democratic societies this is facilitated, albeit crudely, by the party system. In an organization of States based on the principle of sovereign equality, in which the interests of the members change and the relations among them fluctuate, a party system in the conventional sense has not evolved. The *bloc* of Soviet Member States does, it is true, function in the United Nations very much like a disciplined political party in a legislature, and the twenty Latin American republics certainly have some of the characteristics of a loosely organized party.

These are, however, imperfect and perhaps misleading analogies. The outstanding fact about the way States associate in the General Assembly is the tendency of Member States to affiliate differently for different purposes. Liberia and the Philippines, for example, usually associate with the heterogeneous group of States which vote with the United States on cold war issues, but on colonial questions they associate with the even more heterogeneous anti-colonial group. The Western States, to take another example, present a united front on most cold war questions, but split on certain issues involving human rights, colonial matters, the question of domestic jurisdiction, and Chinese representation.

Improvised or organized methods of consultation are an integral part of the ordinary processes of diplomacy. In many cases, the consultation takes place at United Nations headquarters or wherever an organ is meeting, but there are also a great many cases where such consultation takes place by conventional diplomatic methods. Indeed, whenever a delegate receives changed instructions from home, he may wonder whether someone has been " getting at " his foreign ministry.

The forms of organized association which have developed at the United Nations are informal and unofficial, though their existence is recognized. Occasionally a representative may speak at a United Nations meeting on behalf of a group or *bloc*. Informal or formal agreements about the allocation of elective places are often based in part on a regional distribution, though the regions may not correspond exactly to organized groups or *blocs*.

There are, broadly speaking, three types of association among

States at the United Nations. There is, in the first place, the *ad hoc* coalition which is improvised to deal with a particular problem, whether of a long-term or short-term character, and which disappears when the problem passes or changes in character. The Spanish-speaking delegations have on a number of occasions combined to press the claims of the Spanish language in United Nations affairs. The sixteen States which contributed forces to the United Nations Command in Korea have co-operated on Korean questions. States administering Trust or Non-Self-Governing Territories consult each other from time to time on matters of common interest, as do the anti-colonial States. During the eleventh session (1956–57), Canada, Japan and Norway acted jointly in connection with various disarmament matters—giving rise to good-humoured comments about " the new Northern *Bloc*." During the twelfth session (1957), three neutral and uncommitted States (India, Sweden and Yugoslavia) co-operated to present to the Assembly a compromise proposal on " Peaceful and Neighbourly Relations among States."

The second type of association arises when States are organized to meet, either regularly or sporadically, to exchange ideas on issues of common concern, though without any commitment to act in unison. The Latin American Group, the Afro-Asian Group (including the Arab and African sub-groups), and the Commonwealth, are associations of this kind. These Groups have certain common organizational features. All of them meet roughly once every week or fortnight during sessions of the General Assembly, and less frequently at other times of the year. All, except the Commonwealth, have an established system for rotating the chairmanship. All of them discuss any matter which any member wishes to raise. All attempt to reach the maximum of agreement without resort to voting.

The third type of association consists of States which not only consult each other but almost always act in unison. The Soviet *Bloc*, consisting of the Communist Member States belonging to the Warsaw Pact and the Council for Mutual Economic Assistance, together with the Byelorussian S.S.R. and Ukrainian S.S.R., is the only association of this kind at the United Nations. It is rarely that the States of the Soviet *Bloc* vote differently, and when this happens it is almost always due to a misunderstanding.

RESOLUTION 1192 (XII)

The General Assembly has taken one decision concerning the distribution of elective places which goes beyond simply endorsing the representative principle, and establishes a fixed pattern. Since I will frequently be referring to this decision, I give here the full text of the resolution, which was adopted at the 728th plenary meeting on 12 December 1957:

Composition of the General Committee of the General Assembly

The General Assembly,

Taking into account the considerable increase in the membership of the United Nations,

Taking also into account that the General Committee should be so constituted as to ensure its representative character on the basis of a balanced geographical distribution among its members,

Believing that for these reasons it is desirable to enlarge the composition of the General Committee,

Noting that the General Committee is composed of the President, the Vice-Presidents and the Chairmen of the Main Committees,

1. *Confirms* the practice established with regard to the distribution of the chairmanships of the Main Committees, namely, two from Latin American States, two from Asian and African States, two from Western European and other States, and one from an Eastern European State;

2. *Decides* to amend as follows rules 31 and 38 of its rules of procedure:

"Rule 31

" The General Assembly shall elect a President and thirteen Vice-Presidents, who shall hold office until the close of the session at which they are elected. The Vice-Presidents shall be elected, after the election of the Chairmen of the seven Main Committees referred to in rule 101, on the basis of ensuring the representative character of the General Committee."

"Rule 38

" The General Committee shall comprise the President of the General Assembly, who shall preside, the thirteen Vice-Presidents and the Chairmen of the seven Main Committees. No two members of the General Committee shall be members of the same delegation, and it shall be so constituted as to ensure its representative character. Chairmen of other committees upon which all Members have the right to be represented and which are established by the General Assembly to meet during the session shall be entitled to attend meetings of the General Committee and may participate without vote in the discussions ";

3. *Decides* that the thirteen Vice-Presidents shall be elected as provided in the annex to the present resolution.

ANNEX

1. The thirteen Vice-Presidents shall be elected according to the following pattern:

    (a) Four representatives from Asian and African States;

    (b) One representative from an Eastern European State;

    (c) Two representatives from Latin American States;

    (d) Two representatives from Western European and other States;

    (e) Five representatives from the permanent members of the Security Council.

2. The region from which the President is elected will, however, reduce by one the number of vice-presidencies allocated in paragraph 1 of the present annex.

3. At least one of the Vice-Presidents in categories (*a*) or (*d*) above, or the President or one of the Chairmen of the Main Committees, will be from a Commonwealth country, without altering the geographical distribution of seats in the General Committee, as defined in paragraphs 1 and 2 of this annex and in paragraph 1 of the resolution.

The effect of this resolution was to increase the size of the General Committee to twenty-one and to provide not only that it is " representative " of the whole membership of the United Nations, but also that the seats are distributed according to a fixed pattern. There was wide agreement at the time this resolution was adopted that some increase in the size of the General Committee was necessary, but there were differences of view on the extent of the increase, and there was even more disagreement on the proposal that the representative character of the Committee should be ensured by bringing about a fixed pattern of election. Hesitation about the change came mainly from the countries of Western Europe, the United States, the older Commonwealth countries and a few other countries which do not fit easily into any regional group. It was argued by them, in the first place, that a General Committee of sixteen or seventeen members was large enough; to increase its size would reduce its utility. Secondly, some delegations took the view that it was premature to take a decision on the matter. They maintained that the question of the composition of the General Committee should not be separated from the question of the composition of other United Nations organs; in any case, this was a matter on which unanimity was desirable, and it would be unfortunate to force a decision through the Assembly so long as an influential body of Member States remained unconvinced of the merits of the proposed changes.

A third group of objections related to the proposed pattern of regional representation. It was pointed out that most of the advocates of change belonged to organized regional groups, whereas the opponents were being lumped together in a meaningless category of " Western European and other States." It was argued that a decision of the Assembly along the lines proposed would crystallize and perpetuate divisions in the world. It was also objected that the Commonwealth was ignored in the proposal in its original form, though this was remedied in the final resolution.

Support for the change came from the Afro-Asian and Communist countries, and some of the countries of Latin America. It was argued by them that the increase in the membership of the Assembly made an increase in the size of the General Committee appropriate, and that opportunity should be taken to guarantee that the Committee would in the future have a more representative character than it had had previously. Czechoslovakia urged that a pattern of representation should be enshrined in a written text, as a previous "gentlemen's agreement" had not been respected.[2] To the argument that a Committee with twenty-one members would be unwieldy, India replied that the argument was irrelevant as the Committee was only procedural; while Poland asserted that the efficiency of a committee depends on the quality of its members rather than on its size.

In Chapter 3 I describe the way Resolution 1192 (XII) affected the elections in 1958 and 1959, and examine certain difficulties which may arise in the future. I should emphasize here that the regions referred to in the first operative paragraph of the resolution and in the annex do not correspond in all respects to organized groups or *blocs*.

I have throughout this book used a consistent and I hope intelligible system of regional classification which is based, to the greatest extent possible, on Resolution 1192 (XII). Unfortunately the system I have used, like all such systems, differs in some respects from all other such systems.

LATIN AMERICA

Co-operation among Latin American States, which was a feature of the League of Nations, has continued and been intensified in the United Nations. The Latin American Group consists of twenty States. These States differ in size, in social and political organization, and in degree of economic development, and there are rivalries and antagonisms within the Group. However, the twenty Latin American republics inherit a common tradition of thought and religion, and, except for Brazil and Haiti, they use the Spanish language. Moreover, they all belong, with the United States, to the Organization of American States.[3]

Even before the San Francisco Conference, the Latin American States had given evidence of their intention of co-operating on United Nations affairs. A resolution on the establishment of an international organization, adopted at the Inter-American Conference held at Chapultepec in 1945, emphasized "The desirability of giving an

---

[2] This was a reference to an agreement on the composition of the Security Council which was concluded in London in 1946. *Infra*, p. 165 *et seq*.

[3] The Assembly, by Resolution 253 (III), 16 Oct. 1948, invited the Secretary-General of the Organization of American States to be present as an observer at sessions of the Assembly.

adequate representation to Latin America in the Security Council." [4]
The Latin American States co-operated closely at the San Francisco
Conference, and co-operation has continued.

During the first session of the General Assembly in London, the
Latin American States, acutely aware of their relative impotence individually, met together informally in an effort to capitalize on their
joint voting strength. Initially their attention was directed to ensuring
the election of as many Latin Americans as possible to key positions,
by agreeing among themselves on a roster of candidates. As time passed,
the " Group " extended its activities to cover all issues of major concern.
. . . Meetings are held frequently during the Assembly on the call of
the President or at the request of one or more members. . . . Occasionally
a representative from another delegation may also be invited if a matter
of common concern is under discussion. . . .

The Latin Americans are proud of their " Group " and not without
justification. It provided an opportunity for discussion and clarification
of important issues and for the adoption of reasoned positions whether
or not a consensus is reached.[5]

The two Latin Americans elected as Vice-Presidents of the
Assembly (or President and Vice-President) share the chairmanship
of the Group. Meetings of the Group are held about once a week
during the General Assembly, and about once a month at other times
of the year. Occasionally meetings are held at the request of a
delegation not belonging to the Group.

TABLE 2

Latin American Member States

Argentina	Guatemala
Bolivia	Haiti
Brazil	Honduras
Chile	Mexico
Colombia	Nicaragua
Costa Rica	Panama
Cuba	Paraguay
Dominican Republic	Peru
Ecuador	Uruguay
El Salvador	Venezuela

Proceedings at meetings of the Group are relatively informal.
There is free discussion, but the Group does not vote or take binding
decisions on important matters of substance. The one matter on
which every effort is made to achieve unanimity is in the nomination
of persons or States from Latin America for election to United
Nations organs. It has not always been possible to reach total

4 Resolution XXX. Text in the U.S. Department of State *Bulletin*, Vol. XII,
No. 299 (18 Mar. 1945), p. 450.
5 John A. Houston, *Latin America in the United Nations* (New York: Carnegie
Endowment for International Peace, 1956), pp. 6–7.

agreement on such nominations, but lack of agreement is always regarded by the Group as very regrettable.

The membership of the Group has not changed since the Organization was founded, so that its relative voting strength has declined and will continue to decline as additional States are admitted to the Organization. The Group's membership is given in Table 2.

AFRICA AND ASIA

The Afro-Asian Group at the United Nations (which includes the ten Arab States) draws its cohesion and inspiration from the Bandung Conference of 1955. Twenty-nine Member States, including Turkey, are associated with it, and it is the largest single organized group of Members. Three Member States of the Organization which fall within the Afro-Asian region are not members of the Group: China, Israel and the Union of South Africa.

The Afro-Asian Group came into existence in 1950, but from the beginning there had been close consultation among Arab Member States on Middle Eastern and related questions. There were five Arab founder Members of the United Nations: Egypt, Iraq, Lebanon, Saudi Arabia and Syria. Yemen was admitted into membership in 1947, Jordan and Libya in 1955, and Sudan, Morocco and Tunisia in 1956. In 1958 Egypt and Syria joined to form the United Arab Republic. At the present time (February 1960), all of the Arab States belonging to the United Nations are members of the League of Arab States, but Iraq and Tunisia do not actively participate in the affairs of the League. A representative of the Algerian Provisional Government has attended meetings of the Arab Group at the United Nations and of the Council of the Arab League. A Palestinian representative participates in meetings of the Council of the League, and a representative of Oman has attended recent sessions of the General Assembly and participated in the work of the Arab Group when matters relating to Oman and neighbouring territories were under consideration.

The Arab League maintains an office in New York which services and co-ordinates the activities of the Arab Group. The General Assembly, by Resolution 477 (V), invited the Secretary-General of the League of Arab States to attend sessions of the Assembly as an observer.

The Arab Group normally meets about once a month, though meetings are held more frequently during the General Assembly. No votes are taken, and every effort is made to reach a consensus. The Arab Group has always maintained a high degree of solidarity on Middle Eastern and colonial questions, even during the periods when the Arab States of the Middle East have been at odds with one another. Egypt has exercised marked leadership within the Group.

Some decisions affecting Arab States at the United Nations are taken by the Council of the Arab League. The Council has, from time to time, approved the nomination of Arab persons or States to United Nations bodies. The Council of the League, acting on a recommendation of the League's Political Committee, decided in January 1954 that the Arab States should co-operate more closely with the States of Africa and Asia.

The Council decided to approve the following decision of the Political Committee:

The Political Committee surveyed existing close ties between States of the Arab League and the other States of the Asian-African bloc and reviewed the sincere co-operation which has prevailed in this bloc, more especially in the treatment of questions submitted to the United Nations in its various sessions.

The Political Committee, to consolidate these ties, decided that:

1. The Arab States should strengthen their diplomatic representation with the States of the Asian-African bloc.

2. They should exchange political delegations with a view to consolidating the ties of friendship and co-operation in the political domain, as well as consolidating cultural and economic relations.

3. The Secretariat-General should study all means necessary for consolidating relations between States of the Arab League and the Asian-African bloc, including the convening of periodic meetings at a high level.

The Committee holds that it should adopt this same attitude toward States of the Latin American bloc.[6]

At a meeting in Casablanca in September 1959, the Council of the Arab League approved a report regarding the proposals of the Secretary-General for the continuation of United Nations assistance to Palestine refugees (Resolution 1593)[7]; adopted a resolution upholding the right of Oman to independence and asking members to discuss the question during the General Debate in the General Assembly (Resolution 1596); adopted a resolution stressing the grave repercussions of the contemplated tests of nuclear weapons in the Sahara by France, and urging support for the proposal of Morocco that the matter be included in the agenda of the General Assembly [8] (Resolution 1601); adopted a resolution urging that the plebiscites to be held in the British Cameroons be conducted in such a way as to guarantee that the people would be free to exercise self-determination;

[6] Resolution 605, 21 Jan. 1954. Text in *Egypt and the United Nations* (New York: Manhattan Publishing, 1957), p. 139.

[7] Circulated to United Nations Member States under symbol A/4236, 7 Oct. 1959.

[8] United Nations Doc. A/4183, 14 Aug. 1959.

and decided to support Morocco's candidature for one of the vice-presidencies of the Assembly [9] and Iraq for membership of the Advisory Committee on Administrative and Budgetary Questions,[10] and decided that Arab delegations at the United Nations should have discretion regarding other candidatures (Resolution 1227).

Five Arab States (Libya, Morocco, the Sudan, Tunisia and the United Arab Republic) are also members of the African Group, which came into existence after the Conference of Independent African States held in Accra in 1958. The other members of the African Group are Ethiopia, Ghana, Guinea and Liberia; additional members will be added as new African States are admitted to the United Nations. The African Group is still in a formative stage and its machinery of consultation at United Nations headquarters is informal. The Secretariat of the Group consists of members of the Permanent Missions of Ghana, Tunisia and the United Arab Republic. Meetings of the Group are held about once a week; a meeting may be called at the request of any member. Only African and related questions are discussed. There is no voting, and no binding decisions are taken. The chairmanship rotates on an alphabetical basis; meetings are conducted in English, though interpretation into French is sometimes needed.

From time to time both the United Arab Republic and Ghana have sought to exercise leadership within the Group, but the other members of the Group have tended to resist the idea that the Group has a " leader."

The Arab Group and the African Group are sub-groups within the larger Afro-Asian Group. The latter Group began on an improvised basis as an Arab-Asian group of twelve members in 1950, during the early stages of the Korean War. Those attending meetings of the Group in 1950 were: Afghanistan, Burma, Egypt, India, Indonesia, Iran, Iraq, Lebanon, Pakistan, Saudi Arabia, Syria and Yemen. The Philippines and all of these countries except Syria and Lebanon consulted together on the Tunisian question in 1951. Syria and Lebanon returned to the Group in 1952, and Thailand joined in 1954.

It was the Bandung Conference in 1955 that gave the Group a sense of identity and purpose. Ethiopia, Liberia and Turkey joined the Group the same year, and the thirteen States of Asia and Africa which were admitted to United Nations membership during or since

[9] Morocco was elected a Vice-President on 15 Sept. 1959.
[10] This Committee consists of persons rather than States. Ismat T. Kittani of Iraq was appointed by the Assembly on 17 Nov. 1959.

the tenth session have joined the Group. The increase in United Nations membership in Asia and Africa is shown in Table 3.

TABLE 3

Increase in United Nations Membership in Asia and Africa*

Founder Members	1946	1947	1948
Egypt†	Afghanistan	Pakistan	Burma
Ethiopia	Thailand	Yemen	
India			
Iran			
Iraq			
Lebanon			
Liberia			
Philippines			
Saudi Arabia			
Syria†			

1950	1955	1956	1957	1958
Indonesia	Cambodia	Japan	Ghana	Guinea
	Ceylon	Morocco	Malaya	
	Jordan	Sudan		
	Laos	Tunisia		
	Libya			
	Nepal			

* Excludes China, Israel, Union of South Africa and Turkey.
† Egypt and Syria joined in 1958 to form the United Arab Republic.

Turkey's position in the Group is ambiguous. Turkey, though geographically situated in the eastern Mediterranean, is a member of the North Atlantic Treaty Organization (NATO) and of such European bodies as the United Nations Economic Commission for Europe, the Council of Europe, and the Organization for European Economic Co-operation. For some purposes, Turkey has been regarded as being within the category " Western Europe and other States." Turkey has also sometimes been considered an East European State for other purposes, such as Security Council elections. To confuse the picture still further, when Turkey was a candidate for one of the Assembly's vice-presidencies in 1959, it was uncertain until the last moment for which region she was a candidate. Since it would be confusing in this book to regard Turkey as belonging to more than one region, I have (unless there are specific indications to the contrary) regarded Turkey as within the region " Western, Northern and Southern Europe."

The affiliations of members of the Afro-Asian Group, including Turkey, are shown in Table 4.

TABLE 4

Affiliations of United Nations Member States Belonging to the Afro-Asian Group*

	Central Treaty Organization (formerly Baghdad Pact), SEATO, or defence arrangements with U.S.	League of Arab States	Accra Conference of Independent African States
Afghanistan			
Burma			
Cambodia			
Ceylon			
Ethiopia			x
Ghana			x
Guinea			x
India			
Indonesia			
Iran	x		
Iraq		x	
Japan	x		
Jordan		x	
Laos			
Lebanon		x	
Liberia			x
Libya		x	x
Malaya			
Morocco		x	x
Nepal			
Pakistan	x		
Philippines	x		
Saudi Arabia		x	
Sudan		x	x
Thailand	x		
Tunisia		x	x
Turkey	x		
United Arab Republic		x	x
Yemen		x	

* Including Turkey.

The influence of the States of Africa and Asia on United Nations affairs has been growing not only because the number of such States in the United Nations has increased, but also because they are now organized for common action, share some common ideals, and are aware of their strength when united. There are, inevitably, cross currents within the Afro-Asian Group. For a time India exercised considerable influence within the Group, but leadership has recently been more diffused. If the People's Republic of China were to be represented in the United Nations, it would presumably participate in meetings of the Afro-Asian Group.

It is likely that the Group will encounter difficulties in maintaining cohesion in the future. At least six, and probably more, new African States will presumably join the Group during 1960, bringing the total membership (including Turkey) to at least thirty-five. It will probably be necessary to use the French language, as well as English, at Group meetings. With a membership of forty or more, further fissiparous tendencies might develop.

The Afro-Asian Group meets as required, the chairmanship rotating among the members on a monthly basis. The Group as such takes no decisions except by unanimity. The Group has not hitherto put forward regional candidates for election, though it is possible that there will be changes in this respect.

EASTERN EUROPE

I suggested earlier that the only *bloc* at the United Nations consists of the Communist Member States belonging to the Warsaw Pact and the Council for Mutual Economic Assistance, together with Byelorussia and the Ukraine. These Member States are closely bound together by ideological and other ties; though there are occasionally variations in the tone of voice and choice of language of their representatives, their votes are so consistently the same that the rare deviations arouse comment.

United Nations Member States from Eastern Europe were originally six in number: the Soviet Union, the Byelorussian and Ukrainian Soviet Socialist Republics, Czechoslovakia, Poland and Yugoslavia. The creation of the Cominform and the coup in Czechoslovakia increased the solidarity of the group, but its size was diminished to five in 1948 following the break between the Cominform and Yugoslavia. The admission to the United Nations of Albania, Bulgaria, Hungary and Romania in December 1955 increased the number of Member States associated with the Soviet Union to nine.

Little is known about the procedures by which these nine States consult each other. There is continuous and close consultation in their capitals, both on a government and a party level. Their representatives in United Nations bodies share the Marxist ideology and are informed of current Soviet views on foreign policy questions. Moreover, the predominant role of the Soviet Union is accepted by all members of the *Bloc*.

Whether the States of the Soviet *Bloc* reach binding decisions after consultation, or whether identity of view is reached by other means, is immaterial. The fact is that these States have a uniform policy on major questions. Divergencies in voting rarely occur on matters of major importance; deviations on matters of lesser importance happen from time to time, though these may be caused by a misunderstanding either as to what the position of the *Bloc* is or

what exactly was being voted on. If deviations because of misunderstanding occur, members of the *Bloc* usually try to change their votes
subsequently so as to present a united front.[11]

" The Soviet *Bloc*," in this book, means the States of the Warsaw
Pact and the Council for Mutual Economic Assistance, together with
Byelorussia and the Ukraine. Yugoslavia is not now a member of
the Soviet *Bloc* but is part of the geographical region " Eastern
Europe." Although Turkey and Greece have occasionally been
regarded by some as Eastern European States for purposes of
United Nations elections, it has seemed to me that, for the sake
of consistency, it is preferable to regard them as within the area
" Western, Northern and Southern Europe."

TABLE 5

Eastern European Member States of the United Nations

Albania
Byelorussian S.S.R.
Bulgaria
Czechoslovakia
Hungary   Soviet *Bloc*
Poland
Romania
Ukrainian S.S.R.
U.S.S.R.
Yugoslavia

WESTERN EUROPE

The fourth category of States referred to in the Assembly's resolution
of the twelfth session on the composition of the General Committee,
called " Western Europe and other States," is not a regularly
organized group nor even a precise geographical expression. Western
Europe, in this context, is an elastic term, since it extends from
Iceland to Finland in the north and from Spain to Greece in the
south. It would be more exact to refer to these seventeen States as
" Western, Northern and Southern Europe," but for the sake of
brevity I have used the term " Western Europe," except in a few
cases where the more elaborate term is needed for the sake of clarity.

There were nine founder Members of the United Nations from
Western Europe: Belgium, Denmark, France, Greece, Luxembourg,
the Netherlands, Norway, Turkey and the United Kingdom. Iceland
and Sweden were admitted to membership in 1946, and Austria,
Finland, Ireland, Italy, Portugal and Spain in 1955. The Member
States of the region are given in Table 6.

[11] See, for example, G.A.O.R.: 14th Sess., Spec. Pol. Cmtte., 138th Mtg., 28 Oct.
1959 and 139th Mtg., 29 Oct. 1959; also G.A.O.R.: 14th Sess., 4th Cmtte.,
932nd Mtg., 30 Oct. 1959.

TABLE 6

United Nations Member States in Western, Northern and Southern Europe, Including Turkey

Austria	Luxembourg
Belgium	Netherlands
Denmark	Norway
Finland	Portugal
France	Spain
Greece	Sweden
Iceland	Turkey
Ireland	United Kingdom
Italy	

Within this region are a number of associations for political or economic co-operation. Denmark, Finland, Iceland, Norway and Sweden belong to the Nordic Council and consult each other on regional questions, including matters relating to the United Nations. Belgium, Luxembourg and the Netherlands form the Benelux Union; these three States, together with France, the Federal Republic of Germany (not a Member of the United Nations) and Italy are members of the European Economic Community. Austria, Denmark, Norway, Portugal, Sweden, Switzerland (not a Member of the United Nations) and the United Kingdom belong to the European Free Trade Association; Finland is loosely related to this organization. For United Nations purposes, however, it may be convenient to sub-divide the States of this region into:

(*a*) the twelve European members of NATO which belong to the United Nations, together with Spain;

(*b*) the four European neutrals (Austria, Finland, Ireland and Sweden).

" OTHER STATES "

Resolution 1192 (XII) refers to " other States "; the four older Commonwealth countries and Israel are presumably covered by this expression.

Nationalist China and the United States are listed in Resolution 1192 (XII) in the fifth category, being permanent members of the Security Council. Neither China nor the United States belongs to a regularly organized group at the United Nations, though the United States almost always plays a leading role in the various coalitions which oppose Soviet policies.

THE COMMONWEALTH

The Commonwealth was described to me recently in the following way: " The Commonwealth cannot be defined, but it undoubtedly exists. We meet from time to time to exchange ideas on matters on which we are agreed. We always vote for each other, unless we happen to prefer some other candidate. It is a very superior form of co-operation, but it cannot be copied." This is doubtless a caricature, but like all real caricatures it contains an element of truth. The Commonwealth possesses neither ideological nor geographical unity, but Commonwealth States do understand one another rather readily; they have, in varying degrees, been influenced by British political traditions; and their representatives are at home in the English language. Australia, Canada, New Zealand and South Africa are referred to in the book by the admittedly clumsy expression " older Commonwealth States." The ten Member States of the Commonwealth are listed in Table 7.

TABLE 7

United Nations Member States of the Commonwealth

Western Europe	Older Commonwealth States	Afro-Asian Group
United Kingdom	Australia	Ceylon
	Canada	Ghana
	New Zealand	India
	Union of South Africa	Malaya
		Pakistan

The Commonwealth group meets once a fortnight while the Assembly is in session, and irregularly at other times of the year. The meeting is chaired by the senior British representative, though consideration has been given to the possibility of rotating the chairmanship. The agenda consists of all matters whose inclusion has been requested by Commonwealth members. Representatives are free, if they wish, to express the views of their governments on matters as they arise, but no attempt is made at Commonwealth group meetings to reach a consensus. The only matter on which the Commonwealth reaches a common view is in connection with the nominations for " Commonwealth vacancies " on United Nations organs, but this is dealt with by discussion and consultation outside Commonwealth group meetings.[12] If the Afro-Asian Group should decide to nominate candidates for election, there seems to be no reason why that Group rather than the Commonwealth should not nominate Commonwealth States from Asia and Africa in appropriate cases. An important feature of the Commonwealth group is that it overlaps other groups and regions.

[12] During the first session of the Assembly, both Australia and Canada were candidates for the Commonwealth seat on the Security Council. Australia withdrew after the third ballot and Canada was elected. This unhappy situation was avoided on future occasions by reaching prior, informal agreement on a single Commonwealth candidate.

As the membership of the United Nations has changed, so the relative voting strength of the regions has changed. Western European membership has fluctuated between 18 and 22 per cent., Eastern European membership between 10 and 13 per cent. Latin American strength has steadily declined from 39 to 24 per cent., and the Afro-Asian area has increased by a similar amount—from 20 to 35 per cent. It seems certain that Afro-Asian membership will steadily increase in the future, and that the relative strength of the other regions will decline. The Commonwealth, which overlaps the different regions, has varied between 10 and 12 per cent. of the whole membership.

CHART I

PERCENTAGE OF ASSEMBLY SEATS OF MAIN REGIONS AND GROUPS, 1945-1959

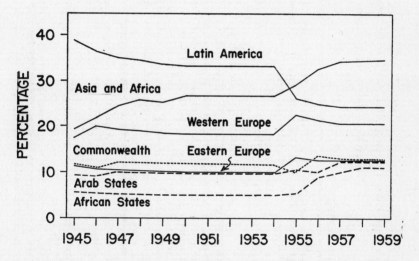

REGIONAL DISTRIBUTION OR ROTATION OF ELECTIVE PLACES

In addition to the regional distribution of members of the General Committee established by Resolution 1192 (XII), certain other elective places are distributed or rotated on a regional basis, either because this is required by the Charter or the Rules of Procedure, or because of some unwritten but generally accepted understanding. The constitutional position is set forth in Table 8.

It is inevitable that systems for the rotation or distribution of elective places should often take priority over personal competence (in the case of individuals) or the contribution made to the purposes of the United Nations (in the case of States). The fact is that it

TABLE 8

Factors to be Taken Into Account in Elections by the General Assembly

Office or organ A. Elected as individuals	Factors to be taken into account	References
1. President of the General Assembly	None specified	—
2. Chairmen, Vice-Chairmen and Rapporteurs of Main Committee	Equitable geographical distribution, experience and personal competence. Resolution 1192 (XII) confirmed the practice regarding the distribution of Chairmanships as follows: Latin America 2 Asia and Africa 2 Eastern Europe 1 Western Europe and other States 2	Rule 105 Resolution 1192 (XII)
3. International Court of Justice	The Court shall be composed of independent judges, elected regardless of their nationality from among persons of high moral character, who possess the qualifications required in their respective countries for appointment to the highest judicial offices, or are jurisconsults of recognized competence in international law. The electors shall bear in mind not only that the persons to be elected should individually possess the qualifications required, but also that in the body as a whole the representation of the main forms of civilization and of the principal legal systems of the world should be assured.	Articles 2 and 9 of the Statute
4. Advisory Committee on Administrative and Budgetary Questions	Broad geographical representation, personal qualifications and experience	Rule 157
5. Committee on Contributions	Broad geographical representation, personal qualifications and experience	Rule 160
6. International Law Commission	Persons of recognized competence in international law and representing as a whole the chief forms of civilization and the basic legal systems of the world	Resolution 174 (III)

B. Elected as States

7. Vice-Presidents of the General Assembly	On the basis of ensuring the representative character of the General Committee. The pattern, as specified in the annex to Resolution 1192 (XII), is as follows:	Rules 31 and 38 Resolution 1192 (XII)

    (a) Latin America   2
    (b) Asia and Africa   4
    (c) Eastern Europe   1
    (d) Western Europe and other States   2
    (e) Permanent members of the
        Security Council   5

The region from which the President of the Assembly is elected has one Vice-President less than is indicated above; furthermore, the President of the Assembly, or one of the Chairmen of the Main Committees, or one of the Vice-Presidents in group (b) or (d) above, should be from a Commonwealth country.

8. Credentials Committee	None specified	
9. Elected members of the Security Council	In the first instance to the contribution of Members to the maintenance of international peace and security and to the other purposes of the Organization, and also to equitable geographical distribution	Article 23 Rule 144
10. Economic and Social Council	None specified	
11. Elected members of the Trusteeship Council	None specified	

would be impossible for governments to agree on an objective method for evaluating the personal competence of individuals or the contribution of States to the purposes of the United Nations, whereas anyone who can count can set down on paper a scheme for the rotation or distribution of elective places which—on the surface, at any rate—looks equitable. The consistent application of such a system has drawbacks. It can, and sometimes does, result in the election of less than the best. It tends to crystallize and even exaggerate regional differences. Its merit, however, is that justice seems to be done.

There has developed a practice by which certain groups of States conduct what are, in effect, primary elections in the hope or expectation that the Assembly will give a formal endorsement to the candidates thus nominated. The Soviet Union, in particular, has held that this should be the normal practice. When, during the fourth session, Yugoslavia defeated Czechoslovakia for a seat on the Security Council vacated by the Ukraine, the Soviet representative protested in most vigorous terms:

There had . . . been a violation of the firmly established tradition that candidates for non-permanent membership were always nominated by the States belonging to the geographical areas concerned. . . . Yugoslavia's entry into the Security Council was not based on a free election held in conformity with the principles of the Charter and established tradition; it was the result of a lobby conspiracy . . . a bargain struck behind the scenes by Yugoslavia, the United States and various delegations which thus hoped to consolidate their position in the Security Council so as better to transform that Council into an obedient tool of the Anglo-American bloc.

The delegation of the Soviet Union wished to state most emphatically that Yugoslavia did not represent the countries of Eastern Europe. . . .[13]

It has been suggested that, as a purely practical matter, the automatic election of States nominated by groups or regions has the merit of excluding from the public meetings of the Assembly controversy regarding elections. This argument should not be pressed too far, however; the dispute concerning the presidency of the Assembly in 1958, to which reference is made in Chapter 3, shows that no arrangement, whether nominations are permitted or prohibited, and whether the election is by secret or public ballot, can guarantee that controversy will be excluded from the public meetings. Moreover, the practice of nominations by groups works to the disadvantage of a State which happens to be at odds with its neighbours in the same region.

13 G.A.O.R.: 4th Sess., 231st Plenary Mtg., 20 Oct. 1949, p. 103, paras. 10–13.

From a strictly constitutional point of view, the nomination of States by groups or regions is not binding; representatives are free to vote for any eligible candidate. In nine cases out of ten, it may be in the general interest that the nominations of regional groups should be endorsed, but this should not interfere with the right of any State to vote for any eligible candidate.

CHAPTER 3

THE FIRST DAY OF THE SESSION

The place of their first session should be central, as much as is possible, afterwards as they agree. . . . To avoid quarrel for precedency, the room may be round, and have divers doors to come in and go out at. . . . They may preside by turns, to whom all speeches should be addressed, and who should collect the sense of the debates, and state the question for a vote. . . . I should think it extremely necessary that every sovereignty should be present under great penalties, and that none leave the session without leave, till all be finished. . . . I will say little of the language in which the session . . . should be held, but to be sure it must be in Latin or French; the first would be very well for civilians, but the last most easy for men of quality.

WILLIAM PENN

EVERY year there take place at United Nations headquarters in New York some 1,500 meetings of United Nations organs. These may be important meetings of the Security Council or routine meetings of technical bodies concerned with such matters as statistics, petitions from trust territories, and the effects of atomic radiation. Most of these meetings are held in public.

Of all these meetings, those of the General Assembly always arouse great public interest. The Assembly normally convenes in New York on the third Tuesday in September and closes or adjourns about three months later. Plenary meetings of the Assembly are held in the large blue and gold hall, which is situated at the north end of the cluster of buildings of the United Nations on the east side of Manhattan. A few days before the Assembly is due to open, there will be a bustle of activity at United Nations headquarters as the staff completes the preparations for the three-month session. Foreign ministers, usually one or two prime ministers, diplomats and members of parliament will be gathering from all parts of the globe. The opening day is characterized by a sense of drama much like that of the State Opening of Parliament in the countries of the Commonwealth. As three o'clock approaches, sleek black cars draw up at the delegates entrance behind the flags of the United Nations and its Member States. Members of the general public wait in the lobby at the north end of the Assembly building for admission to the meeting.

At 3.15 p.m. on the third Tuesday in September 1959, Rachid Karame, Prime Minister of Lebanon, entered the General Assembly hall and took his seat on the dais at the front. He was accompanied by Secretary-General Dag Hammarskjold, who sat on his right, and by Andrew Cordier, Mr. Hammarskjold's executive assistant, who sat on his left. On the delegates' floor, representatives of eighty-two Member Nations had been gathering. Old friends greeted each other; old opponents exchanged pleasantries; new delegates were shown the ropes by the veterans. In the galleries sat a multilingual group of journalists, officials of the Secretariat, representatives of non-governmental organizations, and members of the public.

For five minutes the hubbub continued, and then Mr. Karame rapped the gavel and said, " I declare open the fourteenth regular session of the General Assembly of the United Nations." Mr. Karame spoke in French, but his words were immediately interpreted by officials into the other four languages used by the General Assembly—Chinese, English, Russian and Spanish—and each person present was able to switch the earphones by his seat to the language of his choice.[1]

Mr. Karame then invited the representatives to stand and observe one minute of silence dedicated to prayer or meditation (Rule 64). This practice was initiated in 1950 after the receipt by Secretary-General Trygve Lie of hundreds of letters from individuals and organizations urging that the General Assembly should devote a few moments of its time to prayer. It would hardly be possible to devise a public prayer which would be acceptable to all the faiths of which there are adherents among citizens of the Member States of the United Nations, but a short time of silence is a solemn act which gives offence to none.

When the representatives had sat down, Mr. Karame spoke briefly of the tasks that lay ahead. He mentioned, in particular, the need to achieve progress in the matter of disarmament and of the importance of international action to aid refugees.

THE QUESTION OF CREDENTIALS

The next item of business was the appointment of a Committee to examine the credentials of representatives and report its findings to the full Assembly (Rule 28). The purpose of this practice is to ensure that all representatives have been properly appointed and issued with credentials by the head of the State or the head of the Government or the Minister for Foreign Affairs concerned (Rule 27). The Credentials Committee is appointed during the first meeting of

---

[1] A U.N. delegate is allowed to speak in a language other than the five official languages, but if he does so he must himself make arrangements for the interpretation of his remarks. Victor Andrés Belaúnde of Peru, the President of the fourteenth session, has said that he uses French when he wishes to be precise, English when he wishes to under-state, and Spanish when he wishes to exaggerate.

the session and is asked to " report without delay " (Rule 28). Any representative to whose admission objection has been made is seated provisionally with the same rights as other representatives until the Credentials Committee has reported and the General Assembly has given its decision (Rule 29).

There has never been overt controversy about the composition of the Credentials Committee, which consists of nine members " appointed by the General Assembly on the proposal of the President " (Rule 28). Informal agreement on the membership of the Committee is reached before the opening of the session; the United States and the Soviet Union are usually included among the members. When the time comes to appoint the Committee, the President refers to the relevant Rule of Procedure, names the nine States which he proposes for membership, and says that if there is no objection he will consider that his proposal has been approved. There never is any objection.

The task of the Committee is to see that all representatives are properly accredited. The names of representatives and their credentials should be submitted to the Secretary-General of the United Nations " if possible not less than one week before the date fixed for the opening of the session " (Rule 27). The Secretariat examines these credentials and makes a report to the Credentials Committee. During the first five sessions of the Assembly (1946–50), the Credentials Committee made a first report to the Assembly within a day or so of its appointment, but since the sixth session (1951), the Credentials Committee has been asked to consider not only the question whether representatives have been issued with credentials in proper form, but also the further question whether the issuing authority was legally entitled to act on behalf of the Member State concerned. This question has arisen if two rival governments claim to be the only legitimate authority in a Member State, or if a government has been overthrown in circumstances which create doubts as to the legitimacy of its successor.

The two cases of this kind which have arisen in the General Assembly relate to China and Hungary. The Republic of China is a founding Member of the United Nations and is named in Article 23 of the Charter as a permanent member of the Security Council.[2] The

---

[2] In documents of the United Nations, the Government of China means the Nationalist (Kuomintang) Government headed by President Chiang Kai-shek, now based on Taiwan (Formosa); to avoid confusion, I have sometimes referred to this Government by some such phrase as " Nationalist China " or " the Kuomintang Government." The Communist Government established in Peking in 1949 is officially known as the Central People's Government of the People's Republic of China; in referring to this Government, I have used such phrases as " Communist China " or " the Peking Government."

expulsion of the Nationalist Government from the Chinese mainland and the formal establishment in Peking in October 1949 of the Chinese People's Republic posed an awkward constitutional problem for the General Assembly and other organs of the United Nations, a a problem which was aggravated a year later by the Chinese intervention in Korea. The political and moral arguments in favour of seating Chinese Communist representatives in organs of the United Nations, and the political and moral arguments in favour of maintaining the representation of the Chinese Nationalists, are well known and there is no need to repeat them.[3]

On four occasions the question of the representation of China has been raised as a point of order during the opening meeting of the Assembly, before the appointment of the Credentials Committee (1950), during the process of appointing the Credentials Committee (1954 and 1955), or during the process of electing the President (1953). In 1956 and each year since then India has proposed that the question of Chinese representation should be placed on the Assembly's agenda. The decisions of the Assembly have been as follows:

> 1950: Special Committee established to consider the question of Chinese representation; pending a decision on the matter, representatives of the Nationalist Government of China were seated with the same rights as other representatives. The Special Committee submitted a report which contained no recommendations, and the Assembly merely took note of the report.[4]
>
> 1951, 1952 and 1953: Decision to postpone consideration of proposals to exclude representatives of the Nationalist Government of China or to seat representatives of the People's Republic of China.[5]
>
> 1954–59: Decision " not to consider " proposals to exclude representatives of Nationalist China or to seat representatives of the People's Republic of China.[6]

The Assembly may decide to postpone consideration of a question (as it in effect did in relation to Chinese representation in 1950, and

---

[3] For a discussion of some of the legal aspects of the question, see Secretary-General Trygve Lie's memorandum *Legal Aspects of Problems of Representation in the United Nations*, S.C.O.R.: 5th Yr., Suppl. for 1 Jan.–31 May 1950 (S/1466, 9 Mar. 1950), p. 18 *et seq.*

[4] General Assembly Res. 490 (V), 19 Sept. 1950; 501 (V), 5 Nov. 1951.

[5] G.A.O.R.: 6th Sess., 342nd Plenary Mtg., 13 Nov. 1951, paras. 83–155; 351st Plenary Mtg., 7 Dec. 1951, paras. 1–53; General Assembly Res. 609 (VII), 25 Oct. 1952; Res. 800 (VIII), 15 Sept. 1953.

[6] General Assembly Res. 903 (IX), 21 Sept. 1954; Res. 990 (X), 20 Sept. 1955; Res. 1108 (XI), 16 Nov. 1956; Res. 1135 (XII), 24 Sept. 1957; Res. 1239 (XIII), 23 Sept. 1958; Res. 1351 (XIV), 22 Sept. 1959.

as it explicitly did in 1951, 1952 and 1953) or it may refuse to consider a question (as it has done since 1954). It may be doubted, however, whether the Assembly has fully conformed to its own Rules of Procedure since 1954, because the resolutions on Chinese representation which it has adopted at the beginning of each session have had the effect not only of rejecting the request to discuss Chinese representation (which is not open to objection on legal grounds), but also of excluding the credentials of Chinese representatives from scrutiny by the Credentials Committee. Indeed, when the question of Chinese credentials has arisen in the Credentials Committee, the Chairman has ruled that the question was already decided.[7]

The other problem of credentials has related to representatives of Hungary. During the sessions of the Assembly since the Hungarian uprising, the Credentials Committee has taken no decision regarding the credentials of Hungarian representatives, and on each occasion the report of the Credentials Committee has been approved by the Assembly.[8] In the absence of a decision on their credentials, Hungarian representatives enjoy the same rights as other representatives.

As a result of the sharp differences regarding credentials, the Credentials Committee now meets late in the session; this practice does not conform to the requirement of the Rules of Procedure that it " report without delay " (Rule 28). Indeed, it is somewhat anomalous that the appointment of the Credentials Committee should be a matter of such urgency that it precedes the election of the President for the session, though it is known that the Committee will probably not meet until about twelve weeks later. It is, however, a recognized practice of international conferences to appoint a credentials committee as the first item of business. It is interesting to note that the Security and Trusteeship Councils entrust the examination of credentials to the Secretary-General, while the Economic and Social Council leaves this matter to the President and two Vice-Presidents.[9]

[7] G.A.O.R. Annexes, Agenda item 3 for: 9th Sess., 1954 (A/2752), para. 5; 10th Sess., 1955 (A/3027), para. 6; 11th Sess., 1956 (A/3536), para. 12; 12th Sess., 1957 (A/3773), para. 14; 13th Sess., 1958 (A/4074), para. 5; and United Nations Doc. A/4346, 9 Dec. 1959, para. 6.

[8] General Assembly Res. 1009 (XI), 21 Feb. 1957; Res. 1183 (XII), 10 Dec. 1957; Res. 1346 (XIII), 13 Dec. 1958; Res. 1457 (XIV), 10 Dec. 1959.

[9] Provisional Rules of Procedure of the Security Council (S/96/Rev. 3), 27 Jan. 1948, Rule 15; Rules of Procedure of the Trusteeship Council (T/1/Rev. 5), 1958, Rule 14(2); Rules of Procedure of the Economic and Social Council (E/3063), 1958, Rule 19.

THE ELECTION OF THE PRESIDENT

Until the Assembly has elected a President for the session, the Chairman of the delegation from which the President of the previous session was elected acts as Temporary President. The President of the 1958–59 session was Charles Mâlik of Lebanon, and accordingly the Chairman of the Lebanese delegation presided over the opening of the 1959 session. A Credentials Committee having been appointed, it was now time for Mr. Karame to invite the Assembly to choose a new President which, according to Article 21 of the Charter, shall be by election. Two matters arise in this connection: (a) the factors taken into account in the choice of the President; and (b) the method of election. A further question concerns the powers of the President, but this will be considered in Chapter 6.

It has been the general experience of assemblies of many kinds that the chief criterion to be borne in mind in the selection of officers should be personal competence, while in the establishment of organs of limited membership the main requirements should be that the organs should be sufficiently expert to fulfil the tasks assigned to them and sufficiently representative so as to enjoy the greatest possible degree of confidence of the whole. The more heterogeneous the membership of an assembly, the more the criterion of personal competence in the selection of officers tends to give way to some principle of rotation or equitable distribution. This tendency is clearly apparent in the General Assembly of the United Nations.

The League of Nations was less preoccupied than the United Nations has been with systems for the rotation of offices. Paul Hymans of Belgium was President of the first session of the League Assembly in 1920, and in 1932–33 he presided over the extraordinary session on the Sino-Japanese dispute; Paul van Zeeland, also of Belgium, presided over the resumed sixteenth session of the Assembly in the summer of 1936 on the Italo-Ethiopian dispute. On the two latter occasions, personal competence outweighed the fact that a Belgian had already been President. Similarly, Nicolas Titulesco of Romania presided over the eleventh session of the League Assembly in 1930, and was elected to the same office the following year.

The Rules of Procedure of the United Nations Assembly place no restriction on the Assembly's freedom of choice, but—as in the League—there is a general though informal understanding that it would be undesirable to elect as President a representative of any of the five Powers which are permanent members of the Security Council. The Presidents elected by the Assembly are shown in Table 9.

TABLE 9

Presidents of the General Assembly, 1946–59

Session	Date	President	State
1	10 Jan.–15 Dec. 46	Paul-Henri Spaak	Belgium
1st Spec. Sess.	28 Apr.–15 May 47	Oswaldo Aranha	Brazil
2	16 Sept.–29 Nov. 47	Oswaldo Aranha	Brazil
2nd Spec. Sess.	16 Apr.–14 May 48	José Arce	Argentina
3	21 Sept. 48–18 May 49	Herbert V. Evatt	Australia
4	20 Sept.–10 Dec. 49	Carlos P. Romulo	Philippines
5	19 Sept. 50–5 Nov. 51	Nasrollah Entezam	Iran
6	6 Nov. 51–5 Feb. 52	Luis Padilla Nervo	Mexico
7	14 Oct. 52–28 Aug. 53	Lester B. Pearson	Canada
8	15 Sept.–9 Dec. 53	Mrs. Vijaya Lakshmi Pandit	India
9	21 Sept.–17 Dec. 54	Eelco van Kleffens	Netherlands
10	20 Sept.–20 Dec. 55	José Maza	Chile
1st Emergency Special Sess.	1 Nov.–10 Nov. 56	Rudecindo Ortega	Chile
2nd Emergency Special Sess.	4 Nov.–10 Nov. 56	Rudecindo Ortega	Chile
11	12 Nov. 56–8 Mar. 57	Prince Wan Waithayakon	Thailand
12	17 Sept.–14 Dec. 57	Sir Leslie Munro	New Zealand
3rd Emergency Special Sess.	8 Aug.–21 Aug. 58	Sir Leslie Munro	New Zealand
13	16 Sept. 58–13 Mar. 59	Charles Mâlik	Lebanon
14	15 Sept.–13 Dec. 59	Victor Andrés Belaúnde	Peru

The presidency has rotated from region to region with reasonable equity, though there has not yet been a President from one of the Communist States of Eastern Europe. During the fourteenth session (1959), the countries of the Soviet *Bloc* maintained that this was an injustice, and proposed that the Presidents of the succeeding four sessions should be elected from the four main regions as follows:

1960 Eastern Europe
1961 Asia and Africa
1962 Western Europe and other States
1963 Latin America

In an explanatory memorandum submitted by Czechoslovakia, it was stated that the principle of equitable geographical representation, which was one of the fundamental functional principles of the United Nations, had not been consistently applied in the elections of the President of the Assembly. Representatives of all geographical areas except Eastern Europe had several times held in turn the office of President. The shortcomings connected with the practice of filling the office had not been removed even after the adoption of Resolution 1192 (XII) on the composition of the General Committee. The attainment of an agreement on the correct application of the

" principle of equitable geographical representation in the election of the President " would remove the existing shortcomings and would contribute to a further development of co-operation and the strengthening of mutual confidence among Member States.[10]

The proposal of Czechoslovakia, which was supported by other members of the Soviet *Bloc*, was considered by the Special Political Committee in December 1959. On two aspects of the matter the debate revealed substantial agreement: first, that the principle of equitable geographical representation should be an important factor in the choice of the President; secondly, that personal competence and experience were of great importance. There was thus agreement on two matters of general principle, but on questions of procedure there were important differences. The Soviet *Bloc* countries insisted that discrimination against Eastern Europe should be ended by the adoption of a precise formula for the rotation of the presidency, and that the presidency should always be filled by a candidate nominated by the countries of the region whose turn it was.

There were some objections to the formula proposed on the grounds that it would remedy one injustice by creating others. It was pointed out, for example, that the presidency had gone to the Afro-Asian area in 1949, 1950, 1953, 1956–57 and 1958–59; it was, in the view of some representatives, the turn of " Western Europe and other States " before it was the turn of Africa and Asia. Other speakers held that, because the Afro-Asian region had more members than any other region, it was entitled to the presidency more than once in a four-year period.

But the real objection was not so much to the terms of the proposed formula as to having a formula at all. The opponents of the Communist proposal considered that the adoption of any formula would tend to give a lesser importance to personal competence and experience. This led to an interesting discussion of the relationship of genius to geography. Some representatives insisted that genius knew no frontiers and was as likely to appear in Eastern Europe as in other regions of the world, to which it was retorted that genius might appear twice in one country before visiting the other eighty-one.

One element of confusion entered the debate. The question before the Assembly was " the consistent application of the principle of equitable geographical representation," but several speakers maintained that the real issue was whether it would be appropriate to choose a President from a Communist State. The ideological and geographical aspects were obviously closely linked, but to treat them

[10] United Nations Doc. A/4182, 13 Aug. 1959.

as the same was bound to cause misunderstanding. It is theoretically conceivable that in the future a Member State of the United Nations not in Eastern Europe may have a Communist government, or that an Eastern European State may have a non-Communist government.

It was, I think, understood by most representatives that the initiative of Czechoslovakia in raising the question represented a prelude to an attempt to mobilize sufficient support for the election of Jiři Nosek of Czechoslovakia as President of a future session of the Assembly. The debate served to clarify the issues in this connection, but the complicated manœuvres regarding a draft resolution hardly seemed worth the candle.

The draft resolution adopted by the Special Political Committee by 36–32–8 was as follows:

The General Assembly,

In view of the spirit of the United Nations Charter and of the provisions of the rules of procedure of the General Assembly pertaining to the President of the General Assembly,

Recognizing the importance of ensuring that the President of the General Assembly possesses the highest personal qualifications for the performance of his duties, and of taking into account in his election the principle of equitable geographical representation,

Recommends that in the election of the President of the General Assembly due regard be specially paid to the qualifications that the President of the General Assembly must possess in order to perform the important duties of his office and to the principle of equitable geographical representation.[11]

The first preambular paragraph, beginning with the words *In view*, was part of a draft resolution submitted by Czechoslovakia and Romania. The second preambular paragraph, beginning with *Recognizing*, was part of a proposal of eleven Latin American States, with a minor amendment proposed by Guinea and the United Arab Republic. The operative paragraph, beginning with *Recommends*, was proposed by Guinea and the United Arab Republic, with a slight change of form but not of substance proposed by Mexico. This composite draft resolution might seem unobjectionable though it was, in the event, rejected in plenary meeting by 36–40–6. It was supported by the ten Eastern European Member States, twenty-three members of the Afro-Asian Group, and three Latin American States (Cuba, El Salvador and Mexico). It was opposed by all the States of Western, Northern and Southern Europe except Finland (abstaining), fourteen States of Latin America, four Asian States (Japan,

11 United Nations Doc. A/4340, 8 Dec. 1959, pp. 6–7.

Laos, the Philippines and Thailand), three of the older Commonwealth countries, together with China, Israel and the United States. Canada was one of the six abstainers.[12]

A rigid formula for the rotation of the presidency among regions is, in my view, undesirable. The presidency has, in practice, rotated with reasonable fairness in the past. It is, however, the turn of Eastern Europe and an effort should be made to agree on a candidate from that region for 1960 or, should a West European be elected in 1960, for 1961. There have been five Presidents from the Afro-Asian area, three of them from Asia, one from an Arab country of the Middle East, and one from a non-Arab country of the Middle East (Iran). With a growing African membership, it will no doubt be desirable to have a President from the continent of Africa in 1962.

There is now a certain artificiality about the prohibition of nominations in connection with the election of the President. The Provisional Rules of Procedure did not prohibit nominations, and it was the uneasiness regarding the election of the first President that led to the change in the Rules. Trygve Lie relates how, on Christmas Day of 1945, he received a message that had originated with Adlai Stevenson, who was then acting as head of the United States delegation to the Preparatory Commission of the United Nations. Mr. Stevenson had inquired whether Mr. Lie " would be willing to accept election as President " of the first Assembly, which was to open in London a fortnight later. Mr. Lie replied in the affirmative, being under the impression that Britain and the Soviet Union also favoured his election. When he arrived in London a couple of days before the opening of the Assembly, Mr. Lie learned that Britain " for the last two months had been vigorously supporting Paul-Henri Spaak, the Foreign Minister of Belgium." The next day, Mr. Lie was informed that the United States " now regarded Mr. Spaak's election as certain " and would therefore " refrain from trying to influence the Latin American delegations, who . . . were in many instances strongly inclined to vote for Mr. Spaak." [13] On the morning of the day the Assembly was to convene, Mr. Lie was told by a Soviet representative that the Soviet Union intended to nominate him.

When the time came to elect the President, the Soviet representative stated that his delegation intended to vote for Trygve Lie of Norway. He referred to the heroic role of Norway during the war, and praised Mr. Lie's personal qualities. The Ukrainian, Polish and Danish representatives then stated that they also would vote for Mr.

[12] United Nations Doc. A/PV.852, 10 Dec. 1959, pp. 47–50.
[13] *In the Cause of Peace* (New York: Macmillan, 1954), pp. 4–5.

Lie. Although there was no other nomination, the result of the ballot was that Mr. Spaak received twenty-eight votes and Mr. Lie twenty-three. Mr. Spaak was therefore elected on the first ballot. Mr. Lie comments that this decision left him " both relieved and discontented." [14] Three weeks later he was appointed the first Secretary-General of the Organization, by a vote of forty-five to three in the Assembly.

The direct result of the election of the first President was the adoption of an amendment to the Provisional Rules of Procedure prohibiting nominations in plenary meetings.[15] This did not, of course, get rid of the nominating process: it transferred it from the floor of the Assembly to the corridors. Moreover, it has been impossible to avoid nominations in disguise.

In 1957 Charles Mâlik of Lebanon was the nominee of the Afro-Asian Group for the presidency. It was not, however, the turn of the Afro-Asian area since the retiring President, Prince Wan of Thailand, was an Asian. When the time came to elect a President during the first plenary meeting of the session, a former President of the Assembly took the floor and urged Mr. Mâlik to withdraw. Mr. Mâlik then stated that in the interest of concord, he would yield to his good friend Sir Leslie Munro of New Zealand. This was equivalent to a public nomination, and Carlos P. Romulo, who presided over the fourth session of the Assembly (1949), had ruled (and had not been challenged) " that the withdrawal of one . . . candidature in favour of another was equivalent to a nomination" and was therefore out of order.[16] Be that as it may, when Mr. Mâlik had finished his statement, several representatives stated that they would support his candidature on some future occasion. The ballot gave seventy-seven votes to Sir Leslie Munro and one to Charles Mâlik.

An unusual situation thus existed in 1958. A large number of delegations had agreed privately, and a few publicly, to vote for Mr. Mâlik. It was, however, regarded as virtually certain that within a week of the opening of the Assembly, Mr. Mâlik would cease being Foreign Minister of Lebanon. Moreover, the majority of Arab delegations had stated that they had switched support from Charles Mâlik to M. A. Mahgoub, who was at that time the Sudanese Foreign Minister. To complicate the picture further, the countries of the Soviet *Bloc* had let it be known that Jiří Nosek of Czechoslovakia was also a candidate. When the time came to elect the President,

---

[14] *Ibid.*, p. 10.
[15] General Assembly Res. 17 (I), 26 and 29 Jan. 1956; Rule 94.
[16] G.A.O.R.: 4th Sess., 231st Plenary Mtg., 20 Oct. 1949, para. 22.

the representative of Czechoslovakia stated that " By agreement with the other east European countries, the Czechoslovak delegation withdraws the candidature of Ambassador Jiří Nosek . . . in favour of the candidate of the overwhelming majority of the Arab countries " (that is to say, Mr. Mahgoub).[17] In the event, Mr. Mâlik was elected by forty-five votes to thirty-one for Mr. Mahgoub, with four abstentions.

In 1959 the election was straightforward. It was, by general consent, the turn of Latin America. The States of that area had informally put forward the candidature of Mr. Victor Andrés Belaúnde of Peru, an experienced and highly respected diplomat. Mr. Belaúnde obtained eighty-one votes in the election, and there was one invalid ballot.

The prohibition of nominations in plenary meetings can sometimes be quite unreal. It is no secret that there are nominations. Delegations openly lobby for themselves or their friends. Unofficial papers are circulated stating that a particular person or country is a candidate for a particular post. The Groups inform the Press of their choices. Perhaps the chief merit of the ban on nominations is not that it prevents nominations but that it prevents nomination *speeches*.

THE ELECTION OF COMMITTEE CHAIRMEN

After the newly-elected President has addressed the Assembly, the Chairmen of the seven Main Committees are elected. Much of the basic work of the Assembly is done in the Main Committees, each of which consists of all the Member States of the United Nations. Each Main Committee elects its own Chairman, Vice-Chairman and Rapporteur (Rule 105). Officers of Main Committees are elected in their individual capacities.

The procedure for the election of Chairmen is as follows. The President of the Assembly formally closes the first plenary meeting of the session and immediately calls to order the First Committee. Nominations are permitted in Committees of the Assembly, and the President therefore asks if there are any nominations for the chairmanship of the First Committee. A representative, often the Chairman of the Committee the previous year, mounts the rostrum and nominates a person as Chairman. The nomination is seconded by another representative, although this is not required under the Rules of Procedure. If, as is normally the case, there is only one nomination, the President declares the nominee elected by acclamation; if

[17] G.A.O.R.: 13th Sess., 747th Plenary Mtg., 16 Sept. 1958, paras. 19–20.

there is more than one nomination, an election is held by secret ballot. The procedure lasts about ten minutes. When it is concluded, the President closes the meeting of the First Committee and at once calls the Special Political Committee to order for the election of a Chairman, then the Second Committee, and so on until the seven Chairmen have been elected.

The arrangements for brief speeches of nomination and support are prepared in advance by the Secretariat, in agreement with delegations, in such a way as to distribute the honours and responsibilities as equitably and acceptably as possible. In the 1959 Assembly the arrangements were as follows:

COMMITTEE	NOMINATED AS CHAIRMAN	NOMINATED BY	SUPPORTED BY
First	Franz Matsch, Austria	Padilla Nervo, Mexico	Koto Matsudaira, Japan
Special Political	Charles T. O. King, Liberia	Omar Loutfi, United Arab Republic	A. Quaison-Sackey, Ghana
Second	Marcial Tamayo, Bolivia	Daniel Schweitzer, Chile	Omar Abdel Hameed Adeel, Sudan
Third	Mrs. Georgette Ciselet, Belgium	Christian X. Palamas, Greece	Salvador P. Lopez, Philippines
Fourth	Lambertus Palar, Indonesia	Frederick H. Boland, Ireland	U Thant, Burma
Fifth	Jiří Nosek, Czechoslovakia	Sir Claude Corea, Ceylon	José A. Correa, Ecuador
Sixth	Alberto Herrarte, Guatemala	Riccardo Monaco, Italy	Jorge E. Illueca, Panama

The Rules state that the Chairmen, Vice-Chairmen and Rapporteurs of Committees shall be elected on the basis of equitable geographical distribution, experience and personal competence (Rule 105). Representatives of States which are permanent members of the Security Council have not been elected as Chairmen of Main Committees, with the single exception that T. F. Tsiang of China was elected Chairman of the First Committee by secret ballot during the second special session (1948). The recent practice has been to allocate the chairmanships as follows:

Latin America	2
Asia and Africa	2
Eastern Europe [18]	1
Western Europe and other States	2

[18] Czechoslovakia and Poland head the list of States whose representatives have been most frequently elected to chairmanships of Main Committees.

By Resolution 1192 of the twelfth session, this practice was formally confirmed. There is normally one woman among the Chairmen.

The electoral process in the election of Vice-Chairmen and Rapporteurs is the same as in the election of Chairmen. If there is only one candidate for a vacancy, as is usually the case, election is by acclamation. If there are two or more candidates, as was the case, for example, in connection with the vice-chairmanship of the Fourth Committee during the fourteenth session,[19] an election is held by secret ballot (Rule 105).

A chairmanship or other Committee office can be a rung on a ladder, bringing honour to the person and his country. If a representative has ambitions for himself or his country and aspires to a committee office, he will let it be known that he is " available " and will seek the support of any groups to which his country belongs.

Thus Nasrollah Entezam of Iran, before being elected President of the General Assembly, was successively Chairman of the General Committee of the Executive Committee of the Preparatory Commission of the United Nations, Rapporteur of the Permanent Headquarters Committee, Chairman of the Sixth Committee, and Chairman of the *Ad Hoc* Political Committee.

As a representative mounts the ladder, he learns the tricks of the trade, the arts of good chairmanship. He learns how to look as if he is enjoying boring speeches; he learns how to smooth the ruffled feelings of aggrieved representatives; he learns when to consult members of the Secretariat and when to act on his own initiative; he learns how to rule on a point of order which he has not fully heard or has not understood.

The Assembly's resolution of the twelfth session confirming the practice for the distribution of chairmanships, and the fact that candidatures are in many cases endorsed by groups of States, does not mean that the elections are necessarily mere formalities. An aspirant for a chairmanship who fails to obtain the support of his Group may persist with his candidacy and force a ballot. Such a potentially awkward situation existed immediately before the opening of the fourteenth session (1959). The informal slate of candidates for chairmanships corresponded to the Chairmen subsequently elected, except that a representative of the Philippines was an additional candidate for the chairmanship of the Third Committee. Intensive consultations were necessary, and in the end the matter was resolved without the disagreeable necessity of a contested election. Four days before the session was due to open, the

[19] G.A.O.R.: 14th Sess., 4th Committee, 882nd and 883rd Mtgs., 23 Sept. 1959.

Permanent Missions of Japan and the Philippines issued the following carefully-worded joint Press release:

> The Japanese Permanent Representative proposes to withdraw their candidacy for the Vice-Presidency of the United Nations General Assembly in favour of the Philippines in view of the fact that the Philippines has withdrawn its candidacy for the Chairmanship of the Third Committee.
>
> The Philippine Permanent Representative expressed appreciation for the kind gesture of the Japanese Permanent Representative and stated that the announcement of the withdrawal of the Philippine candidacy for the Chairmanship of the Third Committee was released last night.[20]

THE ELECTION OF VICE-PRESIDENTS

The President of the Assembly and the Chairmen of Main Committees are elected in their personal capacities; the Vice-Presidents are elected as States. The President, Vice-Presidents and the seven Chairmen of Main Committees together constitute the General Committee (Rule 38). The Vice-Presidents are elected after the election of the Chairmen in such a way as to ensure the representative character of the General Committee (Rules 31 and 38). If the President finds it necessary to be absent during all or part of a meeting of the Assembly, he asks one of the Vice-Presidents to take his place (Rule 32); a Vice-President acting as President has the same powers and duties as the President himself (Rule 33).

It has been the custom that the five permanent members of the Security Council are included among the Vice-Presidents, since representatives of these States are not normally elected to the presidency or one of the chairmanships. The single exception to this practice occurred during the second special session (1948), when a member of the Chinese delegation was elected Chairman of the First Committee. Since no two members of the General Committee may be members of the same delegation (Rule 38), China was not included among the seven Vice-Presidents elected for that special session.

The importance of limiting the size of the General Committee was generally recognized during the first decade of the life of the United Nations, but following the admission of sixteen new Members in December 1955, pressure to increase the size of the Committee began to mount. During the eleventh session (1956–57), the size of the General Committee was increased to sixteen by the addition of an eighth Vice-President. At the twelfth session (1957) it was decided to include in the agenda a proposal to establish a ninth vice-presidency on an *ad hoc* basis for the session. After a confused debate

20 No document symbol appears on the Press release.

in the plenary, the Assembly proceeded to elect a ninth Vice-President before it had taken a decision on whether or not to increase the number of Vice-Presidents. The Assembly also agreed, as a separate matter, to consider the question of the composition of the General Committee. As noted earlier, the Assembly decided to confirm what was already the practice regarding the distribution of the chairmanships of the seven Main Committees, to increase the number of vice-presidencies to thirteen, and to establish a regional pattern of distribution of the vice-presidencies.[21]

The decision regarding vice-presidencies has had three important procedural consequences. It has undoubtedly made it easier than it was formerly to constitute the General Committee on a widely representative basis. On the other hand, the increase in the Committee's size makes it doubtful whether the Committee can perform the " steering " functions specified in the Rules of Procedure; this matter is examined in greater detail in Chapter 5.

A third consequence has been to complicate the procedure for the election of Vice-Presidents. This can be illustrated by reference to the two elections that have taken place since the change was approved in 1957. The election of Vice-Presidents is by secret ballot and there are no nominations (Rules 31 and 94). The Assembly's Resolution 1192 provided that the Vice-Presidents should be elected in accordance with the pattern specified in the annex to the resolution; the pattern of distributing vice-presidencies was not incorporated into the Rules of Procedure, though a footnote in the Rules quotes the full text of the annex to the resolution.

In the election of Vice-Presidents during the thirteenth session, eighty Members returned ballot papers, and thus a total of 1,040 votes could have been cast.[22] In fact, only 973 valid votes were cast, distributed among no less than forty-one States, as shown in Table 10. It was theoretically possible for twenty-five Member States to receive a simple majority, though there were only thirteen places to be filled. This, I have no doubt, is carrying theoretical possibilities to excess; all the same, if the sixty-seven votes not cast or not valid, or the seventy-three votes dispersed among the bottom twenty-eight States, had been concentrated on one State, the pattern of representation specified in the annex to Resolution 1192 could have been upset. In spite of the informal understanding among delegations about the election, and in spite of the fact that the annex to Resolution 1192 specifies that the permanent members of the Security Council shall

---

[21] *Supra*, pp. 30–31.
[22] G.A.O.R.: 13th Sess., 748th Plenary Mtg., 16 Sept. 1958, para. 2.

be members of the General Committee, more than one-quarter of the Members did not vote for China.

TABLE 10

Election of Vice-Presidents, 1958

United States of America	78		Canada	4
Ecuador	77		Ethiopia	4
United Kingdom	76		Iraq	3
France	75		India	2
Pakistan	73		Jordan	2
Uruguay	73		New Zealand	2
		elected	Thailand	2
Australia	71		Tunisia	2
Indonesia	71		Turkey	2
Soviet Union	71		United Arab Republic	2
Nepal	65		Argentina	1
			Brazil	1
Czechoslavakia	57		Bulgaria	1
Netherlands	57		Burma	1
			Cambodia	1
China	56		Haiti	1
			Iran	1
Liberia	13		Morocco	1
			Norway	1
Poland	9		Peru	1
			Philippines	1
Austria	7		Ukrainian S.S.R.	1
			Venezuela	1
Ghana	5		Yemen	1

In an attempt to avoid a dispersal of votes to the extent that took place in 1958, the Secretariat circulated the official notice shown opposite to delegations before the opening of the 1959 Assembly.[23]

Before calling on the Assembly to proceed with the election, the President referred to Rules 31 and 94 of the Rules of Procedure and to Resolution 1192; pointed out that the Secretariat had suggested the type of ballot paper to be used; and reminded the Assembly that, as the President came from a Latin American State, the number of vacancies in group C should be reduced from two to one. The President also stated that " if the number of candidates for any of the five groups is greater than the number prescribed, the vote on that group . . . will be considered invalid " [24]; this statement was not challenged.

[23] Journal of the United Nations, 14 Sept. 1959, addendum to No. 2209.
[24] G.A.O.R.: 14th Sess., 796th Plenary Mtg., 15 Sept. 1959, para. 6.

The balloting was conducted quite quickly, but the counting of the votes took about an hour. The result is shown in Table 11. It will be seen that the votes were dispersed among fewer States than in 1958 (25 in 1959, 41 in 1958), and this can be ascribed in large measure to the use in 1959 of a more elaborate ballot paper.

OFFICIAL NOTICE TO DELEGATIONS

The election of the thirteen Vice-Presidents of the General Assembly *en bloc* could lead to a departure from the distribution of seats decided upon by General Assembly resolution 1192 (XII) and referred to in the annex to rule 31 of the rules of procedure. In order to avoid this possibility, the Secretariat suggests the type of ballot cited below:

BALLOT

ELECTION OF VICE-PRESIDENTS OF THE GENERAL ASSEMBLY

1. The annex to rule 31 of the rules of procedure of the General Assembly establishes the following distribution of posts for vice-presidencies:

   A. Asian and African States—4 Vice-Presidents
      1. ....
      2. ....
      3. ....
      4. ....

   B. Eastern European States—1 Vice-President
      1. ....

   C. Latin American States—2 Vice-Presidents
      1. ....
      2. ....

   D. Western European and other States—2 Vice-Presidents
      1. ....
      2. ....

   E. Permanent members of the Security Council—5 Vice-Presidents
      1. ....
      2. ....
      3. ....
      4. ....
      5. ....

2. The region from which the President is elected will, however, reduce by one the number of vice-presidencies allocated for that region.

3. The number of candidates that may be elected from each group is established by the pattern set forth above. If the number of names for any one group in the ballot paper is greater than the number prescribed for that group, the vote on that group will be considered as invalid.

The use of a more elaborate ballot paper in 1959 did not and could not prevent dispersal within each group. Moreover, there is no procedure or form of ballot paper which can compel Member States to vote for candidates if they do not wish to do so, unless the drastic step was taken of ruling that a ballot paper containing fewer names than there are vacancies would be considered invalid.

TABLE 11

Election of Vice-Presidents, 1959

Group A :		Group D :	
Burma	79*	Sweden	71*
Morocco	79*	South Africa	60*
Philippines	78*	Belgium	1
Turkey	77*	Canada	1
Iraq	9	Finland	1
Afghanistan	2	Italy	1
Japan	2	Netherlands	1
Tunisia	1	Norway	1
Group B :		Group E :	
Romania	75*	United Kingdom	79*
Bulgaria	2	United States of America	79*
Group C :		France	78*
Brazil	75*	U.S.S.R.	76*
Uruguay	1	China	61*

* These thirteen States were elected.

Valid ballot papers were returned in 1959 by all eighty-two Member States, so that 1,066 votes could have been cast. In fact, only 986 valid votes were cast. Of the 80 votes which were not cast or were not valid, as many as 21 could have been cast for China, up to 16 could have been distributed among the other four permanent members of the Security Council, and 43 could have been cast for States in the other four groups. It is interesting to note that none of the permanent members of the Security Council received the votes of all Member States.

The number of vacancies in each group and the number of States receiving votes in 1958 and 1959 is shown in Table 12.

TABLE 12

Dispersal of votes for Vice-Presidents, 1958 and 1959

	1958		1959	
	No. of vacancies	No. of States obtaining votes	No. of vacancies	No. of States obtaining votes
Asia and Africa	3	19	4	8
Eastern Europe	1	4	1	2
Latin America	2	7	1	2
Western Europe and other States	2	6	2	8
Permanent Members of Security Council	5	5	5	5
	13	41	13	25

The 1957 decision regarding the composition of the General Committee has, in my view, had some unfortunate practical consequences. The regional distribution of chairmanships had previously been satisfactory, and the 1957 decision merely confirmed what was already the existing and accepted practice. The increase in the number of vice-presidencies to thirteen has made it easier to ensure the representative character of the General Committee, but at the cost of making the General Committee so large that its effectiveness is reduced. The 1957 decision did nothing to clear up an existing anomaly, which is that more States can receive a simple (absolute) majority of votes than there are places to be filled. This possibility was commented on by the delegation of Panama during the second session,[25] and on three occasions (1952, 1953 and 1957) in connection with the election of Vice-Presidents more States received a simple majority of votes than there were places. On each occasion, the Assembly has regarded as elected those States, equal in number to the places to be filled, obtaining the greatest number of votes.

There are two sources of potential difficulty that can be directly attributed to the 1957 decision. First, no provision was made for the possibility that fewer States might receive the required majority than there are vacancies. This possibility had always existed, but under the previous procedure, balloting continued until all places had been filled. It is not clear what procedure would be followed in the future if, for example, one of the permanent members of the Security Council should fail to obtain a simple majority of votes in repeated ballots.

The second potential difficulty is that no provision was made in 1957 for the possibility that the number of States obtaining the required majority might equal the number of vacancies, but that the pattern of election might not conform to the annex to Resolution 1192. No form of ballot paper can entirely eliminate this possibility.

THE QUESTION OF NOMINATIONS

The prohibition of nominations in plenary meetings has been more of a fiction than a fact; and in relation to the presidency, even the fiction has not been maintained in recent years.[26] If the present system should, in time, prove unsatisfactory, consideration might again be given to the possibility of having a nominations committee, an expedient to which the Assembly of the League of Nations was driven by an incident which occurred during its sixteenth session.

[25] G.A.O.R.: 2nd Sess., 1947, 6th Committee, Annex 4c, p. 268.
[26] Rule 94, which prohibits nominations in plenary meetings, does not apply in connection with the election of judges of the International Court of Justice.

Until 1937 the League of Nations used essentially the same method of electing the President and Vice-Presidents of the Assembly and Chairmen of Committees as is now used by the United Nations Assembly. The abandonment of this method by the League was due to two developments which, on first glance, might appear to have been in conflict. On the one hand, it was often alleged by some of the medium and smaller Powers that the General Committee of the League Assembly (which was constituted in much the same way as is the General Committee of the United Nations Assembly) was not representative in character, and in particular that the Great Powers exercised a disproportionate influence. This was similar to the view that was expressed by some representatives in the United Nations Assembly in 1957. If that had been all there was to the problem, the League might well have adopted the same course as did the United Nations and have merely enlarged the General Committee. However, when it came to the election of Vice-Presidents by secret ballot in 1935, it was found that seven States had received an absolute majority of votes, though there were only six places to be filled. The President (Eduard Beneš of Czechoslovakia) announced that the six States which had received the largest number of votes had been elected as Vice-Presidents. The trouble was that the seventh State, the Soviet Union, newly admitted into the League, had received only one vote less than the fifth and sixth States in the list; more important, it was a firmly established custom of the League (as it has been of the United Nations) that the Great Powers should always be represented on the General Committee. The difficulty in 1935 was eliminated when the General Committee proposed, and the Assembly agreed, that the Soviet Union should be elected as an additional Vice-President. This was possible under the League Assembly's Rules of Procedure.

Inevitably there was considerable discussion in the League of how a repetition of the unfortunate 1935 incident could be avoided in the future, and the delegation of Norway suggested the procedure which was approved in 1936 and put into operation in 1937 on a trial basis. By this procedure, the provisional President of the Assembly submitted proposals regarding the composition of an eleven-member committee whose duty it was to nominate candidates for the General Committee. This did not interfere with the right to vote for persons or States other than those proposed by the Committee on Nominations. It was hoped that this procedure would put an end to, or at least reduce the extent of, lobbying for elections and also save the Secretary-General from the situation, which he had found embarrassing, of being the recipient of requests for favours which it was not in his power to grant.

The Executive Committee of the Preparatory Commission of the United Nations considered the possibility of recommending for the General Assembly a nominations committee similar to that which the League had approved in 1936. There was wide support for the idea that there should be a nominations committee, that it should be composed of States rather than individuals, and that its members should be appointed on the proposal of the President of the Assembly. The suggestion was made that such a nominations committee might also make recommendations regarding elections to the three Councils, but the general sentiment did not favour this and it was agreed that these elections should be a matter for informal consultations. However, when the proposal for a nominations committee was finally put to the vote in the Executive Committee, it received a simple, but not the necessary two-thirds, majority; accordingly, no recommendation was made.[27]

During the first part of the first session of the General Assembly (1946) there was considerable discussion of the whole question of nominations and the British and Lebanese delegations referred to the consideration that had been given in the Preparatory Commission to the possibility of creating a special committee on nominations. Philip Noel-Baker of the United Kingdom, a veteran of League affairs, considered it likely that experience in the United Nations would eventually demonstrate the need for such a committee; Camille Chamoun of Lebanon, on the other hand, pointed out that the Preparatory Commission had not recommended that such a committee be established, and he felt that the matter should therefore be regarded as settled. The General Assembly did not pursue the question further but adopted an amendment to the Rules to the effect that in plenary meetings "There shall be no nominations."[28] This provision remains in Rule 94.

During the consideration of the Provisional Rules of Procedure in the course of the second session, the Swedish delegation reintroduced the proposal for a nominations committee. This proposal, after minor amendment, read as follows:

A Nominating Committee consisting of representatives of delegations of which the President, Vice-Presidents and the Chairman [*sic*] of Main Committees of the previous session of the General Assembly were members, shall meet three days before the opening of each session of

---

[27] *Report by the Executive Committee to the Preparatory Commission of the United Nations* (New York: United Nations, 12 Nov. 1945), PC/EX/113/Rev. 1, pp. 19, 31, 36.

[28] G.A.O.R.: 1st Sess., Pt. I, 18th Plenary Mtg., 26 Jan. 1946, pp. 282–283, 288.

the General Assembly for the purpose of suggesting one or more candidates for Chairmen, Vice-Chairmen and Rapporteurs of the Main Committees. The Committee shall present a first report to the President of the General Assembly at the opening of the session and such further reports as may be required. The President shall communicate to each Main Committee the suggestions of the Nominating Committee which concern that Committee. These provisions do not affect the right of Members to make nominations in the Main Committees or to cast votes for any eligible person.[29]

This text was approved by a sub-committee of the Sixth Committee by five votes to two, with the United Kingdom abstaining.

In the Sixth Committee itself, the Soviet Union proposed the deletion of the draft rule; the Scandinavian delegations and Canada spoke in its favour. The Swedish representative said that the intention of the rule was to enable nominations to be prepared by orderly means and to ensure geographical representation.

The Soviet representative opposed the draft rule on the grounds that it would lead to back-door intrigues; the persons nominated would be those who were best known to members of the nominations committee and not necessarily those who were most capable. The British representative on this occasion strongly supported the Soviet point of view. The right of nomination belonged to all delegations, he said, and the matter should be dealt with by " the heads of delegations . . . and not persons who merely happened to be at United Nations headquarters before the Assembly was opened." The Indian representative considered that the result of having a nominations committee would be that small countries would be subjected to great pressure. The Soviet proposal to delete the draft rule was carried by twenty-seven votes to four.[30]

In 1949 a further attempt was made to persuade the Assembly to establish a nominations committee. The Canadian delegation urged, among a number of recommendations submitted to the Special Committee on Methods and Procedures (1949), that the Assembly improve its procedures for the election of officers. In order to ensure the selection at all times of competent and experienced Chairmen of Main Committees, and to maintain the principle of equitable geographical distribution, the Canadian delegation proposed that there be created a nominations committee; that nominations should be submitted in writing to the President and should be announced by him; but that there should be no oral nominations or nomination speeches. If the number of nominations should exceed the number of places to be filled, elections would take place by secret ballot. If

29 G.A.O.R.: 2nd Sess., 1947, 6th Committee, Annex 4c, p. 270.
30 *Ibid.*, 57th Mtg., 12 Nov. 1947, pp. 140–142.

the number of candidates should not exceed the number of places to be filled, the President should declare the candidates elected.[31] The Special Committee considered the Canadian proposal for a nominations committee but decided by 11–0–2 " not to make a recommendation in this respect." [32] The matter has not been formally raised since 1949.

The present system of election undoubtedly has many merits, in particular in allowing negotiations which inevitably involve some discussion of personalities to be conducted informally and privately. This, however, is not an argument in favour of the present or any other system, since informal and private negotiations will take place whatever method is used, and whether the method facilitates or forbids formal nominations.

There are said to be three main disadvantages to the present system. First, that some Member States have virtually no opportunity of influencing the informal negotiations and may encounter real difficulty in discovering what proposals are being considered. For obvious reasons, this difficulty is most acute for States which are not members of any organized group or *bloc*.

The second complaint that is sometimes made about the present system is that time is wasted because several sets of negotiations on the same question may take place simultaneously, but without apparent connection. This happens most frequently during the early stages of negotiation, but it is by no means confined to the early stages.

The third complaint is that the system encourages log-rolling, a practice which is doubtless inevitable but which should be discouraged. When log-rolling is carried to excess, it becomes an abuse of the electoral system.

None of the tendencies complained of in the present system would be eliminated entirely by having a nominations committee, but their intensity might be lessened. Should the present system eventually prove unsatisfactory, as it did in the League Assembly by the sixteenth session, the case for establishing a nominations committee might again be examined. Such a committee would need to be small. Perhaps it would be sufficiently representative if it comprised members of the delegations from which the presiding officers of the two procedural committees (the General Committee and the Credentials Committee) and the seven Main Committees of the previous session were elected.

---

[31] *Report of the Special Committee on Methods and Procedures of the General Assembly*, G.A.O.R.: 4th Sess., 1949, Suppl. No. 12 (A/937), Annex 1, p. 18.
[32] *Ibid.*, para. 16.

The Swedish proposal of 1947 would have entrusted a nominations committee with the task of suggesting candidates for the Chairmen, Vice-Chairmen and Rapporteurs of Main Committees. This limitation of the proposals of a nominations committee to the officers of Main Committees was doubtless due to the fact that, when the Swedish proposal was made, the Provisional Rules of Procedure already prohibited nominations in plenary meetings. If, however, the idea of a nominations committee were revived, it might be desirable for it to be concerned not only with the officers of Main Committees, but also with the President and Vice-Presidents of the Assembly, the members of the Credentials Committee, and possibly also the elected members of the three Councils.

A nominations committee might occasionally perform useful ancillary functions. When dissension arises about the composition of a select committee of the General Assembly, a nominations committee might be entrusted with the task of exploring privately the possibility of agreement. There is no guarantee that in any particular case such an arrangement would be more successful than the present practice, but it could hardly have a positively damaging effect.

CHAPTER 4

THE GENERAL DEBATE

It will beget and increase personal friendship between princes
and States, which tends to the rooting up of wars, and planting
peace in a deep and fruitful soil. . . . It were a great motive to
the tranquillity of the world that they could freely converse face
to face, and personally and reciprocally give and receive marks
of civility and kindness. A hospitality that leaves these impres-
sions behind it will hardly let ordinary matters prevail to mistake
or quarrel one another.

WILLIAM PENN

IN many deliberative assemblies there is an annual debate of a
general character which enables representatives to examine the wood
as well as the trees. In the British House of Commons, for example,
such a debate centres around " an humble address " in reply to the
Gracious Speech from the Throne. During the first part of the
first session of the United Nations General Assembly (1946), there
was a general discussion, in plenary meeting, of the report of the
Preparatory Commission. At the beginning of the second part of the
same session (1946), there took place a general discussion. During
the second and all subsequent regular sessions of the Assembly,
there has taken place in plenary meeting a General Debate.

There is no provision in the Rules of Procedure for a General
Debate. The annotated provisional agenda for a regular session,
which is marked " For use of information media—not an official
record," contains the following explanation:

At the beginning of each session of the Assembly, there is a general
debate in which the heads of delegations usually express the views of
their countries on problems of common concern to the Membership of
the United Nations.[1]

The General Debate concludes when all Members who wish to
participate have done so.

The General Debate in the Assembly is an important diplomatic
occasion, an annual gathering at the summit open to all Members of
the United Nations. More than fifty foreign ministers or other
ministers of cabinet rank now participate each year in the General

---

[1] United Nations Press Release GA/1823, 19 Aug. 1959, p. 5. H. G. Nicholas, in
his recent book, comments acidly: "Anything less like a debate could hardly be
imagined, though its generality is indubitable." *The United Nations as a Political
Institution* (London: Oxford Univ. Press, 1959), p. 97.

Debate. The Debate itself has certain intrinsic values: it has been compared to a barometer, which indicates changes in the international climate; it has also been compared to a safety valve, in that it enables governments to let off steam on contentious issues without causing undue damage. Members are able to discuss issues they consider important without the necessity of proposing them as separate items for the agenda. Year after year, for example, the Assembly has decided not to consider the question of Chinese representation, yet Members freely express their views on this question during the General Debate.

The General Debate also provides the occasion for another kind of diplomatic activity. In addition to the formal plane of public speeches, which are incorporated in the official records of the Assembly, there is also the informal plane of personal contacts, private meetings, casual discussions, exchanges of view, exploratory soundings; the carefully arranged chance meetings in corridors, elevators, lounges or dining rooms; the cocktail parties, receptions, lunches and dinners, even the breakfasts. These events are not recorded in the official documents of the United Nations, but this second plane of activity can be more important than the public debate of formal occasions.

The first speech in the General Debate is, by custom, often made by the representative of Brazil. It is usual for the representatives of the United States and the Soviet Union to speak on the first day; and the representative of India likes to speak last.[2] Not all Members participate every year. In 1958, for example, Finland, Haiti, Honduras, Lebanon, Luxembourg, Nicaragua, Paraguay, Sweden and Uruguay did not participate in the General Debate. The non-participants in 1959 were Luxembourg, Mexico and Nicaragua.

There is, inevitably, a good deal of repetition in the General Debate. Most speakers affirm the devotion of their governments to the purposes and principles of the Charter, and many of them state explicitly that this devotion is in contrast to the indifference, not to say defiance, manifested by certain other governments. Many speakers, particularly those from Latin America, express their admiration for the rule of law. Often a major theme of the General Debate has been that aggression, direct or indirect, must be resisted. In 1959, however, other themes tended to predominate. Many speakers reiterated their support of that principle of the Charter by which States renounce the threat or use of force. Virtually every speaker was in

[2] In 1959 the Soviet representative spoke on the last day, but Nikita S. Khrushchev had visited the United Nations early in the session and, as a visiting head of the government of a Member State, had addressed the Assembly.

favour of disarmament, personal contacts between government leaders, and aid to underdeveloped areas. Many speakers expressed satisfaction that the question of Cyprus had been resolved since the previous session.

When one listens to eighty speeches, delivered at a couple of dozen plenary meetings in an apparently random order, one is at first struck by the apparent lack of relationship between them. A closer analysis suggests, however, that plans of like-minded States are concerted in advance. The fact that in 1959 almost every speaker from Latin America spoke of inter-American collaboration, that every Arab speaker explicitly supported the claim of the United Arab Republic to control access through the Suez Canal, and that speakers from the Soviet *Bloc* placed so much emphasis on West German militarism, can hardly have been due to chance alone. Indeed, in some cases the language of speeches in the General Debate approximated so closely that one wonders whether parts of the speeches of different delegations were not based on a single text.

It is difficult to summarize in a few pages some eighty speeches which, on an average, took thirty or forty minutes each to deliver. Indeed, the Under-Secretary for Conference Services has stated that it takes much longer to summarize a speech than to make it.[3] I have, however, tried in the pages that follow to classify the main emphases of speakers from different regions and groups in the General Debate of the fourteenth session (1959).

Most of the speakers from Latin America praised the system of inter-American consultation and co-operation. Many welcomed the initiative of President Juscelino Kubitschek of Brazil in economic matters. There was much emphasis on self-determination and on the emergence of new States. Speakers from Latin America, as is their custom, tended to speak in terms of general principles. A number of specific issues were raised, however. The representatives of Paraguay and Peru spoke in favour of unrestricted access through the Suez Canal. The Tibetan question was mentioned by the representatives of El Salvador, Paraguay and Peru. Speakers from Argentina, Chile and El Salvador expressed the hope that the Algerian question would soon be settled. The Cuban and Uruguayan representatives stated their support for World Refugee Year, and the Cuban representative expressed opposition to the projected test of a nuclear device by France in the Sahara area.

Speakers from Africa referred to race discrimination and the suppression of colonial peoples, and the Minister for Foreign Affairs of Ghana dealt specifically with the situation in the Central African

[3] United Nations Doc. A/C.4/SR.914, 19 Oct. 1959, pp. 4–5.

Federation. All African and Arab speakers, and many of the Asians, referred to the Algerian question, and it was while the Saudi Arabian representative was speaking on this matter that there took place the only Presidential interruption during the General Debate in order to appeal for moderation of language.

All of the African representatives and most of the Arab and Asian neutrals strongly condemned the French proposal to explode an atomic weapon in the Sahara. The Moroccan and Tunisian representatives referred to the presence of Algerian refugees on their soil. All Arab speakers discussed the plight of Arab refugees from Palestine, and expressed their support for the right of the United Arab Republic to control the passage of shipping through the Suez Canal.

Many of the Afro-Asian speakers deplored the continuance of the cold war; many stressed the need for disarmament, often with the assertion that action must come from the big Powers, the role of the medium and smaller Powers being to offer encouragement and advice. The general refugee question and World Refugee Year received little attention in the speeches of Asian and African representatives, although the speech of the Laotian Minister for Foreign Affairs was a notable exception.

Several Asian speakers supported the Indonesian claim to West Irian. The Indian Minister of Defence referred to the overseas territories of Portugal and to the Charter obligations in connection with non-self-governing peoples; appealed to colonial Powers to place further territories under United Nations trusteeship; and denounced apartheid in South Africa as contrary to the Charter.

The Eastern European speakers in the General Debate expressed support for the disarmament proposals of Mr. Khrushchev, admiration for Soviet technical achievements, belief in peaceful coexistence and the relaxation of tension, opposition to the cold war and German militarism, indignation at the continued exclusion from the United Nations of representatives of the Peking Government, and resistance to attempts by the Government of Laos to stir up trouble in South-East Asia.

In the speeches of NATO representatives, the need for controlled and balanced disarmament was emphasized, though only a few speakers referred to the question of outer space. Several representatives discussed the question of Berlin, and in most of the statements there were brief references to Hungary and Tibet. Many of the speakers from NATO countries (though not the United States) urged that President de Gaulle's plan for Algeria be taken seriously. The British and Canadian Foreign Ministers spoke of the importance of

World Refugee Year, and several representatives referred in particular to Palestinian refugees and other related Middle Eastern questions. The Foreign Ministers of Canada, Denmark, Norway and the United Kingdom spoke of the importance of the United Nations Emergency Force (UNEF). Most of the maritime nations supported the principle of free access through the Suez Canal, and the Ministers for Foreign Affairs of Denmark and Norway discussed the problem of territorial waters. The French Foreign Minister entered a spirited defence of the policy of his government in connection with the projected nuclear test explosion in the Sahara.

Of the speeches of European neutrals, the Irish Minister for External Affairs explained the purpose of his delegation in asking the Assembly to discuss means to prevent the wider dissemination of nuclear weapons, and reiterated the anxiety of his government concerning the concentration of military forces in Central Europe. The Swedish Foreign Minister urged that greater use be made of the International Court of Justice, and spoke of the anachronistic policy of the South African Government in connection with race relations.

The South African Minister for External Affairs dealt at length with conditions in South Africa and South West Africa. He also announced a new emphasis in South African policy towards United Nations activities: South Africa intended to contribute to the extra-budgetary programmes of the United Nations.

Among the matters discussed by the Australian Minister of State for External Affairs were the Soviet demand for " parity " in certain bodies and conferences; demographic problems; and the proposals of the Secretary-General for facilitating high-level intergovernmental co-operation in economic matters. The New Zealand representative referred *inter alia* to the need to face squarely the financial implications of the Assembly's decision to establish UNEF.

The speech of the Minister for Foreign Affairs of Israel (the only woman to speak in the General Debate) was largely concerned with the Arab economic blockade of Israel.

Besides providing an opportunity for governmental representatives to make diplomatic *tours d'horizon,* the General Debate enables speakers to express their views on specific grievances without the necessity of going to the length of requesting the inclusion in the agenda of a complaint against another government. Speeches of this kind almost inevitably lead to replies from the representatives of other governments.

Among such matters raised during the General Debate in 1959 were (in chronological order): an Austrian complaint that the people of South Tyrol did not enjoy the autonomy and rights to which they were entitled, to which charge the Italian Foreign Minister replied in his speech two days later, which led to a further Austrian statement, followed by a further Italian statement; a Panamanian complaint of discrimination by the United States authorities in the Canal Zone; a complaint by Guatemala that British Honduras (or Belize, as it is called by Guatemalans) is Guatemalan territory which is illegally occupied by Britain, followed the next day by a statement by the Mexican representative to the effect that if there were to be any changes in the status of British Honduras, Mexico also had territorial claims, followed a day later by a Guatemalan reply to the Mexican statement; a Cuban complaint of hostility and aggression by the Dominican Republic; a statement by Pakistan on Kashmir; allegations by Saudi Arabia, Iraq and Yemen of British aggression against Oman, the Trucial Sheikhdoms, Aden and other parts of the Arabian peninsula; a complaint by Iceland of the invasion of her territorial waters by British vessels, to which the British representative replied later the same day, followed by a counter-reply by the representative of Iceland; and allegations by Morocco that France and Spain continued to hold territory which rightly belongs to Morocco, to which the representatives of France and Spain replied later during the meeting, followed by a Moroccan counter-reply.

Almost hidden among this collection of complaints and grievances were statements by the representatives of Cambodia and Thailand, who spoke appreciatively of the assistance of the Secretary-General and his personal representative in composing certain differences that had arisen between the two countries.

Few Rules of Procedure are abused as frequently as those relating to the right of reply. It is, after all, a privilege and not a right to speak out of turn. It would be useful if Assembly Presidents could foster a tradition that the right of reply would not be exercised excessively during the General Debate, or would be exercised by the circulation of written statements. This was, in fact, done on one occasion in 1959. The following letter from the British delegation was circulated to all Members of the United Nations:

I have the honour to draw your attention to certain observations on the subject of British Honduras which were made in the general debate by the representative of Guatemala on 23 and 25 September and by the representative of Mexico on 24 September.

In order to remove any possible misunderstanding, I wish to make it clear that the territory to which these representatives referred is under the sovereignty of the United Kingdom.

I should be grateful if this letter could be circulated to all Members of the United Nations.[4]

From time to time questions have been raised about the possibility of using the period of the General Debate to better advantage. One of the most experienced of United Nations officials has summarized his point of view as " more consultation, less debate." This attitude has, in fact, gained increasing support, and it has recently been suggested that the period of the General Debate at the beginning of each regular session of the Assembly might be used not only for informal diplomatic consultation, but also for various meetings of foreign ministers in connection with regional organizations. Presumably such a practice would be facilitated if Assembly sessions were not always held in New York.

It is said, in support of this idea, that foreign ministers are under an increasing burden of work because they are expected, or choose, to be their own ambassadors. Most foreign ministers have important domestic responsibilities of a political and constitutional character. They are invariably cabinet members, and in a democracy they are expected to be in regular contact with members of the legislature. They administer complex departments of government, with as many as a hundred or more offices in foreign countries. Some of them have to stand for re-election from time to time. The speed of communication, far from simplifying their tasks, has made them more difficult; the fact that foreign ministers can easily be consulted has increased the extent to which they take decisions.

Added to the burden is the multiplicity of meetings of inter-governmental organizations which foreign ministers are expected to attend, either because there is a specific council of ministers forming part of the organization or because the occasional presence of national political leaders is deemed essential to the prestige or successful operation of the organization.

The holding of General Assembly sessions away from New York raises considerable (but not insuperable) administrative difficulties. " I am more and more a believer in the wisdom of having General Assembly sessions at United Nations headquarters," Mr. Hammarskjold has said, " for technical reasons, if for no other." [5] The technical difficulties can no doubt be overcome, especially if the session could take place in two parts: a three or four week session, away from headquarters, devoted to preliminary business and the General Debate, and a longer session at headquarters for dealing

---

4 United Nations Doc. A/4227, 30 Sept. 1959.
5 Press Conference by the Secretary-General at U.N. headquarters. Note to Correspondents No. 1918, 16 Jan. 1954, pp. 22–25.

with substantive items of the agenda. This would, however, be a clumsy and expensive arrangement which would be very difficult to justify.

The more serious difficulty, however, is not simply one of administrative inconvenience, but the fact that the period of the General Debate is already one of intensive diplomatic activity; I do not see how additional business, particularly of a formal kind, could receive adequate attention during this period.

As the membership of the Organization has increased, so more time has been needed for the General Debate. During the first six sessions (1946–51), the General Debate occupied all or part of approximately ten plenary meetings each session; during the next five sessions (1952–56), an average of fourteen plenary meetings were needed; during the three most recent sessions (1957, 1958 and 1959), twenty-one, twenty-three and twenty-four plenary meetings respectively have been required. I assume that the number of plenary meetings required for the General Debate will not decrease. If allowance is made for the time required to elect members of the General Committee, for meetings of the General Committee, and for plenary meetings of the Assembly to consider the recommendations of the General Committee, then about three weeks will normally elapse between the opening of the session and the conclusion of the General Debate. By the end of the second week or the beginning of the third week, Committees Two to Six can usually begin their work, but it does not seem possible to get the two Political Committees launched while senior members of delegations are occupied with the General Debate.

It is, of course, natural that many representatives should want to defer their speeches until they have heard what others have to say, but only one representative can speak last. The President of the Assembly and officials of the Secretariat no doubt do their best to keep the Debate moving along without unnecessary delays. A list of speakers is established and, in accordance with Rule 75, the President may, during the course of the Debate and if the Assembly consents, declare the list closed. In 1959, the list of speakers was closed a fortnight after the opening of the session, by which time forty-three representatives had spoken. From that point on, the Debate proceeded without interruption, with seven speeches a day. It might be possible to close the list of speakers somewhat earlier than has hitherto been the custom.

Another way in which a little time might be saved would require a stricter application of Rule 70. This states, *inter alia*, that the

President shall call upon speakers in the order in which they signify their desire to speak. It would be consistent with this Rule that, should a representative not be ready to speak when called upon, the President should call upon the next speaker on the list, and so on until a representative willing to speak should be found. Too often a meeting has to be cancelled, or closed before the usual time, because the next speaker on the list is not ready to speak or is otherwise occupied.

Proposals have been made from time to time to limit the length of speeches in the General Debate. The most drastic proposal, made by Canada in 1946, was that " Each speaker in the opening debate in plenary session . . . might be limited to ten minutes with the right to have his remarks extended in the verbatim record." [6] I doubt very much whether any time limit on speeches which would appreciably shorten the period of the General Debate would now be acceptable. It might be possible to make greater use of the General Debate for consideration of a few matters, many of them hardy perennials, in which debate is considered to be more important than the adoption of a resolution, thus reducing the number of items referred to Main Committees.

[6] G.A.O.R.: 1st Sess., Pt. II, 1946, General Committee, Annex 16 (A/92), para. 6(a), p. 97.

B.

CHAPTER 5

THE AGENDA

> Before which sovereign assembly should be brought all
> differences depending between one sovereign and another that
> cannot be made up by private embassies before the sessions
> begin. . . .
>
> WILLIAM PENN

WHEN I hear complaints that sessions of the General Assembly are
needlessly prolonged, I take courage by recalling that the formal
opening of the Congress of Westphalia was delayed three years while
questions of procedure and ceremonial were being resolved. The
Congress was due to open on 25 March 1642, but the French delegates did not put in an appearance until two years later. Disputes
about the admission of members, credentials, forms of address, and
precedence occupied another year. The Congress finally opened on
10 April 1645.[1]

Sessions of the General Assembly are lengthy simply because
there is a great deal of complicated business to discharge. Governments and peoples place great hopes in the capacity of the Assembly
to resolve problems, and the agenda tends to increase year by year.
The two Committees of the Assembly on procedure concluded that
lengthy Assembly sessions were not primarily caused by faulty procedure. The Special Committee on Methods and Procedures (1949)
considered that

the present length of General Assembly sessions . . . is due, above all, to
the number and complexity of the questions submitted to the Assembly,
and to the political problems raised by these questions.[2]

The Special Committee on Measures to Limit the Duration of
Sessions (1953) commented:

The length of the regular sessions of the Assembly has been determined
mainly by the complexity and number of the international problems
which have been brought to its attention as the result of differences
among the Members, and by the atmosphere of deep-seated international
tension in which the Assembly's discussions have taken place.[3]

---

[1] Sir Ernest Satow, *A Guide to Diplomatic Practice* (Second and rev. ed., New
York and London: Longmans Green, 1922), Vol. II, pp. 5–7.
[2] *Report of the Special Committee on Methods and Procedures of the General
Assembly,* G.A.O.R.: 4th Sess., 1949, Suppl. No. 12 (A/937), para. 7. (Hereafter
to be cited in this chapter as: United Nations Doc. A/937.)
[3] G.A.O.R.: 8th Sess., 1953, Annexes, Agenda item 54 (A/2402), para. 8. (Hereafter to be cited in this chapter as: United Nations Doc. A/2402.)

The decisions of the Assembly regarding the agenda are important, in the sense that these decisions are momentous and weighty, though not in the legal sense that they are among the matters which are decided by a two-thirds majority vote of the Members present and voting. Every deliberative body needs a standard procedure for deciding which of the matters submitted to it shall be discussed. Such a procedure normally takes account of three considerations: (a) any constitutional limits on the powers of the body concerned; (b) the need, as a purely practical matter, to confine the number of matters to be discussed to what can reasonably be attempted in the time available; and (c) a judgment on the wisdom of taking up a particular question at a particular time. The usual practice is for a provisional agenda to be drawn up by officials in accordance with certain rules or customs, and for the deliberative body to decide, sometimes on the basis of recommendations from a subsidiary organ, whether or not to place on the definitive agenda the items included in the provisional agenda.[4]

The question of the legal competence of the Assembly should be considered from two points of view: the power to *discuss*, and the power to *make recommendations*. The Charter grants to the Assembly virtually unlimited power of discussion.

The General Assembly may discuss any questions or any matters within the scope of the present Charter or relating to the powers and functions of any organs provided for in the present Charter.[5]

The power to discuss does not automatically carry with it the power to recommend. A Member State may favour, or at least acquiesce in, discussion of a matter, though opposing the making of recommendations; it may take this position either because it considers that the question of competence can be decided only after the matter has been discussed or, regarding matters which are essentially within the domestic jurisdiction of a State, because it considers that discussion does not constitute intervention but that the making of recommendations (or certain kinds of recommendations) does constitute intervention and is therefore not authorized in the Charter. The Assembly has not been inclined to reject proposals for the inclusion of items in the agenda on constitutional grounds. In the few cases in which items proposed for the agenda have been rejected or repeatedly postponed, practical or political considerations have usually carried more weight than legal considerations.

---

4 Strictly speaking, *agenda* is plural, meaning " things to be done "; one item of an *agenda* is an *agendum*. In practice, *agenda* is usually treated as singular. The French equivalent is *ordre du jour*. It would, perhaps, be useful to revive the word *agendum* when " an item of the agenda " is meant.

5 Article 10.

The agenda of the Assembly has grown year by year. This happens in the case of most continuing organizations; once an item has appeared on the agenda it tends to reappear on the agenda. But two additional factors have been at work in the case of the Assembly. First, the increase in the number of sovereign States since the war, as well as the character and interests of these new States, has added to the number and complexity of international problems and to the time required to deal with them. Secondly, the General Assembly has increasingly overshadowed the three Councils; in certain fields the Assembly duplicates debates which have already taken place in the Councils, and in other fields it has assumed responsibilities that could be more effectively discharged by technical organs of limited membership.

Whatever the number of questions submitted to the Assembly, and regardless of their gravity or complexity, there are practical limits to what the Assembly can do effectively within the present general organizational framework. For purely practical reasons relating to the administration of the United Nations and the schedule of meetings, the Assembly should in normal circumstances conclude its regular session by the third week in December. This, in effect, establishes a maximum duration for regular sessions of thirteen or fourteen weeks, depending on the date of " the third Tuesday in September " on which the regular sessions commence (Rule 1).[6] Within that three-month period, only a limited amount of business can receive adequate consideration. If the agenda is overloaded, some matters will receive insufficient attention.

The Special Committee on Methods and Procedures (1949), at a time when the Assembly's agenda was not as heavy as it is now, laid special emphasis on the need for discrimination in connection with the acceptance of agenda items. The Committee urged that, in order to maintain the duration of sessions within normal limits, proposals for the inclusion of items in the agenda should be scrutinized with greater care than had formerly been the practice. All requests for the inclusion of items in the agenda should be examined, not only with special attention to the importance of the questions in relation to the achievement of the purposes of the United Nations,

---

6 It was thought by the Secretariat in 1947 that regular sessions of the Assembly would last five to seven weeks, of which three weeks would be taken up with meetings of Main Committees. The British delegation commented in 1947 that " grave damage may result to the prestige of the U.N. if Assembly proceedings continue to last as long as two months." The Special Committee on Methods and Procedures (1949) recorded the opinion that sessions should not exceed eight weeks. The average length of regular sessions, including resumed sessions, has in fact been approximately thirteen weeks. G.A.O.R.: 1st Sess., Pt. I, General Committee, 1946, Annex 3 (A/BUR/3), pp. 49–50; United Nations Docs. A/316, 8 July 1947; and A/937, para. 9.

but also in relation to the agenda as a whole and the time available for the session. The Committee reaffirmed the right of the Assembly to exclude certain questions from the agenda, as well as its right to delete questions previously included.[7]

Matters proposed for inclusion in the agenda are of three kinds, depending on the date of their submission. Most matters are included by the Secretary-General in the Provisional Agenda, which is communicated to Member States at least sixty days before the opening of the session (Rule 12); that is to say, approximately the middle of July. An unofficial draft of the provisional agenda is communicated to Members in May.

The Provisional Agenda of a regular session should include (Rule 13):

    (a) Report of the Secretary-General on the work of the Organization;

    (b) Reports from the Security Council,
               the Economic and Social Council,
               the Trusteeship Council,
               the International Court of Justice,
               the subsidiary organs of the General Assembly,
               specialized agencies (where such reports are
                    called for under agreements entered into);

    (c) All items the inclusion of which has been ordered by the General Assembly at a previous session;

    (d) All items proposed by the other principal organs of the United Nations;

    (e) All items proposed by any Member of the United Nations;

    (f) All items pertaining to the budget for the next financial year and the report on the accounts for the last financial year;

    (g) All items which the Secretary-General deems it necessary to put before the General Assembly; and

    (h) All items proposed under Article 35, paragraph 2, of the Charter by States not Members of the United Nations.

In spite of the express terms of Rule 13, the International Court of Justice does not submit a report to the Assembly, and the Provisional Agenda includes no reference to such a report. Practice in this matter does not conform to the Rules, and there would seem no reason why the reference to a report from the Court should not be deleted from Rule 13 when the Rules of Procedure are next revised.

---

[7] United Nations Doc. A/937, para. 10.

The stipulation in Rule 13 that " the provisional agenda of a regular session shall include . . . reports from . . . the subsidiary organs of the General Assembly " has not been interpreted to mean that every subsidiary organ must report every session. Reports of a subsidiary organ are included in the Provisional Agenda only if this has been specifically requested or ordered by the Assembly at a previous session or if the subsidiary organ itself considers that a report is necessary.

Resolutions of the Assembly requesting that reports be prepared have not always indicated clearly what procedure should be followed regarding the inclusion of such reports in the Provisional Agenda of a future session. The Special Committee on Measures to Limit the Duration of Sessions (1953) commented:

The situation would be clarified if the practice were adopted of stating in the resolution whether it is intended that the report should be sub-mitted to the General Assembly for consideration or to Members for their information. . . . As regards, in particular, resolutions calling for the submission of annual reports, it is especially desirable to avoid any possible uncertainty as to whether or not the Secretary-General should include such reports each year in the provisional agenda.[8]

Matters submitted too late for inclusion in the Provisional Agenda, but at least thirty days before the date fixed for the opening of the session, are known as Supplementary Items and are placed on a Supplementary List (Rule 14). The Rules of Procedure provide that " Any Member or principal organ . . . or the Secretary-General " may request the inclusion of items in the Supplementary List. States not Members of the United Nations (which, in accordance with Article 35, paragraph 2, of the Charter, may under certain circum-stances bring to the attention of the Assembly disputes to which they are parties) and subsidiary organs of the Assembly, are not specifically given the right to propose items for the Supplementary List.[9]

Matters which are proposed for inclusion in the agenda after the Supplementary List has been closed (that is to say, matters submitted less than thirty days before the opening of the session or during the session) are known as Additional Items (Rule 15). Such Additional Items, by the very fact of having been submitted late, are presumed

8 United Nations Doc. A/2402, paras. 17–18.
9 If it were thought desirable to make specific provision for the submission of Supplementary Items by States not Members and by subsidiary organs of the Assembly, it would be necessary to revise Rule 14 of the Rules of Procedure. Alternatively, it may be understood that the Secretary-General, as a matter of course, would place on the Supplementary List, on his own authority, any item requested by a State not a Member (if the conditions of Article 35, paragraph 2, had been met) or by a subsidiary organ.

to be both important and urgent. The Rules provide that, unless the Assembly decides otherwise by a two-thirds majority of Members present and voting, an Additional Item may not be considered until seven days have elapsed since it was placed on the agenda; the Rules also provide that no Additional Item may be considered until a committee has reported on the question concerned.

Rule 15 regarding Additional Items, which is based on a similar rule of the League Assembly, does not specify by whom Additional Items may be submitted. It would seem logical that the right to submit Additional Items under Rule 15 should belong to a Member State, a principal organ or the Secretary-General, being the agencies that may submit Supplementary Items under Rule 14. The provision that no Additional Item may be considered until it has been on the agenda for a week, unless a decision to the contrary is taken by a two-thirds majority vote, is intended to prevent the Assembly from taking up a new matter before delegations have received instructions. The difficulty is that if the matter is " important and urgent," the sponsor or sponsors may take the view that it should be considered immediately.

The Rules of Procedure state that each item proposed for the agenda " shall be accompanied by an explanatory memorandum and, if possible, by basic documents or by a draft resolution " (Rule 20). In practice it is not always possible or wise to circulate a draft resolution until the debate is well under way.

It would be a useful practice, in the case of disputes or situations which are in the nature of disputes, if Member States proposing items for inclusion in the agenda would state, in the explanatory memorandum, whether the " peaceful means " which, under Article 33 of the Charter, shall be resorted to " first of all," have been tried. This would help the Assembly to judge the gravity of the situation and the extent to which the parties had already made efforts to reach agreement.

The General Committee: Composition

All proposals for the inclusion of items in the agenda are examined by the General Committee (*le Bureau*), which makes recommendations to the plenary Assembly. The General Committee consists of the officers of the Assembly, that is to say, the President, Vice-Presidents and Chairmen of Main Committees (Rule 38). It has been the experience of most deliberative bodies with more than about twenty members that a small " steering " group or committee is needed if business is to be handled in an orderly manner. Such a " steering " group should be quite small in size, so that a degree of intimacy and cohesion may develop. It should proceed with its work without undue hurry, and, if possible, in private. It need not have the power to act on its own responsibility; its primary function should be advisory.

The Executive Committee of the Preparatory Commission of the United Nations recommended that the General Committee should consist of the following fifteen members:

> (a) the President of the Assembly;
> (b) seven Vice-Presidents;
> (c) the Chairmen of the six Main Committees;
> (d) the Chairman of the Credentials Committee.

The Executive Committee also recommended that the Assembly should have the right to add to the General Committee " the Chairmen of the other Committees of the General Assembly and, in exceptional cases, other members." [10]

The Preparatory Committee itself considered that the General Committee should " have a small membership " and reduced the size of the Committee from fifteen to fourteen members by omitting the Chairman of the Credentials Committee. The Preparatory Committee also stipulated that:

> (a) no two members of the General Committee should be nationals of the same State;
>
> (b) the Vice-Presidents should be chosen on the basis of ensuring the representative character of the Committee;
>
> (c) the Chairmen should be chosen on the basis of equitable geographical distribution, experience and personal competence. [11]

These recommendations were approved during the first part of the first session of the Assembly.

During the fourth session, it was agreed that the Chairman of any sessional committee of the whole membership should be entitled to attend meetings of the General Committee and participate without vote in the discussions. [12] As an *Ad Hoc* Political Committee was created each session, this change in the Rules in effect increased the number of members of the General Committee to fifteen. The Chairman of the *Ad Hoc* Political Committee was made a voting member

---

10 *Report by the Executive Committee of the Preparatory Commission of the United Nations* (New York: United Nations, 12 Nov. 1945), PC/EX/113/Rev. 1, pp. 21, 31.
11 *Report of the Preparatory Commission of the United Nations* (New York: United Nations, 23 Dec. 1945), PC/20, p. 11.
12 General Assembly Res. 362 (IV), 22 Oct. 1949, Annex I.

of the General Committee during the eighth session.[13] During the eleventh session, the *Ad Hoc* Political Committee was made permanent and its name was changed to " Special Political Committee "; and the number of Vice-Presidents was increased from seven to eight.[14] During the twelfth session, the number of Vice-Presidents was increased to thirteen, giving the General Committee a total membership of twenty-one, and at the same time a pattern of representation was established.[15]

The Assembly's eight presiding officers are elected in their individual capacities; if the Chairman of a Main Committee is unable to attend a meeting of the General Committee, he designates the Vice-Chairman rather than a member of his delegation as his substitute. A Vice-Chairman acting as a substitute for a Chairman is not entitled to vote in the General Committee if he is of the same delegation as another member of the General Committee. Vice-Presidents, as in the League of Nations, are States rather than persons. During the election of Vice-Presidents during the first session, the President stated: " I should like to remind the delegations that they should vote for countries and not for individual representatives." [16] If a Vice-President finds it necessary to be absent during a meeting of the General Committee, he may designate a member of his own delegation as his substitute (Rule 39).

During the first part of the first session, it was agreed that a Member of the Assembly which did not have a representative on the General Committee, but which had requested the inclusion of an Additional Item in the agenda, should be entitled to attend any meetings of the General Committee at which its request was being discussed, and might participate, without vote, in the discussion of that item.[17] The word " additional " was eliminated during the 1947 revision of the Rules.[18]

There have been two problems connected with the participation of non-members of the Committee. First, when a large number of governments propose that an item should be included in the agenda, it is undesirable that all of them should participate in the work of the General Committee when the request is being discussed. It is interesting, in this connection, to recall that the League of Nations fixed a limit to the number of States which might propose a new item or sponsor a proposal. The matter was raised by Norway in the following terms:

[13] General Assembly Res. 791 (VIII), 23 Oct. 1953.
[14] General Assembly Res. 1104 (XI), 18 Dec. 1956.
[15] General Assembly Res. 1192 (XII), 12 Dec. 1957.
[16] G.A.O.R.: 1st Sess., Pt. I, 3rd Plenary Mtg., 11 Jan. 1946, p. 69.
[17] General Assembly Res. 17 (I), 29 Jan. 1946.
[18] General Assembly Res. 173 (II), 17 Nov. 1947. The Rule is now numbered 43.

During the last few sessions of the Assembly, it has occasionally happened that proposals have been submitted in the name of an exceptionally large number of delegations. Norway has been happy to be able to vote for these proposals. It is, however, conceivable that proposals might be submitted by so considerable a number of signatories that the other Members of the League would find themselves exposed to moral pressure and would hesitate to express their misgivings or doubts. . . . A proposal signed by more than half the Members of the League would more or less settle the question in advance. . . .

It seems desirable to remedy in good time the drawbacks created by the precedents mentioned above.

This purpose might be attained by stipulating that no proposal for the placing of a new question on the Assembly's agenda and no draft resolution, amendment or motion should be signed by more than a small number of Members. . . .

The Norwegian Government ventures to suggest that the figure should be fixed at ten. . . .[19]

Italy, supported by Venezuela and Cuba, proposed that the number might be increased from ten to fifteen, and Norway agreed.[20] The Rules of Procedure of the League Assembly were revised accordingly.

In the General Assembly of the United Nations there is no limitation on the number of Member States which may propose an item for inclusion in the agenda, and in the early days there was a tendency for all the sponsors to participate in the discussion in the General Committee. During the first special session, for example, the delegations of Iraq, Lebanon, Saudi Arabia and Syria took an active part in the work of the General Committee during consideration of the proposal to include the Palestine question in the agenda, although Egypt was a member of the Committee.[21] There has developed over the years a commendable tradition by which all the sponsors of an item do not insist on participating in the work of the Committee when the request is under discussion; indeed, in the majority of cases, there is now little or no discussion in the General Committee.

The second problem in connection with the participation of non-members in General Committee discussions has been that Rule 43 limits participation to those States which have " requested the inclusion of an item in the agenda "; a Member State which is opposed to the inclusion of an item, or is in some other way directly concerned in the matter, has no specific right of participation. This matter arose during the first part of the third session during consideration of the Indian proposal to include in the agenda the item " Treatment of

19 League of Nations Assembly Official Journal: 13th Ordinary Sess., 1st Committee, Annexes, Spec. Suppl. No. 105, p. 44.
20 *Ibid.*, pp. 11, 12.
21 G.A.O.R.: 1st Spec. Sess., General Committee, 29th–31st Mtgs., 29–30 April 1947, pp. 12–87.

Indians in the Union of South Africa." The South African representative made a formal request to participate in the discussion. The Chairman pointed out that there was no Rule of Procedure which covered this contingency, but he considered that it was only fair to hear the views of the South African representative. He therefore put his proposal to the vote, and it was adopted without opposition.[22]

During the second part of the same session, a similar question arose when India and Australia requested that the Indonesian question should be included in the agenda. The Netherlands was not represented on the General Committee, and Indonesia was not yet a Member of the United Nations. The Chairman suggested that, following the practice of the first part of the session, it would only be fair to allow the representative of the Netherlands to speak. The Soviet and Polish representatives objected to this, but did not press the matter to a vote. Following the statement of the representative of the Netherlands, the Chairman said that a representative of the Republic of Indonesia had " expressed the wish to state his views." It is not clear from the summary in the official records whether there was any objection to this request; the records merely state " the Chairman invited him to make a statement." [23]

During the tenth session, both the Netherlands and Australia requested permission to take part in the discussion in the General Committee on the proposal to include the question of West Irian (West New Guinea) in the agenda, but the Egyptian delegate opposed granting the Australian request. The matter was pressed to a vote, and the Committee decided by a vote of 9–1–4 to invite the Australian representative to take part in the discussion.[24]

THE GENERAL COMMITTEE: FUNCTIONS

The main responsibility of the General Committee is to examine all proposals for the inclusion of items in the agenda and to make recommendations to the plenary Assembly. The five permanent members of the Security Council are, by well-established tradition, always elected to membership of the General Committee, but from the beginning the medium and smaller Powers have feared lest the General Committee should become an instrument of the Great Powers for dominating the Assembly. This apprehension was apparent in the Preparatory Commission, when Belgium proposed to add to the Provisional Rules of Procedure the sentence " The General Committee

---

22 G.A.O.R.: 3rd Sess., Pt. I, General Committee, 43rd Mtg., 22 Sept. 1948, pp. 11–12.
23 G.A.O.R.: 3rd Sess., Pt. II, General Committee, 60th Mtg., 8 Apr. 1949, p. 43.
24 G.A.O.R.: 10th Sess., General Committee, 104th Mtg., 29 Sept. 1955, paras. 2–4.

cannot decide any political question." This proposal received twenty-four affirmative and seventeen negative votes, but as a two-thirds majority was not received, it failed of adoption.

In view of the anxiety which lay behind the Belgian proposal, the United States, British and Soviet delegations made statements regarding their conception of the role of the General Committee. The delegate of the United States emphasized that the plenary Assembly would have complete control over policy and would be the " supreme authority "; the functions of the General Committee would be mainly those of " administrative management." The British delegate denied that the General Committee would be a secret caucus; it would be concerned with procedure, and the plenary must and would stop any political manipulations under the cloak of procedure. The Soviet delegate said that the General Committee would not take decisions of political importance, and in any case its recommendations would be subject to approval by the full Assembly.[25]

During the first part of the first session, a sentence substantially the same as that proposed by Belgium in the Preparatory Commission was added to the Provisional Rules of Procedure. The vote on this in the Sixth Committee was 32–14–5, with China, the Soviet Union, the United Kingdom and the United States opposing the change; the revision was approved in the plenary by thirty-three votes, with three abstentions.[26] The main problem in this connection, however, has not been to prevent the General Committee from deciding political questions; the problem has been to prevent it from engaging in unnecessarily lengthy political debate prior to making procedural recommendations. It is obviously impossible to avoid all political discussion when considering proposals for the agenda, since some facts and opinions of a political nature may have a bearing on the decision whether to accept or reject a request for inclusion.

During the second part of the first session, Canada made a number of suggestions for economizing the time of the Assembly. Among these was the following:

> The General Committee, in discussing matters related to the agenda of the General Assembly, should not debate the substance of a question but should confine itself to discussing whether or not it should recommend that an item be included in the agenda. . . .[27]

Nothing came of this proposal when it was first put forward, but the idea was revived by Canada some years later when the Special

25 *Report of the Preparatory Commission of the United Nations, op. cit.,* pp. 11, 12, 123, 124.
26 G.A.O.R.: 1st Sess., Pt. I, 6th Committee, 3rd Mtg., 21 Jan. 1946, pp. 7–8; and 18th Plenary Mtg., 26 Jan. 1946, pp. 271–274.
27 G.A.O.R.: 1st Sess., Pt. II, 1946, General Committee, Annex 16 (A/92), para. 6 (*d*).

Committee on Methods and Procedures (1949) invited Member States to submit proposals. The Canadian delegation pointed out that Presidents of the Assembly had found it difficult to restrict the discussions in the General Committee to matters within the Committee's jurisdiction. The Committee was precluded from deciding any political question, but nothing was said about the extent to which the Committee might discuss the substance of items proposed for the Assembly's agenda. The Canadian delegation proposed that the Rules should state explicitly that the General Committee should not discuss the substance of an item except in so far as this might bear on the Committee's recommendations. This proposal was approved by the Special Committee on Methods and Procedures and an addition was made to the relevant Rule along the lines of the Canadian proposal.[28]

Until 1949, the General Committee was merely asked to consider the matters proposed for inclusion in the agenda and to " report thereon to the General Assembly." Acting on a suggestion of the British delegation, the Special Committee on Methods and Procedures (1949) proposed that the General Committee should be specifically required to make one of three recommendations with regard to each item proposed: inclusion in the agenda, rejection of the request for inclusion, or inclusion in the provisional agenda of a future session (which is tantamount to postponement).[29] This proposal was approved by the Assembly.

The Special Committee on Methods and Procedures (1949) emphasized that the Assembly had the power " to decide, at the beginning of or during the session, to refer certain items, without preliminary debate, to other organs of the United Nations . . . such as one of the existing subsidiary organs of the General Assembly, an *ad hoc* committee, one of the Councils, a specialized agency or the Secretary-General." [30] It is presumably within the competence of the General Committee, when recommending such action to the plenary, to recommend also that any such item or items be included in the provisional agenda of a future session.

Like other organs of the United Nations, the General Committee did not immediately settle into an established routine. During the first three sessions it met relatively frequently, easily became involved in substantive debate, and discussed a variety of matters which in later sessions were dealt with by other and usually more informal means.

[28] United Nations Doc. A/937, para. 25. This provision is now the last sentence of Rule 40.
[29] *Ibid.*
[30] *Ibid.*, para. 12.

The frequency of meeting of the General Committee is shown in Table 13. In order to illustrate the variety of questions submitted to the General Committee in the early days, I give below some of the matters considered by the Committee during the first session:

Request of the World Federation of Trade Unions for representation in the General Assembly;

Procedure for dealing with communications from non-governmental organizations;

Seating arrangements in committees of the Assembly;

Reply to a congratulatory communication from the Italian Government;

Arrangements for the installation of the Secretary-General;

Terms of reference of the Permanent Headquarters Committee;

Translation of speeches;

Arrangements for heads of principal organs, specialized agencies and other official international organizations to attend the General Assembly.

TABLE 13

Number of Meetings of the General Committee, 1946–59

Regular Session No.	Year	Number of Meetings
1	1946	27
2	1947	7
3	1948–49	22
4	1949	4
5	1950–51	6
6	1951–52	4
7	1952–53	8
8	1953	5
9	1954	10
10	1955	4
11	1956–57	5
12	1957	6
13	1958–59	4
14	1959	5
		117
Special Session No.		
1	1947	7
2	1948	1
	Total	125

During the first flush of enthusiasm for the United Nations, there was a tendency to submit for inclusion in the agenda idealistic proposals of marginal importance. This had been true of the League Assembly, which had been asked to take up such matters as how the teaching of Esperanto could become more general. Among the items submitted for inclusion in the agenda of the first session of the United Nations Assembly were the following:

> Proposal that the Assembly should express " its keen sympathy with the impending start of the construction of the Columbus Lighthouse Memorial. . . ." [31]
>
> Proposal regarding " the translation and publication of the classics into the languages of Members of the United Nations." [32]
>
> Proposal for the " creation of a world university alliance." [33]

Member States soon realized that the Assembly could not perform its own essential functions if it took up too many matters of secondary importance.

The General Committee no longer exercises to the full the functions specified in the Rules. It now makes recommendations to the plenary concerning the following matters:

(1) The inclusion, exclusion or postponement of items proposed for the agenda;

(2) The rewording of items;

(3) The amalgamation of related items;

(4) The allocation of items;

(5) The closing date of the session.

The Committee has the authority to revise resolutions adopted by the Assembly, changing their form but not their substance; any such changes must be reported to the Assembly for its consideration (Rule 44). I am not aware of any instance of this right being exercised. The Committee meets at such times as the President deems necessary, or upon the request of any other of its members (Rule 42).

There are two groups of functions which the Rules state are the responsibility of the General Committee but which in practice are not exercised. First, the General Committee should—but does not—assist the President and the General Assembly in drawing up the agenda for each plenary meeting, in determining the priority of its items, and in the co-ordination of the proceedings of all committees of the General Assembly, and should assist the President in the general conduct of the work of the General Assembly which falls within the competence of the President (Rule 41). This wording is an adaptation of paragraph 2 of Rule 8 of the Rules of Procedure of the League Assembly.

[31] G.A.O.R.: 1st Sess., Pt. I, General Committee, 9th Mtg., 2 Feb. 1946; 13th Mtg., 8 Feb. 1946, Annex 8, pp. 17, 21, 54.

[32] G.A.O.R.: 1st Sess., Pt. II, General Committee, 24th Mtg., 5 Nov. 1946, p. 80.

[33] *Ibid.*, 25th Mtg., 6 Nov. 1946, p. 88.

Secondly, the General Committee should—but does not—meet periodically throughout each session to review the progress of the General Assembly and its committees, and to make recommendations for furthering such progress (Rule 42). This wording is based on a British revision of a proposal of the Special Committee on Methods and Procedures (1949).[34]

The above functions, which formally belong to the General Committee, are in practice discharged by informal means, and in particular by a weekly lunch held throughout the session attended by the presiding officers of the Assembly and officials of the Secretariat specially concerned with the business of the Assembly.[35]

GOVERNMENTS AND THE AGENDA

There are, broadly speaking, two main views concerning proposals to include items in the agenda. There is, first, the view which one may term " unselective " and which seems to be the view of many, perhaps most, Member States. Those holding this view would say that the Assembly should reject the request of a Member State to include an item in the agenda only in the most exceptional circumstances; that the Charter implies the right of Member States to have their grievances and problems aired in the Assembly; that the Assembly is strengthened rather than weakened by having a great deal of work to do; and that the effect of Assembly debate is almost always beneficial. Such a view may not be held with perfect consistency; a government may take this general position and yet at the same time favour rejecting a request that some particularly controversial item be included in the agenda (as, indeed, many governments have done on the question of Chinese representation).

I can best illustrate the point of view just summarized by letting some delegates speak for themselves.

> *Ceylon:* " his delegation . . . attached great importance to the principle that items proposed by Member States should be included in the agenda. . . ."[36]

> *Ecuador:* " his delegation had unreservedly supported the principle that the General Assembly should not refuse to discuss any item which a Member State had requested for inclusion in the agenda. . . ."[37]

---

[34] G.A.O.R.: 4th Sess., 6th Committee, 146th Mtg., 29 Sept. 1949, paras. 28–43; 148th Mtg., 1 Oct. 1949, paras. 95–105.
[35] Herbert V. Evatt, President of the third session, referred in the General Committee to informal meetings between presiding officers and the Secretary-General. G.A.O.R.: 3rd Sess., Pt. II, General Committee, 57th Mtg., 5 Apr. 1949, p. 1.
[36] G.A.O.R.: 13th Sess., General Committee, 118th Mtg., 19 Sept. 1958, para. 25.
[37] *Ibid.*, para. 22.

Ghana: " It is the view of my delegation that any Member of the United Nations has a right to place on the agenda . . . any item that it wishes to propose for discussion." [38]

Guatemala: " he would vote in favour of inclusion of the item . . . in accordance with his delegation's policy of agreeing to the inclusion of all items requested." [39]

India: " An item could not be deleted . . . without a serious infringement of the Assembly's prerogatives." [40]

Iraq: " stated that the General Assembly was the supreme forum of the world and that Member States should have every opportunity to bring their problems before it. To deny them that right would be to deny the very precepts of the Charter. . . . Member States should have the right to secure the inclusion in the agenda of problems they considered to be of importance." [41]

Mexico: " he had voted for the inclusion of the item in the agenda only in order to express his delegation's opinion that any Member of the United Nations could bring any dispute to the attention of . . . the General Assembly." [42]

United States: " would vote in favour of including the item since it believed that the United Nations should hear every complaint brought before it " (1950).[43]

United States: " the United States delegation would not vote against the inclusion of the proposal item in the agenda, because it believed that a Member of the United Nations was entitled to express any views it desired . . ." (1957).[44]

The general approach which these statements express is in contrast to the view which one may term " restrictive." Those holding the latter view ask that every proposal for the inclusion of items in the agenda should be examined with regard to the Assembly's competence, as well as the political wisdom and practical consequences of taking up a question at a particular time. As the British Foreign Secretary has put it:

[38] G.A.O.R.: 13th Sess., 752nd Plenary Mtg., 22 Sept. 1958, para. 33, p. 49.
[39] G.A.O.R.: 12th Sess., General Committee, 114th Mtg., 4 Oct. 1957, para. 17.
[40] G.A.O.R.: 1st Sess., Pt. II, General Committee, 19th Mtg., 24 Oct. 1946, p. 70.
[41] G.A.O.R.: 8th Sess., General Committee, 88th Mtg., 22 Sept. 1953, paras. 51–52.
[42] G.A.O.R.: 10th Sess., General Committee, 103rd Mtg., 22 Sept. 1955, para. 69.
[43] G.A.O.R.: 5th Sess., General Committee, 70th Mtg., 22 Sept. 1950, para. 5.
[44] G.A.O.R.: 11th Sess., General Committee, 110th Mtg., 14 Feb. 1957, para. 19.

We also think . . . that the inscription of items should be approached not just from the legalistic point of view; there also should be a practical political attitude towards the agenda. . . . I cannot accept the conception, although I know it is held by many, that inscription should be automatic.[45]

It is not possible, within the scope of this book, to examine in detail the question of the Assembly's competence. It is significant, however, that several of the delegations which have been most insistent that the Charter limitations on the competence of the Assembly should be strictly applied have, at the same time, taken the view that the issue of competence can be settled only after substantive debate. Even if there are doubts concerning the Assembly's competence in some matter, these delegations do not regard this as a reason to oppose the inclusion of the item on the agenda—though there may well be political or practical reasons for opposing inclusion. Again I let delegates speak for themselves.

Belgium: " The Assembly . . . could not determine whether the Organization was competent to deal with a matter unless that matter was first included in the agenda." [46]

India: " before we can discuss the question of competence, it is essential first to place the item on the agenda." [47]

Mexico: " Whether or not the General Assembly was competent to deal with the proposed item was certainly a political question, and could be decided only by the General Assembly itself, after discussion." [48]

U.S.S.R.: " Only when the time comes to discuss the substance of any given item can the question of the General Assembly's competence be raised. . . . It is absolutely unprecedented to consider the question of whether an item should be included in the agenda or not from the point of view of the Assembly's competence." [49]

United Kingdom: " reserved the right to speak on the question of competence in the General Assembly; a recommendation by the General Committee to include an item in the agenda in no way prejudged that issue." [50]

Mr. F. M. Urquia (El Salvador, Chairman of the *Ad Hoc* Political Committee): " The CHAIRMAN explained that, when the

45 G.A.O.R.: 14th Sess., 798th Plenary Mtg., 17 Sept. 1959, paras. 14–15.
46 G.A.O.R.: 3rd Sess., Pt. II, 190th Plenary Mtg., 12 Apr. 1949, p. 22.
47 G.A.O.R.: 8th Sess., 435th Plenary Mtg., 17 Sept. 1953, para. 52.
48 G.A.O.R.: 10th Sess., General Committee, 102nd Mtg., 21 Sept. 1955, para. 44.
49 G.A.O.R.: 7th Sess., 381st Plenary Mtg., 17 Oct. 1952, paras. 141, 143.
50 G.A.O.R.: 8th Sess., General Committee, 87th Mtg., 16 Sept. 1953, para. 11.

General Assembly included an item in its agenda, it did not prejudge the question of its competence. . . . It had always been agreed that the question of competence was considered by the committee concerned or by the Assembly itself." [51]

The problem of the Assembly's competence has usually centred around one or other of two provisions of the Charter. Article 2 (7) prohibits the Assembly (or any organ of the United Nations) from intervening in matters which are essentially within the domestic juris-diction of any State, except in relation to the application of enforce-ment measures under Chapter VII of the Charter. The following are among the questions raised in connection with this provision:

> What is the meaning of the phrase " matters which are essentially within the domestic jurisdiction of any state "?
> Does the inclusion of an item in the agenda, and consequently the discussion of it, constitute intervention?
> Does a recommendation, whether of a general nature or addressed to a particular State or group of States, constitute intervention?
> Does the creation of a subsidiary organ to study and report constitute intervention?

These questions are not solely legal in character; they have important political implications. Moreover, the interpretation of the Charter changes as new concepts develop regarding the nature of State sovereignty and the purposes of intergovernmental organizations.

The second provision of the Charter which has given rise to discussion regarding the Assembly's competence is Article 12 (1). This states that " While the Security Council is exercising in respect of any dispute or situation the functions assigned to it in the present Charter, the General Assembly shall not make any recommendations with regard to that dispute or situation unless the Security Council so requests." The purpose of this provision was to prevent the Assembly and the Security Council from acting concurrently in the same question, a problem which had troubled the League. Differ-ences concerning the interpretation of Article 12 (1) have, in the main, centred around two questions:

> What is the meaning of the phrase " while the Security Council is exercising . . . the functions assigned to it . . ."?
> What is the scope of the term " recommendation "?

[51] *Ibid., Ad Hoc* Political Committee, 34th Mtg., 25 Nov. 1953, para. 55.

The practice of the Assembly regarding competence has been neither clear nor uniform. Article 12 (1) does not appear to impose any limitation on the Assembly's right of discussion; Article 2 (7) has been widely (but not universally) interpreted as not imposing any limitation on the right of discussion, and it is widely (but not universally) held that in cases where the question of competence is unclear, the question can be decided only after substantive debate.

If governments believe, before substantive debate has taken place, that the Assembly is not competent even to discuss some question submitted to it, the legal objections are usually stated before a vote is taken on whether to include, postpone or reject the item. As a practical matter, however, such legal objections rarely seem to carry weight in influencing the General Committee and the Assembly. At this stage it seems more effective to use a political argument, such as that to include the matter in the agenda will provoke unnecessary discord, or will prejudice negotiations that are taking place or contemplated elsewhere, or will interfere with other efforts to deal with a question. The head of one delegation is said to have told his subordinates: " Whenever possible, use good political arguments. If there are no good political arguments, use bad political arguments. If there are no bad political arguments, use legal arguments."

Practical considerations are often as important as legal or political ones. The practical question in relation to the agenda, though the one mentioned least often by representatives, is the relative importance of different questions. In a limited period of time, only a limited amount of business can receive adequate attention. All proposals for the agenda, whether new items or hardy perennials, should be examined with reference to the important practical consideration that if the Assembly deals with one matter, it almost certainly deals less effectively with some other matter. The question is not whether a particular matter is urgent or important; the question is how urgent and important it is in relation to all the other matters that have been or may be proposed.

PROPOSALS FOR AN AGENDA COMMITTEE

I have indicated above some of the reasons why the General Committee has not exercised a great deal of discrimination regarding proposals for the agenda. There is an additional reason of a practical nature that may be stressed here: the Committee inevitably works under a sense of pressure because it meets at a time when its members are preoccupied with other matters. Various procedures to circumvent this difficulty have been suggested, of which the most widely favoured has been the idea that a small agenda committee might scrutinize proposals for the agenda before the session begins.[52]

The League of Nations had an agenda committee as well as a general committee—the function of the agenda committee being to consider applications for the inclusion of *new* questions in the agenda and to report to the Assembly thereon. The Executive Committee of the Preparatory Commission of the United Nations considered a proposal for the establishment of both a general committee and an agenda committee; the latter would have performed the functions now given to the General Committee by Rule 40. It was argued, in favour of the establishment of an agenda committee, that it would lighten the task of the General Committee. The majority of the members of the Executive Committee, however, considered that the functions which it had been proposed should be entrusted to the agenda committee could be performed by the General Committee. Fears were expressed that the existence of a special agenda committee would create confusion and a conflict of authority with the General Committee, and it was thought that a proliferation of committees should be avoided. The Executive Committee decided, therefore, to transfer to the General Committee the functions originally intended for an agenda committee.

The idea of an agenda committee for the General Assembly has been revived from time to time, and in the case of another United Nations organ an agenda committee was in existence for four years. The Economic and Social Council decided in 1947 to establish an agenda committee consisting of the President, the two Vice-Presidents and two other members of the Council. The agenda committee met between sessions of the Council and was authorized to hear any of the authorities that had proposed the inclusion of items and to make recommendations on the provisional agenda. Various difficulties were encountered in the functioning of the committee; these arose in part because some of its members could not attend all of its meetings, and also because others had ceased to be members of the Council while they were still members of the agenda committee. Various changes were made in the method of constituting the committee, and its terms of reference were widened, but these changes did not eliminate the difficulties. In any case, it was found that the recommendations of the agenda committee did not appreciably reduce discussion of the agenda in the Council itself. In 1951 the Council

[52] See, for example, Waldo Chamberlin, *Memorandum Concerning the Conduct of the Business of the General Assembly of the United Nations* (New York: Carnegie Endowment for International Peace, 1949), para. 42, p. 23; and Eric Stein, *Some Implications of Expanding United Nations Membership* (New York: Carnegie Endowment for International Peace, 1956), p. 42. (Unpublished memoranda.)

discontinued the committee. In its place, a short session of the Council takes place towards the end of or shortly after the regular session of the General Assembly. The Council, during this " resumed session," considers the programme of work for the following year and adopts the agenda for the forthcoming session. This procedure seems generally satisfactory.

At one time it was thought that the Interim Committee of the Assembly might function as a scrutinizing committee in relation to one category of questions. The Interim Committee was empowered to " consider and report, with its conclusions," to the Assembly on any dispute or situation which, in virtue of Article 11 (2), 14 or 35 of the Charter (threats to peace), had been proposed for inclusion in the agenda, provided the Committee considered the matter to be both important and requiring preliminary study.[53]

When the methods and procedures of the Assembly were being reviewed in 1949, three separate proposals for an agenda committee were made. South Africa favoured a standing agenda committee within the Secretariat, under the chairmanship of the Secretary-General.[54] Denmark, Norway and Sweden jointly suggested, as a basis for discussion, the creation of a committee to meet a short time in advance of each session to prepare its work.[55] The United Kingdom proposed that a fifteen-member agenda committee, representative in character and including the five permanent members of the Security Council, should meet not less than three weeks before the opening of each regular session and should be dissolved on or before the opening of the session. This agenda committee should consider matters proposed for inclusion in the agenda and make recommendations to the General Assembly concerning the inclusion, non-inclusion or postponement of each item, the priority to be given to consideration of particular items, and an estimated date for the conclusion of the session.[56]

These three proposals were not aimed directly at securing a closer scrutiny of the agenda. The main argument of those who favoured the proposals was that it would be advantageous to entrust the examination of the agenda to a committee that would be less pressed for time than is the General Committee, thus making it easier for delegations to find grounds for agreement.[57] The Special Committee on Methods and Procedures (1949) considered the proposals and commented as follows:

53 General Assembly Res. 111 (II), 13 Nov. 1947.
54 United Nations Doc. A/937, Annex 1, p. 15.
55 *Ibid.*, para. 2(g), p. 15.
56 *Ibid.*, p. 20.
57 *Ibid.*, para. 15, p. 6.

Several members of the Special Committee doubted whether the establishment of an agenda committee would actually result in a shortening of the General Assembly's sessions. They also had doubts concerning the degree of authority which the agenda committee would possess and the nature of its relationship with the General Committee. Other members were not ready to express a definite opinion on the proposals which had been submitted and thought that the matter should be further studied and re-examined at a later date.

The Special Committee decided, therefore, to bring the question to the attention of the General Assembly and to transmit to the Assembly the various written proposals which it had received. It also decided to request the Secretary-General to assist the General Assembly by preparing a study on proposals, previously examined, to report on such technical, legal and financial aspects of the question as he may consider pertinent, and to submit to the Assembly his views on the composition and functions of an agenda committee.[58]

The Secretary-General, in the report requested by the Special Committee on Methods and Procedures, expressed doubts that an agenda committee could deal more effectively with questions relating to the Assembly's agenda than the General Committee had done. The General Committee, in his view, enjoyed great prestige, and " its recommendations are therefore normally endorsed by the General Assembly without prolonged debate in plenary meetings." That was a considerable factor in accelerating the pace of the session. He was of the opinion that the consideration of the agenda by the General Committee did not delay the beginning of the work of Main Committees.[59] Most members of the Sixth Committee endorsed the Secretary-General's conclusion, though the British and Norwegian representatives still considered that the possibility of establishing an agenda committee deserved further exploration. After a short debate, the Sixth Committee approved the conclusions of the Secretary-General by a vote of 24–4–17.[60]

During a review of procedure during the seventh session, the possibility of establishing an agenda committee was again raised. The British representative emphasized that the agenda should be carefully pruned in order to avoid unnecessary debate; recalled that it had been suggested in the past that an agenda committee should be set up to scrutinize the agenda before the opening of each session; and expressed the hope that this possibility would receive careful attention. The representative of New Zealand also urged that the possibility of establishing an agenda committee should be examined.

58 *Ibid.*
59 G.A.O.R.: 4th Sess., 1949, 6th Committee, Annexes (A/997), paras. 36–39.
60 G.A.O.R.: 4th Sess., 6th Committee, 156th Mtg., 8 Oct. 1949, paras. 1–43.

In general, however, representatives were not in favour of any change of procedure regarding proposals for the agenda.[61]

Since the time when proposals for an agenda committee were last reviewed by the Assembly, the General Committee has been enlarged by fifty per cent. Moreover, it does not seem likely that the representative character of the General Committee can be maintained in the future, after another half-dozen or more African States have been admitted to membership, without a further increase in its size. It seems likely that the General Committee will in future be unable to perform an adequate scrutinizing function, though its work will doubtless continue to be useful by obviating the need for complicated and lengthy discussions in the plenary on the wording, amalgamation and allocation of items. The time may come when an agenda committee will seem the most palatable medicine for dealing with chronic voracity for work.

VOTING IN CONNECTION WITH THE AGENDA

Two earlier studies prepared under the auspices of the Carnegie Endowment for International Peace refer to the possibility of voting in the plenary on agenda questions by secret ballot:

> As mentioned above, the General Assembly in a regular session has never [1949] refused to accept any item on its agenda. There are undoubtedly many reasons why this is so, but one of them is unquestionably the fact that few states care to offend the proposer of an agenda item by voting against such a proposal in public. Were the secret ballot applied to the acceptance of all items it is possible that a considerable number might be kept off the agenda.[62]
>
> A secret ballot in the plenary might also make it easier for a member to support the General Committee's recommendation against inclusion of an item without offending the proposing state.[63]

Although there are some weighty arguments in favour of this proposal, it is possible that the use of secret balloting for matters other than elections would be somewhat cumbersome without the adoption of mechanical voting devices. In any case, there seems to be a widespread dislike of the secret ballot, based on a feeling that governments should not be afraid to " stand up and be counted."

It would presumably not require any change in the Rules of Procedure for the General Committee to recommend that certain matters be included in the agenda for debate only. There are always a number of items that are included in the agenda in order to allow governments to express their views rather than because any recommendation or expression of opinion by the Assembly is thought to

---

[61] G.A.O.R.: 7th Sess., 387th Plenary Mtg., 23 Oct. 1952, paras. 25, 81.
[62] Chamberlin, *op. cit.*, para. 27, p. 17.   [63] Stein, *op. cit.*, p. 41.

be necessary. Certain items of this nature might be considered and discussed during the General Debate. It is presumably open to any Member State, either at the time the decision is taken to include an item in the agenda, or when the item arises in the normal course, to move that the item be discussed but that no proposals arising from the debate be considered or put to the vote.

The United Kingdom delegation suggested to the Special Committee on Methods and Procedures (1949) that consideration be given to amending the Rules of Procedure so that a two-thirds majority of the Members present and voting, rather than a simple majority, would be required in plenary meetings to include in the agenda either an Additional Item of an important and urgent character or any item which had been recommended for rejection or postponement by the General Committee.[64] The British proposal regarding Additional Items was approved by the Special Committee on Methods and Procedures, and a revision of the relevant Rule was proposed.[65]

This proposed revision did not receive the consideration it deserved in the Sixth Committee of the Assembly. The United States representative insisted that a heavy agenda, far from being a sign of weakness, was a sign of strength. The representative of Uruguay regarded the increase in the list of items submitted to the Assembly as a matter for congratulation. The representatives of Yugoslavia and Pakistan did, however, draw attention to a possible anomalous situation that would arise should the Committee's proposal be adopted: important and urgent Additional Items could be included in the agenda only if they received a two-thirds vote of Members present and voting, while a special session of the Assembly could be summoned by simple majority of Members. The text proposed by the Committee was rejected by a vote of 28–13–6.[66]

The possible anomaly to which the representatives of Yugoslavia and Pakistan drew attention would certainly have existed had the Committee's proposal been adopted. However, this possibility already exists in that Supplementary and Additional Items may be added to the agenda during a special session by a two-thirds majority of the Members present and voting (Rule 19), whereas a special session itself can be summoned by a majority of Member States (Rules 8 and 9). It was also suggested, during the consideration of the Special Committee's proposal, that the inclusion of items in the agenda is a procedural question and that procedural matters should be decided by a simple majority.[67] It should be noted, however, that three of

[64] United Nations Doc. A/937, Annex 1, p. 17.
[65] *Ibid.*, para. 11.
[66] G.A.O.R.: 4th Sess., 6th Committee, 143rd Mtg., 27 Sept. 1949, paras. 58, 61, 68, 70.   [67] *Ibid.*, paras. 65, 71, 80.

the Rules relating specifically to procedural matters (Rules 15, 19 and 83) provide that a two-thirds majority is required for a decision.

Although questions relating to the agenda are procedural, they are indubitably important. Article 18 (2) of the Charter requires that important decisions shall be made by a two-thirds majority of Members present and voting. It would thus be in accordance with the letter and spirit of Article 18 for the Assembly to determine, by a simple majority, that any decision to include items in the agenda should require a two-thirds vote in plenary meeting. This is admittedly a drastic proposal, though it would only be making a regular practice of what is already the procedure regarding Supplementary and Additional Items during special sessions. It would ensure that all items included in the agenda would receive serious attention, which is not always the case at present. Anyone familiar with the proceedings of the Assembly can think of matters which have been admitted to the agenda with the knowledge that they will receive hurried attention at the end of a busy session. Moreover, virtually all of the matters included in the agenda are regarded as of sufficient importance that resolutions arising from them require a two-thirds vote for adoption. It would, by the same token, be logical to regard inclusion of the item as requiring the same majority.

TABLE 14

Agenda of the Fourteenth Regular Session, 1959

PLENARY MEETINGS

1. Opening of the session by the Chairman of the delegation of Lebanon.
2. Minute of silent prayer or meditation.
3. Credentials of representatives to the fourteenth session of the General Assembly:
   (a) Appointment of the Credentials Committee;
   (b) Report of the Credentials Committee.
4. **Election of the President.**
5. Constitution of the Main Committees and election of officers.
6. Election of Vice-Presidents.
7. Notification by the Secretary-General, under Article 12 (2) of the Charter, of matters relative to the maintenance of international peace and security which are being dealt with by the Security Council.
8. Adoption of the agenda.
9. Opening of the General Debate.
10. Report of the Secretary-General on the work of the Organization.
11. Report of the Security Council.
12. Report of the Economic and Social Council (Chapters I, VIII and IX relating to constitutional and organizational questions, and relations with specialized agencies and non-governmental organizations).
13. Report of the International Atomic Energy Agency.
14. Election of three non-permanent members of the Security Council.
15. Election of six members of the Economic and Social Council.
16. Election of two members of the Trusteeship Council.
17. Election of a member of the International Court of Justice to fill the vacancy caused by the death of Judge José Gustavo Guerrero.

TABLE 14—*continued*

18. Interim report of the Secretary-General evaluating the Second United Nations International Conference on the Peaceful Uses of Atomic Energy in relation to the holding of similar conferences in the future.
19. United Nations Emergency Force: progress report on the Force.
20. Progress report of the United Nations Scientific Committee on the Effects of Atomic Radiation.
21. Report of the Committee on arrangements for a conference for the purpose of reviewing the Charter.
22. The question of Tibet.
23. Question of Hungary.

First Committee

1. General and complete disarmament.
2. Question of French nuclear tests in the Sahara.
3. Prevention of the wider dissemination of nuclear weapons.
4. Suspension of nuclear and thermo-nuclear tests.
5. Report of the Disarmament Commission: letter from the Chairman of the Disarmament Commission to the Secretary-General.
6. The Korean question: report of the United Nations Commission for the Unification and Rehabilitation of Korea.
7. Question of Algeria.
8. Report of the *Ad Hoc* Committee on the Peaceful Uses of Outer Space.

Special Political Committee

1. Question of amending the United Nations Charter, in accordance with the procedure laid down in Article 108 of the Charter, to increase the number of non-permanent members of the Security Council and the number of votes required for decisions of the Council.
2. Question of amending the United Nations Charter, in accordance with the procedure laid down in Article 108 of the Charter, to increase the membership of the Economic and Social Council.
3. Question of amending the Statute of the International Court of Justice, in accordance with the procedure laid down in Article 108 of the Charter of the United Nations and Article 69 of the Statute of the Court, with respect to an increase in the number of judges of the International Court of Justice.
4. Question of race conflict in South Africa resulting from the policies of apartheid of the Government of the Union of South Africa.
5. Question of the consistent application of the principle of equitable geographical representation in the election of the President of the General Assembly.
6. United Nations Relief and Works Agency for Palestine Refugees in the Near East:
   (a) Report of the Director of the Agency;
   (b) Proposals for the continuation of United Nations assistance to Palestine refugees: document submitted by the Secretary-General.
7. Treatment of people of Indian origin in the Union of South Africa.

Second Committee

1. Progress and operations of the Special Fund.
2. Programmes of technical assistance:
   (a) Report of the Economic and Social Council;
   (b) United Nations assistance in public administration: report of the Secretary-General;
   (c) Confirmation of the allocation of funds under the Expanded Programme of Technical Assistance.

TABLE 14—*continued*

3. Economic development of underdeveloped countries:
   (a) Report by the Secretary-General on measures taken by the Governments of Member States to further the economic development of underdeveloped countries;
   (b) Progress in the field of financing the economic development of underdeveloped countries.
4. Report of the Economic and Social Council (Chapters II, III, IV and V relating to the world economic situation, regional economic activities and other economic questions).
5. United Nations Korean Reconstruction Agency: progress report of the Administrator for Residual Affairs of the Agency.

Third Committee

1. Draft Declaration of the Rights of the Child.
2. Report of the Economic and Social Council (Chapters VI and VII relating to social questions and human rights).
3. Report of the United Nations High Commissioner for Refugees.
4. International encouragement of scientific research into the control of cancerous diseases.
5. Draft International Covenants on Human Rights.
6. Draft Convention on Freedom of Information: text of the draft Convention and report of the Secretary-General on the comments of Governments thereon.

Fourth Committee

1. Question of South West Africa:
   (a) Report of the Good Offices Committee on South West Africa;
   (b) Report of the Committee on South West Africa;
   (c) Study of legal action to ensure the fulfilment of the obligations assumed by the Union of South Africa in respect of the Territory of South West Africa;
   (d) Election of three members of the Committee on South West Africa.
2. Report of the Trusteeship Council.
3. Offers by Member States of study and training facilities for inhabitants of Trust Territories: report of the Trusteeship Council.
4. Information from Non-Self-Governing Territories transmitted under Article 73 e of the Charter: reports of the Secretary-General and of the Committee on Information from Non-Self-Governing Territories:
   (a) Progress achieved by the Non-Self-Governing Territories in pursuance of Chapter XI of the Charter;
   (b) Information on educational conditions;
   (c) Information on other conditions;
   (d) General questions relating to the transmission and examination of information;
   (e) Report of the Secretary-General on new developments connected with the association of Non-Self-Governing Territories with the European Economic Community;
   (f) Offers of study and training facilities: report of the Secretary-General.
5. Election to fill vacancies in the Committee on Information from Non-Self-Governing Territories.
6. The future of the Trust Territory of the Cameroons under United Kingdom administration:
   (a) Organization of the plebiscite in the southern part of the Territory: question of the two alternatives to be put to the people and the qualifications for voting;
   (b) Report of the United Nations Plebiscite Commissioner on the plebiscite in the northern part of the Territory and report of the Trusteeship Council.

TABLE 14—*continued*

7. Question of the frontier between the Trust Territory of Somaliland under Italian administration and Ethiopia: reports of the Governments of Ethiopia and of Italy.

Fifth Committee

1. Financial reports and accounts, and reports of the Board of Auditors, for the financial year ended 31 December 1958:
   (a) United Nations;
   (b) United Nations Children's Fund;
   (c) United Nations Relief and Works Agency for Palestine Refugees in the Near East;
   (d) United Nations Refugee Fund.
2. Appointments to fill vacancies in the membership of subsidiary bodies of the General Assembly:
   (a) Advisory Committee on Administrative and Budgetary Questions;
   (b) Committee on Contributions;
   (c) Board of Auditors;
   (d) Investments Committee: confirmation of the appointment made by the Secretary-General;
   (e) United Nations Administrative Tribunal;
   (f) United Nations Staff Pension Committee.
3. The United Nations Library: gift of the Ford Foundation.
4. Scale of assessments for the apportionment of the expenses of the United Nations: report of the Committee on Contributions.
5. Audit reports relating to expenditure by specialized agencies of technical assistance funds allocated from the Special Account.
6. Proposed amendments to certain provisions of the Pension Scheme Regulations of the International Court of Justice.
7. United Nations Joint Staff Pension Fund:
   (a) Annual report on the United Nations Joint Staff Pension Fund;
   (b) Report on the fifth actuarial valuation of the United Nations Joint Staff Pension Fund.
8. Public information activities of the United Nations: report of the Secretary-General.
9. Construction of the United Nations building in Santiago, Chile: progress report of the Secretary-General.
10. Report of the Economic and Social Council (Chapter X, financial implications of actions taken by the Economic and Social Council).
11. Supplementary estimates for the financial year 1959.
12. Administrative and budgetary co-ordination between the United Nations and the specialized agencies: report of the Advisory Committee on Administrative and Budgetary Questions.
13. Personnel questions:
    (a) Geographical distribution of the staff of the Secretariat: report of the Secretary-General;
    (b) Proportion of fixed-term staff;
    (c) Other personnel questions.
14. United Nations International School: report of the Secretary-General.
15. Report of the Negotiating Committee for Extra-Budgetary Funds.
16. United Nations Emergency Force:
    (a) Cost estimates for the maintenance of the Force;
    (b) Manner of financing the Force: report of the Secretary-General on consultations with the Governments of Member States.
17. Budget estimates for the financial year 1960.

Table 14—*continued*

Sixth Committee

1. Report of the International Law Commission on the work of its eleventh session.
2. Diplomatic intercourse and immunities.
3. Reservations to multilateral conventions: the Convention on the Inter-Governmental Maritime Consultative Organization.
4. Question of the publication of a United Nations juridical yearbook.
5. Question of initiating a study of the juridical régime of historic waters, including historic bays.

Chapter 6

DEBATE

> The fuller the assembly of states is, the more solemn, effectual
> and free the debates will be, and the resolutions must needs
> come with greater authority . . . and then reason, upon free
> debate, will be judge, and not the sword.
>
> WILLIAM PENN

THERE has always been a debating aspect to diplomacy. Diplomats
constantly engage in verbal strife with other diplomats. Indeed,
" debate " and " combat " have a common linguistic origin.

Nor is the practice of public diplomatic debate new, though it
would no doubt have seemed shocking to diplomats of the seven-
teenth to nineteenth centuries. Greek diplomacy, two thousand five
hundred years ago, was essentially oratorical. Ambassadors addressed large assemblies of citizens; covenants could hardly have been
more openly arrived at.[1]

The public debate of contemporary " parliamentary diplomacy "
has, however, altered the nature of this verbal combat. Speeches in
today's intergovernmental assemblies are rarely made with the purpose of convincing opponents by reasoned argument. Speeches are
more usually designed to convince third parties, or to appeal to people
over the heads of governments, or to win the approbation of public
opinion at home, or to ensure that a point of view is on record. The
possibility that a direct confrontation of ideas could lead to greater
understanding, or even agreement, is easily submerged by an out-
pouring of words.

Public debate is, nevertheless, an important part of the
" parliamentary diplomacy " of the General Assembly. Although
public debate sometimes increases hostility and tension, it can also
facilitate agreement. In any case, verbal combat is better than violent
coercion. As a writer in *The Economist* has put it:

> I know that some delegates chatter excessively,
> But this is much better than acting aggressively.[2]

Of some seventy to eighty items that are now included in the agenda
of a regular session of the General Assembly, about twenty are

---

[1] Harold Nicolson, *The Evolution of the Diplomatic Method* (New York: Macmillan, 1954), pp. 2–14.
[2] Vol. CLXXV, No. 5965, 21 Dec. 1957, p. 1059.

normally allocated directly to the plenary Assembly, and the remainder to the seven Main Committees. The items allocated to the plenary are as follows:

(i) Election of the President and Vice-Presidents of the Assembly and members of principal organs, and certain other elections and appointments (see Chapters 3 and 8).

(ii) Consideration of recommendations of the General Committee on matters proposed for inclusion in the agenda (see Chapter 5).

(iii) The General Debate (see Chapter 4).

(iv) Reports, or parts thereof, of principal organs, and certain other reports (see Chapter 7).

(v) Substantive items, usually about three in number.

(vi) Miscellaneous matters, such as the formal opening and closing of the session, the admission of new Members, etc.

From time to time there have been suggestions that a greater number of substantive items should be considered directly in plenary meeting. The Special Committee on Methods and Procedures (1949) suggested that a " means of lightening the task of any given Main Committee would be to consider directly in plenary meeting, without preliminary reference to committee, certain questions which fall within the terms of reference of the Main Committee. This procedure would . . . have the great advantage of reducing to a notable extent repetition of debate." This recommendation now forms part of the first annex to the Rules of Procedure.[3] Discussion in the plenary is more formal than in a Main Committee and is a useful way of permitting statements of view on a matter which is uncontroversial, or on which agreement has already been achieved informally, or on which agreement is not being attempted.

Items not dealt with directly in plenary meeting are referred to one or other of the seven Main Committees. Proceedings in Main Committees differ in a number of ways from proceedings in plenary meetings. Members speak from their places rather than from a rostrum, and this makes for a somewhat less formal atmosphere. One-third of the members of a Committee constitute a quorum, whereas in the plenary a simple majority of Members is required (Rules 110 and 69). Decisions in Main Committees are made by a simple majority of members present and voting, whereas decisions on " important " questions in the plenary require a two-thirds

---

[3] *Report of the Special Committee on Methods and Procedures of the General Assembly*, G.A.O.R.: 4th Sess., 1949, Suppl. No. 12 (A/937), para. 7; Rules of Procedure of the General Assembly (A/3660), 6 Sept. 1947, p. 33. (Hereafter to be cited in this chapter as: United Nations Docs. A/937 and A/3660, respectively.)

majority of Members present and voting (Rules 126 and 85–87). A tie vote in a Main Committee on matters other than elections is regarded as a rejection of the proposal, whereas in the plenary the vote is taken again at a subsequent meeting and, if there is a second tie, the proposal is then regarded as rejected (Rules 134 and 97). There is no prohibition of nominations in Main Committees (Rule 94).

Each Main Committee is a committee of the whole, consisting of representatives of all Member States. A Main Committee exists only for the duration of the session; if it is desired to set up a committee of the whole Membership which can transact business between sessions, the Assembly creates a subsidiary organ. Three inter-sessional committees of the whole are now in existence: the Interim Committee,[4] the Committee on arrangements for a conference for the purpose of reviewing the Charter [5]; and the *Ad Hoc* Disarmament Commission.[6] Unless a specific decision is taken to the contrary, an inter-sessional committee of the whole reaches decisions by a simple majority of the members present and voting (Rules 126 and 162).

Each Main Committee deals with a particular " category of subjects " (Rules 99 and 101). The seven Main Committees are as follows:

> Political and Security Committee (including the regulation of armaments) (First Committee);
> Special Political Committee;
> Economic and Financial Committee (Second Committee);
> Social, Humanitarian and Cultural Committee (Third Committee);
> Trusteeship Committee (including Non-Self-Governing Territories) (Fourth Committee);
> Administrative and Budgetary Committee (Fifth Committee);
> Legal Committee (Sixth Committee).

In the first few sessions of the Assembly, items were occasionally referred simultaneously to two Committees, which met jointly for consideration of such items. This practice, as the Committee on Procedures and Organization (1947) emphasized, " is as a general rule undesirable and often results in unnecessary duplication of debate." [7] It is now the usual practice to allocate each item to one Committee.

---

[4] General Assembly Res. 111 (II), 13 Nov. 1947.
[5] General Assembly Res. 992 (X), 21 Nov. 1955, 1136 (XII), 14 Oct. 1957, 1381 (XIV), 20 Nov. 1959.
[6] General Assembly Res. 1252D (XIII), 4 Nov. 1958, 1403 (XIV), 21 Nov. 1959.
[7] G.A.O.R.: 2nd Sess., 1947, Annex 4 (A/388), para. 24, p. 1459. (Hereafter to be cited in this chapter as: United Nations Doc. A/388.)

B.

Each Committee has a character and personality of its own. The two political Committees and the Fourth Committee engage in robust debate, though the Fourth Committee is unlike the other Committees in that much of its time is now spent in hearing and questioning petitioners. The Sixth Committee is rather like a seminar for lawyers. Debate in the Fifth Committee is often a trialogue between the Secretariat, the Chairman of the Advisory Committee on Administrative and Budgetary Questions, and other representatives.

The Third Committee has often been regarded as the Assembly's problem child. This is partly because the Committee has an exceptionally disparate agenda. Certain of the social questions (such as community development and United Nations Children's Fund [UNICEF]) would easily fit into the "category of subjects" dealt with by the Second Committee. The international control of narcotic drugs is a technical matter with legal and economic, as well as social, aspects. Though the work of the High Commissioner for Refugees is primarily humanitarian in character, it has political undertones. The other items on the Third Committee's agenda relate to human rights, and there has been a tendency on the part of some representatives to treat them in a rather academic way. The Committee has since 1954 been working its way steadily through two draft covenants on human rights prepared by the Human Rights Commission. Progress has inevitably been slow, and one cannot but wonder whether a Main Committee of the Assembly is a suitable organ for giving detailed attention to the text of legal instruments. The Special Committee on Methods and Procedures commented that " some of the Main Committees of the General Assembly had devoted a particularly large number of meetings to the detailed consideration, article by article, of texts of international conventions." It was pointed out that " a Main Committee, by the very fact of its size, was not particularly fitted to draft conventions, and that when it was entrusted with the detailed study of conventions, it often did not have time to deal satisfactorily with the other questions for which it was responsible." [8] The comments and recommendations of the Committee on this matter have been annexed to the Rules of Procedure.[9]

I should add that during the fourteenth session of the Assembly (1959), the Third Committee approached its agenda in a businesslike way. This was partly because the Committee took up as the first item a definite matter which was generally regarded as important and which

[8] United Nations Doc. A/937, para. 12.
[9] United Nations Doc. A/3660, pp. 31–32.

could be completed in a period of three or four weeks.[10] Perhaps an even more crucial factor, however, was that the Committee had an unusually good chairman who combined tact, fairness and authority in the right proportions.

The Fourth Committee now spends much time dealing with petitioners, and this is one of the reasons why the number of its meetings has increased (see Table 15). During the fourteenth session (1959), forty-nine meetings of the Fourth Committee were wholly or partly taken up with discussing whether to grant oral hearings and with the hearings themselves. Both the Trusteeship Council and the Committee on South West Africa hear petitioners, and I have much sympathy with those who think that the Fourth Committee should not spend as much time as it does on this matter. A committee with

TABLE 15

Number of Meetings of the Fourth Committee During Each Regular Session*

No. of session	No. of meetings	
1, Pt. I	12	
		27
1, Pt. II	15	
2		21
3		36
4		57
5		57
6		49
7		66
8		81
9		73
10		81
11		100
12		91
13	103	
		140
13 (resumed)	37	
14		121

* The Fourth Committee met once during the second special session.

more than eighty members, meeting in public, is hardly an appropriate body to give careful attention to the issues raised in oral hearings. It would, as a general rule, be preferable that oral petitions should be considered by bodies of limited membership, and that the Fourth Committee should grant a request for an oral hearing only if it is absolutely clear from the request that:

10 This was the draft declaration of the Rights of the Child, which was discussed and revised during the 907th to 930th meetings of the Committee. The revised text was approved by the plenary by General Assembly Res. 1386 (XIV), 20 Nov. 1959.

(a) the content of the proposed statement is both important and urgent;
(b) the information to be given is not already available to the Committee;
(c) it is essential that the matter be presented in oral rather than written form.

I realize, of course, that oral hearings are intended to be a form of anti-colonial pressure in which nationalist political leaders air their grievances in an international forum. It seems to me, however, that a stage of diminishing returns has now been reached. The Fourth Committee has to devote so much time to these hearings that it can hardly give sufficient attention to the important matters requiring decisions which come before it. Some oral hearings may be unavoidable, nevertheless, and it might be desirable for the Fourth Committee to establish sub-committees of limited membership (under Rule 104) to conduct any such hearings that are deemed essential.

In a world in which scientific questions increasingly arise for international consideration, it may become desirable that a Main Committee of the Assembly should be regarded as specially qualified in scientific matters. During recent sessions the Assembly has considered a number of questions that have been wholly or partly scientific in character: outer space, the effects of atomic radiation, the peaceful uses of atomic energy, scientific research into the control of cancerous diseases, and the possibility of organizing an international public health and medical year. Politics and science are closely interrelated.

It is not possible to allocate items in such a way that each Main Committee has an approximately equal load of business, nor does each Committee necessarily have a similar amount of business from year to year. The Special Political and Sixth Committees now usually require forty to fifty meetings to complete their work; the Second and Fifth Committees hold fifty to sixty meetings; the First and Third Committees require seventy to eighty meetings each session; the Fourth Committee, which during the first eight sessions required about sixty meetings, now has one hundred or more meetings a session.

The two political Committees do not get under way until the fourth or fifth week of the session, and the First Committee almost always has to finish in a rush. The Fifth Committee does not have a particularly heavy agenda, but it cannot complete its work until the session is about to close, since it has to deal with the financial implications of decisions of the Assembly. The schedule of meetings

CHART 2

SCHEDULE OF MEETINGS DURING THE FOURTEENTH REGULAR SESSION

15 SEPTEMBER TO 13 DECEMBER 1959

		Plenary	General C'tee	Credentials C'tee	First C'tee	Special Political C'tee	Second C'tee	Third C'tee	Fourth C'tee	Fifth C'tee	Sixth C'tee
15	September	XX			X	X	X	X	X	X	X
16			XX								
17		XX									
18		X									
21		X									
22		XX	X								
23		XX						X	XX	X	X
24		XX							XX		X
25		XX					X	X	XX	XX	
28		XX						XX	X		X
29		XX						X	X	X	X
30		XX						X	X		X
1	October	XX						X	X		X
2		XX						XX	XX	X	
5		XX					X	X	XX	XX	X
6		XX					X	XX	X		X
7		X				X	X	X	XX	XX	X
8					X			XX	XXX		X
9			X		X		XX	X	XX	X	
12		XX					XX	XX	XX		X
13		X				X	XX	X	XX	X	X
14		X			X	X	X	X	XX	X	X
15						X	X	XX	XX	XX	
16		X			X	X	X	X	XX	X	X
19		X			X	X	XX	X	XX	X	X
20		XX				X	XX	X	XX	X	X
21		XX				X	X	XX	XX	X	X
22					X		X	X	XX	XX	X
23					XX	X	X	XX	XX		
26						X	XX	XX	X	X	X
27					XX	X	X	X	XX	XX	X
28					XX	X	X	X	XX	X	X
29					XX	X	X	X	XX	XX	X
30					XX	X	XX	XX	XX		X
2	November				XX	X	X	X	XX	XX	X
3		XX			X	X	X	X	XX	X	X
4					X	X	XX	X	XX	X	X
5		X			X	X	X	X	XX	XX	X
6					X	XX	XX	XX	X		X
9					XX	X	X	X	XX	X	XX
10					XX	X	X	XX	XX	X	X
11					XX	X	X	X	XX	X	X
12					XX	X	X	XX	XX	X	X
13					X	X	XX	X	XX		X
16					XX	X	X	X	XX	X	X
17		XX				X	X	XX	XX	X	X
18					X		XX	X	XX	X	X
19					XX	X	XX	X	XX	X	X
20		XX			X	X	XX	X	XX	X	X
21	(Saturday)	X.					X		X		
23			X		X	X	X	XX	XXX		X
24					X	X	X	X	XX	XX	X
25		XX			X	X	X	X	XX	X	X
26	(Thanksgiving Day)				X	X	X	X	X		
27		XX			X	X	XX	X	XXX	X	X
28	(Saturday)								X		
30					X	XX	XX	X	XX	XX	X
1	December	X			X	X	XX	X	XX	X	
2			X		XX	X	XX	X	XXX	X	X
3					XX	XX	X	XX	XX	XX	X
4					XX	XX	X	XX	XXX	XX	X
5	(Saturday: date fixed by the Assembly on 22 September for closing the session)	X			XX				X		
7		X			XX	XX		XX	XXX		
8		XX				XX			XX		
9		XX		X					XX		
10		X				X			XX		
11/12	(Meeting continued after midnight)	XX			XX				XXX		
12/13	(Meeting continued after midnight)	XXX			X						

of the plenary Assembly and of Main and procedural Committees during the fourteenth session is shown in Chart 2.

Each Committee establishes its own priorities, taking into account the closing date for the session (Rule 100). The two political Committees often decide at the beginning which item to take first, leaving the decision as to the order of other items until the first is completed, and so on; so far as possible, agreement on the order of items is sought by informal discussion. The other Committees usually decide at the beginning of the session on a definite or tentative order of items; the Second and Third Committees often also decide on the approximate number of meetings to be devoted to each item. The timetable of the Fourth Committee is least predictable, partly because it is not known at the beginning of the session how many petitioners will request oral hearings.

If an informal or formal timetable is drawn up for the guidance of a Committee, night or week-end meetings can be arranged should the Committee fall behind the timetable. The very fact of scheduling a night or week-end meeting sometimes helps a Committee to catch up to its timetable without the necessity of actually holding any extra meeting.

It is natural that there should develop a feeling of professional solidarity and intimacy among representatives in different Committees who meet each other year after year: the lawyers in the Sixth Committee, the economists in the Second Committee, the budget experts in the Fifth Committee, and so on. This feeling of professional solidarity and intimacy facilitates the harmonious conduct of business, though it would be unhealthy should it lead to overt rivalry between Committees.

Sometimes an illusion of conflict between Committees arises from the fact that the internal co-ordination of policy within some delegations is imperfect. The increase in the number of States and of intergovernmental organizations has imposed a severe strain on the diplomatic services of many countries, and not only those newly independent. Sometimes representatives, especially in the non-political Committees, do not have full or precise instructions from their governments; sometimes they have instructions from a particular ministry, but these instructions may in part be inconsistent with the instructions that another member of the same delegation has received from another ministry. Possibly the greatest difficulty occurs when a representative in one Committee votes for some proposal which involves the expenditure of funds, while a member of the same delegation opposes the consequent appropriation in the Fifth Committee. It hardly needs stressing that Main Committees are all composed of the same Member States, and there can be no question of their reaching different conclusions.

In each Main Committee there develops to some extent a feeling that it possesses an expertise that other Committees lack. Members of the Sixth Committee are, perhaps, inclined to give expression to this idea more frequently than do members of other Committees. During the sixth session, for example, the Sixth Committee considered the methods and procedures of the Assembly for dealing with legal and drafting questions. The main focus of debate was not (as one might have expected) on problems arising from the existence of different legal systems, but on the right of legal experts to pronounce on matters within their competence and on the tendency of the Assembly to ignore the legal expertise which was to be found in the Sixth Committee. One representative noted that there was a certain displacement in the balance of the work of the United Nations to the disadvantage of the Sixth Committee. As a result, its agenda was diminishing.[11] A similar point was made by another representative during the fourteenth session. He said his delegation had for long felt that the distribution of work of a juridical nature in the United Nations was not entirely satisfactory and not such as to ensure the maintenance of the highest juridical standards. For example, juridical questions were sometimes discussed by non-legal Committees in which strictly technical considerations might be overshadowed by political and sometimes even purely emotional factors. The preparation of certain legal instruments had been entrusted to the Third Committee, but such instruments involved points of law, and where difficulties arose they should at least be referred to the Sixth Committee for advice. While he fully recognized the fitness of the Third Committee to prepare the draft Covenants on Human Rights, he believed that if the highest standards were to be maintained technical legal matters should be treated by specialists in the subjects concerned. Indeed, that was the reason why the Sixth Committee had been established.[12]

The basic order of business for each item in a Main Committee is as follows. First, a general debate on the item; secondly, discussion of draft resolutions and amendments; finally, voting, including explanations of vote. Each Committee adapts this framework for its own purposes. Some Committees add a further stage, consisting of an examination of the draft report of the Rapporteur. The Fifth Committee examines the budget estimates in two consecutive

11 G.A.O.R.: 6th Sess., 6th Committee, 259th Mtg., 29 Nov. 1951, para. 15.
12 G.A.O.R.: 14th Sess., 6th Committee, 646th Mtg., 4 Dec. 1959, para. 21.

" readings." [13] The Fourth Committee puts before the normal procedure three additional stages for some items: hearing of petitioners,
questioning of petitioners, and introductory statements by governments directly concerned with the matter.[14]

Committees undoubtedly function best if they exercise a high
degree of flexibility in procedure. The Special Committee on
Measures to Limit the Duration of Sessions (1953) noted the tendency
of Main Committees to observe independent and succeeding stages
with respect to each item of the agenda, and considered that this
formal segmentation often provoked duplication of speeches and increased the risk of engaging in protracted procedural discussions.

The mechanics of a Main Committee cannot be simplified or altered
beyond a certain point, it is true, but greater flexibility . . . is desirable.
In general, the discussion on the broad aspects of a subject should be
combined with the consideration of specific proposals.[15]

In order that the business of the Assembly shall be conducted in a
smooth and expeditious manner, three things are required: first,
advance preparation by the Secretariat (including the distribution of
relevant documents at an early stage); secondly, the availability of
presiding officers with " competence, authority, tact and impartiality
. . . respect for the rights both of minorities as well as majorities,
and . . . familiarity with the rules of procedure " [16]; and, finally, the
exercise of good sense and restraint by representatives of Member
States.

All three of the Assembly's Committees on procedure have
emphasized the need for the early submission of relevant documents.[17] There is no doubt that the Assembly's proceedings begin to
" drag " if essential documents have not been available sufficiently
in advance of the session for governments to consider them and
instruct their representatives. In some cases, the Member States
themselves are at fault. The Rules of Procedure require that items
proposed for inclusion in the agenda should, if possible, be accompanied by basic documents (Rule 20), and for these to be of maximum value, they should be available some weeks before the opening
of the session.

Sometimes documents issued by the Secretariat are not available
sufficiently early. This may be caused by the fact that essential
information does not reach the Secretariat on time, or by the uneven

---

13 *Infra*, p. 212.
14 *Supra*, pp. 115–116.
15 G.A.O.R.: 8th Sess., 1953, Annexes, Agenda item 54 (A/2402), paras. 26–27.
   (Hereafter to be cited in this chapter as: United Nations Doc. A/2402.)
16 United Nations Doc. A/937, para. 39.
17 United Nations Docs. A/388, para. 14; A/937, para. 17; A/2402, para. 22.

pressure of work falling on those responsible for preparing or printing the documents. Any change in the basic schedule of United Nations meetings, such as a special session of the Assembly or the late opening of a regular session and the consequent postponement of other meetings, inevitably disrupts arrangements for the production of documents.

The reasons for delay are various, but the consequences are that the Assembly wastes time because Members are insufficiently informed or instructed. In some cases of the late availability of documents, the Assembly might be well advised to postpone consideration of the item until the next session.

PRESIDING OFFICERS

It is difficult to exaggerate the extent to which good chairmanship can facilitate, and bad chairmanship can obstruct, the work of the Assembly. It is true that a good chairman cannot prevent a United Nations organ from getting into a procedural tangle on occasions, since some procedural situations that arise are unpredictable and complicated.[18] But an incompetent presiding officer can, single-handedly, create procedural chaos if he does not understand the Rules, or does not enforce them, or acts in a dictatorial or partisan manner.

The General Assembly is composed of representatives of sovereign Members and, at any rate on important substantive issues, representatives are presumed to act in accordance with official instructions. The problem, though, is that the single category of business on which representatives are usually not under instructions is procedural business. This means that once the Assembly or a Committee becomes involved in a procedural discussion, delegates begin to "free-wheel." I have often sensed the atmosphere of liberation which sweeps over a meeting when debate on the substance of a question is temporarily put aside so that some knotty procedural point can be resolved. One may observe representatives closing their folders of papers and lighting cigarettes so as to deal in a thoroughly relaxed and level-headed way with a matter which requires initiative, tact and imagination rather than fidelity to official instructions.

The Assembly has been reluctant to give substantial authority of a formal kind to its presiding officers, and there has been some decrease in the formal powers of presiding officers since 1946. The first Secretary-General told an Assembly Committee in 1947 that

---

[18] On the day on which I wrote this sentence I heard the eminent President of the fourteenth Assembly preface a vote—quite correctly—with the explanation: "'Yes' will mean 'No' in this case." United Nations Doc. A/PV.843, 25 Nov. 1959, p. 61.

Paul-Henri Spaak, President of the Assembly's first session, had taken important decisions of a procedural or organizational kind without consulting the General Committee or the Assembly " because he considered that the administration of the Assembly was in his hands." [19] It would be unthinkable that an Assembly President would today take decisions of the kind taken by Spaak on his own authority. Indeed, the Assembly amended the Rules of Procedure in 1949 to state specifically that presiding officers exercise their functions " under the authority of " the Assembly or Committee (Rules 36 and 109).

This decline in formal authority is not, perhaps, surprising. In the first years of the life of the Organization, the cold war had not entirely eroded the spirit of co-operation which, in spite of many difficulties, had characterized the relations of the United Nations during the war. During the first session of the Assembly in 1946, there was an evident determination on the part of the permanent members of the Security Council to stick together to the greatest possible extent, especially on matters relating to procedure and the interpretation of the Charter. Moreover, the United Nations began its existence with few exact precedents, though there are certain generally accepted practices relating to the organization and procedure of intergovernmental conferences. With the steady accumulation of a body of precedents, presiding officers have increasingly been called upon to interpret the Rules and the customary practices rather than to establish new precedents. Finally, the Rules of Procedure have been developed and elaborated by successive revisions, thus providing established procedures for matters that were formerly decided in an *ad hoc* manner, often on the basis of proposals from the Chair.

This, however, is not the whole story. The post-war political climate has been characterized by great emphasis on the principle of the sovereignty and equality of nations large and small. This has been held to imply that presiding officers, even in the interests of orderly procedure and the expeditious and harmonious conduct of business, should in no way inhibit the inherent right of representatives to express freely the views of their governments on matters within the scope of the Charter. There is frequent insistence on the notion that each United Nations organ is master of its own proceedings. This seems to me a dangerous half-truth, since no United Nations organ—to take one example—should conduct its procedure in a manner that contravenes the Charter.

Presiding officers are given certain formal powers under the Rules

[19] G.A.O.R.: 1st Spec. Sess., General Committee, 32nd Mtg., 2 May 1947, p. 92.

of Procedure, but these formal powers are no substitute for such personal qualities as courtesy, tolerance and fair-mindedness. The presiding officers of many deliberative bodies acquire authority and respect only by long and continuous tenure of office. One of the most influential of the Speakers of the British House of Commons, Arthur Onslow, achieved his ascendancy and prestige not solely because of his undoubted talents, but also by the fact that he occupied the Chair of St. Stephen's without interruption for thirty-four years. The President of the Assembly or the Chairman of a Main Committee is elected for only one session. At the time of his election, he represents a government which is committed to certain policies. Even the most seasoned and talented diplomat, experienced in the procedures of intergovernmental assemblies, and taking full advantage of the advice and help of the Secretariat, can acquire only limited authority in matters of procedure in a session of three months, and he can never wholly divest himself of the policies, passions and prejudices of his nation.

I do not mean to imply that good chairmanship is unattainable; but good chairmen do not grow on trees, and those who have been endowed with the requisite qualities and have enjoyed appropriate experience often prefer, or are required, to use their talents in other ways.

The formal powers granted to presiding officers are of three kinds: obligatory, discretionary and initiatory. Under their obligatory functions, presiding officers declare the opening and closing of each meeting; direct the discussions, put questions, and announce decisions; accord the right to speak, calling upon representatives in the order in which they have signified their desire to speak; rule on points of order; when debate is limited and a representative has spoken his allotted time, call him to order without delay; ensure observance of the Rules of Procedure; and, subject to the Rules, have complete control of the proceedings and over the maintenance of order.[20]

Under the discretionary functions, a presiding officer may call a speaker to order if his remarks are not relevant to the subject under discussion; limit the time to be allowed to speakers regarding the adjournment or closure of the debate, the suspension or adjournment of the meeting, and explanations of vote[21]; may announce the list of speakers; may accord the right of reply to a representative, even if the list of speakers has been closed; may permit explanations of

[20] Rules 35, 70, 73, 74, 108, 111, 114 and 115.
[21] The President of the Assembly may limit the time to be allowed to speakers in favour of or against a recommendation of the General Committee that an item be included in the agenda.

vote, either before or after the voting; and may permit the discussion and consideration of amendments or of motions as to procedure even though these amendments or motions as to procedure have not been circulated in writing the previous day.[22]

Apart from their obligatory and discretionary functions, presiding officers may initiate proposals for the smooth conduct of business. The Special Committee on Methods and Procedures (1949) emphasized that a presiding officer is entitled to have sufficient authority to exercise leadership in matters of procedure and " should be able, at any time and without any reflection on his impartiality, to draw members' attention to measures likely to expedite their proceedings." [23]

It would be useful if representatives were to emphasize, in speeches of nomination or acceptance, the clear responsibility which presiding officers have to exercise leadership in matters of procedure. Representatives should, as far as possible, uphold the authority and dignity of the Chair—though not all would go as far as the distinguished United States representative who stated laconically " The Chair is always right." [24]

Apart from the general responsibility of a presiding officer to suggest ways of proceeding expeditiously, a presiding officer has the same rights as any other representative to initiate procedural proposals. He may propose that the time to be allowed to speakers or the number of times each representative may speak on any question should be limited; and he may propose the suspension or the adjournment of the meeting, the adjournment of the debate on the item under discussion, the closure of the debate, or the closure of the list of speakers.[25]

Since there is sometimes confusion regarding the responsibilities and rights of presiding officers, it might be useful if each presiding officer, on some convenient occasion early in the session, would state explicitly his or her conception of the responsibilities attaching to the office, particularly in matters where the Rules are imprecise or misunderstanding is likely to occur. Such a statement might include an interpretation of what constitutes a point of order (quoting, where necessary, from reports of committees of the Assembly on procedure) and a reminder that the presiding officer has a duty, under the Rules, to dispose of a point of order before allowing another one to be raised. It might include similar interpretations with regard to the right of reply and explanations of vote, and of the responsibilities of presiding officers

22 Rules 70, 75–78, 80, 90, 111, 116–119, 121 and 129.
23 United Nations Doc. A/937, para. 38.
24 G.A.O.R.: 1st Spec. Sess., General Committee, 33rd Mtg., 2 May 1947, p. 125.
25 Rules 35, 74–78, 108, 115–119.

when requests to exercise these rights are made. It might also include a reminder that presiding officers are under an obligation to ensure observance of the Rules of Procedure. It would be helpful if, following such a statement, a representative were to request that it be made available in verbatim form to all representatives.

Presiding officers can often save time and facilitate the smooth handling of business by reminding the Committee, as each item is taken up, of the history of the matter, of any previous decisions of other organs of the United Nations, and of documents relevant to the item. A chairman can also suggest procedures that would enable a Committee to proceed expeditiously. The majority of Members of the Special Committee on Measures to Limit the Duration of Sessions (1953) considered that when discussion of an item opens, the chairman or any representative might propose that the debate should be confined to observations on draft resolutions or amendments, and that statements of a general character should be allowed only in so far as they might pertain to the specific proposal under discussion. No specific rule to facilitate this practice was recommended, although there is nothing in the Rules which forbids it.[26] As each item is completed, the chairman can remind the Committee of what business still remains to be done, and perhaps suggest some sort of rough timetable for future work.

If procedural suggestions from the Chair come " out of the blue " and appear to be arbitrary or unfair, time may be lost. If, however, they are made after full though informal consultation, a Committee usually accepts them gratefully. To illustrate how proposals from the Chair can assist a Committee, I give below two statements of presiding officers during the fourteenth session. The first deals with the order of items:

THE CHAIRMAN: The next point of the agenda is the order of the items. . . .

Before proceeding with any discussion of priorities, I wish to make a few remarks which may be of assistance in this respect.

Members of the Committee are no doubt acutely aware that our agenda this session is not only heavy but contains several items of great significance for current developments in international relations. I spoke earlier about a spirit of co-operation which I hoped would contribute to the success of our deliberations . . . I am sure that all members of the Committee earnestly wish that our proceedings here would help to promote those favourable trends rather than disturb them.

One of the ways to do this would be to avoid, as far as possible, acrimonious debate, and especially perhaps debate on procedural questions. Experience has shown that sharp differences over procedure may

[26] United Nations Doc. A/2402, para. 28.

serve to charge the air with bitterness or embarrassment and, in fact, to hinder the ultimate discussion of substantive questions, which are the main purpose of our deliberations here.

Members of the Committee will be aware that informal consultations have been taking place among delegations, reflecting various points of view, about the order of priority for the discussion of the items on our agenda. I have tried to keep in touch with those consultations. . . .

In this endeavour there has been a commendable demonstration of co-operation on the part of all concerned and I am happy to state it is my understanding that there is some consensus as to how we are to proceed in the immediate future.

In the light of the circumstances which I have mentioned and of my understanding of various positions, I have been encouraged to make a suggestion, which . . . is that we begin at once with. . . .[27]

The second statement was made by a presiding officer to suggest a timetable for dealing with draft resolutions and amendments:

THE CHAIRMAN considered that the draft resolutions and amendments should be submitted as soon as possible. It would also be desirable for the co-sponsors to hold private meetings as often as practicable, so as to save the Committee's time.

In order for all the draft resolutions to be studied thoroughly, each of them might first be examined during one meeting or a meeting and a half, on the understanding that, if no decision could be reached on the first draft resolution at the end of that time, the Committee would pass on to the examination of the second and so forth, until all the draft resolutions had been examined once for the same length of time. The Committee would then reconsider the draft resolutions on which it had not been possible to take a vote the first time they had been studied. It would also be desirable for all draft resolutions dealing with the same question to be examined together, if the co-sponsors accepted that arrangement. Lastly, the Committee might perhaps find it necessary to limit the time allotted to speakers and to arrange for night meetings or meetings on Saturday mornings.[28]

The above statements were well suited to the needs of the situation and helped the Committees concerned to proceed expeditiously.

There is one other procedural task which is the lot of presiding officers. For those who are habitually punctual, it must be a source of irritation that most United Nations meetings start late. The Secretary-General, in a report to the second session, urged that meetings should begin promptly at the scheduled time,[29] and three Committees of the Assembly on procedure have all emphasized that

27 United Nations Doc. A/C.1/PV.1025, 8 Oct. 1959, pp. 17–21.
28 United Nations Doc. A/C.2/SR.623, 16 Nov. 1959, p. 17.
29 United Nations Doc. A/316, 8 July 1947. See Appendix D.

much time is wasted when meetings begin late.[30] One representative stated in 1950 that he had " spent some forty-six hours in committee rooms between the scheduled period for the opening of a meeting and the actual commencement, that is to say, about the equivalent of a whole week and a half of meetings." [31] Some representatives were under the illusion in 1950 that the late starting of meetings was due to poor transport facilities between Manhattan, Lake Success and Flushing Meadows, and soon after the move to the headquarters building had been effected, the delegate of Uruguay rejoiced that " meetings can now begin within a few minutes of the specified time " and thus valuable time would be saved.[32] A few months later, however, the same representative presided over the Special Committee on Measures to Limit the Duration of Sessions (1953), which once again had to " draw attention to the serious loss of time that results from the lack of punctuality in the opening of meetings. . . ." [33]

A short delay in starting a meeting may on occasion serve a useful purpose, particularly if delicate negotiations are in progress. The presiding officer nearly always knows when this is happening and can adjust the time of starting accordingly. It would be of convenience, in these circumstances, if there could be some means of informing representatives of the approximate time when it was thought the meeting would begin. In any case, it must be admitted that although lack of punctuality is, in some parts of the world, regarded as gross discourtesy, this attitude is not universally accepted.

ORDERLY DEBATE

Many questions arise in connection with maintaining good order in debate, but five seem to me of special importance: the circumstances in which the Rules of Procedure may be suspended; the problem of speeches which include remarks that seem objectionable to the presiding officer or a representative; interruptions during speeches and requests to speak out of turn; procedural motions (such as that a meeting be held in private or that the debate be adjourned); and the limitation of debate.

Enforcing and suspending the Rules

The Rules of Procedure were made for the Assembly, and not the Assembly for the Rules. Although the Rules may be amended by a simple majority of Members present and voting (provided a

---

[30] United Nations Docs. A/388, para. 19; A/937, para. 28; A/2402, para. 49.
[31] G.A.O.R.: 7th Sess., 388th Plenary Mtg., 24 Oct. 1952, para. 3.
[32] *Ibid.*, 387th Plenary Mtg., 23 Oct. 1952, para. 78.
[33] United Nations Doc. A/2402, para. 49.

committtee has reported on the proposed amendment), there is no specific procedure for the suspension of a Rule. The Rules of Procedure of the Economic and Social Council and of the Trusteeship Council both include provisions for the suspension of any Rule.[34] Since the Assembly's presiding officers are required to ensure observance of the Rules of Procedure, and since it is occasionally in the general interest that a particular Rule should not be enforced, it would make for orderly procedure if there were an accepted means by which a Rule could be suspended.

The Canadian delegation drew the attention of the Special Committee on Methods and Procedures (1949) to this matter.

It would save the time of the Assembly if there were a clear provision for the suspension of the rules of procedure. The inclusion of such a rule would, by clarifying the position, render debate on this question unnecessary. Moreover, it would tend to increase respect for the rules of procedure and thus lead to a saving of time.

Canada proposed that a new Rule should provide that a Rule of Procedure should not be suspended, nor should the President put to the vote a motion for the suspension of any Rule, unless (a) the motion had been submitted in writing to the Secretary-General, and (b) copies of the motion had been distributed to all delegations at least forty-eight hours before being put to the vote. The Special Committee did not examine this proposal, and the Canadian representative reserved the right to raise the matter again.[35]

The precise form of the Canadian proposal may seem to place undue obstacles in the way of suspending a Rule, and it might be sufficient, when the Rules are next revised, to provide that any Rule of Procedure may be suspended by a decision of the Assembly taken by a majority of the Members present and voting. It might be desirable to limit the number of speakers in the discussion of any proposal to suspend a Rule to two or three in favour of the suspension and two or three against the suspension, allowing the presiding officer the discretion to limit the time to be allowed to speakers.

Remarks to which objection is made

There are three main grounds on which objection is made to speeches—that the remarks are irrelevant, that they are needlessly repetitious, or that they are abusive.

Presiding officers have the power, though not the obligation, to call a speaker to order if his remarks are not relevant to the subject

[34] United Nations Docs. E/3063, 1958, Rule 87; T/1/Rev. 5, 1958, Rule 106.
[35] United Nations Doc. A/937, para. 36, and Annex 1, pp. 18–19.

under discussion (Rules 70 and 111).[36] The President of the Assembly, when acting as Chairman of the General Committee, should see that the substance of an item is not discussed, except in so far as this bears upon the Committee's recommendation regarding inclusion, rejection, or postponement (Rule 40).

Rules of relevancy are always difficult to apply. For one thing, honest and intelligent people differ as to whether particular matters are or are not relevant to the subject under discussion. For another thing, the relevant merges but gradually into the irrelevant; a presiding officer can rarely be certain at exactly what moment irrelevance begins. In theory it is desirable that a presiding officer should call a speaker to order as soon as his remarks become irrelevant to the subject under discussion. Occasionally a speaker may privately warn the Chair that he proposes to make remarks which may be considered irrelevant by other representatives, but normally the presiding officer has no such warning. In view of the many claims on the attention of a presiding officer, it is impossible for him to detect every trace of irrelevancy; often the matter comes to his attention by means of a point of order raised by a representative other than the speaker. If the presiding officer has momentarily been concerned with some other matter of procedure (for example, if he has been in conversation with the secretary of the meeting), he has to improvise a ruling which will accord with the Rules of Procedure and yet offend neither the representative who was speaking nor the representative who rose on a point of order. Usually this is done by making a general appeal to all speakers to confine their remarks to the subject under discussion.

There is no specific Rule designed to prevent repetition. Indeed, many representatives would claim that they have a right to be long-winded and tediously repetitious if they so desire. There are occasions, though these are rare, when a repetitious speech may be useful as a " screen " for informal negotiations. In the ordinary way, however, tedious repetition is deprecated, and presiding officers, under their general powers and in the interests of orderly procedure, may request speakers to refrain from repeating remarks with which the Committee is already familiar. As a last resort, a presiding officer or any representative may propose a limitation on the time to be allowed to each speaker; in cases of deliberate persistence in

[36] These Rules are similar in intent to Rule 15 (3) of the Rules of Procedure of the League Assembly. It is believed that the League rule was never invoked in the entire history of the Organization. Waldo Chamberlin, *Memorandum Concerning the Conduct of the Business of the General Assembly of the United Nations* (New York: Carnegie Endowment for International Peace, 1949), para. 56, p. 32.

repetition of a filibustering nature, it may be necessary to move the adjournment or closure of the debate on the item under discussion.

There is no specific Rule against making disrespectful or abusive remarks, although presiding officers have invoked the rules on relevancy (Rules 70 and 111) and the rules on the general powers of presiding officers (Rules 35 and 108) in efforts to halt abusive speeches. The South African delegation proposed to the Special Committee on Methods and Procedures (1949) that the Rules should be amended to strengthen the powers of Chairmen

To call speakers to order wherever they resort to invective or display of personal animus directed against either an individual or a State, or where they in any other way detract from the dignity of the proceedings.[37]

The Committee made no recommendation on this question.

It is rarely that representatives resort to gross abuse. More often the problem arises from the use of such phrases as " the Russian satellites " or " the so-called Special Representative on the Question of Hungary." No formal Rule can compel representatives to keep within the bounds of courtesy. There is no reason why a representative should not attack the views or policies of another representative and his government, but it is discourteous and a threat to good order to make abusive personal remarks about other representatives, or accuse other representatives of deliberate falsehood, or impute to other representatives unworthy motives, or charge other representatives with intentional misrepresentation.

Interruptions during speeches and requests to speak out of turn

Although the purpose of the Rules of Procedure is to enable business to proceed smoothly and without interruption, it is necessary to have an emergency procedure by which business can be interrupted if some abnormal development occurs. If, for example, the system of simultaneous interpretation becomes defective so that the Spanish interpretation cannot be heard, it is essential that the situation should be drawn to the attention of the presiding officer without delay. Any procedure that permits a representative to interrupt another representative or to speak out of turn is open to abuse, and in fact the majority of so-called points of order that I have heard raised in the Assembly and its Committees were not points of order at all.

The point of order is believed to have been an English invention, and a French representative has stated that it is unknown in French parliamentary practice.[38] According to the standard work on British

---

37 United Nations Doc. A/937, Annex 1, p. 16.
38 G.A.O.R.: 7th Sess., 6th Committee, 352nd Mtg., 16 Dec. 1952, para. 2.

parliamentary procedure, a point of order in the British House of Commons arises in the following way [39]:

Although it is the duty of the presiding officer to interfere in the first instance for the preservation of order when, in his judgment, the occasion demands his interference, it is also the right of any representative who conceives that a breach of order has been committed, if the presiding officer refrains from interfering (either because he does not consider it necessary to do so, or because he does not perceive that a breach of order has been committed), to rise in his place, interrupting any representative who may be speaking, and direct the attention of the Chair to the matter, provided he does so the moment the alleged breach of order occurs.[40]

The General Assembly has not found it possible to define a point of order. As one representative has put it, " all attempts hitherto made at international conferences and at meetings of international organizations to define points of order have failed . . . because it has obviously been felt that the matter should be left to the good sense of representatives. . . ." [41] This statement is correct as far as it goes, but there are certain attributes of a point of order which are explicit in the Rules of Procedure.[42]

1. A point of order should not concern the substance of the matter under discussion.

2. A point of order raised while voting is in progress should concern only the actual conduct of the voting.

3. A point of order, being a matter for the decision of the presiding officer, should not deal with any matter outside the presiding officer's competence.

4. A point of order should be decided immediately; it takes precedence over all proposals or motions.

5. Presiding officers should decide a point of order in accordance with the Rules of Procedure.

6. A representative may appeal against the ruling of the presiding officer.

7. Any such appeal should not be debated but should be immediately put to the vote.

Two Committees of the Assembly have stated their views on what constitutes a valid point of order, elaborating what is explicitly stated in the Rules.

[39] I have adapted this quotation to the terminology of the United Nations by changing " Speaker " to " presiding officer," and " Member " to " representative."

[40] *Sir Thomas Erskine May's Treatise on the Law, Privileges, Proceedings and Usages of Parliament*, edited by Sir Edward Fellowes and T. G. B. Cocks (16th ed., London: Butterworth, 1957), p. 470.

[41] G.A.O.R.: 7th Sess., 388th Plenary Mtg., 24 Oct. 1952, para. 73.

[42] Rules 73, 90, 114 and 129.

A point of order is, basically, an intervention directed to the presiding officer requesting him to make use of some power inherent in his office or specifically given him under the rules of procedure. It may, for example, relate to the material conditions under which the meeting is taking place. It may be a request that the presiding officer should accord the speaker some privilege which it is in the officer's power to grant. Under a point of order, a representative may request the presiding officer to apply a certain rule of procedure or he may refer to the manner in which the presiding officer should apply a given rule, or the rules of procedure as a whole. . . .

The clear implication . . . is that a point of order must relate to a question which lies within the competence of the presiding officer to dispose of, either by means of his own ruling or, in his discretion, by referring the question at issue to the judgment of the body as a whole. Matters which lie outside his competence clearly cannot be raised as points of order.

Presiding officers must give an immediate ruling on every point of order, and if the ruling is challenged, they must put it to the vote; no discussion may take place. Hence, there can be no question of seconding or debating a point of order.

Moreover, as the presiding officer must immediately dispose of each point of order as it is raised, two or more points of order can never be before the Chair at the same time.[43]

It is discourteous, to say the least, to rise to a point of order in the middle of a speech if it could equally effectively be done at the end of a speech. But there could be no possible objection were a representative to rise to a point of order in the middle of a speech to say that the system of simultaneous interpretation was not working or to question whether a quorum was present. A representative should not, however, interrupt a speech to ask that he be accorded the right of reply or to request the presiding officer to clarify some point in connection with an impending vote.

Two main difficulties are encountered in connection with points of order. The first arises when a presiding officer either fails to rule immediately on a point of order, or fails to put to the vote immediately an appeal against his ruling; these actions are required under Rules 73 and 114. If representatives raise new points of order before any outstanding point of order has been disposed of, and if presiding officers do not insist on disposing of an outstanding point of order before admitting a new one, procedural chaos usually results. I have been assured that a Main Committee once had eighty-four different undecided points of order awaiting rulings from the Chair.

A second difficulty arises when representatives (either deliberately or in ignorance) raise matters under the guise of points of order which are not points of order at all. It is in this regard that the art

[43] United Nations Docs. A/2402, paras. 41–42, and A/937, para. 37.

of good chairmanship is so important. If an inexperienced representative raises what purports to be a point of order but which is in reality nothing of the kind, the presiding officer may explain quite briefly why the alleged point of order is inadmissible. If, on the other hand, such a point is raised by an experienced representative who is deliberately abusing the Rules, the presiding officer faces a more difficult task. If the point appears to be a gross abuse of procedure and a threat to good order, the presiding officer is likely to reply rather succinctly that the matter raised is inadmissible as a point of order; on the other hand, a presiding officer, on a rare occasion, may decide not to reject such a point if he considers that by accepting it he would be facilitating the conduct of business and if he feels confident that he would be supported in so doing by a substantial majority of representatives.

The practice is developing of presiding officers permitting representatives to speak out of turn " on a point of information," or " on a request for clarification," or " on a point of personal privilege." There is no provision for these practices in the Rules, since any legitimate such point or request can be raised as a point of order.

Difficulties also arise regarding the right of reply. The normal practice, in accordance with Rules 70 and 111, is for the presiding officer to call upon representatives in the order in which they signify their desire to speak. If, during the course of debate, a speech is made to which another representative wishes to make a reply, and if the list of speakers has been declared closed, the presiding officer has the discretionary power of according the right of reply if he considers this desirable (Rules 75 and 116). The Rules of Procedure do not provide for the exercise of the right of reply before the list of speakers has been closed. In practice, a representative usually wishes to reply at once to any speech he considers misrepresents the policy of his government or is based on inaccurate information, and in such circumstances presiding officers usually accord the right of reply.

My own impression is that this practice is now carried to excess. It is, after all, a privilege and not a right to speak out of turn. I would make four suggestions designed to prevent undue abuse of the practice.

> 1. Presiding officers should not allow representatives to interrupt the speeches of other representatives in order to make statements of reply.

> 2. Oral statements of reply should, as far as possible, be made at the end of a meeting.

3. Representatives should be encouraged to make statements of reply in written rather than oral form, and such replies should be incorporated into the official records.

4. Presiding officers should be given the power to limit the time allowed to representatives making oral statements of reply.

Representatives spend a great deal of time hearing other representatives explain why they are going to vote, or have already voted, in a particular way. This is permitted under Rule 90 (Rule 129 in Committees), which reads in part:

The President may permit Members to explain their votes, either before or after the voting, except when the vote is taken by secret ballot. The President may limit the time to be allowed for such explanations. The President shall not permit the proposer of a proposal or of an amendment to explain his vote on his own proposal or amendment.

Proposals to limit explanations of vote have been made from time to time. Greece suggested a time limit of five minutes in 1949.[44] The New Zealand representative commented in 1952 that he was " astounded " at the length of speeches delivered in explanations of vote, and added that these explanations often contained " elaborate disputations, rhetorical questions and appeals to the conscience of mankind." [45] Many explanations of vote merely repeat views that have already been expressed during the debate.

It should be emphasized that:

1. The presiding officer is not obliged to permit explanations of vote.

2. It is within the discretion of the presiding officer whether these are heard before or after voting.

3. No explanations of vote are admissible in connection with elections by secret ballot.

4. The proposer of a proposal or of an amendment may not explain his vote on his own proposal or amendment.

5. The presiding officer may limit the time to be allowed for explanations of vote.

6. Explanations of vote may be made in writing and circulated as official documents.

Some years ago Australia proposed that only those Members who had not participated in the debate on a subject should be permitted to explain their votes.[46] This proposal may seem rather drastic, but it might be possible to impose a limit of, say, five minutes on explanations of vote by representatives who have already spoken in the debate

---

44 United Nations Doc. A/937, Annex 1, p. 16.
45 G.A.O.R.: 7th Sess., 387th Plenary Mtg., 23 Oct. 1952, paras. 84–85.
46 G.A.O.R.: 7th Sess., 6th Committee, 349th Mtg., 13 Dec. 1952, paras. 41–43.

on the item being dealt with. Presiding officers should not allow representatives to reopen a discussion which has already concluded under the guise of explaining their votes. Moreover, it would be logical if, in the normal way, explanations of vote were heard after the voting.

Procedural motions

There has been in the past, and no doubt there will continue to be in the future, some confusion between a point of order and a procedural motion; one reason for this, as a representative has suggested, is that in some parliamentary bodies no distinction is made between the two.[47] As far as the General Assembly is concerned, however, the two are clearly distinct. A point of order is a request to the presiding officer to give a ruling; a procedural motion is a proposal which is either automatically accepted by the Chair or, if opposed, is put to the vote.

Motions as to procedure which are automatically accepted by the Chair and not put to the vote are as follows:

(a) the withdrawal by its proposer of an unamended motion before voting on it has commenced (Rules 82 and 123);

(b) the re-introduction of a motion thus withdrawn (Rules 82 and 123); and

(c) a request for a roll-call vote (Rules 89 and 128).

There is only one kind of procedural proposal which, like a point of order, is decided at the discretion of the presiding officer. A presiding officer may " permit the discussion and consideration of amendments, or of motions as to procedure, even though these amendments and motions have not been circulated or have only been circulated the same day " (Rules 80 and 121). Any proposal for the immediate discussion and consideration of an amendment or motion as to procedure which has not been circulated in writing in the normal way is decided by the presiding officer at his discretion and is not put to the vote.

One persistent cause of confusion regarding procedural motions seems to arise in the following way. Speakers are called upon in the order in which they have signified their desire to speak, the only exception being that the discussion of any matter may be interrupted should a representative rise to a point of order. How, then, can a representative move a procedural motion, such as the closure of debate? If he places his name on the list of speakers and awaits his turn, the motion may be irrelevant when his turn comes to speak;

47 G.A.O.R.: 7th Sess., 388th Plenary Mtg., 24 Oct. 2952, para. 73.

if he rises at once on a point of order, he may only raise a matter on which the presiding officer is competent to rule, and therefore may not make a proposal which has to be decided by vote.

It seems that the correct way of moving a motion as to procedure is to do so in the following stages. First, a representative rises to a point of order and states his wish to move a procedural motion, specifying the nature of the motion and the Rule or Rules under which it will be moved. The presiding officer then states whether the proposed motion is admissible. If the ruling of the presiding officer is affirmative, the representative then proposes the motion. In practice, the two stages are frequently merged.

Limitation of debate

No question of procedure arouses more intense feelings than the question of limiting debate.

On the one hand, it has been maintained that it was in the interests of the dignity and prestige of the Assembly to limit the duration of its sessions and so make possible the attendance at its sessions of eminent statesmen of all countries. On the other hand, it was asserted that the sovereign rights of Members to free expression of views and the rights and duties of the Assembly in regard to full discussion of the questions brought before it had to be maintained.[48]

The possibility of imposing some general limitation on the length of speeches has been considered by each Committee of the Assembly on procedure, and the conclusion has been reached on each occasion that no general limitation of debate is feasible.[49] The reason is obvious. If the Rules limit debate at one particular stage, representatives will use another occasion to express their views:

Whatever restrictions were imposed, a representative would always find some way of giving full expression to his views. If restrictions were imposed on the length or number of speeches made by each representative, speakers would resort to points of order, explanations of vote, the right of reply and the like. Even if a point of order was defined as relating only to questions within the President's or the Chairman's competence, a clever speaker would still be able to adjust his speech in order to bring it within that fairly wide definition, and it would only waste more time in the end if the President or the Chairman were to attempt to call him to order.

Again, although an explanation of vote should be brief, the speaker himself was the only judge of what it should cover, and there was no possibility of imposing restrictions in that respect without rendering the right of explanation useless. The right of reply was also difficult to

---

[48] *Repertory of United Nations Practice* (New York: United Nations, 1955), Vol. I, Article 21, para. 81.
[49] United Nations Docs. A/388, para. 20; A/937, para. 30; A/2402, para. 31.

define, and speakers could easily make use of it to evade any limitations on the general debate.[50]

There have been occasions when Committees have successfully applied a time limit, but discussion of the possibility of limiting speeches can be exceedingly time-consuming. During the sixth session, for example, the Chairman of the *Ad Hoc* Political Committee proposed a time limit of five minutes on speeches in explanation of vote or under the right of reply during discussion of a question relating to Germany, and this proposal was upheld by the Committee by a large majority. One representative began a speech of protest and, after he had spoken for five minutes, he was called to order by the Chairman and told that his time was up. The representative protested vigorously at this and proposed the adjournment of the debate so that his delegation could consult the President of the Assembly about the procedural situation. After a confused debate, the Committee voted to give the aggrieved representative an opportunity to explain his views in detail. The representative then proceeded to speak—at great length.[51]

The present practice regarding limitation of debate is set out in Table 16. A number of minor changes of practice regarding limitation of debate may be worth considering. In the first place, it may be noted that the Rules of Procedure of the Economic and Social Council provide for a time limit of five minutes on interventions on procedural questions.[52] This Rule is seldom applied, but the knowledge of its existence has been one means of discouraging lengthy speeches on procedure. It might be desirable for the Assembly to adopt a similar Rule; indeed, Canada made a formal proposal to this effect in 1949.[53]

I suggested earlier in this chapter that presiding officers might be given the right to limit the time of statements of reply. Similarly, presiding officers might be given this right in regard to debate on motions for the division of proposals and amendments (Rules 91 and 130) and on motions to reconsider a proposal that has been adopted or rejected (Rules 83 and 124). Presiding officers already have the right to *propose* the limitation of the time to be allowed to speakers in these matters, and a slight increase in the reserve powers of presiding officers could hardly be open to objection.

It was suggested in a study sponsored by the Carnegie Endowment for International Peace ten years ago that some system should be

---

[50] G.A.O.R.: 7th Sess., 6th Committee, 349th Mtg., 13 Dec. 1952, paras. 40–41.
[51] G.A.O.R.: 6th Sess., *Ad Hoc* Political Committee, 26th Mtg., 19 Dec. 1951, paras. 9–48.
[52] United Nations Doc. E/3063, 1958, Rule 51.
[53] United Nations Doc. A/937, Annex 1, p. 18.

TABLE 16

Practice Regarding Limitation of Debate

	Rule No. Plenary	Rule No. Committees	Number of speakers or number of times each representative may speak	Time to be allowed to each speaker
(a) General practice	35 74	108 115	The presiding officer or any other representative may propose the limitation of the number of times each representative may speak on any question. The Assembly (Committee) may impose such a limitation.	The presiding officer or any other representative may propose the limitation of the time to be allowed to each speaker. The Assembly (Committee) may impose such a limitation. When debate is limited and a representative has spoken his allotted time, the presiding officer shall call him to order without delay.
(b) Appeal against ruling of presiding officer on a point of order	73	114	The appeal shall be immediately put to the vote.	No debate permitted.
(c) Recommendation of the General Committee that an item be included in the agenda	23	—	Three in favour, three against.	The President may limit the time to be allowed to speakers.
(d) Adjournment of debate on the item under discussion	76	117	Proposer of motion, two in favour, two against.	The presiding officer may limit the time to be allowed to speakers.

(e) Closure of debate on the item under discussion	77	118	Two speakers opposing the closure.	The presiding officer may limit the time to be allowed to speakers.
(f) Suspension or adjournment of the meeting	78	119	Proposer of the motion, no debate, motion shall be immediately put to the vote.	The presiding officer may limit the time to be allowed to the proposer of the motion.
(g) Division of proposals and amendments	91	130	Two in favour, two against.	—
(h) Reconsideration of proposals	83	124	Two speakers opposing the motion for reconsideration.	—
(i) Explanations of vote	90	129	Proposer of a proposal or of an amendment may not explain his vote on his own proposal or amendment.	The presiding officer may limit the time to be allowed to speakers.
(j) Report of a Main Committee in plenary meeting	68	—	Discussion takes place only if at least one-third of the Members present and voting consider such a discussion to be necessary. Any proposal to this effect shall not be debated, but shall be immediately put to the vote.	No debate permitted.

adopted by which representatives could incorporate into the official record statements which had not been delivered orally.[54] This possibility was considered by the Special Committee on Measures to Limit the Duration of Sessions (1953), but the Committee concluded that " serious problems would arise regarding such questions as, for example, the relevance of remarks which had been submitted in writing and the exercise of the right of reply with respect to them." [55] I question whether these objections are insuperable. It should surely be possible to impose some limit on the length of such statements, to devise means to ensure that irrelevant remarks could be excluded, and to permit the right of reply or counter-reply. In any case, delegations already have the right to request the Secretary-General to circulate relevant documents. The practice of incorporating undelivered speeches into the official records is not new in United Nations organs. I know of two cases of such statements being incorporated in the records of the Assembly, and this system was also used during the first meeting of the Economic Commission for Africa.[56]

---

[54] Chamberlin, *op. cit.*, para. 73, p. 40.
[55] United Nations Doc. A/2402, para. 29.
[56] G.A.O.R.: 1st Sess., Pt. I, 30th Plenary Mtg., 12 Feb. 1946, pp. 440–442; 3rd Sess., Pt. II, 195th Plenary Mtg., 14 Apr. 1949, pp. 130–140; United Nations Doc. E/CN.14/19, 31 Jan. 1959, pp. 86–87.

Chapter 7

DECISIONS

The composition . . . does, at first look, seem to carry with it
no small difficulty what votes to allow for the inequality of
princes and States. . . . It seems to me that nothing in this
Imperial Parliament should pass but by three quarters of the
whole. . . . In all great points, especially before a final resolve,
they may be obliged to transmit to their principals the merits of
such important cases depending, and receive their last instructions: which may be done in four and twenty days at the most.
. . . If any of the sovereignties that constitute these imperial
states shall refuse to submit their claim or pretensions to them
or abide and perform the judgment thereof, and seek their
remedy by arms, or delay their compliance beyond the time
prefixed in their resolutions, all other sovereignties, united as
one strength, shall compel the submission and performance of
the sentence, with damages to the suffering party. . . .

WILLIAM PENN

WHEN debate has concluded, some procedural mechanism is needed
in order to dispose of the matter and pass to other business. Such a
mechanism may be nothing more than a proposal of the presiding
officer or another representative that the Assembly or Committee
take no further action on the matter. More usually, however, it is a
proposal in express terms, deciding on or recommending some course
of action, or expressing an opinion; and any such proposal is either
accepted without opposition or put to the vote. In this chapter I
am concerned, first, with the rationale of voting; secondly, with the
relationship between " decisions " and " agreement," and the methods
by which the Assembly, in appropriate cases, makes no decision, or
makes only a formal or procedural decision, or seeks to postpone
or avoid a decision; and, finally, I examine the difficult question of
how the General Assembly may best ensure compliance with its
conclusions.

I suppose that the idea of decision by majority vote arose in
primitive societies by empirical observation of the fact that the
majority, being more numerous and therefore usually more powerful
than the minority, was able to coerce the minority. In the most
primitive societies, it was the practice to punish, kill or eat the
dissenting minority; at a later stage of development, it was realized
that the preservation of the community depended on co-operation

141

rather than coercion and that minorities should be granted the right of silent existence, though not the right to challenge overtly the will of the majority; finally, a more advanced stage was reached in which the homogeneity of the community was given a high value, and minorities sought, by persuasion, to become majorities. It is, after all, more civilized to count heads rather than break them, to appeal to the ballot rather than the bullet.

Voting is ostensibly a means of resolving a difference of opinion by the will of the majority and with the acquiescence of the minority. It is thus an attractive system for majorities, or those who expect to become majorities. There are, nevertheless, some differences which no reasonable person would consider should or could be resolved by vote. The weight of numbers has no bearing on questions of fact, such as who wrote the plays ascribed to Shakespeare, or what is the specific gravity of beer, or whether a particular scientific theory is true.

Moreover, the majority is not always right. Alexis de Tocqueville wrote of the possible tyranny of the majority and of the safeguards which might mitigate such tyranny.[1] It is certainly important to distinguish between the rule of law and the rule of the majority, in international as in other forms of politics.

On some matters, unanimity is generally regarded as desirable. This requirement is often encountered in the jury system, for example. Certain organizations never vote. There is no voting at Commonwealth conferences. Informal groups of States at United Nations headquarters do not vote on substantive issues, although the Latin American Group occasionally votes on such procedural questions as the date of the next meeting. The Society of Friends (Quakers) does not resolve differences of opinion by voting; discussion continues until a decision is reached which is acceptable to all.

The use of voting in diplomatic matters is a novel procedure. Before the twentieth century, the principle of unanimity applied in inter-State relations. The same principle was, in theory, the general rule in the League of Nations, and in the case of the permanent members still holds in the United Nations Security Council on non-procedural matters.

The Charter of the United Nations specifies that decisions of the Assembly shall be made by voting. The term " decisions," as used in the Charter, has a broad meaning and " refers to all types of action which the General Assembly takes . . . under the Charter. . . ."[2]

---

[1] *Democracy in America* (New York: Knopf, 1954), Chap. XV.
[2] G.A.O.R.: 5th Sess., 1950, Annexes, Agenda item 49 (A/1356), para. 22.

Very few resolutions of the Assembly include the verb *decides*, though every resolution is a " decision " within the meaning of Article 18.

An election or appointment, whether by secret ballot or acclamation, is also a decision; but its nature is different from a decision, expressed in a resolution, relating to some action or recommendation by the Assembly. A ballot is, to a considerable extent, a mathematical process in the sense that it is not possible to " amend " a candidate for office; each ballot cast is, in this formal sense, unconditional. It is true that there may be informal or under-the-counter understandings and conditions. Q may vote for W on condition that W will support Q on another issue; or on the understanding that W intends, on some future occasion, to act in a particular way; or on the assumption that a second ballot will probably be required, in which event support will be switched to Z.

When two or more elective places are to be filled, the " amending " concept enters in to a somewhat greater degree. When the General Assembly elects its Vice-Presidents or the members of the Economic and Social Council, for example, each vote for a group of States may be unconditional in the formal sense, but the distribution of choices within the vote may represent an element of adjustment to meet the views of others.

All the same, voting as a method of electing persons to offices is to a considerable extent a mathematical process. The mathematical element in voting takes on a different significance once the possibility of amendment exists. In matters where amendment is permitted, there is always the possibility of adjusting the text of a proposal in the interests of wider agreement.[3] No representative in a United Nations organ can know for certain the form a resolution will take until the final vote is taken. The drafting of proposals and amendments, and the anticipation of procedural situations, is today one of the most important of the diplomatic arts. Yet even the most skilled representative cannot foresee every contingency, since there are elements of irrationality and fortuity in any human situation. The mere order of voting is often important. Moreover, there is a voting paradox (which I need not elaborate here) by which, if there are more than two choices, the final result may in part be determined by the order in which the alternatives are put to the vote.

A resolution of the Assembly usually consists of one or more preambular paragraphs and one or more operative paragraphs. The preambular paragraphs may refer to Articles of the Charter, or to principles of international law, or to previous decisions of a United

[3] Occasionally a representative explains that he will vote or has voted in a certain way on the understanding that the proposal has a particular meaning; such a reservation does not affect the validity of the decision.

Nations organ, or to some other sentiment having a bearing on the operative paragraphs. The operative paragraphs of a resolution are, broadly speaking, of two kinds. They may, in the first place, relate to some action which the Assembly, under the Charter, is competent to take; the approval of the budget or the establishment of a subsidiary organ are actions of this kind. The operative paragraphs may, secondly, be such recommendations as the Assembly, under the Charter, is competent to make; they may be straightforward recommendations (the General Assembly . . . appeals to, or calls upon, or invites, or suggests, or urges) or they may be in the nature of expressions of opinion (the General Assembly . . . affirms, or commends, or declares, or deplores, or regrets).[4]

The following resolution of the fourteenth session of the General Assembly consists of four preambular paragraphs; one operative paragraph (the second) taking action which the Assembly is empowered to take under the Charter; one operative paragraph (the fourth) being an invitation or recommendation addressed to Member States; and one operative paragraph (the first) being an expression of opinion. The third operative paragraph, though phrased as a request to the Secretary-General, should probably be regarded as an action which the Assembly is empowered to take under the Charter.

General questions relating to the transmission and examination of information [regarding economic, social, and educational conditions in non-self-governing territories].

The General Assembly,
Having regard to the provisions of Chapter XI of the Charter of the United Nations, and in particular to the obligations to transmit information under Article 73e accepted by Members which have or assume responsibilities for Territories whose peoples have not yet attained a full measure of self-government,
Recalling that, by its resolution 334 (IV) of 2 December 1949, the General Assembly considered that it is within its responsibility to express its opinion on the principles which have guided, or may in future guide, the Administering Members in enumerating the Territories for which the obligation exists to transmit information under Article 73e of the Charter,
Recalling also that, by its resolution 742 (VIII) of 27 November 1953, the General Assembly approved a list of factors to be taken into account in deciding whether a Territory is or is not a Territory whose people have not yet attained a full measure of self-government,
Noting that Member States have expressed differing opinions as to the application of the provisions of Chapter XI to Territories whose peoples have not yet attained a full measure of self-government, including the

---

4 The League Assembly made " decisions " by a unanimous vote, but a recommendation (or *vœu*) could be adopted by a simple majority.

obligation to transmit the information called for in Article 73e of the Charter of the United Nations,

1. *Considers* that it would be desirable for the General Assembly to enumerate the principles which should guide Members in determining whether or not an obligation exists to transmit the information called for in Article 73e;

2. *Decides* to establish a special committee consisting of six members, to be elected by the Fourth Committee on behalf of the General Assembly, three of whom shall be Members who transmit information under Article 73e and three non-administering Members, to study these principles and to report on the results of its study to the fifteenth session of the General Assembly;

3. *Requests* the Secretary-General to prepare for the use of this committee an account of the history of this matter, including a summary of the opinions on the subject which have been expressed by Member States in the past and of the relevant legal treatises on the interpretation of the Charter;

4. *Invites* Member States to submit to the Secretary-General, in writing, before 1 May 1960, their views on these principles, in order that the committee may take them into account.[5]

I suggested in Chapter 5 that the inclusion of an item in the agenda of the Assembly does not necessarily mean that the Assembly is competent to adopt a resolution.[6] Article 12 (1) of the Charter provides that " While the Security Council is exercising in respect of any dispute or situation the functions assigned to it in the present Charter, the General Assembly shall not make any recommendations with regard to that dispute or situation unless the Security Council so requests." The Assembly has not applied this provision of the Charter in a completely consistent manner, although one precedent gives some indication of how Member States interpret the phrase " shall not make any recommendations." A Main Committee of the Assembly decided during the fourth session, in connection with a matter of which the Security Council was seised, that a proposal containing the words " Deems it essential to take the following measures " would have constituted a recommendation within the meaning of Article 12 (1); but that a resolution welcoming an announcement and a forthcoming event, and commending the parties concerned and a United Nations organ, did not constitute a recommendation within the meaning of Article 12 (1).[7]

Article 2 (7) states that the United Nations is not authorized to intervene in matters that are essentially within the domestic jurisdiction of a State except in regard to the application of enforcement

---

[5] Res. 1467 (XIV), 12 Dec. 1959.   [6] *Supra*, pp. 83, 99–100.
[7] G.A.O.R.: 4th Sess., *Ad Hoc* Political Committee, 56th Mtg., 3 Dec. 1949, paras. 116, 118, p. 339.

B.   10

measures if peace is threatened. Most Member States have held either that discussion does not constitute intervention, or at any rate that the Assembly can reach a decision on competence only after discussion has taken place. It is entirely consistent with either one of these positions to insist, after the discussion has been concluded, that the Assembly is not competent to adopt a resolution which includes a recommendation. Some governments have held that, while Article 2 (7) does not prevent the Assembly from making a recommendation of a general nature regarding the domestic matters of all States, the Assembly is not competent to make a specific recommendation regarding the domestic matters of a particular State, since that would constitute intervention.

Belgium: in matters essentially within domestic jurisdiction it could make recommendations directed not against any particular State or States, but of a general nature, directed to all States. . . .[8]

France: the United Nations could address recommendations of a general nature to all Member States, even if those recommendations might affect their domestic affairs; but the recommendations referred to were addressed to the community of States as a whole and not to one individual State.[9]

Sweden: The United Nations could not . . . refrain from concerning itself with respect for human rights. . . . His delegation also considered that the Assembly had every right to make general recommendations in the matter. . . . However, his delegation was not prepared to accept resolutions recommending a Member State to adopt specific measures.[10]

A Member State might thus regard discussion of some question as not constituting intervention, or might consider that discussion was necessary as a preliminary to taking a decision on competence; yet when it came to voting, it might regard as *ultra vires* all resolutions of any kind, or all resolutions containing general recommendations, or all resolutions containing specific recommendations regarding the domestic affairs of a particular State.

Whatever views may be taken about the interpretation of Articles 2 (7) and 12 (1) in regard to the adoption of resolutions, Rules 81 and 122 provide that, at any time before a vote is taken on a proposal which has been submitted, it is in order to move that the Assembly or Committee is not competent to adopt such a proposal. Such a motion calling for a decision on competence must be put to the vote before a vote is taken on the proposal in question.

8 G.A.O.R.: 8th Sess., *Ad Hoc* Political Committee, 32nd Mtg., 23 Nov. 1953, para. 40, p. 159.

9 *Ibid.*, 38th Mtg., 2 Dec. 1953, para. 6, p. 197.

10 *Ibid.*, 33rd Mtg., 24 Nov. 1953, para. 49, p. 168.

THE SEARCH FOR AGREEMENT

" The art of diplomacy," an American diplomat has written, " consists of making the policy of one government understood and if possible accepted by other governments." [11] Applying this definition to the General Assembly, one may say that one purpose of debate is to help governments to understand the policies of other governments, and that one purpose of adopting resolutions is to express the greatest possible degree of consensus. In traditional diplomacy, it was often in the interests of all parties that any differences should be kept private while the search for agreement continued. In contemporary diplomacy, by contrast, it is often difficult to avoid a premature disclosure of differences, and this may seriously hamper the search for agreement.

If conference diplomacy is to serve the interests of governments, constant efforts are needed to devise procedures and practices which can resolve rather than expose differences. Thus when a situation of conflict is being debated in the Assembly, attention should initially be directed towards the reconciling of differences. If the situation is deteriorating while the matter is under consideration, it may be desirable to mobilize the support of governments in favour of an appeal to the parties to exercise restraint, or to discontinue threatening actions, or in other ways to refrain from aggravating the situation. This may be followed at a later stage by the creation of machinery of a fact-finding character, either because some of the facts are in dispute or because of a wish to establish the culpability of one or more of the parties. In some circumstances it may be useful to establish new negotiating machinery, in other circumstances to recommend to the parties the general principles of a settlement. But whichever approach or combination of approaches may be used, someone has to take the initiative. Sometimes this may be done by one or more of the States directly involved; at other times the initiative may come from relatively disinterested third parties; at still other times the Secretary-General or a senior official of the Secretariat may informally initiate procedures designed to facilitate a solution. Sometimes the problem is not to find candidates to exercise this function of leadership but to co-ordinate a number of simultaneous but unrelated efforts.

Moreover, sponsorship of a draft resolution has now become a matter of prestige, and Member States may compete for the privilege. In the first years of the United Nations, a draft resolution usually had a small number of sponsors, but the practice gradually developed of trying to secure a representative group of sponsors, and more recently

[11] James Rives Childs, *American Foreign Service* (New York: Holt, Toronto: Oxford Univ. Press, 1948), p. 64.

of having not simply a representative group but the largest possible number of sponsors.[12] Member States can indicate their positions by voice and by vote without co-sponsoring a draft resolution. The greater the number of sponsors, the less the scope for manœuvre; a Member State may cheerfully acquiesce in a slightly objectionable phrase in a resolution sponsored by another State, but it is much more difficult to be on record as sponsoring an objectionable phrase.

There are differences of opinion regarding the extent to which a presiding officer should initiate substantive proposals designed to foster agreement. During the thirteenth session, the Chairman of the Second Committee submitted a draft resolution combining all the points common to two similar proposals, on the understanding that the two proposals would be withdrawn. This initiative was widely welcomed, although it is interesting to note that the delegation of which the Chairman was a member was one of twenty-seven co-sponsors of one of the proposals that was withdrawn.[13]

The presiding officer has a primary responsibility to give leadership in matters of procedure, however, and this may be endangered if he becomes too much involved in matters of substance. The Rapporteur does not have the same responsibility for procedural leadership, though nowhere are the functions or duties of the Rapporteur defined in the Rules of Procedure.

The Rapporteur filled a vital role in the practice of the League of Nations. In the case of the League Council, a Rapporteur was normally appointed for each matter with which the Council was dealing. In committees of the Assembly, normal procedure was to appoint a Rapporteur for each major subject or group of subjects rather than to have one Rapporteur for all the matters committed to it, as is the practice in committees of the United Nations Assembly.

Sometimes the League Assembly appointed the Rapporteur at the beginning of the discussion, sometimes at the end. The Council usually appointed a Rapporteur at the end of the general discussion. In any event, it was the normal practice for the Rapporteur to begin his duties before formal proposals were submitted, and as a result proposals were submitted to him rather than to the body which had appointed him. A Rapporteur was a delegate, or was appointed a delegate by his government so that he could serve as Rapporteur, but Östen Undén of Sweden has suggested that a different practice might sometimes have been appropriate:

---

12 The summit was reached in 1959 when a proposal on disarmament was sponsored by all eighty-two Member States. This was the *reductio ad absurdum* of the trend towards large numbers of sponsors, since the Member States were presumably addressing the proposal to themselves.

13 G.A.O.R.: 13th Sess., 2nd Committee, 523rd–524th Mtgs., 9–10 Oct. 1958.

The system of appointing Rapporteurs from among the members of the Council itself . . . would not appear to be entirely rational. The Rapporteurs, who frequently are Ministers for Foreign Affairs or are engaged on other highly absorbing duties, cannot be expected to devote to the examination of, usually, complicated questions all the time and attention which would be desirable. In many cases it would, no doubt, be more satisfactory to entrust such duties to private individuals or to a special conciliation commission consisting of members in no way dependent on their Governments, who after exhaustive negotiations with the parties would endeavour to bring about an amicable settlement of the dispute and would ultimately put forward proposals for such a settlement. . . .

The Inter-American Treaty on Good Offices and Mediation of 1936 includes an interesting provision in this respect: " When a controversy arises between them that cannot be settled by the usual diplomatic means, the High Contracting Parties may have recourse to the good offices or mediation of an eminent citizen of any of the other American countries, preferably chosen from a general list made up in accordance with the following article." [14]

The League Rapporteur, like his counterpart in the United Nations, was expected to submit an objective report of the debate, and in this task he was assisted by the Secretariat. But, in cases of disagreement, his duties did not end there.

The task of the Rapporteur was to elucidate the issues involved in the dispute and to make proposals for its solution. To this end it was his duty to study the documents relating to the dispute, to engage in private conversations with the disputants and to guide discussion in the Council. In several instances, he was authorized to call upon outside experts for advice and assistance. Between sessions . . . the Rapporteur in several instances entered into negotiations with the disputants in the capital of his own country. . . . In his report the Rapporteur would submit . . . proposals for the solution of the dispute in the form of a draft resolution. When the report came before the Council the Rapporteur might intervene at any time in the discussion. It was a common practice . . . to adopt the draft resolution submitted by the Rapporteur without discussion, after the President had invited the parties to make their observations and state any objections they might have to raise.[15]

The Rapporteur in the League system thus exercised a variety of functions. He accumulated and reported information which was formally communicated to him, and he requested whatever additional information he deemed necessary. This was an important weapon in the hands of the Rapporteur. " Even when facts were asked for, the object was not fact-finding, but pressure on the disputants to mend the facts." [16] An advisory opinion could be sought on legal aspects from a committee of jurists or from the Permanent Court of

---

[14] United Nations Doc. A/Ac. 18/68, 29 June 1948, para. 19n.   [15] *Ibid.*, para. 20.
[16] Julius Stone, *Legal Controls of International Conflict* (New York: Rinehart, London: Stevens, Sydney: Maitland Publications Pty., 1954), p. 172.

International Justice. Diplomatic pressures of various kinds might be brought to bear on the parties.

The object of the system was to produce a report, with proposals, that would be unanimously accepted. In the Assembly this was not normally difficult. The Council Rapporteur, being concerned with disputes, had a harder task. Disputes tended to be protracted while the search for agreement continued, but disputes of the kind which were dealt with by the League Council were likely to be protracted whatever the procedure.

In 1948 the British delegation suggested that the rapporteur system which had been used by the League should be revived.

The United Kingdom representative explained, first, that any conflict with existing procedures should be avoided, and, second, that conciliation proceedings should not be rigid or formal in character. What was proposed was that a practice be established under which the parties would at the outset automatically meet with the conciliator and ascertain whether their differences could be eliminated.[17]

After extensive discussion of the British proposal, the Interim Committee proposed changes in the Assembly's Rules of Procedure which would have empowered the President of the Assembly to appoint a Rapporteur or conciliator accepted by the parties in any questions relating to the maintenance of international peace and security brought before the Assembly. The Interim Committee, in a separate proposal, referred approvingly to the experience of the League Council " whereby cases were presented . . . by a rapporteur who had the function of conciliator, and that this practice allowed private conversations among the parties and the rapporteur and avoided the crystallization of views that tend to result from taking a stated public position "; the Interim Committee went on to recommend that " such a practice be developed in the Security Council as an integral part of the system of pacific settlement." [18]

When the proposed change in the Rules of Procedure of the Assembly came before the *Ad Hoc* Political Committee during the third session, the British representative proposed that a decision on the matter be postponed, and this was approved by 25–4–2.[19] The official records give no indication as to why the British delegation did not persist with the proposal, but the Assembly can, of course, adopt the method whenever it wishes to do so, no revision of the Rules being needed to permit this.

17 *Report of the Interim Committee of the General Assembly*, G.A.O.R.: 3rd Sess., 1948, Suppl. No. 10 (A/605), para. 47, p. 29.
18 *Ibid.*, Annexes II, III, pp. 34–35.
19 G.A.O.R.: 3rd Sess., Pt. I, *Ad Hoc* Political Committee, 28th Mtg., 9 Dec. 1948, p. 327.

One potential danger of likening the General Assembly to a parliamentary or legislative body is that it may encourage the idea that every debate must terminate with a decision of substance which is arrived at by means of a vote. I incline to the view that some of the contentious questions of which the Assembly has been seised have been prematurely pressed to a vote on a proposal of substance. When a matter is proposed for inclusion in the agenda; and when such a proposal is considered both by the General Committee and by the plenary Assembly; and when the item is the subject of debate —a substantial impact is made whether or not a resolution of substance is adopted. Indeed, it seems to me essential to facilitate practices whereby the Assembly can, without difficulty, debate some question without necessarily reaching a conclusion of substance.

A number of democratic legislatures have found it useful to devise procedures by which a general discussion on some topic can take place without the necessity of putting a question to the vote at the conclusion of the debate. In the British House of Commons, for example, every debate takes place on a motion moved by a Member. Circumstances may arise, however, when a debate is desired but no decision is necessary. The Opposition may wish to ventilate a subject without challenging the authority of the Government, or the Government may wish to test the feeling of the House though without causing a division on a motion in express terms. In such circumstances a debate may be arranged, by informal agreement between the parties, on the motion " That this House do now adjourn " without any intention of pressing to a conclusion a motion which, if approved, would result in the termination of the sitting. This " substantive " motion for the adjournment is a technical form devised for the purpose of enabling the House to discuss matters without recording a decision in express terms. When its purpose has been served, the motion is withdrawn and the House turns its attention to other business.[20]

This kind of adjournment debate is in some respects akin to the General Debate held in plenary meetings of the General Assembly. In the case of the Assembly, however, a debate can take place without a motion of any kind being moved, and can be terminated simply by acquiescence in a declaration of the presiding officer that the matter has been disposed of.

Although the normal practice of the Assembly is that items included in the agenda (other than elections and appointments) are debated and then decided by the adoption of substantive resolutions,

20 *Sir Thomas Erskine May's Treatise on the Law, Privileges, Proceedings and Usages of Parliament*, edited by Sir Edward Fellowes and T. G. B. Cocks (16th ed., London: Butterworth, 1957), pp. 298–300, 305–306.

there are significant exceptions to this general rule. An item may be included in the agenda, but there may be no debate and either no resolution or only a formal resolution; or the item may be debated in the ordinary way but, for some reason or another, disposed of either without the adoption of a resolution or by the adoption of a resolution of which the operative parts are formal or procedural in character.

1. No debate, no resolution

Article 98 requires the Secretary-General to make an annual report to the General Assembly on the work of the Organization. This report now constitutes item 10 of the agenda. Under Article 12 (2) of the Charter, the Secretary-General is required, with the consent of the Security Council, to notify the Assembly at each session of any matters relative to the maintenance of international peace and security which are being dealt with by the Security Council. This notification constitutes item 7 of the agenda. Neither the report nor the notification is debated by the Assembly, and no resolution is adopted in connection with either. In the case of the notification under Article 12 (2), the President draws the attention of the Assembly to it, and the Assembly takes note of it.

Important substantive items may be disposed of without debate and without a resolution. During the eleventh session (1956–57), for example, the Assembly agreed to include in the agenda three items relating to the amendment of the Charter, and to consider them in plenary meeting. When these items were reached, the President stated, " I am informed that there is general agreement to postpone the consideration of these three items until the twelfth session. As there is no objection, this will be done." [21]

The Secretary-General submitted to the thirteenth session a report summarizing the experience derived from the establishment and operation of the United Nations Emergency Force. The General Assembly decided that the report should be referred to the Special Political Committee. After the Special Political Committee had considered a separate report on another aspect of the Force and had adopted a draft resolution, the Committee turned to the Secretary-General's study of the experience of the Force. The Secretary-General made a few remarks about this study and stated that he and his colleagues were at the disposal of the Committee, should there be any need for clarifications. The Secretary-General concluded: " I feel no need for the General Assembly to take any action at the present time." An informal understanding had been reached that there

[21] G.A.O.R.: 11th Sess., 661st Plenary Mtg., 26 Feb. 1957, para. 108.

would be no debate on this aspect of the matter and that no draft resolutions would be submitted. The Chairman of the Committee stated that in view of the Secretary-General's statement, the Committee now need hardly enter into a discussion of the question; since no one had asked for the floor, he took it that the Committee was in agreement that the item was disposed of. The Report of the Committee to the plenary stated:

At its 100th meeting, on 5 November 1958, after hearing the statement of the Secretary-General on agenda item 65(*c*), the Committee decided not to discuss the matter at that time.[22]

2. No debate, only a formal resolution

The three Councils report annually to the Assembly. The report of the Security Council is not discussed, but a formal resolution is adopted in the following terms:

The General Assembly,

Takes note of the report of the Security Council to the General Assembly covering the period . . .

3. Debate, no resolution

There are three ways by which a matter included in the agenda may be debated and then disposed of without the adoption of a resolution: if no draft resolution is submitted, if all draft resolutions are withdrawn, or if none of the draft resolutions obtains the required majority.

An item included in the agenda may be the subject of debate but no resolutions may be submitted either because that is the conventional practice for the item or, in special circumstances, because there is informal agreement that this is appropriate in a particular case. An example of the first kind is the General Debate. When all delegations wishing to participate have done so, the President simply declares " The general debate is concluded " or words to that effect. The Assembly then proceeds to other business.

Certain chapters of the report of the Economic and Social Council become agenda items for the Second and Third Committees of the Assembly. During the thirteenth session part of the first chapter of the Council's report was considered by the Special Political Committee along with a proposal to increase the membership of the Council. In addition, the thirteenth session in plenary meeting formally took note of parts of the Council's report. I assume this was done to enable the Soviet representative to make a statement about the decision of the Economic and Social Council not to grant

---

[22] G.A.O.R.: 13th Sess., 1958, Annexes, Agenda item 65 (A/3943 and A/3989, para. 12); *ibid.*, Special Political Committee, 100th Mtg.

consultative status to the Women's International Democratic Federation, to which statement the United States representative made a brief rejoinder.[23]

The report of the Trusteeship Council is considered by the Fourth Committee, which adopts a resolution as follows:

The General Assembly,

Having examined the report of the Trusteeship Council covering the work of its . . . sessions,

1. *Takes note* of the report of the Trusteeship Council ;

2. *Recommends* that the Trusteeship Council, in its future deliberations, should take into account the comments and suggestions made during the discussion of its reports at the . . . session of the General Assembly.[24]

The Assembly may occasionally find that, having debated a matter, all draft resolutions are withdrawn. During the twelfth session, for example, Syria proposed that the Assembly should take up the question of " threats to the security of Syria and to international peace " caused by " the heavy, unprecedented and unwarranted concentration of Turkish troops . . . in close proximity to the Syrian–Turkish border." [25] The Syrian delegate stated that it was urgently necessary for the Assembly to set up a commission to investigate the Turkish threat to Syria. His government had turned to the Assembly only after exhausting all other diplomatic resources. The Turkish representative affirmed the friendly feelings of his country towards Syria, and welcomed the proposal that the Assembly should take up the Syrian request. The Soviet representative complained that two days had elapsed since the urgent and grave Syrian request had been made; the matter should be discussed without further delay. After other representatives had spoken, the General Committee agreed to recommend that the item be included in the agenda and discussed in plenary meeting.[26]

The matter was considered in a rather strident atmosphere at six plenary meetings of the Assembly during the succeeding two weeks. Syria proposed that a commission be set up to investigate the situation

---

23 *Ibid.*, 788th Plenary Mtg., 12 Dec. 1958, paras. 72–93.

24 The Special Committee on Measures to Limit the Duration of Regular Sessions (1953) emphasized that " consideration of the reports of the Economic and Social Council and the Trusteeship Council would be facilitated if the General Assembly were to encourage the Councils to continue the practice of indicating in their annual reports those matters on which they desire that the Assembly should take action. This trend, which should be strengthened, does not prejudice the right of the Assembly to debate any aspect of the reports, and it has the advantage of providing Members in advance with more precise information on what questions covered in the reports would be the subject of debate. . . ." G.A.O.R.: 8th Sess., 1953, Annexes, Agenda item 54 (A/2402), para. 22.

25 G.A.O.R.: 12th Sess., 1957, Annexes, Agenda item 69 (A/3699).

26 G.A.O.R.: 12th Sess., General Committee, 116th Mtg., 18 Oct. 1957.

on the spot. Canada and six other States submitted a draft resolution which would have expressed confidence that the Secretary-General, in the exercise of his responsibilities under the Charter, would be available to undertake discussions with the parties. Throughout the period of the public debate, there took place intensive private consultations in an effort to ease the tension and assist the two countries to compose their differences. At the conclusion of the debate, the Indonesian representative appealed to the parties to the dispute and to the sponsors of draft resolutions not to press any of the proposals to a vote. Syria, Turkey and the seven sponsors of the second draft resolution agreed to the Indonesian proposal; the President of the Assembly stated, " I feel sure that the Assembly will regard this . . . as a satisfactory outcome "; and the Assembly proceeded to other business.[27]

A similar situation arises in the case of a dispute in which disinterested governments may attempt to produce a compromise draft resolution acceptable to the parties. If it should transpire that one or more of the parties find the proposed compromise unacceptable, the sponsors may prefer to withdraw a draft even if it seems likely that it might secure the majority required. Thus a report of the Fourth Committee concerning the frontier between Italian Somaliland and Ethiopia in 1958 included the following paragraphs:

13. At the same meeting, the sponsors of the three-Power draft resolution withdrew their proposal in view of the fact that, despite their efforts to revise it to meet objections, they had not been able to produce a text acceptable to both parties concerned.

14. In the absence of any other proposal, the Committee is therefore unable to present a draft resolution for adoption by the General Assembly.[28]

When the same question came before the Assembly's Fourth Committee a year later, no proposals were submitted formally although several informal suggestions were made. The representatives of Japan and New Zealand, in particular, had consulted with the two parties concerned and with other delegations in the hope that a proposal acceptable to both parties could be worked out. These efforts were, in the event, abortive and the Rapporteur reported to the plenary that " the Fourth Committee regrets to inform the General Assembly that it has no draft resolution to recommend." [29] It is clear from the wording of the Rules and the practice of the Assembly that a Main Committee is under no obligation to recommend a draft resolution to the plenary Assembly.

[27] *Ibid.*, 708th, 710th–714th Plenary Mtgs., 22 Oct., 25 Oct.–1 Nov. 1957.
[28] G.A.O.R.: 13th Sess., 1958, Annexes, Agenda item 41 (A/4073), paras. 13–14.
[29] United Nations Doc. A/4350, 11 Dec. 1959.

Another way in which a matter may be debated but no resolution adopted arises when a draft resolution passes in a Main Committee (where a simple majority is sufficient) and later fails in the plenary (where a two-thirds majority is required for " important " questions). In recent years, draft resolutions relating to Algeria, Cyprus, West Irian (West New Guinea) and information from non-self-governing territories have been adopted by majority votes in Main Committees but have failed to secure two-thirds votes in the plenary.

It should be emphasized that once a draft resolution has been adopted by a Committee, it becomes the proposal of the Committee and not of the original sponsor or sponsors; the question whether or not to vote in the plenary on a draft resolution recommended by a Main Committee is a matter for the decision of the plenary.

4. Debate, followed by a formal or procedural resolution

Finally, a substantive conclusion may be avoided or postponed by the adoption of a resolution of which the operative parts are formal or procedural. Opinions may differ as to precisely what constitutes a resolution of which the operative parts are formal or procedural, but I suggest that such a resolution is one of which the operative parts do not go beyond: (a) an expression of satisfaction that certain steps are taking place or contemplated; (b) an expression of confidence that the matter will be resolved in accordance with the Charter; (c) a decision not to consider the matter further, or to postpone further consideration. Examples of resolutions of this kind are:

(a) *The General Assembly,*
Having examined the Moroccan question,
Noting that some delegations declared that negotiations between France and Morocco would be initiated regarding this question,
Expressing confidence that a satisfactory solution will be achieved,
Decides to postpone for the time being further consideration of this item.[30]

(b) *The General Assembly,*
Considering that, for the time being, it does not appear appropriate to adopt a resolution on the question of Cyprus,
Decides not to consider further the item. . . .[31]

(c) *The General Assembly,*
Decides not to consider further the item entitled " The question of Algeria " and is therefore no longer seized of this item on the agenda of its tenth session.[32]

(d) *The General Assembly,*
1. *Decides* to give further consideration at its thirteenth session to items 19, 20 and 21 of the agenda of the twelfth session ;

---

30 General Assembly Res. 812 (IX), 17 Dec. 1954.
31 General Assembly Res. 814 (IX), 17 Dec. 1954.
32 General Assembly Res. 909 (X), 25 Nov. 1955.

2. *Requests* the Secretary-General to include these items in the provisional agenda of the thirteenth session of the General Assembly.[33]

DEVELOPING A TRADITION OF COMPLIANCE

The problem of compliance in the Assembly arises from the fact that the world of States is in a period of transition. Nations treasure the concept of sovereignty as much as ever they did; yet nations never were, and are not now, wholly sovereign. The limitation on State sovereignty is given legal expression in Article 25 of the Charter, by which Member States agree to accept and carry out the decisions of the Security Council in accordance with the Charter. The limitation on sovereignty is, perhaps, even more drastic in its non-legal forms. Nations are not entirely free to act as they will in external affairs: they are inhibited by the concrete power of others, and by such intangible qualities as reason and justice.

A government should not disregard the national interest, but the national interest must constantly be reviewed in the light of the national interests of others. A chief purpose of diplomacy is to make what is apparently incompatible compatible. National interest is transcended by international interest.

This is the theory. In practice, international issues rarely present themselves in simple terms. The United Nations is a centre for harmonizing the actions of nations in the attainment of certain common ends, but true harmony in international affairs is elusive. Institutions for peaceful international co-operation have been created, governments realize that the alternative to using them wisely is disaster, they weigh the relative risks of alternative courses of action; yet too often the wise things that are said are submerged by the foolish things that are done.

The General Assembly is not a world parliament. It cannot legislate, but it can " recommend." Its recommendations may relate to general principles of international co-operation, or they may be specific measures for the peaceful adjustment of a situation which seems likely to impair friendly relations among nations or lead to a breach of peace. Increasingly the Assembly has interpreted its right of recommendation as including the right to deplore or condemn.

A substantive resolution adopted by the General Assembly usually attempts to express the greatest possible degree of consensus of Member States. Numbers are often significant, since decisions on " important " questions require a two-thirds majority, but there are other considerations besides numbers. The minority is sometimes wiser than the majority. Moreover, although the votes of States are

[33] General Assembly Res. 1190 (XII), 12 Dec. 1957.

equal in a numerical or juridical sense, they have different values in a political or moral sense.

The Assembly wavers between conflicting conceptions of its main role. " It seems obvious," H. Field Haviland has written, " that the principal task of the Assembly is to harmonize conflicting views rather than to impose a decision contrary to these views. Yet at times pressure may be necessary to break a deadlock." [34] The predicaments the Assembly often faces can be simply stated. Should the Assembly frame its decision in such a way as to make compliance as easy as possible, or in such a way as to endorse the highest standards of conduct? Should it seek by quiet diplomacy to persuade an erring government to mend its ways, or should it publicly condemn all departures from the noble principles on which the Organization is based? Does reconciliation or censure best serve the interests of Member States and of the United Nations itself?

There is no general answer to these questions. Each issue is unique each time it arises. Certainly there are policies and incidents that come to the attention of the Assembly which cause a general sense of moral affront. Military or other forms of aggression, the subjugation of a helpless people, doctrines of race superiority, the contemptuous disregard of agreements—these cannot be condoned by any person or government that cares for the principles on which the United Nations was founded. But the essential task, it seems to me, is not to strike an attitude; it is to rectify the situation which is objectionable. The former is relatively easy, the latter requires such rare qualities as imagination, wisdom and patience. As a former United States Secretary of State has noted,

To express collective indignation may bring the glow of moral principles vindicated without effort ; but it is usually futile, and, more often than not, harmful.[35]

I do not mean that intractable problems should be swept under the carpet nor that the Assembly should turn a blind eye when the principles of the Charter are flouted. But I find it difficult to believe that resolutions which regret, deplore or condemn, repeated year after year in some cases, have a consistently beneficial effect. Repetition can be vain.

The General Assembly cannot, by fiat, abolish prejudice, or free slaves, or liberate the oppressed; but it can declare that these are desirable goals and it can often take technical steps to bring their attainment nearer. The heart of the problem is to frame the

---

[34] *The Political Role of the General Assembly* (New York: Carnegie Endowment for International Peace, 1951), p. 93.

[35] Dean Acheson, *Power and Diplomacy* (Cambridge: Harvard Univ. Press, 1958), p. 80.

Assembly's decisions in such a way that they exert pressure without increasing intransigence.

The adoption of a resolution expressing an opinion may represent pressure, or the resolution may authorize action which amounts to pressure. The General Assembly may formally use the prestige of the Organization and the Secretary-General in an attempt to secure compliance with some principle which is stated in the Charter. The Assembly may establish a subsidiary organ to elucidate the facts or to exercise good offices. It may call upon governments to report on the implementation of a resolution. But whatever form the decision takes, restraint of language is important. In examining those resolutions of the Assembly which have not been complied with, I cannot help wondering whether in every case it was wise to formulate the decision in such blunt language. If defiance of a United Nations recommendation is to be regarded as a grave matter, it will be because compliance is the normal policy of a civilized government. What is needed is a tradition of compliance.

ANNEX: METHODS OF MAKING DECISIONS

The Rules of Procedure provide for five methods of making decisions; in practice, a method of making decisions which is not provided for in the Rules of Procedure is also used.

1. Voting is " normally . . . by show of hands "

In a vote by a show of hands, the presiding officer first requests those in favour of a proposal to raise their hands, then those who are against the proposal, and finally those wishing to abstain; those who do not raise their hands are considered absent. The secretary of the meeting counts the votes and communicates the result to the presiding officer.

2. Voting may be " by standing "

In a vote by standing, the presiding officer first requests those in favour of a proposal to rise from their seats, then those who are against the proposal, and finally those wishing to abstain; those not rising are considered absent. The counting of votes is done in the same way as in a vote by show of hands. I know of no case in which the Assembly or one of its committees has voted by standing.

3. In connection with a vote other than a secret ballot, " any representative may request a roll-call "

A vote by roll-call is taken in the English alphabetical order of the names of Members, beginning with the Member whose name is drawn by lot by the presiding officer from a special box. The name of each Member is called by the secretary of the meeting, and representatives reply " yes," " no," or " abstain." If no reply is heard, the name is repeated; if again no reply is heard, that Member is considered absent. The vote of each Member is marked by the secretary on a special form; upon conclusion of the roll-call, the votes are counted by the secretary and the result communicated to the presiding officer.

When voting is by show of hands, by standing, or by roll-call, the presiding officer announces the result in some such terms as:

" The result of the vote is as follows: . . . in favour, . . . against, . . . abstentions. The proposal is adopted (*or* is not adopted, *or*, having failed to secure a two-thirds majority, is not adopted)."

4. " All elections shall be held by secret ballot"; " There shall be no nominations" for elections held in plenary meetings

In the case of voting conducted by secret ballot, the presiding officer designates two tellers from among the representatives. One ballot paper is distributed to each delegation by conference officers, and a member of the delegation writes on the paper the name of the State(s) or person(s) his delegation wishes to vote for. A ballot box is placed at the head of the meeting, and the secretary calls the names of Members in the English alphabetical order, beginning with the Member whose name is drawn by lot by the presiding officer from a special box. Representatives deposit their ballots in the ballot box in the presence of the tellers. When the voting is completed, the box is opened in the presence of the tellers, who count the votes with the assistance of the Secretariat, and communicate the result to the presiding officer.

The system of election by secret ballot used in committees of the Assembly, and in plenary meetings where only one elective place is to be filled and a simple majority is sufficient for election, is known as Second or Exhaustive Ballot. In the first ballot, votes may be cast for an eligible candidate.[36] If no candidate obtains a simple majority of Members present and voting, the ballot is inconclusive and a second ballot is taken restricted to the two candidates obtaining the largest number of votes. If in the second ballot the votes are equally divided, and a simple majority is required, the presiding officer decides between the candidates by drawing lots.

If in plenary meeting two or more elective places are to be filled, those obtaining in the first ballot the majority required are elected. If more candidates obtain the required majority than there are places

---

[36] The word " candidate " is a little misleading in connection with ballots in plenary meeting, since candidates are not publicly named. Aspirants for elective places are, however, usually candid in private. In any case, the word " candidate " is used in the Rules of Procedure.

to be filled, it has been the practice to regard as elected those candidates obtaining the greatest number of votes, to a number equal to the places to be filled. If all the places are not filled, additional ballots are held to fill the remaining places, the voting being restricted to the candidates obtaining the greatest number of votes in the previous ballot, to a number not more than twice the places remaining to be filled. Similarly, if only one place is to be filled and a two-thirds majority is required, and if in the first ballot no candidate obtains the majority required, additional ballots are held, restricted to the two candidates obtaining the largest number of votes, until one candidate secures two-thirds of the votes cast.

The additional ballots referred to in the previous paragraph are known as restricted ballots. If three restricted ballots are inconclusive, not more than three unrestricted ballots are held in which votes may be cast for any eligible candidate, followed by not more than three additional restricted ballots, followed by not more than three unrestricted ballots, and so on until all the places have been filled.

A system of election which combines a secret ballot, a ban on nominations, the requirement of a two-thirds majority for election in certain cases, and an alternation between restricted and unrestricted ballots in groups of three, is inevitably cumbersome.

In the case of an election by secret ballot, the presiding officer announces the result in some such terms as:

" The result of the vote is as follows: A   votes ; B   votes ; C   votes.

" A (and/or B, and/or C) is elected ; *or* as no candidate has obtained the majority required, another ballot will be taken, by the following method . . ."

5. *A method of making a decision which is not explicitly provided for in the Rules is by acquiescence (or, in the case of elections, by acclamation)*

When a presiding officer believes that a proposal does not meet with objection, he may decide not to put the question to a vote; he declares that, if there is no objection, the proposal will be adopted. If objection is made, a vote is held in accordance with the Rules of Procedure. Occasionally, after a resolution has been adopted by acquiescence, abstentions or negative votes have been recorded at the request of one or more Members.

6. *When the Assembly is not in session, decisions relating to the place of meeting of the Assembly or the summoning of a special session may be made by consultation of Members*

B.   11

Sessions of the Assembly may be held elsewhere than at head-quarters, and special sessions may be summoned, at the request of a majority of Members or at the request of any Member with the concurrence of a majority of Members.

The Secretary-General has twice reported on the possibility of using mechanical voting devices. The first report was prepared at the request of the Special Committee on Methods and Procedures (1949); the second formed part of a report dealing with the correction of votes.[37] Electrical voting equipment is used in a number of legislative bodies. The system is rapid, taking only ten seconds for a vote in the House of Assembly of New Jersey (sixty members) and thirty seconds in the *Riksdag* of Sweden (231 members). It is simple to use; mechanical failures are said to be rare, and the equipment gives warning if it is out of order.

Each representative has a small panel with buttons or switches for voting; there is a larger wall panel on which the vote of each representative and the totals can be shown; the presiding officer has a device for initiating the vote and being informed of the result; a permanent record of the result may be made by means of a punched card or photography. The equipment could also be used for purposes other than voting. Representatives could use it when they wish to inform the presiding officer of their wish to be included in the list of speakers; the equipment could also be used to determine whether a quorum is present.

It was estimated in 1949 that electrical voting equipment would cost $271,000 (£97,000) to instal, but the Secretary-General commented in 1955 that "It may be that the estimate [of cost] will be lower than that made in 1949, since the main expense would be for the purchase of equipment, and . . . the General Assembly Hall already has all the necessary electrical circuits and the conference rooms have most of them. . . ."

Mechanical voting equipment could save time, particularly in connection with roll-call votes on paragraphs of draft resolutions and amendments. It presumably could not be used for elections by secret ballot.

---

[37] *Report of the Special Committee on Methods and Procedures* . . . G.A.O.R.: 4th Sess., 1949, Suppl. No. 12 (A/937), Annex II; G.A.O.R.: 10th Sess., 1955, Annexes, Agenda item 51 (A/2977), paras. 55–70.

CHAPTER 8

THE ELECTION OF MEMBERS OF THE PRINCIPAL ORGANS

> [A] vote . . . in my opinion, should be by the ballot . . . which, in a great degree, prevents the ill effects of corruption, because if any of the delegates . . . could be so vile, false, and dishonourable as to be influenced by money, they have the advantage of taking their money that will give it them and of voting undiscovered to the interest of their principles and their own inclinations; as they that do understand the balloting box do very well know.
>
> WILLIAM PENN

THERE are, in addition to the General Assembly, five " principal organs " of the United Nations: the three Councils, the International Court of Justice and the Secretariat. The General Assembly is composed of all the Members of the Organization. The Assembly elects some members of the Security and Trusteeship Councils, all the members of the Economic and Social Council, and participates in the election of the Judges of the International Court. The Secretary-General of the Organization is " appointed by the General Assembly upon the recommendation of the Security Council," and the staff is appointed by the Secretary-General under regulations established by the General Assembly.[1]

In every case, the composition of a body is intimately related to its functions. It is useless to review election procedure as though it were an end in itself—though this may often seem to be the case to the candidates. All the same, I am concerned in this book with the procedure and practice of the General Assembly and not with the activities of those organs some or all of whose members are elected by the Assembly. I do not intend, therefore, to discuss the functions of United Nations organs except to the extent that these have a direct bearing on the Assembly's electoral responsibilities.

THE SECURITY COUNCIL

The Assembly fills six seats on the Security Council by election. Members are elected for terms of two years, three elected members retiring each year; and retiring members are not eligible for

[1] Articles 7, 23, 61, 86, 97 and 101 of the Charter, and Articles 4, 8, 10–12 and 14 of the Statute of the Court.

163

immediate re-election. The non-elective seats are held by the five permanent members: the Republic of China, France, the Soviet Union, the United Kingdom and the United States (Article 23). The election of non-permanent members of the Security Council is one of the important questions for which a two-thirds majority of the Members present and voting is required (Article 18).

The importance of the Security Council hardly needs stressing. Member States have, in the Charter, specifically conferred on the Council primary responsibility for the maintenance of international peace and security (Article 24). Moreover, Member States have agreed to accept and carry out the Council's decisions (Article 25).

The Charter lays down principles that should govern the election of non-permanent members of the Council:

due regard being specially paid, in the first instance to the contribution of Members of the United Nations to the maintenance of international peace and security and to the other purposes of the Organization, and also to equitable geographical distribution.[2]

The history of this part of Article 23 of the Charter is of some interest. The British delegate at Dumbarton Oaks had suggested that the Charter should specify that in the election of non-permanent members of the Security Council, due regard should be paid to the military contributions of States to the maintenance of international peace and security. Both the United States and the Soviet Union had reservations about the proposal in this form, and the British delegate therefore suggested the omission of " military." It seemed for a time that this revised formula might be acceptable, but it was withdrawn when the Soviet delegate stated that he would accept it on the understanding that it would apply to all sixteen Soviet republics, which at that time were being sponsored by the U.S.S.R. as potential Members of the Organization.[3]

The idea of linking the election of non-permanent members of the Council to contributions to peace and security was revived at San Francisco, though " military " was left out. Britain suggested adding " equitable geographical distribution " as another criterion, and the phrase " contribution . . . to the other purposes of the Organization " was inserted because of the difficulties the League of Nations had experienced in collecting financial contributions.[4]

During the first session of the Assembly, the following five States received more than the required two-thirds majority on the first ballot: Brazil, Egypt, Mexico, the Netherlands and Poland; Australia and

[2] Article 23 (1).
[3] Ruth B. Russell, assisted by Jeannette E. Muther, *A History of the United Nations Charter* (Washington: Brookings Institution, London: Faber, 1958), p. 444.
[4] *Ibid.*, pp. 648–649.

Canada were runners-up. Australia withdrew after the third ballot, and Canada was accordingly elected.[5] The pattern of election at the first session was thus as follows:

Latin America	2
Middle East	1
Eastern Europe	1
Western Europe	1
Commonwealth	1

This pattern was not fortuitous, since it was based on an informal understanding between the Council's five permanent members.

TABLE 17

Distribution of Non-permanent Seats on the Security Council, 1946–60

	Latin America	Asia and Africa	Eastern Europe	Western, Northern & Southern Europe	"Older" Common-wealth States
1946	Brazil Mexico	Egypt	Poland	Netherlands	Australia
1947	Brazil Colombia	Syria	Poland	Belgium	Australia
1948	Argentina Colombia	Syria	Ukraine	Belgium	Canada
1949	Argentina Cuba	Egypt	Ukraine	Norway	Canada
1950	Cuba Ecuador	Egypt India	Yugoslavia	Norway	
1951	Brazil Ecuador	India	Yugoslavia	Netherlands Turkey	
1952	Brazil Chile	Pakistan		Greece Netherlands Turkey	
1953	Chile Colombia	Lebanon Pakistan		Denmark Greece	
1954	Brazil Colombia	Lebanon		Denmark Turkey	New Zealand
1955	Brazil Peru	Iran	Yugoslavia (resigned)	Belgium Turkey	New Zealand
1956	Cuba Peru	Iran		Belgium	Australia
1957	Colombia Cuba	Iraq Philippines		Sweden	Australia
1958	Colombia Panama	Iraq Japan		Sweden	Canada
1959	Argentina Panama	Japan Tunisia		Italy	Canada
1960	Argentina Ecuador	Tunisia Ceylon	Poland	Italy	

Table 17 shows the distribution of non-permanent seats on the Security Council since the Organization was founded. It will be seen

[5] G.A.O.R.: 1st Sess., Pt. I, 4th and 5th Plenary Mtgs., 12 Jan. 1946.

that there have always been two non-permanent members from Latin America, at least one from Western Europe, and one from the Commonwealth, the latter seat being held by Asian Commonwealth States in 1950–53 and again in 1960. The Middle East has been continuously represented if the area is regarded as including Turkey and Tunisia. Eastern Europe has been represented for half of the period, but for three years by a State which had parted company with the Soviet *Bloc* in 1948.

The dispute about Eastern European membership of the Security Council has been one of the most unpleasant controversies with which the United Nations has been plagued. If Eastern Europe is regarded as consisting of the States of the Soviet *Bloc* together with Yugoslavia, and if the Byelorussian and Ukrainian Republics are regarded for this purpose as being States in no way different from other Members of the United Nations, then a strict application of the principle of equitable geographical distribution without reference to other considerations would entitle Eastern Europe to a seat on the Council most years, but not every year. The Soviet complaint, however, has been based not so much on the Charter as on the informal understanding reached in 1946 by the Council's five permanent members. The Soviet Union maintains that the five permanent members of the Security Council

undertook to support the election to the Council of candidates nominated by the countries of the five main regions of the world. In accordance with that plan it was agreed that in the election of non-permanent members support would be given to two countries from the Latin-American region . . . while one seat would be allotted to the British Commonwealth, one to the Middle East, one to Western Europe, and one to Eastern Europe.[6]

The United States, for its part, maintains that the 1946 agreement was intended to apply to the first election; that the only factors now to be taken into account in connection with the elections are those specified in Article 23 (1) of the Charter; that the States of the Soviet *Bloc* have not contributed to the maintenance of international peace and security; and that the principle of equitable geographical distribution has usually been maintained by the election of Eastern European States not belonging to the Soviet *Bloc* (Greece, Turkey and Yugoslavia). Underneath these legal arguments has been the wish to have the Security Council so constituted that there are always seven members which can be relied upon to stand together in the case of threats to the peace and which, should the Security Council be unable to act because of the veto, would vote in favour of an

---

[6] G.A.O.R.: 8th Sess., 450th Plenary Mtg., 5 Oct. 1953, para. 19, p. 219.

emergency special session of the Assembly under the " Uniting for Peace " resolution.

It should be emphasized that some States which were not parties to the 1946 understanding have not felt bound by it. The Indian representative made this point during the second session (1947), after having withdrawn from the contest to permit the election of the Ukraine to the Council:

> We have been told that the allocation of seats on the Security Council is based on some arrangement privately arrived at among some of the Powers. But the distribution of Council seats by secret diplomacy to which the members of the General Assembly are not a party cannot, I am sure, find any support in this august body.
>
> Without in any way desiring to offend any of the Powers concerned, the delegation of India must challenge this arrangement.
>
> Our withdrawal should not be taken to mean, nor does it imply, that we accept the so-called agreement between certain Powers for the distribution of seats.[7]

It is, perhaps, now fruitless to invoke the 1946 agreement. The main questions are essentially political in character, and are as follows:

(1) Does the strict application of Article 23 (1) mean that Eastern Europe should have one non-permanent seat on the Security Council?

(2) Which States, for this purpose, are East European?

(3) Should the East European seat go to a State favoured by a majority of Member States in the East European area, or should the Assembly have unfettered freedom of choice in the matter?

(4) Could the problem be eliminated by increasing the number of non-permanent members of the Council?

I would like to deal with the last point first. I have suggested elsewhere that much can be done to improve the working of the United Nations without revising the Charter. I am not opposed to Charter revision as such, but I have been struck by the tendency to blame the Charter for the failure of Member States to make better use of the Organization, and to imply or assert that if only the Soviet *Bloc* would abandon its opposition to reviewing or revising the Charter, all would be well.

In this book I do not advocate any changes in the Charter (though I happen to favour some). As regards a possible revision of Article 23 so as to increase the number of permanent or non-permanent members of the Security Council, which would necessarily mean a

[7] G.A.O.R.: 2nd Sess., 109th Plenary Mtg., 13 Nov. 1947, p. 750.

consequential revision of Article 27 relating to voting and the veto, I would merely suggest that no increase in numbers is likely to eliminate controversy concerning the distribution of the seats of non-permanent members.

As regards the application of Article 23 (1) to elections, there are inevitably difficulties in defining or applying such a subjective criterion as " the contribution of Members." It would, from every point of view, be undesirable to elect to the Security Council a State which had recently been condemned by the Assembly for some action or policy that threatened world peace and security or, in some other way, seemed to conflict with the purposes of the Organization. But this surely does not mean that any State or group of States should be permanently blackballed.

A strict application of "equitable geographical distribution" would now mean frequent, though not continuous, representation of Eastern Europe. If Eastern Europe is regarded as consisting of the nine Soviet *Bloc* Member States, together with Yugoslavia, then the area would be entitled to representation roughly four years out of every six. But let me emphasize again that this is on the basis of " equitable geographical distribution" only, and that the Charter states that in elections to the Security Council " due regard " shall be " specially paid, in the first instance to the contribution of Members. . . ."

The Soviet answer to the question whether the Assembly should necessarily endorse the nomination of a regional group, or whether it should exercise unfettered freedom of choice, is unequivocal: the Assembly, in the Soviet view, should ratify choices already made informally and privately by the regional groups.

I have suggested in Chapter 2 that this principle is inadmissible. Indeed, in the case of the Security Council, the Charter does not refer to equitable geographical *representation* but equitable geographical *distribution*. The representative principle is not mentioned in the Charter. Member States are free to vote as they choose, and the use of a secret ballot is one guarantee of freedom of choice. It may be politically desirable to vote for the candidate favoured by the majority of Member States in some region, but it is in no way mandatory.

The Charter requirement that a two-thirds majority of the Members present and voting is required for the election of non-permanent members of the Security Council means that, if a seat is contested, balloting can be a tedious and lengthy process. Indeed, a determined minority of one-third of the Members plus one has the power to compel the Assembly to engage in inconclusive ballots for an indefinite period and, in the case of extreme intransigence, might render the Security Council ineffective.

During the second session (1947) there were eleven inconclusive ballots for one of the seats before India withdrew in favour of the Ukrainian S.S.R. There were thirteen inconclusive ballots during the fifth session (1950) before Lebanon withdrew in favour of Turkey. It was not until the nineteenth ballot during the sixth session (1951) that Greece received a two-thirds majority. It was during the tenth and fourteenth sessions, however, that the most acute difficulties developed.

During the tenth session balloting began on 14 October. On the first ballot, thirty-nine votes were needed for election, and Cuba and Australia obtained the required majority; Poland and the Philippines had thirty-four and thirty-three votes respectively. After four ballots, Poland withdrew in the hope that Yugoslavia might be acceptable as a compromise candidate. Twenty-five further inconclusive ballots were held, with Yugoslavia varying between twenty-three and twenty-eight votes and the Philippines varying between twenty-five and thirty-three votes; on all these ballots, except the nineteenth, the Philippines was in the lead, but was always at least seven votes short of the required two-thirds majority.

After the twenty-ninth inconclusive ballot had taken place on 6 December, the President of the Assembly drew the attention of hungry delegates to the serious situation.

If no agreement is reached, I for my part am ready to assist the Assembly [the verb was nicely chosen] in reaching a decision by calling a meeting which would not rise until the vacant seat has been filled. . . .[8]

The session was due to close on 10 December, but, two days before this, the closing date was changed to 16 December. The admission of sixteen new Member States on 14 December introduced a new element into balloting for the Security Council. For the next five ballots, which were held on the morning of 16 December, the required two-thirds majority of Members present and voting fluctuated between forty-four and forty-six. On the thirty-second ballot, the Philippines obtained forty votes, its highest vote, but still six short of two-thirds.

At 9 o'clock on the evening of 16 December (the revised date for the closing of the session), after all other business of the session had been disposed of, the Assembly returned to the election. Thirty-four ballots had been taken without the eleventh seat on the Security Council being filled. The President announced that there had been

[8] G.A.O.R.: 10th Sess., 551st Plenary Mtg., 6 Dec. 1955, para. 64, p. 407.

consultations with a number of delegations, including the two rivals for the Security Council seat, with the object of finding an acceptable solution.

It was felt that this purpose would be achieved if lots were drawn in the President's office between the two candidates I have already mentioned to decide which should withdraw from the present elections. After completing the first year of the term, the other candidate would offer its resignation from the Security Council. The agreement is that the vacant seat would then be filled for the remainder of the term by the election of the other candidate at the eleventh session.

The spirit of this compromise solution, for which I do not hesitate to assume a moral responsibility that will certainly be shared by the other representatives, must ensure that the agreement will be faithfully observed.

In accordance with the procedure I have outlined, lots were drawn in the President's office; as a result, the Philippines has withdrawn its candidature at this time in favour of Yugoslavia.

I am sure that the Assembly, in approving this procedure, will recognize that it does not set a precedent and will further agree that, in view of the unusual circumstances, the arrangement should be accepted and carried out.[9]

Following the President's statement, several representatives mounted the rostrum to express reservations about the procedure which had been outlined. A few stated flatly that it was illegal; others announced that they had no instructions in connection with such a new and unexpected development; others expressly stated that they could not at that time commit their governments regarding the future, and in particular regarding how they would vote in 1956 if Yugoslavia should resign the seat after one year. After an inconclusive debate, the Philippines suggested that a further ballot be held. This time Yugoslavia received thirty-four votes and the Philippines nineteen (forty votes required for election). The President thereupon declared that he released the two parties from the agreement. The Assembly, having at 10.30 p.m. rejected a motion to suspend the meeting and resume it one hour later, decided to extend the session until 20 December.[10]

On the morning of 20 December the Assembly returned to the question, and on the thirty-sixth ballot Yugoslavia received forty-three votes, five more than the required majority. The three-month session closed, as is the custom, with one minute of silent prayer or meditation.

Having served on the Council during 1956, Yugoslavia informed the Secretary-General that she would not be in a position to serve on

9 *Ibid.*, 559th Plenary Mtg., 16 Dec. 1955, paras. 197–201, pp. 494–495.
10 *Ibid.*, paras. 271, 301–302, pp. 499–500.

the Council in 1957.[11] A by-election to fill the vacancy was therefore held in accordance with Rule 141, and the Philippines was elected on the first ballot, obtaining one vote more than the required majority. Following the election, the Soviet representative stated that there had been a flagrant violation of the rights of the Eastern European Members. He referred to the informal agreement of 1946 and said that the decision just reached illustrated the fact that the United Nations was dwindling in importance.[12]

A similar situation developed during the fourteenth session (1959). The terms of office of Canada, Japan and Panama were due to expire at the end of 1959. After a certain amount of preliminary manœuvring, it was agreed informally that Ceylon and Ecuador should succeed Canada and Panama respectively, and the two first-named States were duly elected on the first ballot. Poland and Turkey were both candidates for the other seat.

Poland's candidature was announced in July, though for some months before that Polish diplomats in New York and elsewhere had been preparing the ground. Poland had the virtually unwavering support of the East European Members, seven West European States, about ten members of the Afro-Asian Group, six or seven Latin American States, and two of the older Commonwealth countries.[13]

At one time it seemed likely that Greece would be Poland's rival for the seat, but at the last moment Greece withdrew and Turkey was substituted. It was the view of Turkey's supporters that the seat for which she was a candidate should, if possible, be filled by an Eastern European country. One difficulty was that Turkey had, for a time in 1959, been a candidate for one of the vice-presidencies of the Assembly reserved for " Western European and other States " but at the last moment had switched her candidature to one of the Afro-Asian vacancies. By contesting an East European vacancy on the Security Council, Turkey was in effect claiming to belong to three different regions at once. The announcement of Turkey's candidature was not made until after the session had begun, and this meant that some States which might have supported her had already made certain commitments to Poland. Turkey apparently had the virtually unwavering support of fifteen States belonging to NATO, SEATO or CENTO, eleven States of Latin America and seven other Members with close associations with the United States.

---

[11] *Cf.* G.A.O.R.: 11th Sess., Annexes, 1956–57, Agenda item 68 (A/3332).
[12] *Ibid.*, 612th Plenary Mtg., 7 Dec. 1956, paras. 18–22, pp. 584–585.
[13] As the ballots were secret, I have made the best guesses I could on the basis of the information available to me.

Fifty-two ballots were needed to resolve the question. The two-thirds majority required for election varied between fifty and fifty-four votes, with the result that a State which could get at least twenty-nine votes on every ballot could prevent any other State from being elected. In the event, Poland's vote never fell below thirty-six, and —until the last ballot—Turkey's vote never fell below thirty-three. To put it another way, Poland's highest vote was six short of the necessary majority, and Turkey's highest vote was ten short of the necessary majority. About a dozen States were " floating " voters, but even if all these had " floated " in the same direction on any single ballot, this would still not have given either candidate the required majority. The results of the balloting are given in Chart 3.

The motives that influenced the voting can only be guessed at. The ten Eastern European States supported Poland for obvious reasons. Those Afro-Asian neutrals and the West European States which supported Poland probably did so because they believed that the election of Poland would give the Security Council a more representative character than the election of Turkey. The Latin American supporters of Poland doubtless felt that to adhere firmly to the 1946 agreement might help to ensure that Latin America always had two places on the Council.

The motives of Turkey's supporters were presumably less mixed. The overriding consideration was to constitute the Security Council in such a way that a pro-Western majority could, so far as possible, be relied on.

Balloting began on 12 October. Thirty-one ballots were held during that month, twelve more during November and six more on 1 December. The Assembly was due to close on 5 December, though the closing date was eventually changed to 12 December. During October and the first half of November, there seemed to be little serious talk of a compromise. Steadily, as the session progressed, the word " compromise " was heard more frequently. It seems likely that several of Poland's supporters took the position that they could not persist with their support if this meant that the Assembly would be unable to discharge its responsibilities.

Turkey had let it be known in mid-November that she would consider " splitting the term " with Poland, and discussions about this were entered into during the last few days of the session. Even if agreement could be reached on this, it still remained to be settled which of the two would be elected in 1959 and serve the first year, what guarantees there would be that this country would resign at the end of 1960, what guarantees there would be that the other country would be elected during the fifteenth session to serve during 1961,

CHART 3

BALLOTING FOR ELECTION OF NON–PERMANENT MEMBERS OF THE SECURITY COUNCIL, FOURTEENTH SESSION

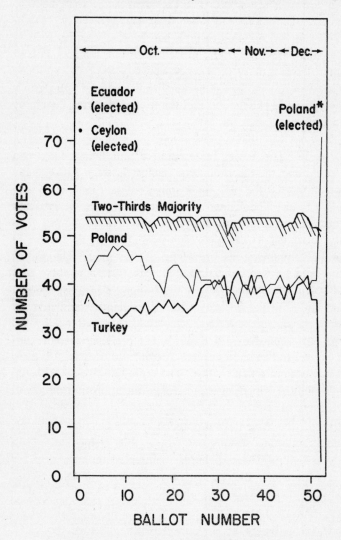

*It is understood that Poland will resign at the end of 1960 and that Turkey will be the only candidate for the vacancy.

whether any of the arrangements should be linked with any other question, and what implications the arrangements would have for the elections after 1961.

At the night meeting at the end of the session, 12/13 December, the Assembly was able to endorse an agreement which had been negotiated in private discussions. The President stated that, because of the impasse, consultations had taken place between the two candidates and their supporters. As a result it had been agreed that Poland was the only candidate during the fourteenth session, but that Poland would resign at the end of 1960. Turkey would be the only candidate during the fifteenth session for the vacancy thus created. " In participating in the vote, it is understood that the Members of the Assembly will confirm such an agreement." [14]

Before the vote was taken, several not entirely consistent statements were made. The Soviet representative said that the election of Poland would end the discrimination against Eastern Europe; the Soviet Union supported the plan for a split term as a temporary way out of the situation. The United States representative denied that there had been any discrimination against any area or nation. The United States intended to examine each candidacy in the future in the light of the circumstances prevailing at the time. The Polish representative said he was convinced that there was agreement that there would not, in the future, be any discrimination against Eastern Europe in elections to the Security Council. Poland would give an assurance that, should she be elected, she would resign after one year. The Turkish representative said that his country's agreement with Poland did not extend to the question of principle involved: Turkey maintained its position in that matter. The representatives of Canada, Brazil and the United Kingdom expressed gratification that the deadlock had been ended.[15]

At 2.30 a.m., the Assembly proceeded to the election by secret ballot, Poland obtaining seventy-one votes, thus being elected on the fifty-second ballot. Three diehards maintained their support for Turkey, and Greece and the Yemen obtained one vote each. Four Members abstained, and two were absent.

It is apparent from the public statements which preceded the ballot in 1959 that there still seems to be some disagreement about the distribution of non-permanent seats on the Security Council. With

[14] United Nations Doc. A/PV.857, 12 Dec. 1959, pp. 141–142.
[15] *Ibid.*, pp. 148–155.

only six seats to be shared among those Member States which are not permanent members of the Security Council, some inequities are inevitable, even if the only factor taken into account is equitable geographical distribution. Latin America has always had one-third of the elective places, and this was reasonable during the first ten years. With the large increase in the membership of the United Nations in December 1955 and since, and assuming the Security Council is not enlarged by amending the Charter, it seems inevitable that pressure will mount to give Latin America one rather than two seats occasionally. Western, Northern and Southern Europe will no doubt continue to have one non-permanent seat, in addition to the two permanent Western European members of the Council. The Middle East will presumably continue to have one seat, and the Commonwealth seat will probably go half of the time to one of the Commonwealth States in Asia and Africa. This would mean that the States of Africa and Asia which are neither Middle Eastern nor members of the Commonwealth [16] could be represented fairly continuously, and still leave a seat for Eastern Europe roughly two years out of every three.

I admit that I have been juggling with figures rather than States, and that every group (with the possible exception of the Middle East) would regard such a distribution of seats as inequitable. In any case, the admission to the Organization of more African States will add to the difficulties of paying due regard to equitable geographical distribution in filling the six elective places.

THE ECONOMIC AND SOCIAL COUNCIL

Acute difficulties have not hitherto arisen in connection with the election of members of the Economic and Social Council. The Council consists of eighteen members elected for three-year terms. A retiring member is eligible for immediate re-election (Article 61). Elections to the Council are among the important questions for which a two-thirds majority vote of Members of the Assembly present and voting is required (Article 18). No criteria are laid down for the selection of members or the distribution of seats.

The five permanent members of the Security Council have been continuously re-elected to the Economic and Social Council, and have also been members of most of the Council's subsidiary organs. The distribution of seats has, since 1953, been as follows:

[16] Afghanistan, Burma, Cambodia, Ethiopia, Guinea, Indonesia, Japan, Laos, Liberia, Nepal, the Philippines and Thailand.

Latin America	4
Asia and Africa	4
Eastern Europe	3
Western, Northern and	
Southern Europe	5
Older Commonwealth States	1
United States	1

For the period 1946–59, with the exception of one year—1948—at least one Asian member of the Commonwealth has had a seat on the Council, in addition to the United Kingdom and at least one of the older Commonwealth States. In the election during the fourteenth session India and Japan were both candidates for the seat being vacated by Pakistan. After six inconclusive ballots in which Japan led, the Indian representative stated that as Japan had consistently obtained a simple majority of votes, and in order to establish a good practice and a good convention, India would withdraw.[17] Japan was accordingly elected on the seventh ballot, thus reducing the Commonwealth representation to two.

From the very first session of the Assembly, there has been pressure to increase the size of the Economic and Social Council. This would, of course, be possible only by amending Article 61 of the Charter. It has been argued that an increase in the number of the members would make it possible for the Council to be more representative of the whole membership of the United Nations, which in turn would improve the effectiveness of the Council and the quality of its work. Pressure for such an increase has mounted since the admission to the United Nations of sixteen new Members in 1955. A resolution in support of an increase in the membership of the Council was adopted by the Council in July 1958, and by the Assembly during the thirteenth and fourteenth sessions (1958 and 1959). The Soviet *Bloc* has opposed any increase, but the opposition has not been related to the merits of the proposals but has been part of a general opposition to any amendment to the Charter so long as the present representation of China continues. Most, if not all, of the countries abstaining in the Assembly in 1958 and 1959 favoured an increase in the size of the Council but were doubtful about the wisdom or utility of adopting the resolution in the face of Soviet opposition.

I question whether the Council has in reality been as unrepresentative as is sometimes implied by speakers in the Assembly. If it is assumed that the five permanent members of the Security Council should be continuously re-elected, and that in filling the remaining thirteen places account should be taken of such factors as fair regional

17 United Nations Doc. A/PV. 826, 12 Oct. 1959, p. 15.

TABLE 18

Distribution of Seats on the Economic and Social Council, 1946–60

	Latin America	*Asia and Africa**	*Eastern Europe*	*Western, Northern and Southern Europe*	*Older Commonwealth States*	*United States*
1946	Chile Colombia Cuba Peru	China India Lebanon	Czechoslovakia Ukraine U.S.S.R. Yugoslavia	Belgium (resigned) France Greece Norway United Kingdom	Canada	United States
1947	Chile Cuba Peru Venezuela	China India Lebanon	Byelorussia Czechoslovakia U.S.S.R.	France Netherlands Norway Turkey United Kingdom	Canada New Zealand	United States
1948	Brazil Chile Peru Venezuela	China Lebanon	Byelorussia Poland U.S.S.R.	Denmark France Netherlands Turkey United Kingdom	Australia Canada New Zealand	United States
1949	Brazil Chile Peru Venezuela	China India Lebanon	Byelorussia Poland U.S.S.R.	Belgium Denmark France Turkey United Kingdom	Australia New Zealand	United States
1950	Brazil Chile Mexico Peru	China India Iran Pakistan	Czechoslovakia Poland U.S.S.R.	Belgium Denmark France United Kingdom	Australia Canada	United States

TABLE 18—*continued*

Distribution of Seats on the Economic and Social Council, 1946–60 (Continued)

	Latin America	Asia and Africa*	Eastern Europe	Western, Northern and Southern Europe	Older Commonwealth States	United States
1951	Chile Mexico Peru Uruguay	China India Iran Pakistan Philippines	Czechoslovakia Poland U.S.S.R.	Belgium France Sweden United Kingdom	Canada	United States
1952	Argentina Cuba Mexico Uruguay	China Egypt Iran Pakistan Philippines	Czechoslovakia Poland U.S.S.R.	Belgium France Sweden United Kingdom	Canada	United States
1953	Argentina Cuba Uruguay Venezuela	China Egypt India Philippines	Poland U.S.S.R. Yugoslavia	Belgium France Sweden Turkey United Kingdom	Australia	United States
1954	Argentina Cuba Ecuador Venezuela	China Egypt India Pakistan	Czechoslovakia U.S.S.R. Yugoslavia	Belgium France Norway Turkey United Kingdom	Australia	United States
1955	Argentina Dominican Rep. Ecuador Venezuela	China Egypt India Pakistan	Czechoslovakia U.S.S.R. Yugoslavia	France Turkey Netherlands Norway United Kingdom	Australia	United States

Year						
1956	Argentina Brazil Dominican Rep. Ecuador	China Egypt Indonesia Pakistan	Czechoslovakia U.S.S.R. Yugoslavia	France Greece Netherlands Norway United Kingdom	Canada	United States
1957	Argentina Brazil Dominican Rep. Mexico	China Egypt Indonesia Pakistan	Poland U.S.S.R. Yugoslavia	Finland France Greece Netherlands United Kingdom	Canada	United States
1958	Brazil Chile Costa Rica Mexico	China Indonesia Pakistan Sudan	Poland U.S.S.R. Yugoslavia	Finland France Greece Netherlands United Kingdom	Canada	United States
1959	Chile Costa Rica Mexico Venezuela	Afghanistan China Pakistan Sudan	Bulgaria Poland U.S.S.R.	Finland France Netherlands Spain United Kingdom	New Zealand	United States
1960	Brazil Chile Costa Rica Venezuela	Afghanistan China Japan Sudan	Bulgaria Poland U.S.S.R.	Denmark France Netherlands Spain United Kingdom	New Zealand	United States

* Nationalist China, though not a member of the Afro-Asian Group, is included in this table as part of the area "Asia and Africa."

representation and the contribution of States to the regular activities and extra-budgetary programmes for which the Economic and Social Council has general responsibility, the present composition may be regarded as reasonable. It is true that if equitable geographical distribution were the only factor that should be taken into account, then every regional group except Africa and Asia has been over-represented. Furthermore, one of the four members of the Council from Afro-Asia has been Nationalist China, which is not a member of the Afro-Asian Group. But equitable geographical distribution has not been, and should not be, the sole factor of which account is taken. Moreover, it does not follow that a Council which does not mirror the whole membership with precision is necessarily less effective than it need be, though this might be inferred from the Council's own resolution of 31 July 1958.[18] The operative part of the resolution expresses the view that " an increase in the membership of the Council would provide a more effective organ for carrying out the obligations placed upon the Council," and invited the Assembly to give favourable consideration to an increase in the membership of the Council. The Assembly's resolution of 1958 is even more explicit in that it asserts that an increase in membership " is desirable in order to achieve a wider representation." [19]

The fact remains, however, that many Member States believe that it is the inadequate representation of the underdeveloped countries, especially those of Asia and Africa, that has accounted for the Council's problems. I question whether this is the main or even an important source of difficulty. Certainly the record of the Council does not suggest that the Council has been indifferent to the needs and problems of the less-developed countries.

I also question whether schemes to increase the participation of Member States in the work of the Council's functional commissions are directed to the main problem. The President of the Council's twenty-eighth session stated that most of the new Members of the United Nations were anxious to participate in the Council's activities, and that to satisfy this demand the functional commissions should be increased in size and means devised to prevent the continuous re-election of a small number of States.[20] The difficulty is that technical bodies concerned with such matters as transport and population problems cannot do their work properly if they are unduly large and if some of their members lack the necessary expertise. A change in

18 Economic and Social Council Res. 690B (XXVI).
19 General Assembly Res. 1300 (XIII), 10 Dec. 1958.
20 Economic and Social Council Official Records (ECOSOC, O.R.): 28th Sess., 1089th Mtg., 31 July 1959, paras. 36–40, pp. 162–163.

the size or composition of a technical organ inevitably affects its procedures and functions.

The real problem, it seems to me, is that the Council has wavered between divergent conceptions of its own role and functions. At times it has aspired to become a periodic " summit " conference on major economic and social questions; at other times it has sought to be a body concerned primarily with reviewing and co-ordinating the activities of the specialized agencies and its own functional and regional commissions; at still other times it has been content to be a debating club, passing resolutions of a general character. Because the growth of economic regionalism has led to the creation of organs of regional economic co-operation (both within the framework of the United Nations and outside it), and because the General Assembly provides an attractive forum for major policy initiatives in the economic and social field, the Economic and Social Council has increasingly tended to become a procedural body concerned with the review and co-ordination of programmes of work. It is true that the Council often prepares the ground for action by the Assembly, and has recently embarked on a five-year appraisal of programmes of the United Nations and related agencies in the economic, social and human rights fields.[21] This has not, however, changed the basic nature of the Council; nor has it prevented the Assembly from taking the initiative in matters that lie within the Council's field of responsibility. This is undesirable, since in a body with eighty-two or more members, there is nearly always a tendency for propaganda considerations to assume undue importance. Complicated technical matters in the economic and social field are best dealt with in an expert body of limited membership.

Steps that might be taken to reinvigorate the Council itself lie outside the scope of this book, except in so far as procedural action by the Assembly would help. If the main problem is, as it is thought by many to be, that wider participation in the work of the Council is desirable, two alternative possibilities that do not involve amendments to the Charter may be envisaged.

In the first place, the Charter provides that members of the Economic and Social Council serve for three-year terms (as do the elected members of the Trusteeship Council), compared with two-year terms for the non-permanent members of the Security Council. It might be possible to develop a convention that some of the members elected to the Economic and Social Council, other than the five permanent members of the Security Council, would resign

[21] General Assembly Res. 1094 (XI), 27 Feb. 1957; Economic and Social Council Res. 665C (XXIV), 1 Aug. 1957 and Res. 694D (XXVI), 31 July 1958.

after two years in favour of other States from the same regions. This would not change the distribution of places on the Council but would increase the speed of rotation of seats.

A second possibility would be based on Article 69 of the Charter and Rules 75 and 76 of the Council's Rules of Procedure. These provisions empower the Council to invite a Member of the United Nations which is not a member of the Council to participate in the Council's deliberations. Such a Member may take part in debate and submit proposals, but does not have the right to vote. In accordance with these provisions, the Assembly might designate a number of States not elected to the Council as " Consulting Members," which would participate regularly in the business of the Council. If there were six such " Consulting Members," they might be distributed as follows:

Latin America	1
Asia and Africa	3
Eastern Europe	1
Western, Northern and Southern Europe	1

Such an arrangement, like the one examined earlier, would not alter the voting situation in the Council; the less-developed countries of Asia and Africa might still continue to regard the Assembly as a more advantageous forum for debate and decision than the Council. Nevertheless, it might help in some degree, since the less-developed countries would feel that their problems and needs would have fuller expression in the Council before decisions were taken.

A third and rather different possibility would be to accept the likelihood that the Council will continue to devote its main attention to programmes of work rather than major problems of policy, and to initiate some new means of consultation and co-operation on important economic and social questions, supplementing the machinery already in existence. Action along these lines could be taken whether or not the Council were increased in size by Charter amendment, and whether or not other arrangements were devised to increase the participation of States in the work of the Council and its subsidiary organs.

At the twenty-eighth session of the Council held in Geneva in July 1959, a number of proposals for improving consultation on economic matters were made. The British and Dutch representatives, as well as the Secretary-General, expressed doubt as to whether the

Council had been living up to its responsibilities.[22] The Secretary-General suggested that the time had come for the United Nations to deal more directly with the formulation of international economic policies, or at least to serve in a more systematic way as a forum for the co-ordination of such policies. The Council, and perhaps the Assembly, might consider the possibility of arranging special meetings at, say, five-year intervals for the purpose of reviewing long-term economic questions.

The Secretary-General's ideas were developed further in the light of the debate and consultations in Geneva. At a Press conference on his return to New York, the Secretary-General said:

> There is a difficulty with United Nations procedures as they are at present in the sense that they tend to develop into what I might call routine. There are very many questions partly of a household nature which have to be tackled by, for example, the Economic and Social Council or the appropriate committee at the General Assembly, and it is difficult to get concentration on the key issues. . . . It is also difficult to organize the work in those permanent bodies in such a way as to make it possible for key people in governments to attend. They cannot spare too much time.
>
> The classical alternative is economic conferences on a large scale. I do not believe too much in that because they have their own weaknesses. There is something in between, namely to develop procedures around, for example, the Economic and Social Council, in such a way that there is a concentration on a few key problems or perhaps on one key problem.[23]

In the introduction to his annual report, the Secretary-General dealt with the matter somewhat more formally.

> I believe that short special meetings at the ministerial level, within or under the aegis of the Economic and Social Council, might make an invaluable contribution to the formulation of international economic policies adequate to vital requirements for concerted action. . . . It is my opinion that . . . efforts should now be made to add to the usefulness of the Economic and Social Council and to give to the United Nations, through this Council, better possibilities of playing a role of the same significance in the economic field as the one which is entrusted to it in the political sphere.[24]

A draft resolution, asking the Secretary-General to " study this question more fully and submit proposals to the Economic and Social Council in due course," was introduced by the Mexican representative in the Assembly's Third Committee during the fourteenth session (1959). After a short debate, the draft resolution was withdrawn, it being understood that the Rapporteur would include in his report an

---

22 ECOSOC, O.R.: 1069th Mtg., 6 July 1959, paras. 39–47; 1074th Mtg., 10 July 1959, paras. 13–17, 47–52.

23 Press conference by the Secretary-General at United Nations headquarters. Note to Correspondents No. 2015, 23 July 1959.

24 G.A.O.R.: 14th Sess., 1959, Suppl. No. 1A (A/4132/Add. 1), p. 3.

adequate account of the views which had been expressed, and that the records of the discussion would be transmitted to the Council.[25]

At the resumed twenty-eighth session of the Council held in December 1959, the Secretary-General reported that governments had expressed the view that any discussions of economic questions at the ministerial level should be kept as informal as possible and should be held in private whenever appropriate. Such discussions should not necessarily result in the adoption of resolutions or other formal action, their importance lying primarily in the influence they might exercise within governments and on later actions of the Council. Meetings at the ministerial level should be organized as part of the regular meetings of the Council itself, and the agenda should be so arranged that ministerial discussions could be concentrated within a few days. Such discussion should focus on major issues of economic policy, with special reference to the promotion of the economic development of less-developed countries, and on the better integration of the world economy. The documentation should include a summary of major events or policy decisions affecting the international economy, and the Secretary-General might highlight those problems or policy which, in his view, should receive the Council's attention.[26]

The proposals of the Secretary-General were welcomed by members of the Council, but several representatives considered that discussions at the ministerial level should be open to all States, whether or not they were members of the Council. The Council approved a resolution requesting the Secretary-General to proceed with arrangements for a meeting as suggested in his report, taking account of the views expressed at the resumed twenty-eighth session in December 1959.[27]

It seems clear that the success of the Secretary-General's proposal will depend to a considerable extent on advance preparation. Ministers of senior rank will attend only if they consider that the subjects to be discussed are of major and definite importance, and that discussion will get beyond the expression of pious generalities. Perhaps the ground should be prepared by advance visits of the Secretary-General or other senior officials of the Secretariat to some of the capitals.

THE TRUSTEESHIP COUNCIL

So fast has been the development of trust territories toward self-government or independence that a situation will arise in 1960 which seems not to have been foreseen by the founding fathers of the United

25 United Nations Docs. A/C. 3/SR. 941, 30 Oct. 1959, pp. 5–8; A/4250, 17 Nov. 1959, paras. 74–81.
26 United Nations Doc. E/3311, 2 Dec. 1959.
27 Economic and Social Council Res. 745 (XXVIII), 15 Dec. 1959.

Nations. The Trust Territories of the Cameroons and Togoland under French administration and of Somaliland under Italian administration ceased to be trust territories on 1 January 1960, 27 April 1960 and 1 July 1960 respectively. France, as a permanent member of the Security Council, remains a member of the Trusteeship Council; Italy's membership of the Trusteeship Council will, in the near future, come to an end. These changes have implications for the balance of membership of the Council which, according to the Charter, is divided equally between States which administer trust territories and States which do not administer such territories.

The idea of parity of representation in the Trusteeship Council originated in the United States Government. At the San Francisco Conference, the United States proposed that the Trusteeship Council should consist of " specially qualified representatives, designated (a) one each by the States administering trust territories; and (b) one each by an equal number of other States named for three-year periods by the General Assembly." [28] The Soviet Union, for its part, proposed that parity be applied in a different form, so that the Big Five would always be members of the Council. On one side would be representatives of States administering trust territories and of permanent members of the Security Council not administering such territories, balanced by an equal number of representatives of other States named by the General Assembly.[29]

In the light of the Soviet view that permanent members of the Security Council should also be permanent members of the Trusteeship Council, the original United States proposal was modified to provide for a Trusteeship Council in essentially the same form as was subsequently provided in the Charter as finally approved. This revised United States proposal led the delegate of Egypt to revive the earlier Soviet idea.

In favour of this proposal it was argued that the permanent members of the Security Council resembled the administering States in that they were interested parties, and that the peoples of the trust territories would be better protected if half the seats on the Trusteeship Council were held by elected members. To this, it was objected that there was no distinction in humanitarian purpose between the three categories . . . but only of practical experience, and that what was required on the Trusteeship Council was the greatest possible sum of knowledge and wisdom.[30]

The revised United States text was, however, adopted and later became Article 86 (1) of the Charter.

[28] *Documents of the United Nations Conference on International Organization* (New York and London: U.N. Information Orgs., 1945), Vol. III, p. 600.
[29] *Ibid.*, p. 619.
[30] *Ibid.*, Vol. X, pp. 516–517.

The theoretical possibility that the objectives of the trusteeship system might eventually be achieved in respect of some territories seems not to have been discussed at San Francisco. It was, however, raised by the British delegation to the Executive Committee of the Preparatory Commission of the United Nations the following September. In a memorandum on the composition of the Trusteeship Council, the United Kingdom pointed out that reductions in the number of members administering trust territories might occur, and would be of two kinds. If a permanent member of the Council should cease to be an administering State, it would displace two elected members. If a non-permanent member of the Council should cease to be an administering State, it would lose its seat on the Council unless subsequently elected by the Assembly as a non-administering member, and would displace one elected member. The decision which elected member should be displaced " would presumably lie with the General Assembly." [31]

The possibility raised by the British delegation seemed so remote in 1945 that it evidently evoked no discussion. Interest at that time was concentrated on getting the trusteeship system into effective operation, and there was no overt interest in such long-term problems as how the system might be dismantled as its objectives were progressively achieved. [32]

By the end of 1946, it became possible to constitute the Trusteeship Council. Australia, Belgium, France, New Zealand and the United Kingdom had submitted trusteeship agreements which had been approved by the Assembly, and they thus became Administering Authorities; China, the Soviet Union and the United States were members of the Council by virtue of their permanent membership of the Security Council; Mexico and Iraq were elected for a three-year term each to establish parity. After approval and ratification of the trusteeship agreement for the Pacific Islands under United States administration in 1947, the United States became an Administering Authority, and in order to restore the balance, Costa Rica and the Philippines were elected to membership of the Council during the second session of the Assembly. Italy, as Administering Authority for the Trust Territory of Somaliland, began to participate without vote in relevant proceedings of the Trusteeship Council in 1950. After the admission of Italy to the United Nations in December 1955, Burma was elected as an additional non-administering member in order to maintain the balance.

The principle of parity of membership between administering and

[31] Doc. PC/EX/TC/4, para. 5.
[32] Docs. PC/EX/TC/6, 8 and 9.

non-administering members has been observed in almost all of the Visiting Missions and other subsidiary organs of the Council.

In two cases, non-administering members have resigned from the Council before expiration of their terms of office. On each occasion, the Assembly has elected a member to fill the remainder of the term, though I question whether this practice conforms strictly to the letter of Article 86 of the Charter (" as many other Members elected for three-year terms ") or the Rule of Procedure of the Assembly based on that Article (now Rule 149). The elected members of the Council have comprised two Latin American States and two States from the Afro-Asian area for the period 1948–55, with a third member from the Afro-Asian area since 1956. No European State has been elected to membership of the Council. The elected members are listed in Table 19.

TABLE 19

Elected Members of the Trusteeship Council, 1947–60

Year*	Latin America		Asia and Africa		
1947	Mexico		Iraq		
1948	Mexico	Costa Rica	Iraq	Philippines	
1949	Mexico	Costa Rica (resigned)	Iraq	Philippines	
1950	Argentina	Dominican Republic	Iraq	Philippines	
1951	Argentina (resigned)	Dominican Republic	Iraq	Thailand	
1952	El Salvador	Dominican Republic	Iraq	Thailand	
1953	El Salvador	Dominican Republic	Syria	Thailand	
1954	El Salvador	Haiti	Syria	India	
1955	El Salvador	Haiti	Syria	India	
1956	Guatemala	Haiti	Syria	India	Burma
1957	Guatemala	Haiti	Syria	India	Burma
1958	Guatemala	Haiti	Syria	India	Burma
1959	Paraguay	Haiti	United Arab Republic	India	Burma
1960	Paraguay	Bolivia	United Arab Republic	India	Burma

* According to the Rules of Procedure of the General Assembly, the term of office of Members of the Council shall begin on 1 January following their election, except as provided in Rule 148: " When a Trusteeship Agreement has been approved and a Member of the United Nations has become an Administering Authority of a Trust Territory . . . the General Assembly shall proceed to such election or elections to the Trusteeship Council as may be necessary. . . . Members elected at any such election . . . shall take office immediately upon their election and shall complete their terms . . . as if they had begun their terms of office on 1 January following their election."

A possible reduction in the size of the Trusteeship Council now looms on the horizon. When elections to the Council took place during the thirteenth session of the Assembly (1958), the President stated that

in the foreseeable future . . . one of the Members ceases to be an Administering Authority and therefore ceases to be a member of the Council. This will occur in 1960. In the light of the elections which will take place today, it will be necessary for the General Assembly, at its next regular session, to consider the procedure to be followed in order that the . . . balance may be maintained after the number of Administering Authorities has been reduced.

There was no discussion of the President's statement, and the election of Paraguay, Burma and the United Arab Republic took place in the normal manner.[33]

The problem to which the President of the thirteenth session referred was a legal one but, like all legal problems, it had political implications. The legal aspect involved an interpretation of Article 86 of the Charter and the means by which elected members should be displaced if this should be necessary in order to maintain parity. The political aspect involved France's position on the Council, which until 1960 was that of a member administering trust territories.

France may maintain that whether a particular State sits on the Council as an administering member or a non-administering member is a technicality; the obligation on all members of the Council is to uphold the purposes and principles of the Charter. France, in the future as in the past, will be no less faithful to the Charter than any other Member of the United Nations. Moreover, the fact that the only two trust territories under French administration have become independent may be cited as evidence of France's devotion to the objectives of the trusteeship system.

As for the legal situation, the French representative outlined France's position in the following terms:

We have a disinterested attitude in this question since, in any event, we shall be a member of the Trusteeship Council. . . . Just as we have spoken in the Fourth Committee in defence of our rules of procedure, so have we always stood, in the Assembly and in other Committees, for the defence of the Charter, and there is no reason why we should not continue to do so when it comes to matters relating to the Trusteeship Council. . . .

We are accustomed not only to reply to questions, but to do so clearly and specifically. On 27 April 1960, France will no longer consider itself as an Administering Authority and will be a part of the Trusteeship Council because of being a permanent member of the Security Council and, therefore, will draw all the practical consequences from that new situation in its participation in the work of the Council.

---

[33] G.A.O.R.: 13th Sess., 775th Plenary Mtg., 8 Oct. 1958, paras. 13–20, pp. 376–377.

This position of principle being clearly stated, we have no preference regarding the solutions which might be considered by the Assembly.[34]

It is understandable that anti-colonial countries might look at the matter somewhat differently. They doubtless consider that whether a State sits on the Council as an administering or a non-administering authority is not a technicality; if it were, the Charter would not have provided for parity. France's record in the United Nations on trusteeship and related questions, according to this view, has demonstrated beyond all doubt that France takes a position in regard to those parts of the Charter concerning non-self-governing and trust territories that is different from that of the majority of Member States. The independence of Togoland and the Cameroons was achieved in large measure as a direct result of anti-colonial pressures within the United Nations.

Those who hold this view may believe that the Trusteeship Council can function effectively only if there is parity of point of view, rather than parity between administering and non-administering States. Parity of point of view cannot be guaranteed by any formal arrangement. Whatever the formal composition of the Council, the balance can be upset—for example, by the absence of a member. Indeed, the Soviet Union did not participate in several of the Council's early sessions.

Let me deal here with some of the legal aspects of the problem. The Cameroons and Togoland achieved independence on 1 January 1960 and 27 April 1960 respectively. It has been argued that, immediately France ceased to exercise administrative responsibilities, she should occupy a seat on the Trusteeship Council by virtue of being a permanent member of the Security Council rather than as a State administering trust territories. In order to maintain parity thereafter, the Assembly in 1959 could have done one of two things. The Assembly could have elected two members upon the expiry of the terms of office of Haiti and India, to serve during the period of about four months during which France would continue to exercise administering responsibilities. Such a procedure would not have accorded exactly with the letter of the Charter (" elected for three-year terms "), but there are precedents for elections for less than three-year terms. Alternatively, the Assembly could have decided on a procedure for displacing two of the five elected members at the end of April 1960, assuming that two members did not indicate the intention of retiring.

Two means of displacing elected members may be envisaged. In the first place, lots could be drawn. This method is prescribed in the

[34] United Nations Doc. A/PV.857, 12 Dec. 1959, pp. 93–96.

Assembly's Rules of Procedure in certain cases of equally divided votes in elections (Rules 95 and 133), and it was resorted to in 1955 in an attempt to break the deadlock over the Security Council election. It is, however, one thing to use this method if it is prescribed in the Rules or accepted by the candidates before an election takes place, and quite another thing to resort to it after valid elections have been held and without the express consent of the parties. Secondly, the Assembly might decide that all elected members should retire simultaneously, and a new election held to fill the proper number of vacancies.

Either of these methods of reducing the number of elected members is open to some objection. During discussion of this matter in 1959, the Indian representative, after informing the Assembly that India was a candidate for election, stated that " once a country is elected for a three-year period there is no provision . . . for premature termination of membership without consent. . . . The compulsive premature cessation or termination of membership would indeed infringe on the fundamental right of an elected member under the Charter." [35]

In any event, any procedure for reducing by two the number of elected members at the end of April 1960 would provide only an interim solution. On 1 July 1960, Somalia attained independence, and the question arose whether Italy and an elected member should leave the Council.[36] Should this happen, the Council would then be constituted as follows:

Administering members	*Non-administering members*	
Australia	China	Permanent members
Belgium	France	of the
New Zealand	U.S.S.R.	Security Council
United Kingdom	Two elected members	
United States		

As additional trust territories achieve self-government or independence, the size of the Council would contract still further. The trusteeship agreement for Western Samoa is likely to be terminated by the end of 1961 and at that time New Zealand will cease to exercise administering responsibilities. It is true that the trusteeship agreement for Nauru designates New Zealand, Australia and the United Kingdom jointly as " the Administering Authority," although Australia has administered the territory on behalf of the three governments. But Article 86 (1a) of the Charter refers to " Members

---

35 *Ibid.,* pp. 63–68.
36 It was anticipated that, contrary to normal practice, the Council would complete the work of its two sessions in 1960 before 1 July.

administering trust territories " and not to " Administering Authorities." If New Zealand leaves the Council at the end of 1961, the size of the Council would drop to eight members, of which only one would be elected by the Assembly. When the two African trust territories, Ruanda-Urundi and Tanganyika, have attained self-government or independence, the Trusteeship Council would be composed as follows:

Administering members	*Non-administering members*	
Australia (administering Nauru and New Guinea) United States (administering the Pacific Islands)	China France U.S.S.R. United Kingdom	Permanent members of the Security Council

At this stage, there will be no elected members of the Council and no way of constituting the Council on the basis of parity.

I should make it clear that what I have written above is based on an interpretation of the Charter which is not accepted by all Member States. There are those who maintain, in private if not in public, that the phrase in Article 86 " Members administering trust territories " means members who, at the time the Charter was signed, were administering territories which were subsequently placed under the international trusteeship system. According to this interpretation, all the members at present administering trust territories except Italy should be regarded as permanent members of the Trusteeship Council. I confess that I do not find this interpretation of the Charter wholly convincing.

Some Member States have, in any case, maintained that an administering member's responsibilities do not cease with the termination of a trusteeship agreement. This view was stated forcefully in the Assembly by the Indian representative.

It is also the view of my delegation that, though a trusteeship agreement may be terminated on a particular date, the obligations of the Administering Authority *vis-à-vis the* General Assembly and the Trusteeship Council need not and in fact will not in most cases terminate on the same date. Article 88 of the Charter makes it mandatory on the Administering Authority to submit annual reports to the General Assembly. These reports must necessarily be examined by the Trusteeship Council. For the consideration of these reports, the presence of the Administering Authority in the Council is necessary and even obligatory. In the present situation, the final report in respect of the French Cameroons and French Togoland and indeed of Italian Somaliland will not be submitted by the Administering Authority concerned until some time after these dates when the Administering Authority will be able to report definitively on the termination of trusteeship and the attainment of independence by the Territories, including the processes immediately preceding such independence. So far, the General Assembly has received the Administering Authority's reports on Togoland and the French

Cameroons and Italian Somaliland only up to 1958 and 1957 respectively. Further reports of the Administering Authority in respect of these three Territories up to the date of independence are called for under Article 88 of the Charter. We submit that such reports are indispensable, if only for the record and to conform to the requirements, legal and other, necessarily involved in the winding up of United Nations supervisory functions and of the trust undertaken by the Administering Authorities through the Trusteeship Council right up to the date of independence.

Therefore, it seems to us that there will really be no stretching of the Charter if the countries concerned stay on in the Council until the next session of the General Assembly.[37]

There are some Member States which, while not accepting either of these interpretations of the Charter, considered that the Assembly, during its fourteenth session in 1959, should not officially take cognizance of future developments but only of the situation existing at the time. Two seats on the Trusteeship Council were vacant and, in accordance with the Charter and the Rules of Procedure, the Assembly should proceed to elect two members for a period of three years. The administering responsibilities of France and Italy would cease during 1960, but France would continue as a member of the Council in virtue of permanent membership of the Security Council and Italy would remain until the expiration of the terms of office of the non-administering members elected in 1958. The future of the Trusteeship Council might be considered at the sixteenth session of the Assembly (1961), by which time the possibility of agreement on limited Charter amendment might be examined.

The informal discussions before and during the fourteenth session of the Assembly were concerned with political as well as legal aspects of the question. The general approach of the administering States was based on a wish to preserve the Trusteeship Council as an effective organ, and it seemed to be assumed that parity of point of view within the Council had been one of the reasons for the success of the trusteeship system. Neither the administering members nor the non-administering members have been able to force through the Council a decision which is unacceptable to the other " side." The fact that there have been two " sides," equal in voting strength, has induced an attitude of moderation, a search for the acceptable compromise. This has led to the further consequence that the Council has, by and large, adopted a technical rather than a political approach. It was, however, widely felt that parity of point of view

---

[37] United Nations Doc. A/PV.857, 12 Dec. 1959, pp. 71–72. In the case of Togoland under United Kingdom administration, no report was submitted to the Trusteeship Council by the Administering Authority after the territory had left the trusteeship system.

could be maintained only if France remained on the Council as one of the administering States.

Some of the anti-colonial countries also had reasons for wanting to prevent a steady diminution in the size of the Council. They saw the possibility that the number of elected members of the Council might drop from five to two during 1960, and to one before 1962. While the anti-colonial countries welcomed the rapid development of trust territories towards self-government or independence, they hoped that the Trusteeship Council would continue to have some elected members. This would be possible in the unlikely event that additional territories might be brought under the trusteeship system; or because a procedure had been agreed upon, either within the present Charter or after revision of the Charter, to keep the Council as it was constituted before France's administering responsibilities ceased.

There was a further consideration. If trusteeship questions were not dealt with effectively in an expert body of limited membership, they would be dealt with in the Fourth Committee of the General Assembly. In this eighty-two member body (soon to be increased in size still further), there would be the danger that the interests of the inhabitants of trust territories would be submerged in an ocean of propaganda and counter-propaganda. Everything possible should be done to maintain and increase the effectiveness of the Trusteeship Council. As the Assembly increases in size and its agenda becomes clogged with old and new business, it becomes more rather than less important to use to the full the other principal organs of the United Nations.

The provisional agenda of the fourteenth session (1959) included, in the normal way, an item entitled " Election of two members of the Trusteeship Council," to which was appended a footnote reading as follows:

Procedure to be devised in order to comply with the provisions of Article 86 of the Charter as France and Italy will cease to be Administer-ing Authorities in 1960. . . .[38]

This footnote was not included in the agenda recommended by the General Committee and approved by the plenary Assembly.[39]

The question raised in the footnote in the provisional agenda did not come formally before the Assembly until 9 p.m. on the final evening of the session. Consideration of the question was interrupted for about an hour in order to complete the election of members of the Security Council; except for this break, the matter occupied the attention of weary delegates until 4 a.m.

[38] United Nations Doc. A/4150, 17 July 1959, p. 2.
[39] United Nations Doc. A/4214, 17 Sept. 1959, p. 4.

B.   13

It was probably difficult, during a night meeting at the end of a busy three-month session, to give the matter the attention it deserved. Some representatives were familiar with the problem in all its ramifications, but others were apparently taken by surprise. The representative of Israel, for example, said that his delegation had had no opportunity to study the implications of what was being proposed.[40] The outcome of the debate did not represent a clear-cut decision but merely registered the fact that agreement was not possible.

There were, in effect, three proposals before the Assembly. The first was submitted by the Soviet Union in two different but similar versions. One would have decided to elect two members of the Trusteeship Council upon the expiry of the terms of office of Haiti and India, and to have resumed the fourteenth session of the Assembly on 28 April 1960 to decide on the composition of the Trusteeship Council thereafter; the other would have convened a special session of the Assembly on 28 April 1960.[41] The first Soviet proposal was not adopted as it failed to obtain the required two-thirds majority; the second Soviet proposal was rejected.

The second proposal was submitted by Tunisia and, in its revised form, consisted of three preambular and four operative paragraphs.[42] The Assembly approved by majorities of at least two-thirds of the Members present and voting the following paragraphs:

The General Assembly,

Guided by the provisions of Article 86 of the Charter of the United Nations,

Considering the desirability of studying the situation which would result both from the fact that it will soon be impossible to observe simultaneously the principles of parity and of the inclusion of the permanent members of the Security Council in the membership of the Trusteeship Council, and from the fact that the category of elected members whose role in the work of the Trusteeship Council has proved important will be eliminated in the very near future,

Decides [to] elect two members of the Trusteeship Council at the present session, in accordance with Article 86 of the Charter;

Decides to resume consideration of the whole question of membership of the Trusteeship Council at its next session.

A preambular paragraph stating that France and Italy would cease being administering members of the Trusteeship Council during 1960, and that the composition of the Council would have to be modified in consequence, failed of adoption, receiving a simple but not a two-thirds majority. An operative paragraph recommending

---

40 United Nations Doc. A/PV.857, 12 Dec. 1959, p. 97.
41 United Nations Docs. A/L.274, 8 Dec. 1959, A/L.277, 12 Dec. 1959.
42 United Nations Doc. A/L.275/Rev. 1, 12 Dec. 1959.

that " consideration should be given to equitable geographical distribution among the . . . elected members, namely, that the two main groups at present represented by the elected members [Latin America and Afro-Asia] should continue to be so represented " also failed to obtain a two-thirds majority.

The Assembly rejected the paragraphs of the Tunisian proposal which would have decided that two elected members of the Council should cease being members on 27 April 1960; that an additional elected member should cease being a member on 1 July 1960; and that, in the absence of voluntary resignations, the Trusteeship Council should draw lots to designate the elected members to be displaced.

The Assembly, having voted on the Tunisian proposal paragraph by paragraph, then voted on the draft resolution as a whole, in its revised form. Surprisingly, it was not adopted as it failed to obtain the required two-thirds majority.

It should be assumed that representatives of sovereign States, when voting in the Assembly, know the implications of what they are doing. All the same, it is difficult to evaluate the full significance of the vote on the amended Tunisian proposal. Of the seven States administering trust territories, three supported the amended proposal (New Zealand, the United Kingdom and the United States), one opposed (Belgium), and three abstained (Australia, France and Italy). Fifteen Latin American States voted " yes " and five " no "; of the Afro-Asians, sixteen voted " yes " and nine " no "; of the West Europeans (excluding the States administering trust territories), nine voted " yes " and three " no "; the Soviet *Bloc* voted " no."

This was, indeed, a freak vote. There surely has never been a draft resolution on a colonial question in the United Nations in which Britain and Portugal have found themselves voting " yes " along with the United Arab Republic and Indonesia; in which Belgium and Nationalist China have joined Albania and Guinea in voting " no "; in which both Ghana and South Africa have been among the abstainers.

I referred earlier to " three proposals before the Assembly." Having rejected the two versions of the Soviet proposal and the amended Tunisian proposal, the Assembly by implication adopted the third proposal. At 3.30 a.m., by secret ballot, the Assembly elected Bolivia and India to the Trusteeship Council, succeeding Haiti and India. The future was left to take care of itself.

This was, in fact, the result which several Member States had favoured, though the result was achieved by unsatisfactory means. The representatives of Ceylon, India and the United Kingdom had specifically urged the Assembly to hold the election in the ordinary way.[43] In the event, the Assembly took that course in the absence of agreement on any other proposal. Some Member States regarded the Assembly's action as the acme of political wisdom, while others considered that the Assembly had merely swept an awkward problem under the carpet. But whichever view one takes, the fact is the problem remains. It has not been solved, though its solution has been deferred.

JUDGES OF THE INTERNATIONAL COURT

The Assembly, in conjunction with the Security Council, elects the judges of the International Court of Justice. The procedure of nomination and election is very cumbersome.

According to Articles 2 and 9 of the Statute of the International Court, the Court should be composed of independent judges, elected regardless of their nationality from among persons of high moral character, who possess the qualifications required in their respective countries for appointment to the highest judicial offices, or are jurisconsults of recognized competence in international law. The electors should bear in mind not only that the persons to be elected should individually possess the qualifications required, but also that in the body as a whole the representation of the main forms of civilization and of the principal legal systems of the world should be assured.

The nominating procedure is set forth in Articles 4 to 7 of the Statute. Candidates are nominated by the national groups in the Permanent Court of Arbitration established by the Hague Conferences of 1899 and 1907; or, in the case of Members of the United Nations not represented in the Permanent Court of Arbitration, by national groups appointed by their governments under the same conditions prescribed for members of the Permanent Court of Arbitration. Each nominating group consists of not more than four persons, selected by governments, " of known competency in questions of international law, of the highest moral reputation. . . ."

These national groups are somewhat amorphous.

[They] have actually no organic consistency; each is rather four separate individuals having no provision for acting together as a unit. They have no address. . . . [They] are supposed to act independently of their governments; presumably they would transmit their nominations to the Secretary-General directly. No procedure for this has been provided. . . .[44]

This system of nominations can, and often does, lead to the valid nomination of many more candidates than there are vacancies. Thus

43 United Nations Doc. A/PV.857, 12 Dec. 1959, pp. 57–77, 86–95.
44 Clyde Eagleton, " Choice of Judges for the International Court of Justice," *The American Journal of International Law*, Vol. 47, No. 3 (July 1953), pp. 462–463.

there were seventy-eight nominations in 1946 for the original fifteen vacancies. Similarly, when it was necessary to appoint a member of the Court to fill the unexpired part of the term of Judge José Gustavo Guerrero, who died on 25 October 1958, no fewer than eleven candidates were nominated. Eleven national groups (Belgium, France, Iran, Paraguay, Peru, Sweden, Switzerland, the United Kingdom, the United States, Uruguay and Yugoslavia) nominated two candidates for the one vacancy; and two of the candidates nominated were of the same nationality (Spanish). Rule 94 of the Rules of Procedure of the Assembly, which prohibits nominations in plenary meetings, does not apply in connection with the election of judges of the Court, although the only nominations permitted are those made in accordance with the Statute of the Court; a candidate whose name does not appear on the ballot paper may not be nominated in a meeting of the Assembly.

The procedure of election is based on Articles 2 to 4 and 7 to 14 of the Statute of the Court, Rules 40 and 61 of the Provisional Rules of Procedure of the Security Council, Rules 151 and 152 of the Rules of Procedure of the General Assembly, and to some extent on precedents established during the first session of the Assembly (23rd to 26th plenary meetings) and the 9th meeting of the Security Council. In accordance with Article 4 (3) of the Statute and Resolutions 91 (I), 264 (III), 363 (IV) and 806 (VIII) of the General Assembly, Liechtenstein, San Marino and Switzerland are parties to the Statute of the Court but not Members of the United Nations and may participate in the General Assembly in electing members of the Court in the same manner as the Members of the United Nations.

Regular elections take place every three years and are for five vacancies; an election to fill a single vacancy is held if a judge ceases to serve before the completion of his term. The system of election in the case of a single vacancy is as follows. The Secretary-General of the United Nations submits to the General Assembly and the Security Council the nominations which he has received, and the *curricula vitae* of the candidates. On the day of the election, the General Assembly and the Security Council proceed, independently of one another, to elect a member of the Court, and the candidate who obtains " an absolute majority of votes " in both bodies is elected. The expression " absolute majority of votes " is not used in the United Nations Charter, the Rules of Procedure of the General Assembly, or the Provisional Rules of Procedure of the Security Council, except in connection with the election of members of the Court. In practice, " absolute majority " has been interpreted as meaning a majority of all the qualified electors, whether or not they vote. The qualified electors in the General Assembly are all the

Members of the United Nations, together with Liechtenstein, San Marino and Switzerland. Thus in the election of a successor to Judge Guerrero held in 1959, eighty-two Member States and three parties to the Statute of the Court but not Members of the United Nations were qualified to participate, so that forty-three votes constituted " an absolute majority " in the General Assembly. In the Security Council, six votes constitute an absolute majority, no distinction being made between permanent and non-permanent members. This is the only matter on which six votes in the Security Council are sufficient to make a decision; indeed, there is an inconsistency between Article 10 of the Statute of the Court (" an absolute majority of votes . . . of the Security Council ") and Article 27 of the Charter (" an affirmative vote of seven members ").

The electors in the General Assembly and the Security Council indicate the candidate for whom they wish to vote by placing a cross in the box on the left opposite the name of the candidate on the ballot paper. A ballot paper on which more names are marked than there are vacancies is considered invalid. With an exception noted below in the event of a deadlock, only those candidates who have been nominated and whose names appear on the list prepared by the Secretary-General are eligible for election. The withdrawal of a candidate before balloting begins, or between ballots, has been allowed.

If in the first ballot in either the General Assembly or the Security Council no candidate receives an absolute majority of votes, a second ballot is held, and balloting continues in the same meeting until a candidate has obtained an absolute majority. When this occurs in either organ, and not until that time, the President of that organ notifies the President of the other organ of the name of that candidate. Such notification is not communicated by the President to the members of the other organ until that organ has itself given a candidate the required majority of votes.

If, upon comparison of the names of the candidates receiving the required majority in each organ, it is found that different persons have received absolute majorities, the organs proceed, again independently of one another, in a second meeting, and if necessary a third meeting, to elect a candidate by further ballots, the results being again compared after a candidate has received an absolute majority in each organ.

This procedure continues until the two organs have given an absolute majority of votes to the same candidate. If, after the third of these meetings, the vacancy remains unfilled, however, the Assembly and the Council may, at any time, at the request of either body, form a joint conference consisting of six members, three appointed by each body. This joint conference may, by an absolute majority, agree upon a candidate and submit his name for the approval of the Assembly and the Council. If unanimously agreed, the

TABLE 20

Members of the International Court of Justice, 1 January 1960

Order of precedence	Nationality	Date of expiration of term (on 5 February)
Helge Klaestad,* President	Norway	1961
Sir Mohammad Zafrulla Khan, Vice-President	Pakistan	1961
J. Basdevant*	France	1964
G. H. Hackworth*	United States of America	1961
B. Winiarski*	Poland	1967
A. H. Badawi*	United Arab Republic	1967
E. C. Armand Ugón	Uruguay	1961
F. I. Kojevnikov	U.S.S.R.	1961
Sir Hersch Lauterpacht	United Kingdom	1964
L. M. Moreno Quintana	Argentina	1964
R. Córdova	Mexico	1964
V. K. Wellington Koo	China	1967
J. Spiropoulos	Greece	1967
Sir Percy Spender	Australia	1967
Ricardo J. Alfaro	Panama	1964

* Judges who have served continuously since the establishment of the Court.

joint conference may submit the name of a candidate which was not included in the list of nominations. If a joint conference is satisfied that it will not be successful in procuring an election, those members of the International Court who have already been elected proceed, within a period fixed by the Security Council, to fill the vacant seat by selection from among those candidates who obtained votes in the General Assembly or the Security Council. In the event of a tie vote, the eldest judge has a casting vote.

These procedures are unquestionably complicated and time-consuming. The nominating procedure is designed to achieve, to the greatest extent possible, the independence of judges. The election procedure is intended to ensure the election of judges representing the main forms of civilization and the principal legal systems of the world. The procedures are in large measure based on the Statute of the Court, which forms an integral part of the Charter of the United Nations (Article 92), and they can be changed only by the same procedure as is laid down for amendments to the Charter (Article 69 of the Statute).

The composition of the Court has been as follows:

Latin America	4
Asia and Africa	initially 2, now 3
Eastern Europe	initially 3, now 2
Northern, Western and Southern Europe	usually 4
Older Commonwealth countries	1
United States	1

It is likely that there will be some pressure in 1963 to elect an additional judge from Asia or Africa. The names and nationalities of the present members of the Court, and the years in which their terms expire, are given in Table 20.

CHAPTER 9

SUBSIDIARY ORGANS OF THE GENERAL ASSEMBLY

> If men of sense and honour and substance are chosen . . . one
> may be a check upon the other, and all prudently limited by
> the sovereignty they represent.
>
> WILLIAM PENN

A COMMITTEE can, of course, consist of all members of the appointing body, or it can be a single individual. A committee is merely an agency to which something is committed. The Rules of Procedure of the Assembly refer to three types of committees: procedural committees (the General Committee and the Credentials Committee); Main Committees; and the two committees concerned with administration and budget (the Advisory Committee on Administrative and Budgetary Questions and the Committee on Contributions). In addition to these eleven committees, the methods of appointment of which are laid down in the Rules of Procedure, the Assembly may establish such subsidiary organs as it deems necessary for the performance of its functions (Article 22 of the Charter and Rule 162). Such subsidiary organs of the Assembly are of three kinds:

(a) Committees upon which all Members have the right to be represented (Committees of the Whole);

(b) Committees composed of a limited number of Member States (Select Committees);

(c) Subsidiary organs composed of one or more persons appointed in their individual capacities.

Subsidiary organs composed of States are usually called committees, but several are called commissions, and there is one council; these semantic variations seem to have no particular significance.[1]

SELECT COMMITTEES COMPOSED OF STATES

The composition of Select Committees of States is shown in Table 21. The appropriate size of a Select Committee depends on its functions and purposes. Most Committees are too large, and they tend to

---

[1] Sir Eyre Crowe once explained to Mr. (later Sir) Harold Nicolson the difference between a commission and a committee in the following terms: " My dear Nicolson, a Commission is a body which is despatched to a definite place, a body that sits at the centre is a Committee." Harold Nicolson, *Peacemaking* (New York ; Houghton Mifflin ; London : Constable, 1933), p. 261.

TABLE 21

Membership of Select Committees of the General Assembly, 1 January 1960*

	Advisory Commission on the Relief and Works Agency for Palestine Refugees	Advisory Committee on the U.N. Emergency Force	Advisory Council for Somaliland	Collective Measures Committee	Commission for the Unification and Rehabilitation of Korea	Commission on Permanent Sovereignty over Natural Resources	Commission to Investigate Conditions for Free Elections in Germany	Committee on Information from Non-Self-Governing Territories	Committee on South West Africa	Committee on the Peaceful Uses of Outer Space	Conciliation Commission for Palestine	Negotiating Committee for Extra-Budgetary Funds	Peace Observation Commission	Scientific Advisory Committee	Scientific Committee on Effects of Atomic Radiation	Special Committee to Study the Principles Regarding the Transmission of Information under Article 73e
Afghanistan						×										
Albania																
Argentina				×				×		×		×			×	
Australia					×			×		×					×	
Austria										×						
Belgium	×			×				×		×					×	
Bolivia										×						
Brazil		×		×			×	×	×	×		×		×	×	
Bulgaria				×						×						
Burma																
Byelorussian S.S.R.																
Cambodia																
Canada		×		×						×		×		×	×	

			1	2	3	4	5	6	7	8	9	10	11	12	13	14	15	16
Ceylon	...	...	...		x						x							
Chile	...	...	...				x	x										
China	...	...	...												x			
Colombia	...	...	...		x	x												
Costa Rica	...	...	...															
Cuba	...	...	...															
Czechoslovakia		...	...							x			x		x		
Denmark	...	...	...						x								
Dominican Republic		...							x								
Ecuador	...	...	...														
El Salvador	...	...	...														
Ethiopia	...	...	...						x								
Federation of Malaya	...															
Finland	...	...	...														
France	...	...	...	x			x			x		x	x	x	x	x	x
Ghana	...	...	...							x							
Greece	...	...	...														
Guatemala	...	...					x		x							
Guinea	...	...	...													
Haiti	...	...	...													
Honduras	...	...	...										x			
Hungary	...	...	...							x						
Iceland	...	...	...						x							
India	...	...	...		x				x		x		x	x	x	x
Indonesia	...	...	...							x						
Iran	...	...	...							x					
Iraq	...	...	...						x				x			
Ireland	...	...	...						x						

* The Committee, established under Resolution 1181 (XII), on the question of defining aggression, is composed of " the Member States whose representatives have served on the General Committee at the most recent regular session of the General Assembly."

TABLE 21—*continued*

	Advisory Commission on the Relief and Works Agency for Palestine Refugees	Advisory Committee on the U.N. Emergency Force	Advisory Council for Somaliland	Collective Measures Committee	Commission for the Unification and Rehabilitation of Korea	Commission on Permanent Sovereignty over Natural Resources	Commission to Investigate Conditions for Free Elections in Germany	Committee on Information from Non-Self-Governing Territories	Committee on South West Africa	Committee on the Peaceful Uses of Outer Space	Conciliation Commission for Palestine	Negotiating Committee for Extra-Budgetary Funds	Peace Observation Commission	Scientific Advisory Committee	Scientific Committee on Effects of Atomic Radiation	Special Committee to Study the Principles Regarding the Transmission of Information under Article 73e
Israel										×			×			
Italy										×						
Japan															×	
Jordan	×															
Laos										×						
Lebanon	×											×				
Liberia																
Libya																
Luxembourg																
Mexico				×						×					×	×
Morocco																×
Nepal																
Netherlands					×	×	×	×								×
New Zealand								×				×	×			
Nicaragua																

Norway											×	×		
Pakistan									×	×	×	×	×	×
Panama														
Paraguay														
Peru														
Philippines					×	×	×				×			
Poland					×	×			×				×	×
Portugal														
Romania					×	×			×				×	×
Saudi Arabia														
Spain														
Sudan														
Sweden					×	×	×		×				×	×
Thailand					×									
Tunisia														
Turkey	×			×	×	×		×						
Ukrainian S.S.R.														
Union of South Africa														
U.S.S.R.	×			×	×	×	×	×	×	×	×		×	×
United Arab Republic	×			×	×	×	×	×	×	×	×		×	×
United Kingdom	×				×	×	×	×	×	×	×	×	×	×
United States of America	×			×	×	×		×	×	×	×	×	×	×
Uruguay				×										
Venezuela														
Yemen														
Yugoslavia	×													

increase in size as efforts are made to increase their representative character. The British House of Commons has a standing order that " No select committee shall, without leave of the House, consist of more than fifteen members. . . ." [2] and Alexander Loveday comments that " international committees of more than fifteen members are certain to waste time. . . . When a committee exceeds fifteen in number it tends to change its nature altogether. It ceases to be a working group and becomes a debating society." [3] There is no magic in the number fifteen, but it is a fact that fifteen people can just manage to sit round one table and engage in discussion; when there are sixteen people, it seems that two tables are required.

The composition of a committee, like its size, depends on its purposes and functions. Occasionally the only factor to be taken into account in constituting a subsidiary organ is that it should be as representative as possible of the whole membership. In the case of organs of small size, this is difficult to achieve in practice. Even a fifteen-nation committee cannot include a representative of a group or region numbering five or less (such as the West European neutrals) unless some other group or region is prepared to accept less than the share to which it is entitled. Moreover, the choices within regions may give rise to dissension. Is Yugoslavia, in present circumstances, " representative " of Eastern Europe, or China of Asia, or Tunisia of the Arab States? It is difficult enough to agree on the composition of an organ if the sole factor of which account is taken is that it should be representative; how much more difficult it is when other factors also enter the picture. Yet this almost always happens. In constituting the Scientific Advisory Committee and the Scientific Committee on Effects of Atomic Radiation, for example, account was taken of the degree of scientific and technological development in the countries belonging to the Committee. Furthermore, some subsidiary organs are deliberately unrepresentative in order that they may have the best chance to discharge their functions with any hope of success. The Palestine Conciliation Commission is an example of this kind. Some subsidiary organs of the Assembly, such as the Advisory Committee on UNEF, the Advisory Council for Somaliland, the Commission for the Unification and Rehabilitation of Korea and the Commission to Investigate Conditions for Free Elections in Germany, did not include any of the permanent members of the Security Council. Several organs, such as the Advisory Commission on the United Nations Relief and Works Agency for Palestine Refugees in the Near East (UNWRA), the Collective Measures

2 Standing Order No. 66.
3 *Reflexions on International Administration* (Oxford: Clarendon, 1956), p. 185.

Committee and the Negotiating Committee for Extra-Budgetary Funds, consist of States directly concerned with and supporting particular activities.

There can be no uniform method of constituting organs with widely differing functions. The membership of each organ should be determined in the light of three main considerations: does the organ possess, or can it develop, the necessary expertise to discharge the functions entrusted to it; is it small enough so that there can emerge a reasonable degree of intimacy, cohesion and consensus; and is its composition such that its reports and recommendations will command wide support by the full membership of the Assembly?

The drafting of appropriate terms of reference for subsidiary organs concerned with controversial issues is always difficult. To some extent this arises from the inevitable process of compromise, whereby paragraphs are added or deleted in order to win wider support.

I doubt whether the creation of committees of the whole United Nations membership is, in the ordinary way, a useful proceeding. The Interim Committee was an attempt to give the Assembly a continuous existence, but it has not in practice proved a useful institution. The Committee concerned with Charter review has been a device to keep open an issue that could be neither evaded nor resolved in 1955. The Disarmament Commission consisting of all Member States has still to be put to the test.

In examining the elections to the three Councils and to Select Committees of the Assembly, one is struck by the fact that there is a nucleus of about a dozen States (in addition to the five permanent members of the Security Council) which have been repeatedly elected to United Nations bodies: Argentina, Australia, Belgium, Brazil, Canada, India, Mexico, Netherlands, New Zealand, Pakistan, the Philippines and the United Arab Republic. These States have, in a sense, become " experts " in matters relating to intergovernmental organizations. It is also interesting to note that some of the States which have been most active in promoting conciliation in the Assembly (Ireland, Norway, Sweden and Yugoslavia, for example) have not been frequently elected to membership of United Nations organs. In a number of cases, uncommitted States may have preferred not to serve on organs dealing with controversial topics so as not to risk endangering their neutral status; it is also known that some States refuse to commit themselves in support of any candidate for election, and for this reason are themselves not frequently elected.

THE FINANCIAL COMMITTEES

The committees of the Assembly concerned with budget and administration have a special importance in the United Nations system because of the predominant role in financial matters given to the Assembly under the Charter. Control of the purse-strings has traditionally been an important political weapon. The Council of the

TABLE 22

Estimated Gross Expenditures (1959) of the United Nations, including Extra-budgetary Programmes

		millions	
		$	£
1.	Regular U.N. budget	61·7	(22·0)
2.	UNEF	19·0	(6·8)
3.	Extra-budgetary programmes:		

	$	£		
(1) Expanded Programme of Technical Assistance	32·8	(11·7)		
(2) United Nations Special Fund	25·8	(9·2)*		
(3) UNICEF	28·0	(10·0)		
(4) High Commissioner for Refugees	4·5	(1·6)		
(5) UNRWA	34·1	(12·2)	125·2	(44·7)

$205·9 (£73·5)

* This figure represents pledges of income, not expenditure, as the Special Fund had not begun field operations in 1959.

League of Nations at first intended to exercise general financial control of the Organization, but the Assembly soon asserted its primacy in financial matters. The United Nations Charter expressly gave to the Assembly the responsibility of considering and approving the budget, apportioning the expenses among the Members, considering and approving financial and budgetary arrangements with specialized agencies, and examining " the administrative budgets " of such agencies " with a view to making recommendations to the agencies concerned " (Article 17).

The regular expenses of the United Nations, the expenses of the United Nations Emergency Force, and the extra-budgetary programmes of the United Nations in 1959 amounted to approximately $206 million (£73·5 million).[4]   Intergovernmental agencies related to the United Nations spent an additional $80 million (£28·6 million).

The annual budget estimates for the United Nations Organization are prepared within the Secretariat, consolidated in the Office of the Controller, and issued by the Secretary-General. They are submitted

[4] The accounts of the United Nations are in dollars; I have given the sterling equivalents, at the rate of £1 = $2.80, in parentheses.

to the Advisory Committee for Administrative and Budgetary Questions (hereafter called " the Advisory Committee ") at least twelve weeks prior to the opening of the regular session of the Assembly, that is to say, usually by about the middle of June; and they are submitted to Member States, with the report of the Advisory Committee, at least five weeks before the opening of the Assembly.[5]

The Advisory Committee consists of nine persons, including at least two financial experts of recognized standing. Members are selected on the basis of broad geographical representation, personal qualifications and experience. No two members may be nationals of the same State (Rules 156 and 157). The Secretary-General informs Member States when vacancies occur by death, resignation or expiration of term. Nominations are not specifically requested, but in practice they are made. After a reasonable interval, the Secretary-General informs Member States of the names of the persons who have been proposed to fill the vacancies.

The members of the Committee are appointed by the Assembly, and the practice is for the Fifth Committee to conduct a secret ballot and submit to the Assembly a draft resolution containing the names of the persons recommended for appointment. Representatives may vote for any eligible candidate, regardless of whether the name has been included in the Secretary-General's note.

The membership of the Committee on 1 January 1960 was as follows:

Thanassis Aghnides (Greece), *Chairman*

Albert F. Bender (United States) A. H. M. Hillis (United Kingdom)
Carlos Blanco (Cuba) Ismat T. Kittani (Iraq)
Eduardo Carrizosa (Colombia) Agha Shahi (Pakistan)
André Ganem (France) Alexei F. Sokirkin (U.S.S.R.)

There has been remarkable continuity in the membership of the Advisory Committee. Mr. Aghnides, a veteran of intergovernmental organizations, has been Chairman since the Committee's inception; and nationals of France, the Soviet Union, the United Kingdom and the United States have been on the Committee continuously. An Indian national served on the Committee from its creation until the end of 1959. Nationals of Colombia and Cuba have three times been appointed for three-year terms, and nationals of Brazil have twice been so appointed. With such stability of representation and membership, the Advisory Committee has acquired considerable homogeneity and expertise.

---

[5] Financial Regulation 3. The Financial Regulations are annexed Res. 456 (V), 16 Nov. 1950.

It is by no means clear to what extent members of the Committee act as individuals or as representatives of governments. Some members of the Committee are probably briefed by their governments on all important questions; others may not receive detailed instructions, though they are doubtless familiar with the policies of their governments since they often serve in national delegations to the General Assembly.

In 1952, the first Secretary-General pointed out that some members of the Advisory Committee also represent their governments in the General Assembly " where they may act as advocates for the Advisory Committee, or may argue and vote against its recommendations." This situation was, he considered, a source of confusion and not in keeping with the intentions of the Assembly. The Secretary-General suggested that membership in the Advisory Committee should disqualify a person from service in the Fifth Committee of the Assembly.[6] The Secretary-General's proposals, along with a number of other matters, were referred to a committee, which was asked to report to the eighth session.[7]

Mr. Hammarskjold, on taking office as the second Secretary-General, found himself unable to maintain the proposals of his predecessor, and the matter was accordingly dropped.[8]

A basic problem of any system of financial control is that a committee whose duty it is to review estimates of expenditure usually feels that it has to justify its existence by proposing some reductions. The officials who prepare the estimates, knowing that some cuts are likely, are tempted to inflate the figures. A second problem is to keep financial control separate from policy decision. A budget review committee should examine the estimates and recommend economies that might be effected, but only in a way that is consistent with the decisions of policy on which the estimates are based.

The United Nations has not escaped these two problems entirely. The first has, however, gradually assumed less importance as the Advisory Committee has acquired experience and cohesion. The second problem can never disappear entirely, since honest men and women may disagree on the exact location of the line which separates policy from administration.

A further difficulty, which is peculiar to international organizations, arises when different members of the same delegation advocate

6 G.A.O.R.: 7th Sess., 1952–53, Annexes, Agenda item 69 (A/2214), paras. 39, 40; *ibid.*, 5th Committee, 371st Mtg., 9 Dec. 1952, paras. 31–34.
7 General Assembly Res. 681B (VII), 21 Dec. 1952.
8 G.A.O.R.: 8th Sess., 1953, Annexes, Agenda item 49 (A/2429), para. 6; General Assembly Res. 764 (VIII), 3 Nov. 1953.

inconsistent policies in various organs. This may arise because of a lack of co-ordination within delegations, or because representatives have not received sufficiently precise instructions. It is interesting, for example, to note the impassioned appeal for economy by the representatives of Czechoslovakia, Ceylon and India in the Fifth Committee during October 1959,[9] and to compare it with the indignation of the representatives of the same Member States in the Fourth Committee during the same month when the Under-Secretary for Conference Services appealed to delegations to bear in mind budgetary restrictions before incurring abnormal expenditures.[10] The Fourth Committee is particularly prone to incur expenses for the preparation of documents beyond the standard practice. During the 1958 session of the Assembly, the Fourth Committee asked that, contrary to the usual policy, certain records in connection with South West Africa be issued in verbatim form.[11] The States voting in favour of this together contributed less than 10 per cent. of the budget.

The Advisory Committee usually recommends to the Assembly that some of the estimates be reduced.[12] The Secretary-General may, in the light of such recommendations, agree that some of the reductions are reasonable, though he may point out that the reductions recommended by the Advisory Committee are based on certain assumptions, and if the assumptions turn out to be incorrect, supplementary estimates may be required. Occasionally the Secretary-General may insist on maintaining some of the original estimates, in spite of a recommendation of the Advisory Committee that they be reduced. In that event the Assembly, acting on a recommendation of its Fifth Committee, would be the arbiter. Each year the Assembly authorizes the Secretary-General to incur " unforeseen and extraordinary expenses " within certain established limits and subject to certain conditions.

The Assembly considers the budget estimates in the following stages:

1. The Secretary-General introduces the budget estimates with an oral statement in the Fifth Committee.

[9] G.A.O.R.: 14th Sess., 5th Committee, 715th Mtg., 7 Oct. 1959, paras. 9–16; 718th Mtg., 13 Oct. 1959, paras. 13–16; 720th Mtg., 15 Oct. 1952, paras. 1–6.

[10] *Ibid.*, 4th Committee, 19 Oct. 1959, paras. 5, 7, 8.

[11] G.A.O.R.: 13th Sess., 4th Committee, 777th Mtg., 29 Oct. 1958, para. 55.

[12] In 1959, the Secretary-General submitted estimates of expenditure for 1960 amounting to $63·7 million (£22·7 million). The Advisory Committee recommended reductions amounting to $866,000 (£309,000). The Assembly accepted the recommendations of the Advisory Committee except that in three cases, amounting to $338,000 (£120,000), the original estimates of the Secretary-General were restored. Income from all sources was estimated at $11·7 million (£4·2 million), giving an estimated net expenditure for 1960 of $51·4 million (£18·3 million).

2. The Chairman of the Advisory Committee introduces his Committee's report on the budget estimates with an oral statement in the Fifth Committee.
3. The Fifth Committee discusses the budget estimates as a whole.
4. The Fifth Committee makes a detailed examination (the " first reading ") of the budget estimates.[13]
5. The Fifth Committee reviews the budget estimates in a " second reading," in the light of the provisional decisions taken during the " first reading."
6. The recommendations of the Fifth Committee are embodied in the report of the Rapporteur.
7. Finally, the Rapporteur's report is considered by the Assembly in plenary meeting, and a resolution is adopted, a two-thirds majority being required for decisions on budgetary questions (Article 18).

Debate on the budget estimates enables delegations to express their views on a wide range of financial and administrative questions. At the same time, it is of little value, except for purposes of propaganda, to make speeches in the Fifth Committee to the effect that some activity of the United Nations is undesirable and that therefore there should be no financial provision for it in the budget. There is little value in generalized complaints of extravagance or suggestions for an across-the-board reduction of a fixed percentage. There is little value in proposing a budget ceiling. Opposition to the policy on which the the estimates are based should be voiced in the policy organs; the task of the Fifth Committee is to review the financial and administrative implementation of policy.

Expenses necessitated by extraordinary or unforeseen circumstances are met provisionally from the Working Capital Fund.[14] Supplementary estimates are later submitted by the Secretary-General, and are dealt with in the same manner as the original estimates. The Working Capital Fund is also used to meet the expenses of the Organization pending the receipt of contributions. The Fund consists of advances from Member States in accordance with the regular scale of assessments, and the present amount is $25 million (£8·9 million).[15]

The amount of the Working Capital Fund is now insufficient to meet the demands on it, and on 30 June 1959, the cash and investments of the Fund had fallen as low as $178,000 (£63,546).[16] The

---

[13] The expressions " first reading," " second reading," etc., originated in the British Parliament. Before the invention of mechanical printing, every proposal to change the statute law was read in full by the Clerk each time it was debated.
[14] General Assembly Res. 14H (I), 13 Feb. 1946.
[15] General Assembly Res. 1340 (XIII), 13 Dec. 1958.
[16] United Nations Doc. A/C.5/L.575, 19 Oct. 1959.

cash position was such that, in June and July 1959, the Secretary-General had to borrow $1 million (£357,000) from the account of the Expanded Programme of Technical Assistance and $1 million (£357,000) from the United Nations Special Fund.[17] The low cash position of the Working Capital Fund in June and July is caused by the fact that only about one-fifth of the income of the United Nations is received during the first half of the calendar year, by the fact that some Member States are habitually in arrears with their contributions, and by the fact that the Secretary-General has had to draw on the Fund because of the deficit on the UNEF account.

The amount of the Working Capital Fund has been increased from $22 million (£7·8 million) for 1958, to $23·5 million (£8·4 million) for 1959, to $25 million (£8·9 million) for 1960. The Fund should be progressively increased over the next few years to a figure of about $30 million (£10·7 million).

The Charter states that the expenses of the Organization shall be borne by the Member States as apportioned by the General Assembly.[18] The Assembly decided during the first session that the apportionment of the expenses should be " broadly according to capacity to pay," and a Committee on Contributions was set up to advise the Assembly on this matter. On the basis of the original terms of reference of the Committee and later directives, the Committee takes account of the following factors: [19]

(a) Comparative income per head of population;

(b) ability of Member States to secure foreign currency;

(c) the principle that the maximum contribution of any one Member State shall not exceed 30 per cent. of the total [20];

(d) in normal times the *per capita* contribution of any Member shall not exceed the *per capita* contribution of the Member which bears the highest assessment (the United States);

(e) the assessment for countries with low *per capita* income may be reduced by amounts which, for countries with the very lowest incomes per inhabitant, approach a maximum of 50 per cent.;

---

[17] *Annual Report of the Secretary-General* . . . , G.A.O.R.: 14th Sess., 1959, Suppl. No. 1 (A/4132), p. 103; *Advisory Committee: Tenth Report to the General Assembly at its Fourteenth Session, ibid.*, Suppl. No. 7 (A/4170), para. 98.

[18] Article 17 (2).

[19] General Assembly Res. 14A (I), 13 Feb. 1946; Res. 69 (I), 14 Dec. 1946; Res. 238 (III), 18 Nov. 1948; *Report of the Committee on Contributions*, G.A.O.R.: 7th Sess., 1952, Suppl. No. 10 (A/2161), paras. 11, 12; Res. 665 (VII), 5 Dec. 1952; Res. 1137 (XII), 14 Oct. 1957.

[20] If it were not for this provision, the United States assessment would be about 45 per cent. of the total. The United States assessment is 32·51 per cent. and will eventually be reduced to 30 per cent.

(f) the minimum assessment shall be 0·04 per cent.

The Committee on Contributions is described in the Rules of Procedure as " an expert Committee " (Rule 159). It consists of ten members, no two of whom shall be nationals of the same State, selected on the basis of broad geographical representation, personal qualifications, and experience (Rule 160). The Committee is appointed by the same procedure as is used to appoint the Advisory Committee. The membership of the Committee on 1 January 1960 was as follows [21]:

Georgy P. Arkadev (U.S.S.R.)	F. Nouredin Kia (Iran)
Raymond F. Bowman (U.S.A.)	Jerzy Michalowski (Poland),
René Charon (France)	*Vice-Chairman*
José A. Correa (Ecuador)	José Pareya Paz Soldan (Peru)
A. H. M. Hillis (United Kingdom)	Sidney Pollock (Canada),
Chandra Shekhar Jha (India)	*Chairman*

There has been considerable continuity in the membership of the Committee on Contributions. Nationals of France, the Soviet Union, the United Kingdom and the United States have served continuously since the Committee was established. A Mexican served continuously from 1946 to 1957, and Canada, Czechoslovakia and India have each been represented for three three-year terms. As in the case of the Advisory Committee, there is some imprecision about the extent to which members of the Committee are supposed to act on the instructions of their governments.

The Committee operates as far as possible on an objective basis, but it is hampered by technical difficulties which cannot easily be overcome. Statistical information is not available for some countries and the available information varies in degree of reliability. Moreover, there is no generally accepted method of converting estimates of *per capita* income into a common currency. In addition, the Committee faces a number of questions which are partially subjective. What is meant by " broadly according to capacity to pay "? Is it possible to determine " the ability of Members to secure foreign currency "? In spite of these difficulties, the Committee is able to present an annual report to the Assembly which is, in the main, acceptable to Members.

The report of the Committee on Contributions is considered by the Fifth Committee, and the Rapporteur embodies the Fifth Committee's recommendations in a report, which is considered and approved in plenary meeting.

---

[21] On at least one occasion, a member who was unable to attend meetings of the Committee has designated a fellow-national to represent him.

TABLE 23

Budgetary Assessments on United Nations Member States for 1960

	Per cent.		Per cent.
Afghanistan	0·06	Israel	0·14
Albania	0·04	Italy	2·25
Argentina	1·11	Japan	2·19
Australia	1·79	Jordan	0·04
Austria	0·43	Laos	0·04
Belgium	1·30	Lebanon	0·05
Bolivia	0·04	Liberia	0·04
Brazil	1·02	Libya	0·04
Bulgaria	0·16	Luxembourg	0·06
Burma	0·08	Mexico	0·71
Byelorussian S.S.R.	0·47	Morocco	0·14
Cambodia	0·04	Nepal	0·04
Canada	3·11	Netherlands	1·01
Ceylon	0·10	New Zealand	0·42
Chile	0·27	Nicaragua	0·04
China	5·01	Norway	0·49
Colombia	0·31	Pakistan	0·40
Costa Rica	0·04	Panama	0·04
Cuba	0·25	Paraguay	0·04
Czechoslovakia	0·87	Peru	0·11
Denmark	0·60	Philippines	0·43
Dominican Republic	0·05	Poland	1·37
Ecuador	0·06	Portugal	0·20
El Salvador	0·05	Romania	0·34
Ethiopia	0·06	Saudi Arabia	0·06
Federation of Malaya	0·17	Spain	0·93
Finland	0·36	Sudan	0·06
France	6·40	Sweden	1·39
Ghana	0·07	Thailand	0·16
Greece	0·23	Tunisia	0·05
Guatemala	0·05	Turkey	0·59
Guinea	0·04	Ukrainian S.S.R.	1·80
Haiti	0·04	Union of South Africa	0·56
Honduras	0·04	U.S.S.R.	13·62
Hungary	0·42	United Arab Republic	0·32
Iceland	0·04	United Kingdom	7·78
India	2·46	United States of America	32·51
Indonesia	0·47	Uruguay	0·12
Iran	0·21	Venezuela	0·50
Iraq	0·09	Yemen	0·04
Ireland	0·16	Yugoslavia	0·35

NOTE: This table totals 100·04 per cent. as Guinea's assessment is in addition to the assessments agreed upon in 1958.

Separate from the regular budget of the United Nations, but theoretically financed by assessments in accordance with the ordinary scale, is the account for the United Nations Emergency Force. The Secretary-General's second report to the Assembly on the plan for UNEF had this to say on the financial question:

A basic rule which, at least, could be applied provisionally would be that a nation providing a unit would be responsible for all costs for equipment and salaries, while all other costs would be financed outside the normal budget of the United Nations.[22]

The Secretary-General has expressed the view that decisions which are taken by the General Assembly, and which have important financial consequences, carry with them an obligation on the part of Member States to make available the resources or other means for their implementation.[23] In accordance with this principle, the Secretary-General recommended that the expenses of the Force be allocated to Member States on the basis of the regular scale of assessments; and the Assembly so decided.[24]

The cost of maintaining the Force in 1960 is estimated at $20 million (£7·1 million); on 31 December 1959, accumulated arrears of $18·7 million (£6·7 million) were due from Member States. The arrears of Member States are shown in Table 24. By the end of 1959, UNEF had borrowed more than $6 million (£2·1 million) from the Working Capital Fund and had over $12 million (£4·2 million)

TABLE 24

United Nations Emergency Force Arrears, 1957–59
(as of 31 December 1959)

			1957	1958	1959	Total
			$	$	$	$
Afghanistan	...	...	2,814	15,000	9,092	26,906
Albania	...	...	5,876	10,000	6,062	21,938
Argentina	...	...	171,869	285,000	168,180	625,049
Australia	...	...	—	—	—	—
Austria	...	...	—	—	22,500	22,500
Belgium	...	...	—	—	—	—
Bolivia	...	...	7,345	12,500	6,056	25,901
Brazil	...	...	—	—	—	—
Bulgaria	...	...	20,565	35,000	24,257	79,822
Burma	...	...	—	—	—	—
Byelorussian S.S.R.	...		70,510	117,500	71,219	259,229
Cambodia	...	...	—	—	—	—
Canada	...	...	—	—	—	—
Ceylon	...	...	—	—	—	—
Chile	...	...	14,069	72,500	40,900	127,469
China	...	...	605,048	1,252,500	759,151	2,616,699
Colombia	...	...	—	—	46,946	46,946
Costa Rica	...	...	1,876	10,000	6,062	17,938
Cuba	...	...	12,662	65,000	37,874	115,536
Czechoslovakia	...		123,393	205,000	131,856	460,249
Denmark	...	...	—	—	—	—
Dominican Republic	...		—	—	—	—

22 G.A.O.R.: 1st Emergency Special Sess., 1956, Annexes, Agenda item 5 (A/3302), para. 15.
23 G.A.O.R.: 12th Sess., 1957, Annexes, Agenda item 65 (A/3694), para. 106.
24 G.A.O.R.: 11th Sess., 1956–57, Annexes, Agenda item 66 (A/3383), para. 6 (a); General Assembly Res. 1089 (XI), 21 Dec. 1956; Res. 1151 (XII), 22 Nov. 1957; Res. 1337 (XIII), 13 Dec. 1958.

United Nations Emergency Force Arrears, 1957–59
(as of 31 December 1959)—continued

	1957	1958	1959	Total
	$	$	$	$
Ecuador	—	11,500	9,097	20,597
El Salvador	8,814	15,000	7,571	31,385
Ethiopia	16,159	27,500	9,067	52,726
Federation of Malaya	—	—	—	—
Finland	—	—	—	—
France	—	—	—	—
Ghana	—	—	—	—
Greece	29,379	47,500	34,847	111,726
Guatemala	—	—	7,566	7,566
Guinea	—	—	—	—
Haiti	—	—	6,062	6,062
Honduras	—	10,000	6,062	16,062
Hungary	67,572	97,500	63,627	228,699
Iceland	—	5,000	6,062	11,062
India	155,775	725,000	372,529	1,253,304*
Indonesia	—	—	—	—
Iran	—	27,000	31,792	58,792
Iraq	5,627	30,000	13,623	49,250
Ireland	—	—	—	—
Israel	—	—	—	—
Italy	—	—	341,053	341,053
Japan	—	—	—	—
Jordan	5,876	10,000	6,062	21,938
Laos	—	—	—	—
Lebanon	—	12,269	7,576	19,845
Liberia	—	1,828	6,048	7,876
Libya	5,876	10,000	6,062	21,938
Luxembourg	—	—	—	—
Mexico	32,828	170,000	107,564	310,392
Morocco	—	—	—	—
Nepal	1,876	10,000	6,062	17,938
Netherlands	—	—	—	—
New Zealand ...	—	—	—	—
Nicaragua	—	—	6,062	6,062
Norway	—	—	—	—
Pakistan	—	—	—	—
Panama	7,345	12,500	6,056	25,901
Paraguay	5,876	10,000	6,062	21,938
Peru	7,034	37,500	16,649	61,183
Philippines	—	85,227	65,172	150,399
Poland	229,159	380,000	207,514	816,673
Portugal	—	—	—	—
Romania	73,448	122,500	51,442	247,390
Saudi Arabia	10,283	17,500	9,087	36,870
Spain	167,462	277,500	140,826	585,788
Sudan	16,159	27,500	9,067	52,726
Sweden	—	—	—	—
Thailand	—	—	—	—
Tunisia	—	—	—	—
Turkey	—	—	75,545	75,545

* Invoices, when received for services rendered in connection with the contingents provided by India to UNEF, will be set off against the unpaid contributions.

United Nations Emergency Force Arrears, 1957–59
(as of 31 December 1959)—continued

	1957	1958	1959	Total
	$	$	$	$
Ukrainian S.S.R. ...	271,759	450,000	272,747	994,506
Union of South Africa	—	—	—	—
U.S.S.R.	2,050,676	3,405,000	2,063,805	7,519,481
United Arab Republic	64,635	107,500	48,432	220,567
United Kingdom ...	—	—	598,737	598,737
United States of America	—	—	—	—
Uruguay	7,503	40,000	18,164	65,667
Venezuela	20,165	105,000	75,806	200,971
Yemen	5,876	10,000	6,062	21,938
Yugoslavia	—	—	—	—
	$4,303,189	$8,377,824	$6,055,722	$18,736,735
	(£1,536,853)	(£2,992,080)	(£2,162,758)	(£6,691,691)

in unliquidated obligations. On 24 November, the representatives of the United States and the United Kingdom, while stating that their Governments maintained their position that the expenses of the Force should be financed on the regular scale of assessments, announced that, subject to parliamentary approval, their Governments would make voluntary contributions to the 1960 expenses of the Force in the approximate amounts of $3·2 million (£1·1 million) and $275,000 (£98,175) respectively.[25] The Assembly decided that these voluntary contributions should be applied so as to reduce by 50 per cent. the contributions of as many governments of Member States as possible, commencing with those governments assessed at the minimum percentage of 0·04 per cent. and then including, in order, those governments assessed at the next highest percentages until the total amount of voluntary contributions has been fully applied.[26] The effect of this was to reduce, by half, the normal assessment for 1960 of all Member States wishing to take advantage of the arrangement, except the fourteen Member States with the highest assessments, that is to say, all Member States except Australia, Belgium, Canada, China, France, India, Italy, Japan, Poland, the Soviet Union, Sweden, the Ukraine, the United Kingdom and the United States.

In addition to the regular budget of the United Nations, there are five programmes of the United Nations which are financed by voluntary contributions of governments, and also of non-governmental agencies and private individuals. The task of securing contributions for these programmes from governments is entrusted to a Negotiating

[25] United Nations Doc. A/4335, 4 Dec. 1959, para. 14.
[26] General Assembly Res. 1441 (XIV), 16 Dec. 1959.

Committee for Extra-Budgetary Funds (hereafter referred to as " the Negotiating Committee "). In practice, the Negotiating Committee has in recent years given its main attention to the two refugee programmes, which have encountered special difficulties in raising funds.

The members of the Negotiating Committee are not elected but are appointed by the President of the Assembly. The Committee consists of States rather than persons. The members on 1 January 1960 were as follows: Argentina, Brazil, Canada, France, Lebanon, New Zealand, Pakistan, the United Kingdom and the United States.

The Negotiating Committee consults with States, whether Members of the United Nations or not, regarding contributions to the programmes in group 3 of Table 22. The Committee is charged by the Assembly to proceed with its work in such a way as to maintain the identity and integrity of each programme. In addition to informal activities, the Chairman of the Committee addresses letters to delegations outlining the financial requirements of the programmes falling within the Committee's purview. The Chairman and members of the Committee visit delegations and make personal approaches to governments in order to stimulate interest in and obtain support for extra-budgetary programmes. In addition, one or more " pledging conferences " are held at which representatives announce what the contributions of their governments to the different programmes will be.

TABLE 25

Pledges of Extra-Budgetary Contributions for 1959, *as at* 31 *October* 1959
(in U.S. dollars)

	Expanded Programme of Technical Assistance	Special Fund	UNRWA	High Commissioner for Refugees	UNICEF
Member States					
Afghanistan	12,500	6,000	—	—	10,000
Albania	2,000	—	—	—	—
Argentina	99,692	100,000	—	—	—
Australia	625,000	—	95,200	224,000 §	—
Austria ...	57,692	—	2,000	12,000	38,462
Belgium	437,500	250,000	30,000	50,000	200,000
Bolivia	20,789	—	—	—	—
Brazil	832,432	208,108	—	30,000 ‖	1,009,564
Bulgaria	14,706	14,706	—	—	2,206
Burma	35,000	10,000	—	—	56,000
Byelorussian S.S.R. ...	50,000	50,000	—	—	37,500
Cambodia	6,171	2,000	486	571	—
Canada	2,000,000	2,000,000	2,075,000	303,956	679,073
Ceylon	20,000	5,000	—	1,000 ‖	14,726
Chile	55,612	55,612	—	8,520 ‖	80,000
China	20,000	20,000	—	5,000	—
Colombia	126,800	16,393	—	—	253,869
Costa Rica	10,053	—	—	—	30,000
Cuba	125,000	—	—	5,000 ‖	—
Czechoslovakia ...	104,444	69,444	—	—	34,722
Denmark	651,513	332,996	21,720	72,390	72,400
Dominican Republic ...	—	—	—	5,000	20,000
Ecuador	11,333	10,000	—	—	10,000
El Salvador	7,700	—	—	—	20,000

Table 25 cont.	Expanded Programme of Technical Assistance	Special Fund	UNRWA	High Commissioner for Refugees	UNICEF
Member States					
Ethiopia	20,000	29,187	—	—	12,000
Federation of Malaya ...	20,000	5,000	3,000	2,000 §	24,500
Finland	25,000	—	—	—	19,687
France	1,555,288	1,072,068	245,828†	177,143	669,809**
Ghana	44,100	28,000	3,000	3,000	14,000
Greece	30,000	25,000	15,000	9,000	10,000
Guatemala	12,000	8,000	—	—	—
Guinea	—	—	—	—	—
Haiti	14,400	22,000	—	—	—
Honduras	10,000	—	—	—	20,000
Hungary...	42,608	42,608	—	—	12,876
Iceland	3,888	—	—	—	16,560
India	525,000	500,000	21,008	—	483,000
Indonesia	49,207	19,815	—	—	100,000
Iran	50,495	50,000	6,000	—	240,000
Iraq	56,000	28,006	—	—	56,000
Ireland	14,000	—	2,814	4,693	7,000
Israel	50,000	15,000	—	5,000	25,000
Italy	400,000	600,000	120,000	3,000	288,000
Japan	135,000	480,000	10,000	—	130,000
Jordan	5,881	—	100,000	—	2,244
Laos	3,000	3,000	1,000	—	500
Lebanon...	7,813	15,625	15,000	—	—
Liberia	25,000	10,000	5,000	—	5,000
Libya	6,000	10,000	10,000	—	—
Luxembourg ...	4,000	3,000	2,000	3,000	5,000
Mexico	113,600	34,000	—	20,000‖	500,000
Morocco	10,000	20,000	4,796	2,381	17,887
Nepal	5,000	1,000	—	—	—
Netherlands ...	1,202,000	2,440,105	65,790	139,211	78,947
New Zealand ...	210,000	70,000	140,000	56,000	210,000
Nicaragua	—	—	—	—	10,000
Norway	461,991	377,992	42,000	98,000	67,200
Pakistan	170,000	104,998	20,964	—	75,534
Panama	4,000	1,000	—	—	10,000
Paraguay	12,000	10,000	—	—	10,000
Peru	30,000	10,000	—	—	74,947
Philippines	66,000	66,000	—	—	102,462
Poland	75,000	125,000	—	—	50,000
Portugal	15,000	10,000	—	—	—
Romania	16,667	16,667	—	—	25,000
Saudi Arabia ...	25,000	—	212,000	—	—
Spain	50,000	—	—	—	23,810
Sudan	119,350	27,000	—	—	—
Sweden	902,764	2,103,228	57,915	144,984 §	260,618
Thailand	38,186	160,000	—	—	150,000
Tunisia	2,000	2,000	2,000	2,000	8,160
Turkey	210,000	210,000	5,000	2,667	161,071
Ukrainian S.S.R. ...	125,000	125,000	—	—	75,000
Union of South Africa...					
U.S.S.R.... ...	1,000,000	1,000,000	—	—	500,000
United Arab Republic...	114,877	287,191			
Egyptian Region ...	—	—	340,000	—	106,907
Syrian Region ...	—	—	83,000	—	8,108
United Kingdom ...	2,240,000	1,000,000	5,400,000	280,000	658,000
United States of America	12,000,000*	10,312,511*	11,500,000‡	1,750,000 §¶	9,500,000††
Uruguay...	120,000	—	—	—	—
Venezuela	350,000	40,000	—	6,000	—
Yemen	—	—	—	—	—
Yugoslavia	116,667	150,000	40,000	15,000	200,000
Non-Member States					
Germany, Federal Republic of	1,190,476	476,190	238,095	209,524	523,810
Holy See	1,000	1,000	—	3,000 §	1,000
Korea, Republic of ...	3,500	—	—	—	2,000
Liechtenstein	—	—	—	1,100	702
Monaco	1,013	2,026	203	2,041 §	2,041
Switzerland	348,837	465,116	35,047	156,977	269,100
Viet-Nam	25,714	16,686	2,500	2,500 §	5,000

	Expanded Programme of Technical Assistance	Special Fund	UNRWA	High Commissioner for Refugees	UNICEF
Other Contributors					
Bahrein	—	—	—	—	—
British Honduras ...	—	—	—	—	350
Brunei	—	—	—	—	1,633
Gaza Authority ...	—	—	78,000	—	—
Hong Kong	—	—	—	—	3,500
North Borneo	—	—	—	—	327
Rhodesia and Nyasaland, Federation of ...	—	—	—	2,823	—
Sarawak	—	—	—	—	3,267
Singapore	—	—	—	—	6,533
West Indies Federation:					
Antigua	—	—	—	—	117
Grenada	—	—	—	—	583
Jamaica	—	—	—	—	5,621
Trinidad and Tobago	—	—	—	—	7,000
TOTALS ...	29,810,259 (£10,646,571)	25,781,278 (£9,207,599)	21,051,366 (£7,518,345)	3,818,481 (£1,363,743)	18,425,933 (£6,580,690)

Expanded Programme of Technical Assistance (EPTA) and Special Fund

* *United States of America*: Estimated amount $38 million has been pledged to EPTA and the Special Fund subject to the condition that it will not exceed 40 per cent of the total contributions to each of the two programmes.

UNRWA

† *France*: Includes contribution for scholarships and rent of camps and warehouse sites.

‡ *United States of America*: This amount represents half of the total pledge for the fiscal year 1958-1959. The contribution is subject to the condition that it must not exceed 70 per cent of the total contributions to the programme.

High Commissioner for Refugees

§ Includes a contribution for World Refugee Year.

‖ Represents a contribution for World Refugee Year.

¶ *United States of America*: The contribution is subject to the condition that it will be at the rate of one-third of the total governmental contributions to the Fund.

UNICEF

** *France*: Part of 1959 contribution.

†† *United States of America*: Estimated amount: a total of $11 million was pledged subject to the condition that the contribution shall not exceed 50 per cent of total governmental contributions to the Fund.

The separation of expenditures into an ordinary budget and a number of extra-budgetary accounts was dictated by the harsh realities of each case; it would have been impossible to have established the programmes had it been necessary to finance them by normal assessments on governments. From one point of view it might seem logical to integrate the expenses into a common budget, with a uniform method of assessing contributions. In favour of this it might be argued, first, that a single, integrated budget would be easier and cheaper to administer than the present system; secondly, that once the teething troubles were over, it would increase the element of stability in the financing, and thus in the planning, of United Nations programmes; and, finally, that Member States should feel a sense of loyalty to the Organization to the extent of upholding the decisions of its most representative principal organ.[27]

On the other hand, it seems beyond the realm of immediate possibility to combine the different budgets. The most that could be attempted, in present circumstances, would be a progressive transfer to the regular budget of the United Nations of the administrative expenses of extra-budgetary programmes, continuing to finance field operations by voluntary contributions.

The General Assembly, by Article 17 (3) of the Charter, is supposed to " examine the administrative budgets of . . . specialized agencies with a view to making recommendations to the agencies concerned." By the terms of the agreements with the United Nations, the International Bank for Reconstruction and Development, and the International Monetary Fund are not required to transmit their budgets for examination by the United Nations. The agreement between the United Nations and the International Atomic Energy Agency provides that the administrative aspects of the Agency's budget shall be examined by the United Nations. These functions are entrusted to the Advisory Committee,[28] which also examines the budget estimates of the Technical Assistance Board and the administrative budget of the United Nations Special Fund. The Advisory Committee reports on these matters to the General Assembly.

The Advisory Committee thus conducts a broad review of the problems of administrative and budgetary co-ordination of the United Nations family of agencies. The exchange of information between the agencies on financial procedures, personnel matters, and the question of common premises is facilitated, though without any interference with the autonomy of the separate agencies. The Advisory Committee, as a subsidiary organ of the Assembly, has certain parallel responsibilities to the Administrative Committee on Co-ordination, which consists of the Secretary-General of the United Nations and the executive heads of the agencies. The Advisory Committee cannot compel an agency to change its administrative and budgetary procedures, but it can make available the experience of different agencies and emphasize the importance of the highest practicable degree of co-ordination and uniformity of practice.

---

27 In the case of one extra-budgetary programme—the Korean Reconstruction Agency (UNKRA)—more than 90 per cent. of the funds were provided by four Member States: the United States, the United Kingdom, Australia and Canada (United Nations Doc. A/4263, 9 Nov. 1959, Annex I, p. 1). UNKRA has now terminated its activities. The same four governments contributed more than 90 per cent. of the funds of UNRWA during 1959 (United Nations Doc. A/4267, 10 Nov. 1959).

28 General Assembly Res. 14A (I), 13 Feb. 1946.

The accounts of the United Nations are audited by a Board of Auditors composed of the Auditors-General (or equivalent officers) of three Member States, appointed by the Assembly for three-year terms.[29] The certified annual accounts, a financial report of the Secretary-General, and the report of the Board of Auditors are considered by the Advisory Committee, then by the Fifth Committee, and finally by the Assembly in plenary meeting. Defalcations have been rare, and the amounts trivial. In 1959 the Board of Auditors reported defalcations by a locally recruited book-keeper at an information centre, totalling $12,803 (£4,570); of this amount $1,029 (£367) had been reimbursed, and some further recovery of funds was anticipated. The Advisory Committee was satisfied that this was an exceptional case and did not detract from the general efficacy of the controls that are applied.[30]

[29] General Assembly Res. 74 (I), 7 Dec. 1946.
[30] *Financial Reports and Accounts for the year ended 31 December 1958 and Reports of the Board of Auditors*, G.A.O.R.: 14th Sess., 1959, Suppl. No. 6 (A/4116), p. 27; United Nations Doc. A/4153, 12 Aug. 1959, para. 5.

Chapter 10

THE QUESTION OF TIBET: A CASE STUDY

I am come now to the . . . objection, that sovereign princes
and states will hereby become not sovereign: a thing they will
never endure. But this also, under correction, is a mistake. . . .
And if this be called a lessening of their power, it must be only
because the great fish can no longer eat up the little ones. . . .
What cannot be controlled or resisted must be submitted to;
but all the world knows the date of the length of such empires.

WILLIAM PENN

Much of this book has necessarily been in general terms. I have
described procedural machinery, and only incidentally referred to the
political uses to which the machinery is put. In this penultimate
chapter, I want to show in political, as well as procedural and legal,
terms how one specific issue has been handled by the General
Assembly.

I had intended to select for study a typical item from the
Assembly's agenda, but there are no typical items. Each question is
unique. I therefore abandoned the search for a typical item and have
chosen one that is merely interesting. On two occasions, 1950 and
1959, delegations have proposed that the Assembly should take up
the Tibetan question, and each time significant procedural, legal and
political questions have arisen. Moreover, the discussion of the situation in Tibet by the General Assembly in 1959 illustrated the contention of a growing number of Member States that the question of
human rights, though a matter of domestic jurisdiction, is a proper
subject for international concern and action.

In describing the consideration given by the Assembly to the
Tibetan question, I have tried to record events in logical sequence—
but history is not like that. Events rarely have single causes; they
rarely occur in a rational order; they rarely have the results that the
chief actors intend. I am reminded of Sir Harold Nicolson's warning
in his account of the Congress of Vienna:

Nobody, in fact, who has had occasion actually to witness history in the
making, and to observe how infrequent and adventitious is the part
played in great affairs by "policy" or planned intention, can believe
thereafter that history is ever quite so simple, or quite so deliberate, as
it seems in retrospect; or that the apparent relation between cause and
effect was the relation which at the time, and in the circumstances,

actually determined the course of affairs. . . . Nobody who has not actually watched statesmen dealing with each other can have any real idea of the immense part played in human affairs by such unavowable and often unrecognisable causes as lassitude, affability, personal affection or dislike, misunderstanding, deafness or incomplete command of a foreign language, vanity, social engagements, interruptions and momentary health. Nobody who has not watched " policy " expressing itself in day to day action can realise how seldom is the course of events determined by deliberately planned purpose or how often what in retrospect appears to have been a fully conscious intention was at the time governed and directed by that most potent of all factors, " the chain of circumstance." Few indeed are the occasions on which any statesman sees his objective clearly before him and marches towards it with undeviating stride ; numerous indeed are the occasions when a decision or an event, which at the time seemed wholly unimportant, leads almost fortuitously to another decision which is no less incidental, until, little link by link, the chain of circumstance is forged.[1]

I am concerned in this chapter with three phases of the Tibetan question: (a) the request of El Salvador in November 1950 that the General Assembly should consider the Tibetan question; (b) developments relating to Tibet from 1951 until the middle of 1959; and (c) the Assembly's consideration of the Tibetan question in 1959.

THE REQUEST OF EL SALVADOR, 1950

The juridical status of Tibet has for long been ambiguous. Although successive Chinese Governments (including the Kuomintang and Communist Governments) have regarded Tibet as under Chinese suzerainty, the Tibetans themselves have often claimed the right to autonomy, and even full independence. China has usually had a special relationship to Tibet, and this was implicit in the Anglo-Chinese Convention of 1906 by which Britain agreed not to annex Tibet and not to interfere in the internal administration of Tibet; and China undertook not to permit any other foreign State to interfere with the territory or internal administration of Tibet. A Chinese attempt in 1910 to incorporate Tibet as a province of China caused the Dalai Lama to flee to India, and Chinese troops occupied parts of Tibet. Shortly after the Chinese revolution which overthrew the Manchu dynasty in 1911, the Chinese garrisons in Tibet were wiped out or expelled, and the Dalai Lama returned.

The republican Government of China, like its Manchu predecessors, regarded Tibet as a Chinese province; and Tibet, evidently under some pressure from Britain, agreed to accept Chinese suzerainty. The Convention of 1914, which was drawn up at a tripartite conference in Simla, recognized that Tibet was under

---

[1] *The Congress of Vienna* (New York: Harcourt, Brace; London: Constable; Toronto: Longmans, 1946), pp. 19–20.

Chinese suzerainty. China agreed not to convert Tibet into a Chinese province, and Britain agreed not to annex Tibet or any portion of it. This Convention was signed by the Dalai Lama for Tibet and by Sir Arthur McMahon for Britain; the Chinese initialled the agreement but later refused to sign or ratify it.

For the next thirty-five years the juridical status of Tibet remained obscure. The Kuomintang Government continued to regard Tibet as a province of China and, from time to time, tried to establish complete or partial Chinese authority in Tibet. The Tibetans, while not forcing the juridical issue, regarded themselves as independent, and Britain took a similar view. Britain enjoyed certain extraterritorial rights in Tibet, and these rights were inherited by India in 1947.

After the establishment of a Communist Government in Peking in 1949, negotiations were opened in New Delhi between a Tibetan delegation and the Chinese Ambassador to India. After a few weeks, the negotiations were suspended on the understanding that they would be resumed in Peking at a later date. Before the negotiations could be resumed, however, Chinese troops entered Tibet, and representatives of the Tibetan Government, in exile in India, addressed three appeals for help to the Secretary-General of the United Nations. The first communication stated that the people of Tibet wished to be independent and desired to be " uncontaminated by the germ of a highly materialistic creed "; reported the willingness of the Tibetan authorities to negotiate with the Peking Government; complained that their country was the victim of unprovoked aggression; asserted the determination of the Tibetan people to resist the invaders; and asked for the help of the United Nations.

We understand the United Nations have decided to stop aggression whenever it takes place. . . . We Ministers [of the Tibetan Government], with the approval of His Holiness the Dalai Lama, entrust the problem of Tibet in this emergency to the ultimate decision of the United Nations, and hoping that the conscience of the world would not allow the disruption of our State by methods reminiscent of the jungle.[2]

Before the next communication to the Secretary-General had been received, El Salvador had asked the General Assembly to consider the Tibetan appeal. The General Assembly was in session at the time and was much preoccupied with the Korean question. A month earlier, troops of the United Nations Command had crossed the 38th parallel and, two days before the first Tibetan appeal had been addressed to the United Nations, General Douglas MacArthur had confirmed that Communist Chinese forces had intervened in Korea. On the day that the request of El Salvador was considered by the

2 United Nations Doc. A/1549, 24 Nov. 1950.

General Committee, General MacArthur had launched a massive offensive in Korea, and Communist Chinese troops had immediately counter-attacked.

El Salvador was not a member of the General Committee but, in accordance with the Assembly's Rules of Procedure, her representative participated without vote in the discussion of the matter on 24 November 1950. The representative of El Salvador stated that unprovoked aggression had been committed against Tibet. He considered that the Assembly would be neglecting its responsibilities if it failed to condemn this aggression. He proposed that the Assembly should adopt the following resolution:

The General Assembly

Taking note that the peaceful nation of Tibet has been invaded, without any provocation on its part, by foreign forces proceeding from the territory controlled by the government established at Peiping,

Decides :

1. To condemn this act of unprovoked aggression against Tibet ;
2. To establish a Committee composed of . . . (names of nations) . . . which will be entrusted with the study of the appropriate measures that could be taken by the General Assembly on this matter ;
3. To instruct the Committee to undertake that study with special reference to the appeal made to the United Nations by the Government of Tibet, and to render its report to the General Assembly, as early as possible, during the present session.[3]

The British, Indian and Australian representatives urged the General Committee to defer a decision on the matter. They pointed out that the actual situation in Tibet was not clear, and the legal status of Tibet was ambiguous. The question should be resolved by peaceful means, and it was doubtful that the inclusion of the item in the agenda would facilitate a peaceful settlement. The United States representative agreed to postpone consideration of the request of El Salvador, since the governments most directly concerned favoured this course.

The Soviet representative, while not opposing postponement, said that Tibet was an inalienable part of China and the question was within China's domestic jurisdiction; the United Nations had no right to interfere in the internal affairs of China. The representative of Nationalist China did not object to adjourning the discussion. He, too, asserted that Tibet was part of China. The Peking régime was, however, a satellite and the invasion of Tibet had shocked the peace-loving Chinese people and was without justification.

---

[3] United Nations Doc. A/1534, 18 Nov. 1950.

The decision to adjourn consideration of the request of El Salvador was unanimous, and discussion of the request of El Salvador was not resumed at later sessions.[4]

From a procedural point of view, the General Committee's action on this occasion is of interest. The Rules state that the General Committee " shall make recommendations to the General Assembly with regard to each item proposed, concerning its inclusion in the agenda, the rejection of the request for inclusion, or the inclusion of the item in the provisional agenda of a future session "—in other words, postponement (Rule 40). The decision of 24 November 1950 " to adjourn consideration of the inclusion of the item proposed by El Salvador " was not specifically covered by the Rules of Procedure. The General Committee sent no recommendation to the Assembly, nor did it provide for its own resumption of consideration of the request. Moreover, neither El Salvador nor any other Member State subsequently asked the Assembly, and through it the General Committee, to continue its consideration of the proposed item.

Politically, however, the General Committee's action in 1950 was generally acceptable. It was acceptable to the Communist States, as they had no wish to see the United Nations discussing the dispatch of missions of enquiry to Tibet or adopting resolutions condemning the Peking Government. It was acceptable to the Indian and British Governments because it provided a breathing space for further negotiations on the matter. It did not rebuff El Salvador and other States which would have preferred more vigorous United Nations action. It was, in other words, a typical diplomatic compromise.

Following the decision of the General Committee to defer consideration on the request of El Salvador, two further communications from the Tibetan delegation in India were addressed to the Secretary-General. The first would appear to have been sent before the Tibetan delegation had been apprised of the General Committee's decision. A cablegram dated 28 November 1950 stated that the Tibetan delegation had " received instructions from our Government by wireless to request the United Nations for an early settlement of Tibet's problem. . . ."[5] The second communication, dated 8 December 1950, expressed " grave concern and dismay . . . great surprise and regret " at the General Committee's decision; insisted that Tibetans would accept any decision of the United Nations; stated that they were willing to send a delegation to the United Nations; suggested that if the facts were in dispute, a fact-finding mission of the United Nations

---

[4] G.A.O.R.: 5th Sess., General Committee, 72nd–73rd Mtgs., 20, 24 Nov. 1950, pp. 15–20.
[5] United Nations Doc. A/1565.

should be sent to Tibet; disclaimed any intention of provoking a world conflict over Tibet; and said that the appeal to the United Nations had the consent and blessing of the Dalai Lama.[6]

DEVELOPMENTS RELATING TO TIBET, 1951–59

It was clear that the Tibetans, left to their own resources, would have to negotiate with Peking. How these negotiations took place can best be told in the candid words of the agreement of 23 May 1951 between the Peking Government and the Government of Tibet.

The CPG [Central People's Government of the People's Republic of China], when it ordered the People's Liberation Army (PLA) to march into Tibet, notified the local government of Tibet to send delegates to the central authorities to conduct talks for the conclusion of an agreement on measures for the peaceful liberation of Tibet. At the latter part of April 1951 the delegates with full powers of the local government of Tibet arrived in Peking.[7]

The Tibetan delegation engaged in the negotiations with the Peking authorities in the knowledge that Chinese troops had entered Tibet, and the Dalai Lama has since confirmed that the agreement of 23 May 1951 was signed under duress. In a statement after his escape to India, the Dalai Lama said:

When Chinese armies violated the territorial integrity of Tibet they were committing a flagrant act of aggression.

The agreement which followed the invasion of Tibet was also thrust upon its people and Government by threat of arms. It was never accepted by them of their own free will. Consent of the Government was secured under duress and at the point of bayonet.

My representatives were compelled to sign the agreement under a threat of further military operations against Tibet by invading armies of China. . . .[8]

The agreement of 23 May 1951 authorized the entry into Tibet of Chinese forces, and empowered the Peking Government to handle the external affairs of Tibet. The Peking Government agreed not to alter the existing political system in Tibet, and not to interfere with the established status, functions, and powers of the Dalai Lama or the Panchen Lama. The Tibetan people were to have regional autonomy, and their religious beliefs and customs were to be respected. Internal reforms in Tibet would be effected after consultation with leading Tibetans, and there would be no compulsion. A committee, which

6 United Nations Doc. A/1658.
7. Text in *The Question of Tibet and the Rule of Law* (Geneva: International Commission of Jurists, 1959), p. 140.
8 Statement of Dalai Lama in Mussoorie, India, 20 June 1959. *The New York Times*, 21 June 1959, p. 24. Hereafter cited as: Mussoorie Statement.

would include patriotic Tibetans, would be set up to ensure the implementation of the agreement.[9]

A significant feature of the 1951 agreement was the attempt to increase the prestige of the Panchen Lama. Traditionally the two Grand Lamas had been of equal status, the Panchen Lama having a special authority in secular matters and the Dalai Lama having a special authority in spiritual matters. In modern times, the prestige and status of the Dalai Lama had increased, and he had come to be regarded as supreme in both religious and secular affairs.

The 1951 agreement stated that " the central authorities " would not alter the established status, functions, and powers of the Dalai Lama. This could be interpreted to mean that the Peking Government would not be under any obligation to interfere if any initiative to alter the position of the Dalai Lama were taken by Tibetans. In regard to the Panchen Lama, however, his position was to be maintained unconditionally. " The established status, functions and powers of the Panchen Ngoerhtehni . . . shall be maintained." Moreover, the phrase " established status, functions and powers " was defined as meaning those of the thirteenth Dalai Lama and the ninth Panchen Ngoerhtehni " when they were in friendly and amicable relations with each other "; meaning the status, functions and powers of the immediate predecessors of the present Grand Lamas.[10]

This aspect of the 1951 agreement has a special significance in view of the fact that the Panchen Lama and his recent predecessors had been under strong Chinese influence. The ninth Panchen Lama had left Tibet in 1924, never to return. He had died in exile in China in 1937. The tenth incarnation of the Panchen Lama had not been discovered until 1941, and he was not installed until August 1949, in the Chinghai province of China. Within a month he had fallen into the hands of the Chinese Communists, and it was not until April 1952 that he reached Lhasa. By the 1951 agreement, he regained some of the formal authority his predecessor had enjoyed until 1924.

The Panchen Lama has co-operated closely with the Communist authorities. He did not accompany the Dalai Lama into exile in 1959, and he has vigorously denounced the Dalai Lama as a dupe, a traitor and a stooge of imperialists.

The events of 1949–50 and the agreement of 1951 brought the Chinese Communist revolution to the Indian borders. Mr. Nehru had made it clear that India had no wish to retain the extraterritorial privileges she had inherited from Britain. At the same time, the

---

9 *The Question of Tibet and the Rule of Law*, pp. 140–141.
10 *Ibid.*, p. 140.

Indian Government had greatly regretted the Chinese invasion of Tibet, and had so informed the Peking Government. It was, in the Indian view, natural that the Tibetans would consider that the 1951 negotiations were conducted under duress.

In April 1954 an agreement was concluded between the Indian Government and the People's Republic of China concerning trade between India and the " The Tibet region of China." A preamble to the agreement contained the *Panchsheel,* or five principles, which were later to acquire much renown. They were incorporated into several agreements between Asian governments, and were endorsed a year later at the Bandung Conference. These lofty principles affirmed mutual respect for each other's territorial integrity and sovereignty, mutual non-aggression, mutual non-interference in each other's internal affairs, equality and mutual benefit, and peaceful co-existence.[11]

In September 1954 the Dalai Lama (who was then nineteen years old) and the Panchen Lama, accompanied by an entourage of leading Tibetans, arrived in Peking, where they remained until March 1955. The Tibetan delegation at that time agreed to the creation of a new body, known inelegantly as the Preparatory Committee for the Formation of a Tibetan Autonomous Region. This Committee was given wide paper powers, though the Dalai Lama now says that it " had little power and decisions in all important matters were taken by the Chinese authorities." [12]

The Tibetans, according to Chinese Communist sources, evinced no great enthusiasm for the 1955 plan for Tibet. The Preparatory Commission did not get launched until the middle of 1956, by which time reports of armed clashes between Tibetan and Chinese units were reaching India. There was, therefore, considerable interest in the visit of the two Grand Lamas to India in connection with the observance of the 2,500th anniversary of the birth of the Buddha.

The Tibetan party reached New Delhi on 25 November 1956 and remained in India until April of the following year. The young Dalai Lama evidently considered the possibility of not returning to Tibet, and sought Prime Minister Jawaharlal Nehru's advice on the matter. Mr. Nehru states that he " told him [the Dalai Lama] of Premier Chou En-lai's . . . assurance that he would respect the autonomy of Tibet. I suggested to him that he should accept these assurances in good faith and co-operate in maintaining that autonomy and bringing

11 India, Ministry of External Affairs, *Notes, Memoranda and Letters Exchanged and Agreements Signed Between the Governments of India and China, 1954–1959: White Paper* (New Delhi: 1959), p. 98. Hereafter cited as: *Indian White Paper.*
12 Statement of Dalai Lama in Tezpur, India, 18 Apr. 1959, *The New York Times,* 19 Apr. 1959. Hereafter cited as: Tezpur Statement.

about certain reforms in Tibet." [13]   "Mr. Nehru advised me to change my decision," the Dalai Lama has said; " I followed his advice and returned to Tibet. . . ." [14]

Throughout 1957 and 1958 there were frequent reports of fighting in Tibet and of opposition to the Chinese measures of reform. These reports at first suggested little more than sporadic and isolated guerrilla activity, but by the middle of 1958 it seemed certain that unrest was widespread and that a serious revolt was in progress. Even so, the uprising of March 1959 seems to have been spontaneous. The Dalai Lama's account is as follows:

The relations of Tibetans with China became openly strained from the early part of February 1959.

The Dalai Lama had agreed a month in advance to attend a cultural show in the Chinese headquarters and the date was suddenly fixed for the 10th of March. The people of Lhasa became apprehensive that some harm might be done to the Dalai Lama and as a result about 10,000 people gathered around the Dalai Lama's summer palace at Norbulingka and physically prevented the Dalai Lama from attending the function.

Thereafter the people themselves decided to raise a bodyguard for the protection of the Dalai Lama. Large crowds of Tibetans went about the streets of Lhasa demonstrating against the Chinese rule in Tibet. . . .

On the 17th of March two or three mortar shells were fired in the direction of the Norbulingka palace. . . .

After this the advisers became alive to the danger to the person of the Dalai Lama and in those difficult circumstances it became imperative for the Dalai Lama, the members of his family and his high officials to leave Lhasa. The Dalai Lama would like to state categorically that he left Lhasa and Tibet and came on to India of his own free will and not under duress.[15]

Mr. Nehru has made it clear that the Dalai Lama and his party sought, and were granted, political asylum. The Dalai Lama entered India entirely of his own volition, is not held under duress, and may return to Tibet or go wherever he wants. The Panchen Lama, the Chinese Ambassador in New Delhi or any other emissary of the Chinese Government may visit the Dalai Lama to discover whether or not he is a free agent.[16]

THE UNITED NATIONS AND TIBET, 1959

The events in Tibet between 1951 and 1959, culminating in the flight of the Dalai Lama and 13,000 other Tibetans, had shocked non-Communist opinion in all parts of the world. It was admitted that, by the standards of the middle of the twentieth century, Tibet was

---

13 Statement in the Indian Parliament, 27 Apr. 1959. Text in *The Question of Tibet and the Rule of Law*, p. 175.   14 Mussoorie Statement.
15 Tezpur Statement.
16 Statement in the Indian Parliament, 27 Apr. 1959, *Indiagram*, No. 19 (8 May 1959). See also *Indian White Paper*, p. 69.

backward. The social system was feudal and static, and the conditions of life of the mass of the Tibetan people were poor. It was not doubted that the Chinese Communists had encountered difficulties in effecting reforms. Nevertheless, the fact that the Dalai Lama's party had successfully reached India in spite of all attempts to intercept it suggested that the Tibetans, at any rate in the areas through which the party passed, felt a strong loyalty to the Dalai Lama and his advisers.

It would have been possible (though this does not come easily to governments) for the Chinese authorities in Peking to have been somewhat apologetic about events in Tibet, to have admitted that mistakes had been made, to have given assurances that Tibetan opinion would in future be respected, and to have invited the Dalai Lama and his entourage to return.

A contrary policy was followed. In April the National People's Congress was in session in Peking, and advantage was taken of this occasion to let loose a torrent of abuse directed against the Dalai Lama and the " reactionary clique of the upper social strata " in Tibet, as well as " the imperialists and Indian expansionists." [17]

Moderate Asian opinion was as shaken by the virulence of the Chinese attacks on India as it had been by the events in Tibet. Mr. Nehru, in a characteristic understatement, said he was " greatly distressed at the tone of the comments and charges made against India by responsible people in China." He described the charges as " so fantastic that I find it difficult to deal with them . . . unbecoming and entirely void of substance." [18]

During the period preceding the opening of the 1959 regular session of the Assembly, there was naturally a good deal of speculation about the likelihood of the Tibetan question being brought formally before the United Nations. At a press conference in June, Mr. Hammarskjold had stated that he had the question of Tibet under continued observation. " As regards action, I believe that this would be an issue which would take us beyond the routine of human rights and that, for that reason, some government may wish to raise it as an item for debate in the General Assembly." [19]

At first, however, governments were disposed to wait and see. It was felt that India, because of what Mr. Nehru had described as " a long tradition of cultural and religious ties between India and the

---

[17] *The Question of Tibet and the Rule of Law*, pp. 163–170.
[18] Statement in the Indian Parliament, 27 Apr. 1959, *Indiagram, loc. cit.*, pp. 2–3.
[19] Note to Correspondents, No. 2006, 18 June 1959, p. 9.

Tibet region of China," [20] and more particularly because of India's strategic interests and recent association with the Tibetan question, should be allowed the opportunity of raising the matter at the United Nations in the form and at the time of her own choosing.

In the event, the Indian Government took no initiative in formally raising the matter at the United Nations. For one thing, India was gravely concerned at the deterioration of her relations with China and at the intrusion of Chinese forces into territory that India regarded as her own. For another thing, the arrival of the Dalai Lama and his chief advisers on Indian soil was a matter of some embarrassment to the Indian Government. The Tibetans sought asylum, and the Indian Government did not hesitate to grant it. For several years, however, the Chinese Government had been complaining about the activities of Tibetan refugees in India.[21] In a note of July 1958, the Chinese Government had alleged that the activities of Tibetan émigrés in India represented " another malicious scheme of United States imperialists to create tension. . . ." The Indian note of reply expressed great surprise at these allegations which " must have been based on a complete misunderstanding of facts." [22]

Be that as it may, the Indian Government was clearly anxious to avoid offending China by allowing India to become a base for provocative activities. The Indian Government had no wish to place formal restraints on the political activities of the Dalai Lama, yet at the same time was concerned lest the Dalai Lama and his entourage should, explicitly or implicitly, constitute themselves as a Tibetan government-in-exile.[23] Moreover, it was always possible that, should the Tibetan question come before the United Nations, some delegation might propose that the Dalai Lama be heard in person by a United Nations organ. Indeed, the United States representative in the General Committee of the Assembly stated subsequently that " The United States for its part would have welcomed giving the Dalai Lama the opportunity to present his case personally to this body." [24] Such a development, had it occurred, might have made the continued presence in India of the Dalai Lama additionally embarrassing.

The Indian Government may also have been influenced by the knowledge that its proposal that the Assembly discuss the representation of China would again be defeated during the fourteenth session.

20 Statement in the Indian Parliament, 23 Mar. 1959, *Indiagram*, No. 14 (3 Apr. 1959), p. 3.   21 *Indian White Paper, op. cit.*, pp. 60–66.
22 *Ibid.*, pp. 61–63.   23 United Nations Doc. A/PV.834, 21 Oct. 1959, p. 42.
24 This remark is quoted from the verbatim text of the statement of the United States representative issued by the U.S. Mission to the U.N., Press Release No. 3247, 9 Oct. 1959. It does not appear in the summary record issued by the United Nations (G.A.O.R.: 14th Sess., General Committee, 124th Mtg., 9 Oct. 1959).

To discuss the situation in Tibet without the Peking Government being represented in the General Assembly would, in the Indian view, have been absurd. Moreover, the Indian Government took the position that the Universal Declaration of Human Rights and the human rights provisions of the Charter could not properly be invoked in this case.

Violation of human rights applies to those who have accepted the Charter of the United Nations, in other words, those members of the United Nations who have accepted the Charter. Strictly speaking, you cannot apply the Charter to people who have not accepted the Charter, who have not been allowed to come into the United Nations.[25]

Finally, the Indian Government believed that to discuss Tibet would inflame international relations. India had played a leading role in fostering the idea that an area of peace could be created in Asia, and the Indian Government felt that public debate on such a contentious issue as Tibet would heighten tension and add to the difficulties of direct negotiations with Peking on the outstanding questions between the two countries. During a statement on the Tibetan question in the Assembly on 21 October, the Indian representative repeatedly returned to the point:

We think that the welfare of the people concerned and their future largely depend upon the degree of restraint that can be exercised. . . . We would never depart from the belief that reconciliation is not impossible. . . . We shall not tighten this deadlock, we shall not add to this by being parties to any acrimonious discussion here. . . . It is the hope of my people and my government that the plight of the Tibetan people will be resolved by the process of reconciliation. . . . Any warming up of these issues or any exacerbation of them cannot lead in any way to reconciliation.[26]

This argument, taken in isolation, has some merit. Public debate of contentious questions may undoubtedly increase tension. On the other hand, the cause of the tension is not the debate but the events or situations being debated. There can hardly be a government which has not, at some time or another, supported the discussion of a

25 United Nations Doc. A/PV.834, 21 Oct. 1959, p. 42. It should, however, be noted that the People's Republic of China supported the final communiqué of the Bandung Conference, in which " full support " was declared for " the fundamental principles of Human Rights as set forth in the Charter of the United Nations "; noted the Universal Declaration of Human Rights as " a common standard of achievement for all peoples and all nations "; declared full support for " the principles of self-determination of peoples and nations as set forth in the Charter of the United Nations "; and, in the final section of the communiqué, reaffirmed " Respect for fundamental human rights and . . . the purposes and principles of the Charter of the United Nations." Text in George McTurnan Kahin, *The Asian-African Conference* (Ithaca: Cornell Univ. Press; London: Oxford Univ. Press, 1956), pp. 76–85.
26 United Nations Doc. A/PV.834, 21 Oct. 1959, pp. 39–40, 44–45, 46, 47.

contentious question by an organ of the United Nations with the full realization that such discussion might inflame passions.

The Indian Government made it clear later, during the debate in the plenary Assembly, that it was opposed to discussion of the Tibetan item but had not tried to prevent it. This opposition was " not, as has been suggested, because of our fear of anybody or because we are too near China and do not want to displease her." Nor was it based on the provisions of the Charter relating to domestic jurisdiction. " We think the Assembly has a right to discuss it [the Tibetan question] if it so decides to do, but discussion does not mean intervention, and we have always held that point of view." [27]

But the momentum of history is outside the control of any one government. The situation in Tibet was, from the point of view of the United Nations, transformed on 9 September 1959. On that date, the Secretary-General made public the text of a message he had received that day from the Dalai Lama. It read as follows:

Your Excellency,

Kindly refer to the proceedings of the General Committee of the United Nations General Assembly held on Friday the 24th November 1950 at which it was resolved that the consideration of El Salvador's complaint against invasion of Tibet by foreign forces should be adjourned in order to give the parties the opportunity to arrive at a peaceful settlement. It is with the deepest regret that I am informing you that the act of aggression by Chinese forces has not terminated. On the contrary the area of aggression has been substantially extended with the result that practically the whole of Tibet is under the occupation of the Chinese forces. I and my Government have made several appeals for peaceful and friendly settlement but so far these appeals have been completely ignored. In these circumstances and in view of the inhuman treatment and crimes against humanity and religion to which the people of Tibet are being subjected, I solicit immediate intervention of the United Nations and consideration by the General Committee on its own initiative of the Tibetan issue which had been adjourned. In this connection I and my Government wish to emphasize that Tibet was a sovereign state at the time when her territorial integrity was violated by the Chinese armies in 1950. In support of this contention the Government of Tibet urge the following:

(1) No power or authority was exercised by the Government of China in or over Tibet since the declaration of independence by the 13th Dalai Lama in 1912.

(2) The sovereign status of Tibet during this period finds conclusive evidence in the fact that the Government of Tibet concluded as many as five international agreements immediately before and during these years.

[27] *Ibid.*, pp. 33, 37, 38.

(3) The Government of Tibet take their stand on the Anglo-Tibetan Convention of 1914 which recognized the sovereign status of Tibet and accorded the same position to the Tibet Plenipotentiary as was given to the representatives of Great Britain and China. It is true that this Convention imposed certain restrictions on the external sovereignty of Tibet but these did not deprive her of her international position. Moreover, these restrictions ceased to have any effect on the transfer of power in India.

(4) There is no valid and subsisting international agreement under which Tibet or any other power recognizes Chinese suzerainty.

(5) The sovereign status of Tibet is equally evident from the fact that during the Second World War Tibet insisted on maintaining her neutrality and only allowed the transport of non-military goods from India to China through Tibet. This position was accepted by the Governments of Great Britain and China.

(6) The sovereign status of Tibet has also been acknowledged by other powers. In 1948, when a trade delegation from the Government of Tibet visited India, France, Italy, the United Kingdom and the United States of America, the passports issued by the Tibetan Government were accepted by the Governments of these countries.

Your Excellency, I and my Government also solicit immediate intervention of the United Nations on humanitarian grounds. Since their violation of the territorial integrity of Tibet, the Chinese forces have committed the following offences against the universally accepted laws of international conduct:

(1) They have dispossessed thousands of Tibetans of their properties and deprived them of every source of livelihood and thus driven them to death and desperation.

(2) Men, women and children have been forced into labour gangs and made to work on military construction without payment or on nominal payment.

(3) They have adopted cruel and inhuman measures for the purpose of sterilizing Tibetan men and women with the view to the total extermination of the Tibetan race.

(4) Thousands of innocent people of Tibet have been brutally massacred.

(5) There have been many cases of murder of leading citizens of Tibet without any cause or justification.

(6) Every attempt has been made to destroy our religion and culture. Thousands of monasteries have been razed to the ground and sacred images and articles of religion completely destroyed. Life and property are no longer safe and Lhasa, the capital of the State, is now a dead city.

The sufferings which my people are undergoing are beyond description and it is imperatively necessary that this wanton and ruthless murder of my people should be immediately brought to an end. It is in these circumstances that I appeal to you and the United Nations in the confident hope that our appeal will receive the consideration which it deserves.[28]

[28] This document bore no reference number or symbol.

From this point on, it was virtually certain that a move would be made to have the Tibetan question examined by the Assembly, and on 28 September Ireland and the Federation of Malaya formally proposed the inclusion in the agenda of an item, " The question of Tibet."

It is no secret that the original initiative in this matter came from the Irish delegation. Since her admission to the United Nations in December 1955, Ireland has played an independent, imaginative, and constructive role in United Nations affairs. Her Minister for External Affairs, Frank Aiken, had favourably impressed the Assembly by advancing a number of proposals for the easing of tension in Central Europe and in the Middle East. Frederick Boland, Ireland's Permanent Representative at United Nations headquarters, is a veteran diplomat who has won a great deal of personal respect, particularly for his chairmanship of the Fourth Committee during the 1958–59 session. Ireland has been active in support of United Nations action to prevent the dissemination of nuclear weapons. Ireland was the only European country which in 1959 joined in proposing that the Assembly should discuss the question of race conflict in South Africa. Finally, Ireland voted in 1957, 1958 and 1959 in favour of discussing the representation of China. Ireland's record in the United Nations is unquestionably that of a vigorously independent country, and her initiative in this case was consistent with her general policy and her position on similar questions.

The fact that a country is independent does not mean that it always acts alone. During the first fortnight of the Assembly, the Irish delegation engaged in informal consultations concerning the possibility of additional sponsors of the Tibetan item, the timing and procedure of debate should the item be accepted, and the sort of resolution that might gain a two-thirds majority in the Assembly.

In the course of those informal consultations, two points were emphasized. First, that it would not encourage a temperate handling of the matter if the item were co-sponsored by a large number of the so-called " pact-countries," that is to say, anti-Communist countries having military and political ties with the United States. It is a matter of speculation how many such countries would have agreed to co-sponsor the item had their co-sponsorship been actively sought.

Secondly, the Irish delegation attached considerable importance to having at least one neutral Asian country as co-sponsor. The Federation of Malaya was willing to join Ireland in this matter, and on 28 September a formal request was made for the inclusion of the Tibetan item in the agenda.

It is possible that Ireland would have been happy to have had one or two more co-sponsors. The request to include the item in the agenda might have carried a little more weight if the co-sponsors had included such countries as Burma, Canada, Ceylon, Ghana, Mexico, Morocco, Nepal, New Zealand, the Scandinavian countries, Sudan or Tunisia.

Some of the reasons why Ireland and Malaya decided to propose the item for inclusion in the agenda were made clear in subsequent debate; other reasons can only be guessed at. By the end of the second week of the Assembly, it seemed clear that an item on Tibet would be proposed by someone. Ireland and Malaya may have felt— and this would be consistent with their position on other questions— that a maximum effect would be created by a minimum of passion. It may well have been in the minds of members of the Irish and Malayan delegations that if they did not proceed with the matter, others would do so, and perhaps in an extravagant manner.

Rule 20 of the Rules of Procedure states that all items proposed for inclusion in the agenda shall be accompanied by an explanatory memorandum and, if possible, by basic documents or by a draft resolution. In accordance with this Rule, Ireland and Malaya submitted the following explanatory memorandum: [29]

The Governments requesting the inscription of this item are convinced that under the Charter the United Nations cannot ignore the present situation in Tibet, as described in reliable and consistent reports over a long period culminating in the official statements of the Dalai Lama dated 18 April, 22 April and 20 June 1959, and his appeal to this Organization of 9 September 1959. After study of the material available, the conclusion is inescapable that there exists *prima facie* evidence of an attempt to destroy the traditional way of life of the Tibetan people and the religious and cultural autonomy long recognized to belong to them, as well as a systematic disregard for the human rights and fundamental freedoms set out in the Universal Declaration of Human Rights.

In such circumstances, the United Nations has both a moral obligation and a legal right to discuss the situation.

The Governments concerned further consider that this Assembly has a duty to call for the restoration of the religious and civil liberties of the people of Tibet.

To these ends the inscription is requested on the agenda of the General Assembly at this fourteenth session of an item to be entitled " The Question of Tibet ".

While informal discussions were going on in the corridors, the General Debate was taking its desultory course in the General Assembly hall, and it was notable how few of the speakers referred to Tibet.[30] Sixty-four speakers (including the Irish Minister for

---

29 General Assembly Doc. A/4234, 29 Sept. 1959, p. 2.
30 There were a few references to Tibet during the debate on the Indian proposal to discuss Chinese representation.

External Affairs) engaged in a diplomatic *tour d'horizon* without even mentioning Tibet. Representatives of France, Italy, Laos, Nepal, Norway, Paraguay, Thailand, Turkey, the United Kingdom and the United States referred to Tibet *en passant,* but in no case devoted more than one minute of their speeches to this question.

The representative of Nationalist China expounded the views of Kuomintang leaders on the Tibetan question, and quoted the remarks of a member of the Chinese Nationalist delegation when the Tibetan question had come before the General Committee in 1950. The representative of El Salvador quoted at some length from the proposal of El Salvador in 1950, including the draft resolution which his delegation had suggested, and the remarks of the Indian representative on that occasion.[31] The representative of Malaya described events in Tibet as a new and more devilish and sinister form of colonialism. He denied a Communist charge that in this matter Malaya was acting under the influence of the United States.

The representatives of Hungary and the Soviet Union objected briefly that the peaceful atmosphere was being disturbed by raising the so-called question of Tibet. The Soviet representative alleged that Ireland and Malaya were merely acting as puppets in sponsoring the Tibetan item, while the Hungarian representative declared flatly that the United States was the real villain of the piece. Exercising the right of reply, the Irish Minister for External Affairs denied that Ireland was acting at the behest of any other delegation. The human rights of the Tibetan people had been violated. Ireland had consistently acted in the United Nations in support of human rights and in accordance with the Charter, and not because of adherence to any *bloc.* Alarm about events in Tibet was not caused by the machinations of a particular State or group of States; it was caused by the events themselves, which were repugnant to the moral conscience of mankind.

On the afternoon of 9 October 1959, the Assembly's General Committee met to consider *inter alia* the request of Ireland and Malaya that the question of Tibet be included in the agenda. This request had been submitted in accordance with Rule 15 of the Rules of Procedure, which provides that items may be proposed for inclusion in the agenda less than thirty days before the session opens or during the course of the session, so long as the items are " of an important and urgent character." The quoted phrase is difficult to interpret, since almost all items proposed for inclusion in the agenda are regarded

---

31 *Supra,* p. 227.

by their sponsors as important and urgent. In this particular case, the criterion of importance and urgency was peculiarly difficult to apply as the other two matters considered by the General Committee on the same occasion, though undoubtedly important, had acquired urgency only through the fact of not having been included in the original provisional agenda—and for perfectly good reasons.[32]

Rule 43 provides that a Member of the Assembly which is not represented on the General Committee, and which has requested the inclusion of an item in the agenda, may attend meetings of the General Committee at which the request is discussed and may participate, though without the right to vote, in the discussion of the item. In accordance with this Rule, Ireland and Malaya were invited by the Chairman of the General Committee to take their places at the Committee table.

The explanatory memorandum of Ireland and Malaya had presented the Tibetan question as being of concern to the United Nations because human rights had been violated, and this point was made in the Irish and Malayan statements before the General Committee (paras. 4–5, 6, 8 and 51).[33] The representatives of Guatemala, the Philippines and the United States supported this view (paras. 13, 42 and 47). The three members of the Committee from the Soviet *Bloc* denied that there had been any violation of human rights by the Chinese Communists; indeed, the Chinese were trying to change an inherently cruel and feudal system in Tibet, and had been obstructed by the Dalai Lama and other reactionary elements (paras. 16, 28 and 36). The South African representative took the position that however precious might be the traditional values of a people, the suppression of these values could not form the basis of a charge against a State, whether a Member of the United Nations or not (para. 22).

The Irish representative recognized that the facts regarding the matter might not have been sufficiently established, but the statements of the Dalai Lama and other reports constituted prima facie evidence that human rights had been disregarded (para. 9). The British representative, while not necessarily supporting the explanatory memorandum, considered it right that the world should know exactly what was happening in Tibet (para. 27). The representative of the

[32] These items were: International encouragement of scientific research into the control of cancerous diseases (proposed by the Byelorussian S.S.R.); and the United Nations Library: gift of the Ford Foundation (proposed by the Secretary-General).

[33] The official record of the meeting (G.A.O.R.: 14th Sess., General Committee, 124th Mtg., 9 Oct. 1959) constitutes an objective chronological account of the debate. I have not tried to duplicate the official records of the United Nations, but rather to summarize and classify the main points discussed. The references in parentheses in the text are to the paragraphs of the official printed record of the meeting.

B.   16

Philippines said he would vote for the inclusion of the item in the agenda, though without prejudging the question of whether the appeal was justified (para. 47). The Soviet representative, on the other hand, considered that doubt as to the facts was an argument in favour of rejecting the proposed item; indeed, the so-called facts had been fabricated to suit the needs of the case (para. 16).

The absence of representatives of the Peking Government was commented on by the Irish delegate, but he considered that this would not justify the Assembly in ignoring what had happened in Tibet (para. 8). The Indonesian representative, by contrast, considered that the Assembly had deprived itself of the sole means of clarifying the situation in Tibet when it had refused to consider the question of Chinese representation (para. 31). This point was also made by the representative of Romania (para. 37).

The view that events in Tibet were essentially within the domestic jurisdiction of China, and therefore outside the competence of the United Nations, was expressed by the representatives of Czecho-slovakia and the Soviet Union (paras. 15 and 28). The representatives of Belgium, Britain, South Africa and Turkey also expressed doubts as to the competence of the United Nations (paras. 22–24, 33 and 40). The representative of China, while pointing out that Tibet was part of China, did not consider that an examination of the Tibetan ques-tion would contravene the " domestic jurisdiction " provisions of the Charter (para. 18).

The Soviet representative alleged that an unidentified statement of the Dalai Lama had, in reality, been prepared in the United States State Department. It was, in his view, easy to guess for whom the delegations of Ireland and Malaya were acting (para. 15). The Soviet, Czechoslovak and Romanian representatives considered that the attempt to bring the so-called Tibetan question before the United Nations was a manœuvre to revive the spirit of the cold war (paras. 15, 17, 29, 35 and 43), while the Liberian delegate said that he would vote against the inclusion of the item in order to preserve the relaxa-tion of tension (para. 39). The Irish representative insisted, however, that in raising the question of Tibet, his delegation had no wish to create acrimony (para. 7).

Two other points were made by the Irish representative. First, Ireland was anxious not to add to the difficulties of States which were neighbours of China and Tibet, that is to say, Burma, India and Nepal. Secondly, though it might be said that any decision reached by the Assembly would probably be ignored by the People's Republic of China, the majority of Member States had taken the view that no

State could afford to remain obdurate in the face of world opinion, endorsed by the General Assembly (paras. 10 and 11).

Representatives of Morocco and France explained why they intended to abstain from voting. The representative of Morocco said the matter was very complex and difficult to decide (para. 41), and the French representative said that from the legal standpoint there was insufficient justification for acceding to the request of Ireland and Malaya (para. 48).

It can be imagined that the discussion at times became tense, strident, and repetitious; and when the Soviet representative referred to oppression in Oman, Northern Ireland and the Belgian Congo (para. 44), the Chairman intervened and asked the Soviet representative to moderate the tone of his remarks and avoid any reference to matters not related to the item under discussion (para. 45). Later in the meeting, the Soviet representative protested that the Chairman had acted unfairly, but the Chairman insisted that in his conduct of the meeting he had shown an excess of restraint (paras. 54–55).

At the conclusion of the debate, the General Committee voted 11–5–4 to recommend to the plenary that the item " The question of Tibet " be included in the agenda (para. 53); the votes are given in Table 26 (pages 249–250).

The General Committee had one further task: to recommend whether the Tibetan item should be dealt with directly in plenary meeting or in the first instance in a Main Committee; and, in the latter event, which Committee. Although most items are referred in the first instance to a Main Committee, this is not an invariable practice. In recent sessions the plenary Assembly has dealt directly with such questions as the detention in China of personnel of the United Nations Command, the Hungarian question, and the Turkish-Syrian dispute of 1957.

There was an informal understanding, to which there was no real opposition, that the Tibetan question would be taken up in plenary meeting. This method avoids some duplication of debate and is especially appropriate for the consideration of questions that do not require intensive procedural manœuvres before an acceptable resolution can be prepared. The Irish representative had, in his opening statement, suggested that the matter be referred to the plenary Assembly, and the United States and British representatives supported the suggestion (para. 14).[34] This proposal was approved by 12–0–6, with two States present and not voting.

Two interesting procedural points arise in connection with this

---

[34] The remarks of the Irish and British representatives on this matter have been squeezed out of the summary records of the meeting.

vote. First, the Rules of Procedure provide that in a roll-call vote, three ways of voting are possible: " Yes," " No," or " Abstention " (Rule 128). If a member of the General Committee is absent when the vote is taken, he obviously cannot participate in the voting. The Chairman often does not participate in the voting, as a way of demonstrating his impartiality. It is, however, unusual (though by no means unknown) for members to be recorded as " Present and not voting "—to abstain from abstaining.[35]

The second interesting point of procedure concerns the footnote on page 17 of the official records, which reads: " After the meeting, the representative of Indonesia informed the Secretariat that he wished to have his delegation recorded as having voted against," although he had, in fact, voted " yes." The question of the correction of votes in the General Assembly and its Committees was the subject of a special report by the Secretary-General in 1955.[36] With regard to clerical errors in the counting or recording of votes, no particular difficulty arises if the correction of an error does not affect the result. If a representative discovers an error, he may, on a point of order, draw the attention of the presiding officer to it. If the error is discovered by the Secretariat, the presiding officer is informed, and he in turn brings the matter to the attention of the Assembly or Committee. Similarly, no particular difficulty arises in connection with requests by members to change their votes before the results have been announced.

Difficulties may arise, however, if clerical errors are discovered or Members request that their votes be changed after the result has been announced. If clerical errors which would change the result are brought to light, there would seem to be no alternative but to change the decision or repeat the vote. With regard to requests by Members to change their votes after the result has been announced, the usual practice of the Assembly and of virtually all legislative bodies is that a change of vote can be permitted only if such a change does not affect the result. In the case under consideration, the change of vote requested by Indonesia had no effect on the result. The official records give the result of the vote as announced by the Chairman at the time, with the Indonesian request in a footnote.

On 12 October the plenary Assembly considered the recommendations of the General Committee with regard to the proposed Tibetan

---

[35] I heard recently of a representative who was called away from a meeting, and in his absence a roll-call vote was requested. He was hastily recalled by a friendly representative so that it could be recorded that he was present and not voting.

[36] G.A.O.R.: 10th Sess., 1955, Annexes, Agenda item 51 (A/2977).

item. The Assembly had just concluded the thirteenth inconclusive ballot of the day in connection with the election of non-permanent members of the Security Council (together with two roll-call votes on matters of procedure), and seven ballots in connection with the election of members of the Economic and Social Council. It can be imagined that tempers were somewhat frayed—though they might have been even more frayed had representatives known that some forty further ballots for the Security Council would be necessary.

When the General Committee has recommended that an item be included in the agenda, debate on the recommendation in the plenary is limited to three speakers in favour of inclusion and three speakers against; the President may limit the time to be allowed to speakers (Rule 23). There is no specific Rule in the plenary, as there is in the General Committee (Rule 40), that prohibits discussion of the substance of a matter proposed for inclusion in the agenda, though it may be assumed that the President may call to order a speaker who enters unnecessarily into matters of substance, under the Rule relating to relevancy (Rule 70).

The representatives of Indonesia, the Soviet Union, and Romania were the three speakers against inclusion. As they were all members of the General Committee and had already expressed themselves on the question, it is not surprising that their remarks in the plenary did not raise any new points.

The three speakers in favour of including the Tibetan item in the agenda were the representatives of New Zealand, El Salvador and Thailand. The representatives of New Zealand and Thailand did not raise new points. The representative of El Salvador, however, referred to the initiative of his delegation in 1950, and added:

Who knows whether much suffering could not have been avoided for the martyrized people of Tibet if nine years ago the General Committee had acted with the same wisdom and the same spirit of justice which it has demonstrated today [*sic*] and which it did not manifest when we Salvadorians denounced the attack which was launched at that earlier date.[37]

After the debate, a vote was taken by roll call on the recommendation of the General Committee that the question of Tibet be included in the agenda and be discussed in plenary meeting without reference to a Committee. The result of the vote was 43–11–25, with India present but not voting; the votes are given in Table 26 (pages 249–250).

Following the vote, the United States representative spoke under the " right of reply " (Rule 75), and the Soviet representative made

[37] United Nations Doc. A/PV.826, 12 Oct. 1959, p. 36.

a counter-reply. At the next meeting of the Assembly, the representatives of Yugoslavia, Spain and Belgium spoke in explanation of vote (Rule 90).

Immediately after the Assembly had decided to place the item " The question of Tibet " on the agenda, the delegations of Ireland and the Federation of Malaya formally submitted the following draft resolution:

The General Assembly,

Recalling the principles regarding fundamental human rights and freedoms set out in the Charter of the United Nations and in the Universal Declaration of Human Rights adopted by the General Assembly on 10 December 1948,

Considering that the fundamental human rights and freedoms to which the Tibetan people, like all others, are entitled include the right to civil and religious liberty for all without distinction,

Mindful also of the distinctive cultural and religious heritage of the people of Tibet and of the autonomy which they have traditionally enjoyed,

Gravely concerned at reports, including the official statements of His Holiness the Dalai Lama, to the effect that the fundamental human rights and freedoms of the people of Tibet have been forcibly denied them,

Deploring the effect of these events in increasing international tension and in embittering the relations between peoples at a time when earnest and positive efforts are being made by responsible leaders to reduce tension and improve international relations,

1. *Affirms its belief* that respect for the principles of the Charter of the United Nations and of the Universal Declaration of Human Rights is essential for the evolution of a peaceful world order based on the rule of law;

2. *Calls* for respect for the fundamental human rights of the Tibetan people and for their distinctive cultural and religious life.[38]

Provisional texts of a draft resolution had been circulating informally for some weeks, and the draft finally submitted by Ireland and Malaya differed in a few respects from the first draft. Of these differences, two were of some importance.

In the first place, the original draft contained a reference to " The People's Republic of China." This proved embarrassing to the United States and other countries which had voted not to discuss the question of Chinese representation. It was expected that these States would form the core of those supporting the Irish-Malayan resolution, and the reference to the People's Republic of China was accordingly eliminated.

[38] United Nations Doc. A/L.264, 12 Oct. 1959; after its adoption, this proposal became General Assembly Res. 1353 (XIV), 22 Oct. 1959.

Secondly, there was a reference in the original draft to Article 73 of the Charter, which relates to non-self-governing territories. The Member States administering such territories have opposed the adoption by the Assembly of any resolution mentioning such a territory by name. This reference was also removed.

Two comments on the draft, as finally submitted, may be made. First, the basis of Assembly concern was to be the human rights provisions of the Charter and the Declaration of Human Rights. There was no reference to any international dispute, or to any threat to the peace, or to any act of aggression. The security provisions of the Charter were not invoked.

Secondly, there was no proposal for action (other than the adoption of a draft resolution). It was not proposed that fact-finding machinery be established, or that good offices or mediation be exercised. Once the resolution had been put to the vote, the Tibetan question could come before the Assembly again only as a result of a new request.

Debate on the substance of the Tibetan question took place in four plenary meetings of the Assembly on 20 and 21 October. Thirty speakers took part in the debate, but there was nothing to be said that had not already been said. There were, broadly speaking, four points of view.[39]

1. The following eleven countries, in addition to the two sponsors, declared themselves in sympathy with the initiative of Ireland and Malaya and in support of the draft resolution: Australia, Brazil, China, Cuba, Ecuador, El Salvador, Netherlands, New Zealand, Pakistan, the United States and Venezuela.

2. The following four countries, while expressing sympathy with the substance of the proposal of Ireland and Malaya, had doubts about the competence of the Assembly to adopt a resolution: Belgium, France, Spain and the United Kingdom.

3. The following four countries, though distressed by events in Tibet, doubted the political wisdom of adopting the draft resolution: Ethiopia, Finland, India and Nepal.

4. The nine countries of the Soviet *Bloc* expressed strong opposition to the attempt to inflame passions by illegally bringing the non-existent question of Tibet before the Assembly.

There were no amendments to the draft resolution of Ireland and Malaya, and it was adopted by a roll-call vote, 45–9–26. The votes are given in Table 26 (pages 249–250).

[39] The final printed records will be issued as G.A.O.R.: 14th Sess., 831st–834th Plenary Mtgs.

During the course of the debate, the representative of Guatemala exercised the right of reply in connection with some remarks of the representative of Cuba, and the Cuban representative made a brief rejoinder (Rule 75). After the voting had concluded, the following representatives explained their votes (Rule 90): Guatemala, Israel, South Africa, the Soviet Union, and Turkey. The representative of Costa Rica explained that an extremely urgent call had made it impossible for him to be present when the vote was taken, but he wished it to be understood " very clearly, absolutely and categorically " that he would have voted in favour of the resolution had he been present.[40]

In the votes on the Tibetan question, forty-two Member States voted " yes " on each occasion. These comprised eighteen Latin American States, eleven States of Western Europe, seven Asian States, together with Australia, Canada, China, Israel, New Zealand and the United States.

The nine States of the Soviet *Bloc* voted " no " on each occasion.

There were twenty-two States consistently abstaining or absent, comprising sixteen Afro-Asians, four countries of Western Europe (Finland, France, Portugal and Spain), the Dominican Republic and the Union of South Africa.

Belgium and the United Kingdom voted in favour of including the matter in the agenda but abstained on the substantive draft resolution. Indonesia and Yugoslavia opposed inscription and abstained on the draft resolution of substance. Jordan, Peru and Tunisia abstained on the question of inscription and voted in favour of the draft resolution of substance.

India did not vote on the question of inscription and abstained on the draft resolution of substance. Liberia voted " no " on the question of inscription in the General Committee, abstained on the same question in the plenary, and voted in favour of the substantive proposal—a remarkable *volte face*.

The Assembly devoted about sixteen hours of its fourteenth session to the Tibetan question, at first in the General Committee and then in the plenary Assembly. What was achieved?

In the first place, the fact that the item was proposed, recommended for inclusion in the agenda by the General Committee, inscribed by the plenary, and then discussed, was significant. The adoption of a resolution was significant, too, though it is easy to exaggerate the importance of this. By the time the Assembly came

40 United Nations Doc. A/PV.834, 21 Oct. 1959, pp. 93–95.

TABLE 26

Votes on " the question of Tibet "

	Recommendation of the General Committee that " the question of Tibet " be included in the agenda	Decision of the plenary to include in the agenda " the question of Tibet "	Resolution on Tibet sponsored by Ireland and Malaya
Afghanistan		abstain	abstain
Albania		no	no
Argentina		yes	yes
Australia		yes	yes
*Austria	yes	yes	yes
*Belgium	yes	yes	abstain
*Bolivia	yes	yes	yes
*Brazil	yes	yes	yes
Bulgaria		no	no
*Burma	abstain	abstain	abstain
Byelorussian S.S.R. ...		no	no
Cambodia		abstain	abstain
Canada		yes	yes
Ceylon		abstain	abstain
Chile		yes	yes
*China	yes	yes	yes
Colombia		yes	yes
Costa Rica		yes	absent, but would have voted yes if present
Cuba		yes	yes
*Czechoslovakia	no	no	no
Denmark		yes	yes
Dominican Republic ...		abstain	abstain
Ecuador		yes	yes
El Salvador		yes	yes
Ethiopia		absent	abstain
Federation of Malaya ...		yes	yes
Finland		abstain	abstain
*France	abstain	abstain	abstain
Ghana		abstain	abstain
Greece		yes	yes
*Guatemala	yes	yes	yes
Guinea		abstain	absent
Haiti		yes	yes
Honduras		yes	yes
Hungary		no	no
Iceland		yes	yes
India		not voting	abstain
*Indonesia	no	no	abstain
Iran		yes	yes
Iraq		abstain	abstain
Ireland		yes	yes
Israel		absent	yes
Italy		yes	yes
Japan		yes	yes
Jordan		abstain	yes
Laos		yes	yes
Lebanon		abstain	abstain

	Recommendation of the General Committee that " the question of Tibet " be included in the agenda	Decision of the plenary to include in the agenda " the question of Tibet "	Resolution on Tibet sponsored by Ireland and Malaya
*Liberia	no	abstain	yes
Libya		abstain	abstain
Luxembourg		yes	yes
Mexico		yes	yes
*Morocco	abstain	abstain	abstain
Nepal		abstain	abstain
Netherlands		yes	yes
New Zealand		yes	yes
Nicaragua		yes	yes
Norway		yes	yes
Pakistan		yes	yes
Panama		yes	yes
Paraguay		yes	yes
*Peru	the Chairman did not vote	abstain	yes
*Philippines	yes	yes	yes
Poland		no	no
Portugal		abstain	abstain
*Romania	no	no	no
Saudi Arabia		abstain	abstain
Spain		abstain	abstain
Sudan		abstain	abstain
*Sweden	yes	yes	yes
Thailand		yes	yes
Tunisia		abstain	yes
*Turkey	yes	yes	yes
Ukrainian S.S.R. ...		no	no
*Union of South Africa ...	abstain	abstain	abstain
*U.S.S.R.	no	no	no
United Arab Republic ...		abstain	abstain
*United Kingdom	yes	yes	abstain
*United States of America	yes	yes	yes
Uruguay		yes	yes
Venezuela		yes	yes
Yemen		abstain	abstain
Yugoslavia		no	abstain

* These twenty-one States were represented on the General Committee.

to vote on the evening of 21 October, the main impact had been made.

It was the hope of the sponsors that the effect of the Assembly's concern with Tibet would strengthen the forces of moderation within the Peking Government. There had been unmistakable evidence since the summer of 1957 of a " hardening " of policy in Communist China's internal and external affairs. Ireland and Malaya, and the States supporting their initiative, hoped that world opinion would be mobilized against violent attempts to change the way of life of a people. It was significant that not a single State outside the Soviet *Bloc* voted against the final resolution.

No less important than the public speeches and votes were the informal discussions and soundings. As a result of the initiative of Ireland and Malaya, governments were again forced to review their attitude to the question of the Peking Government's relations to the United Nations. Events in Tibet in 1959 had a dual effect. Some governments were strengthened in their conviction that the Peking régime is unfitted for membership of the United Nations. Other governments were strengthened in their conviction that the exclusion of representatives of Peking from the United Nations weakens the capacity of the Organization to have a beneficial influence on developments in the Far East.

Member States were forced to consider the usefulness of public debate, and whether it is worth adopting a resolution that will be regarded as illegal by those to whom it is addressed.

Governments had to examine again the limits of the competence of the United Nations regarding human rights. It is no secret that some of the colonial Powers, which had on other occasions invoked Article 2 (7) of the Charter relating to domestic jurisdiction, would have preferred that the Tibetan question should not have arisen. They thought that a precedent might be created which would later be cited if an attempt were made to bring before the Assembly a complaint that human rights were not respected in some territory for which one or another of these Powers were responsible. Indeed, at one stage it seemed possible that a move would be made to adjourn the debate on Tibet *sine die* before the draft resolution had been put to the vote; the British representative hinted at such a possibility in his speech on the substance of the question.[41]

Few Members take a completely consistent attitude to questions involving human rights in particular countries. The Assembly, during its fourteenth session in 1959, considered proposals relating to Tibet, Hungary, Algeria, and race relations and the treatment of persons of Indian origin in South Africa. These questions raised different problems, and the draft resolutions that were submitted were intended to serve different purposes. All the same, I think it is significant that only the following ten of the eighty-two Member States voted " yes " on the resolutions of substance on each occasion in plenary meeting:

Africa: Liberia, Tunisia.

Asia: the Federation of Malaya, Pakistan, the Philippines.

[41] *Ibid.*, p. 16.

Europe: Sweden.

Latin America: Argentina, Mexico, Panama, Venezuela.

Finland, too, was consistent; she abstained on each occasion.

Considering the contentious nature of the subject, debate on the question of Tibet was reasonably temperate. Indeed, it was notable that the most acrimonious remarks were made by speakers who took the view that the Tibetan question had been brought before the United Nations with the sole purpose of reviving the cold war.

Chapter 11

THE FUTURE OF THE ASSEMBLY

> It now rests to conclude the discourse in which, if I have
> not pleased my reader or answered his expectation, it is some
> comfort to me that I meant well, and have cost him but little
> money and time.
>
> WILLIAM PENN

THE General Assembly occupies a key position in the network of
organs of the United Nations. Some of its main procedural problems
have arisen from the fact that it has had to do things for which
it is not fully equipped, legally or politically. This, in itself, should
occasion no regret. Political institutions progress towards maturity
by a process of trial and error, but perfect maturity is a mirage that
is never achieved. Success consists of striving.

Of all organs of the United Nations, the Assembly has received
the greatest impact from the increase in the number of sovereign
States since the war, since it is the only principal organ to which all
Member States belong. The new and emerging States pin great hopes
on the United Nations. Some, like Indonesia, have owed their very
existence to the United Nations; many regard the United Nations as
a midwife. The United Nations helped them to achieve sovereignty:
can it not also ensure that they achieve security and prosperity?

Moreover, the United Nations can help these new and emerging
States to find their place in the world. The Secretary-General has
emphasized the important role of the Organization during this period
of transition.

The United Nations is now, or will be, their Organization. The United
Nations can give them a framework for their young national life which
gives a deeper sense and a greater weight to independence. The United
Nations has not had a past in any of these regions in the sense that any
one country necessarily has had. The United Nations, for these reasons,
without pushing, without, so to say, becoming a party in their development, can through proper means, even on the basis of fairly small
amounts of money, come into the picture in such a way as to help
considerably in the framing of their political life after independence and
in the building up of the national state.[1]

Membership in the United Nations is a mark of sovereignty. Each
State, as it attains independence, applies for membership, and failure

---

[1] Press conference by the Secretary-General at U.N. headquarters. Note to
Correspondents, No. 2108, 4 Feb. 1960.

to gain admission to the Organization might be thought to cast doubts on the reality of the applicant's independence. Moreover, no State has withdrawn from the Organization, whereas nearly a score of States withdrew from the League, in many cases for reasons which now seem trifling.

There are, at the present time (February 1960), eighty-two Members of the United Nations. During the fifteenth regular session of the Assembly, due to convene in 1960, the membership will no doubt increase to over ninety, and within a few years the number of Members will rise to more than one hundred. This will add to the difficulties of dealing both expeditiously and effectively with all the matters submitted to the Assembly. I have, in this book, examined certain of the Assembly's procedural difficulties, but I must emphasize that these difficulties are in many cases only incipient. I have been concerned not just with the existing situation but with the situation that may develop if the procedures and practices of a living institution remain static.

One of the bases of the United Nations is the principle of the sovereign equality of its Members. This is a juridical concept which, if applied consistently, would mean that no State should be coerced by external means to act contrary to its own wishes. In actuality, no principle can be applied consistently since equally valid principles may be in conflict. But, leaving this aside, it should be stressed that juridical equality is not the same as political equality. The newer States do not differ from other States in this respect. Each Member of the General Assembly has one vote, and no distinction is made between large and small, old and new, wise and foolish. The relationship between power and influence has never been a direct one, but in traditional diplomacy a State could be influential in spite of its folly; in conference diplomacy a State may be influential in spite of its weakness.

One purpose of the United Nations is to ensure that reason and justice take the place of coercion in inter-State relations, and it is thus natural that States which lack the means of physical coercion should repose special trust in the Organization. Yet the United Nations is not like the widow's cruse of oil, which was never exhausted; it is more like a bank, in the sense that disaster will follow if more is withdrawn than is deposited.

The impetus and focus of the United Nations will increasingly be based on the aspirations and ambitions of States which played little or no role in traditional diplomacy. These newer and emerging States face internal and external problems different from those of the older States. The latter have inherited a legacy of obligations, enmities and grievances. The newer States, by and large, start from scratch, without allies, without obligations and with few specific grievances. To be sure, they soon find that other States proffer alliance, they soon incur obligations, they soon discover or invent grievances. But from the moment of birth, these States are thrust upon the world stage. Their representatives in the General Assembly are asked to pronounce on a variety of questions which are of marginal interest. I recall Neville Chamberlain's reference, at the time of the Munich crisis, to "a quarrel in a far-away country between people of whom we know nothing." [2] Today it does not seem surprising that governments and peoples should be concerned about distant tragedies or quarrels; the General Assembly, almost as a matter of course, considers events in Tibet or along the Somali-Ethiopian frontier. There are no longer any far-away countries.

The point I wish to stress, however, is not that we are all involved in mankind, for to understand this is a mark of civilization. What I am concerned about is the temptation to cover the incapacity to deal with one's own problems by moralizing about other people's. A diplomat for whom I have great admiration said to me some time ago that the internal problems facing his people at home seemed insoluble, but that the one thing his country could do to make the world a better place for all people was to vote in the General Assembly for Algerian independence. These remarks were not made cynically, and I have not repeated them cynically. All the same, they seem to me to exemplify one of the dangers to which any political body is subject. It is easy for governments, as it is for individuals who write about governments, to dramatize and thus exaggerate the inadequacies and mistakes of others.

As the Assembly increases in size, it will become even more important than it was in the past to use to the best advantage the other principal organs of the United Nations: the three Councils, the Secretariat and the International Court. It may well be that the Security Council can never fill the role which the founding fathers intended for it. It is often said that the Council was predicated on the assumption that the Great Powers would co-operate in peace as they had in war, and that the icy blasts of the cold war have unexpectedly swept away the foundations of co-operation. I doubt whether the expectations of foreign offices were ever as rosy as such statements imply, but the task now is not to regret the past or deplore the present, but to see what can be done to ensure that there is a future.

[2] *In Search of Peace* (New York: Putnam, 1939), p. 174. Broadcast address, 26 Sept. 1938.

The Security Council may yet come into its own. Guillaume Georges-Picot, former Permanent Representative of France, has suggested that the Council would " render a great service to peace if it got in the habit of meeting in closed session, and of appointing small committees which could try to work out quietly with the Secretary-General " solutions to the problems submitted to it.[3] The Secretary-General made a similar point in the introduction to his annual report in 1959.[4] If the Council could in this way become a better instrument of quiet diplomacy, the Assembly would be relieved of responsibilities relating to the maintenance of international peace and security which it is not well fitted to discharge.

The Economic and Social Council has recently taken steps which, if hopes are realized, will give it a more vital role in the formulation of national and international economic policies. Here again, it seems likely that relatively informal private meetings may serve a useful purpose, as an adjunct to public debate.

The expectation of useful life of the Trusteeship Council is a matter for speculation. Western Samoa will presumably leave the trusteeship system in 1961, and the two African territories that will remain under trusteeship after 1960 (Ruanda-Urundi and Tanganyika) are evolving rapidly towards self-government or independence. The functions formally conferred on the Trusteeship Council by the Charter will remain, even when the only territories under the trusteeship system are Nauru, New Guinea and the Pacific Islands. If the Trusteeship Council is not to decline in importance, it will be because the non-administering Members of the United Nations recognize an interest in seeing that the Council performs its functions with a minimum of passion and propaganda.

A primary task of the Secretariat is to service the policy-making organs, but its responsibilities cannot end there. The Secretariat is a source of ideas, a reservoir of creative imagination. It can never escape the ills that befall any large bureaucracy. Bigness tends to stifle creativity, because bigness necessarily requires system, and even the best systems do not make sufficient allowance for the eruption of creative ideas in unexpected places.

The International Court has, perhaps, been maligned beyond its deserts. It is true that our age is highly political; nations have been reluctant to submit crucial issues for judicial settlement. All the same, the Court has performed some vital tasks. In any case, the value of a judicial system cannot be judged simply by counting the number of times it is overtly resorted to. The usefulness of the Court should

---

[3] Note to Correspondents No. 1938, 12 Feb. 1959.
[4] G.A.O.R.: 14th Sess., 1959, Suppl. No. 1A (A/4132/Add. 1), p. 3.

be determined, in the first place, by the wrongs that were not done and the disputes that were not allowed to fester simply because the Court existed, and only secondarily by the manner in which the Court has discharged its responsibilities.

I have not, in this book, proposed any amendments to the Charter. I have not even written in favour of an increase in the number of members of the Security Council, the Economic and Social Council or the International Court of Justice. Indeed, I question whether an enlargement of these bodies would enable them to perform their essential tasks more adequately than they do at present, or would reduce dissension about the distribution of elective places on them.

The continuing increase in the membership of the United Nations will probably necessitate greater reliance on inter-sessional subsidiary organs. If organs of limited membership are to be of optimum value, it will be important to ensure not only that their composition is such as to command the confidence of the whole Assembly, but also that Member States are represented in such organs by the most competent persons rather than by those who happen to be stationed wherever these organs are to meet.

The competition for Assembly offices, for places on the Councils and for membership of subsidiary organs has caused some distortion of what is important; the contest has tended to become an end in itself, leading to preoccupation with such mutually exclusive concepts as equitable geographical representation and " parity." The important thing is that organs should be so constituted that they can function effectively and enjoy general confidence, and this is rarely achieved by the automatic application of mathematical formulas. The Assembly's need for competent and experienced presiding officers will become greater as the membership increases still further.

It seems to me essential that matters proposed for inclusion in the agenda should be scrutinized more carefully than has been the practice in the past. The Assembly has been reluctant to reject requests for the inclusion of items in the agenda, but there are inter-mediate steps between unconditional inclusion and outright rejection. The Assembly may include an item in the agenda for consideration during the course of the General Debate or on some other occasion, with the proviso that the item is included for discussion only. The Assembly may refer an item, without debate of its substance, for consideration and report by an organ meeting between sessions, or may postpone consideration of an item by deciding to include it in the provisional agenda of a future session. The Secretary-General reported in 1956 that, in informal consultations with the Permanent

Representatives of Member States, it had been suggested that certain items be considered on a biennial rather than an annual basis.[5]

The distribution of work between Main Committees seems to me generally satisfactory, with one exception. The Fourth Committee has had more business than it can cope with effectively in a three-month session. Means might be devised to relieve the Fourth Committee of the necessity of conducting oral hearings, perhaps by the creation of one or more sub-committees that can meet during the course of a session of the General Assembly. It might be useful to establish a sub-committee composed of the Member States that are members of the Trusteeship Council to hear petitioners in connection with trust territories during sessions of the Assembly, and a sub-committee composed of the Member States that are members of the Committee on South West Africa to hear petitioners in connection with South West Africa.

I see very few possibilities of improving the conduct of debate by changing the Rules of Procedure. Arbitrary limitation of the length or number of speeches is a drastic measure, and I doubt whether it would lead to any significant saving of time. Much would be gained, however, if the Rules relating to points of order, the right of reply and explanations of vote were better understood and more strictly applied.

I am inclined to think that the one area in which the Assembly could effect a substantial improvement in procedure is that of the means by which it reaches conclusions. Most of the matters with which the Assembly deals must, in the last resort, be decided by vote. If there is a difference of opinion among Member States about an item in the budget, for example, this can be settled only by a vote. But it seems to me that in contentious questions of a political or quasi-political nature, the primary task is to cause an improvement in the situation rather than to place on the public record the views of Member States. The United Nations is a centre for harmonizing the actions of nations, not just a place where differences are recorded. The impact of quiet diplomacy and public debate may be much reduced or altogether lost if a substantive proposal is pressed to a vote prematurely.

These matters of procedure have no intrinsic importance; they are merely means to achieve the ends for which the United Nations was created. The chief purpose of good procedure is not to save time, but to ensure that international business is well handled.

---

[5] G.A.O.R.: 11th Sess., 1956–57, Annexes, Agenda item 8 (A/BUR/142), para. 13.

A NOTE ON FURTHER READING

THE main bibliographic sources on the procedure and practice of the General Assembly are the official records of Assembly debates. It is impossible, in the space available, to list all the debates which have had a direct or indirect bearing on procedure. Table 27 gives the numbers of the Main Committee and plenary meetings of the Assembly at which some of the more important procedural questions have been discussed.

Three committees of the General Assembly have reported on the procedures, methods, and organization of the Assembly, as follows:

Date	Name of Committee	Ref. No. of Report
1947	Committee on Procedures and Organization of the General Assembly	A/388
1949	Special Committee on Methods and Procedures of the General Assembly	A/937
1953	Special Committee on Measures to Limit the Duration of Regular Sessions of the General Assembly	A/2402

Extracts from these reports will be found in Appendices E, F and G.

The standard work on the League Assembly is *The Assembly of the League of Nations,* by Margaret E. Burton, University of Chicago Press, 1941. A useful study of the procedure and organization of inter-governmental assemblies is *A Guide to the Practice of International Conferences,* by Vladimir D. Pastuhov, Carnegie Endowment for International Peace, 1945.

The Carnegie Endowment for International Peace has sponsored two studies relating wholly or partly to the procedure and practice of the General Assembly of the United Nations. Both studies were issued by the Endowment for limited circulation. The first, *Memorandum Concerning the Conduct of the Business of the General Assembly of the United Nations,* was prepared by Waldo Chamberlin in 1949; it is now out of print. The second, *Some Implications of Expanding United Nations Membership,* was prepared by Eric Stein in 1956; a few copies are still available. An important book on the politics, rather than the procedure, of the Assembly is *The Political Role of the General Assembly,* by H. Field Haviland, Jr., Carnegie Endowment for International Peace, 1951.

TABLE

Main Committee and Plenary Meetings at which

Session No.	*Subject*	
1 (Pt. I)	Provisional Rules of Procedure	
1 (Pt. II)	Measures to economize the time of the General Assembly	
2	,, ,, ditto ,, ,,	
3 (Pt. II)	Methods and procedures of the General Assembly	*Ad Hoc Political Committee* 23rd mtg.
4	,, ,, ditto ,, ,,	
5	"Uniting for Peace"	*First Committee* 354th–371st mtgs.
5	Majority required for amendments to and parts of proposals relating to "important questions"	
6	Methods and procedures for dealing with legal and drafting questions	
7	,, ,, ditto ,, ,,	
6	Measures to limit the duration of regular sessions	*Fifth Committee* 340th mtg.
7	,, ,, ditto ,, ,,	
8	,, ,, ditto ,, ,,	
9	Examination of reports and petitions from South West Africa	*Fourth Committee* 399th–403rd mtgs.
9	Correction of votes	
10	,, ,, ditto ,, ,,	
11	Number of Vice-Presidents: composition of the General Committee	*Special Political Committee* 79th–83rd mtgs.
12	,, ,, ditto ,, ,,	
14	Equitable geographical representation in connection with the Presidency	163rd–169th mtgs.

27

some Important Procedural Questions were Discussed

Sixth Committee	Plenary Meetings	Resolution No.
2nd–5th, 9th–10th mtgs.	2nd, 18th–19th mtgs.	17 (I)
	67th mtg.	102 (I)
56th–57th mtgs.	118th meeting.	173 (II)
	201st mtg.	271 (III)
142nd–158th, 166th mtgs.	235th–236th mtgs.	362 (IV)
	299th–302nd mtgs.	377 (V)
213th–214th mtgs.	290th mtg.	475 (V)
256th–263rd, 266th mtgs.	356th mtg.	597 (VI)
306th–312th mtgs.	391st mtg.	684 (VII)
	373rd mtg.	
346th–354th mtgs.	387th–388th, 410th mtgs.	689 (VII)
360th–366th mtgs.	453rd mtg.	791 (VIII)
	494th mtg.	844 (IX)
439th mtg.	512th mtg.	901 (IX)
455th–458th mtgs.	549th mtg.	983 (X)
480th mtg.	623rd mtg.	1104 (XI)
	728th mtg.	1192 (XII)
	852nd mtg.	

APPENDICES

ARTICLES OF THE UNITED NATIONS CHARTER
quoted or referred to in the book

Chapter I. Purposes and Principles

ARTICLE 1

The Purposes of the United Nations are:

1. To maintain international peace and security, and to that end: to take effective collective measures for the prevention and removal of threats to the peace, and for the suppression of acts of aggression or other breaches of the peace, and to bring about by peaceful means, and in conformity with the principles of justice and international law, adjustment or settlement of international disputes or situations which might lead to a breach of the peace;

2. To develop friendly relations among nations based on respect for the principle of equal rights and self-determination of peoples, and to take other appropriate measures to strengthen universal peace;

3. To achieve international cooperation in solving international problems of an economic, social, cultural, or humanitarian character, and in promoting and encouraging respect for human rights and for fundamental freedoms for all without distinction as to race, sex, language, or religion; and

4. To be a center for harmonizing the actions of nations in the attainment of these common ends.

ARTICLE 2

.   .   .

4. All Members shall refrain in their international relations from the threat or use of force against the territorial integrity or political independence of any state, or in any other manner inconsistent with the Purposes of the United Nations.

.   .   .

7. Nothing contained in the present Charter shall authorize the United Nations to intervene in matters which are essentially within the domestic jurisdiction of any state or shall require the Members to submit such matters to settlement under the present Charter; but this principle shall not prejudice the application of enforcement measures under Chapter VII.

.   .   .

Chapter IV. The General Assembly

ARTICLE 9

1. The General Assembly shall consist of all the Members of the United Nations.

2. Each Member shall have not more than five representatives in the General Assembly.

ARTICLE 10

The General Assembly may discuss any questions or any matters within the scope of the present Charter or relating to the powers and functions of any organs provided for in the present Charter, and, except as provided in Article 12, may make recommendations to the Members of the United Nations or to the Security Council or to both on any such questions or matters.

ARTICLE 11

1. The General Assembly may consider the general principles of cooperation in the maintenance of international peace and security, including the principles governing disarmament and the regulation of armaments, and may make recommendations with regard to such principles to the Members or to the Security Council or to both.

2. The General Assembly may discuss any questions relating to the maintenance of international peace and security brought before it by any Member of the United Nations, or by the Security Council, or by a state which is not a Member of the United Nations in accordance with Article 35, paragraph 2, and, except as provided in Article 12, may make recommendations with regard to any such questions to the state or states concerned or to the Security Council or to both. Any such question on which action is necessary shall be referred to the Security Council by the General Assembly either before or after discussion.

3. The General Assembly may call the attention of the Security Council to situations which are likely to endanger international peace and security.

4. The powers of the General Assembly set forth in this Article shall not limit the general scope of Article 10.

ARTICLE 12

1. While the Security Council is exercising in respect of any dispute or situation the functions assigned to it in the present Charter, the General Assembly shall not make any recommendation with regard to that dispute or situation unless the Security Council so requests.

2. The Secretary-General, with the consent of the Security Council, shall notify the General Assembly at each session of any matters relative to the maintenance of international peace and security which are being dealt with by the Security Council and shall similarly notify the General Assembly, or the Members of the United Nations if the General Assembly is not in session, immediately the Security Council ceases to deal with such matters.

ARTICLE 13

1. The General Assembly shall initiate studies and make recommendations for the purpose of:

(a) promoting international cooperation in the political field and encouraging the progressive development of international law and its codification;

(b) promoting international cooperation in the economic, social, cultural, educational, and health fields, and assisting in the realization of human rights and fundamental freedoms for all without distinction as to race, sex, language, or religion.

2. The further responsibilities, functions, and powers of the General Assembly with respect to matters mentioned in paragraph 1 (b) above are set forth in Chapters IX and X.

ARTICLE 14

Subject to the provisions of Article 12, the General Assembly may recommend measures for the peaceful adjustment of any situation, regardless of origin, which it deems likely to impair the general welfare or friendly relations among nations, including situations resulting from a violation of the provisions of the present Charter setting forth the Purposes and Principles of the United Nations.

ARTICLE 15

1. The General Assembly shall receive and consider annual and special reports from the Security Council; these reports shall include an account of the measures that the Security Council has decided upon or taken to maintain international peace and security.

2. The General Assembly shall receive and consider reports from the other organs of the United Nations.

ARTICLE 16

The General Assembly shall perform such functions with respect to the international trusteeship system as are assigned to it under Chapters XII and XIII, including the approval of the trusteeship agreements for areas not designated as strategic.

ARTICLE 17

1. The General Assembly shall consider and approve the budget of the Organization.

2. The expenses of the Organization shall be borne by the Members as apportioned by the General Assembly.

3. The General Assembly shall consider and approve any financial and budgetary arrangements with specialized agencies referred to in Article 57 and shall examine the administrative budgets of such specialized agencies with a view to making recommendations to the agencies concerned.

ARTICLE 18

1. Each member of the General Assembly shall have one vote.

2. Decisions of the General Assembly on important questions shall be made by a two-thirds majority of the members present and voting. These questions shall include: recommendations with respect to the maintenance of international peace and security, the election of the non-permanent members of the Security Council, the election of the members of the Economic and Social Council, the election of members of the Trusteeship Council in accordance with paragraph 1 (c) of Article 86, the admission of new Members to the United Nations, the suspension of the rights and privileges of membership, the expulsion of Members, questions relating to the operation of the trusteeship system, and budgetary questions.

3. Decisions on other questions, including the determination of additional categories of questions to be decided by a two-thirds majority, shall be made by a majority of the members present and voting.

ARTICLE 19

A Member of the United Nations which is in arrears in the payment of its financial contributions to the Organization shall have no vote in the General Assembly if the amount of its arrears equals or exceeds the amount of the contributions due from it for the preceding two full years. The General Assembly may, nevertheless, permit such a Member to vote if it is satisfied that the failure to pay is due to conditions beyond the control of the Member.

ARTICLE 20

The General Assembly shall meet in regular annual sessions and in such special sessions as occasion may require. Special sessions shall be convoked by the Secretary-General at the request of the Security Council or of a majority of the Members of the United Nations.

ARTICLE 21

The General Assembly shall adopt its own rules of procedure. It shall elect its President for each session.

ARTICLE 22

The General Assembly may establish such subsidiary organs as it deems necessary for the performance of its functions.

Chapter V. The Security Council

ARTICLE 23

1. The Security Council shall consist of eleven Members of the United Nations. The Republic of China, France, the Union of Soviet Socialist Republics, the United Kingdom of Great Britain and Northern Ireland, and the United States of America shall be permanent members of the Security Council. The General Assembly shall elect six other

Members of the United Nations to be non-permanent members of the Security Council, due regard being specially paid, in the first instance to the contribution of Members of the United Nations to the maintenance of international peace and security and to the other purposes of the Organization, and also to equitable geographical distribution.

2. The non-permanent members of the Security Council shall be elected for a term of two years. In the first election of the non-permanent members, however, three shall be chosen for a term of one year. A retiring member shall not be eligible for immediate re-election.

3. Each member of the Security Council shall have one representative.

ARTICLE 24

1. In order to ensure prompt and effective action by the United Nations, its Members confer on the Security Council primary responsibility for the maintenance of international peace and security, and agree that in carrying out its duties under this responsibility the Security Council acts on their behalf.

2. In discharging these duties the Security Council shall act in accordance with the Purposes and Principles of the United Nations. The specific powers granted to the Security Council for the discharge of these duties are laid down in Chapters VI, VII, VIII, and XII.

3. The Security Council shall submit annual and, when necessary, special reports to the General Assembly for its consideration.

ARTICLE 25

The Members of the United Nations agree to accept and carry out the decisions of the Security Council in accordance with the present Charter.

. . .

ARTICLE 27

1. Each member of the Security Council shall have one vote.

2. Decisions of the Security Council on procedural matters shall be made by an affirmative vote of seven members.

3. Decisions of the Security Council on all other matters shall be made by an affirmative vote of seven members including the concurring votes of the permanent members; provided that, in decisions under Chapter VI, and under paragraph 3 of Article 52, a party to a dispute shall abstain from voting.

ARTICLE 28

1. The Security Council shall be so organized as to be able to function continuously. Each member of the Security Council shall for this purpose be represented at all times at the seat of the Organization.

2. The Security Council shall hold periodic meetings at which each of its members may, if it so desires, be represented by a member of the government or by some other specially designated representative.

3. The Security Council may hold meetings at such places other than the seat of the Organization as in its judgment will best facilitate its work.

. . .

Chapter VI. Pacific Settlement of Disputes

ARTICLE 33

1. The parties to any dispute, the continuance of which is likely to endanger the maintenance of international peace and security, shall, first of all, seek a solution by negotiation, enquiry, mediation, conciliation, arbitration, judicial settlement, resort to regional agencies or arrangements, or other peaceful means of their own choice.

2. The Security Council shall, when it deems necessary, call upon the parties to settle their dispute by such means.

. . .

ARTICLE 35

1. Any Member of the United Nations may bring any dispute, or any situation of the nature referred to in Article 34, to the attention of the Security Council or of the General Assembly.

2. A state which is not a Member of the United Nations may bring to the attention of the Security Council or of the General Assembly any dispute to which it is a party if it accepts in advance, for the purposes of the dispute, the obligations of pacific settlement provided in the present Charter.

3. The proceedings of the General Assembly in respect of matters brought to its attention under this Article will be subject to the provisions of Articles 11 and 12.

. . .

Chapter IX. International Economic and Social Co-operation

ARTICLE 60

Responsibility for the discharge of the functions of the Organization set forth in this Chapter shall be vested in the General Assembly and, under the authority of the General Assembly, in the Economic and Social Council, which shall have for this purpose the powers set forth in Chapter X.

Chapter X. The Economic and Social Council

ARTICLE 61

1. The Economic and Social Council shall consist of eighteen Members of the United Nations elected by the General Assembly.

2. Subject to the provisions of paragraph 3, six members of the Economic and Social Council shall be elected each year for a term of three years. A retiring member shall be eligible for immediate re-election.

3. At the first election, eighteen members of the Economic and Social Council shall be chosen. The term of office of six members so chosen shall expire at the end of one year, and of six other members at the end of two years, in accordance with arrangements made by the General Assembly.

4. Each member of the Economic and Social Council shall have one representative.

· · ·

ARTICLE 69

The Economic and Social Council shall invite any Member of the United Nations to participate, without vote, in its deliberations on any matter of particular concern to that Member.

· · ·

Chapter XI. Declaration Regarding Non-Self-Governing Territories

ARTICLE 73

Members of the United Nations which have or assume responsibilities for the administration of territories whose peoples have not yet attained a full measure of self-government recognize the principle that the interests of the inhabitants of these territories are paramount, and accept as a sacred trust the obligation to promote to the utmost, within the system of international peace and security established by the present Charter, the well-being of the inhabitants of these territories, and, to this end:

(a) to ensure, with due respect for the culture of the peoples concerned, their political, economic, social, and educational advancement, their just treatment, and their protection against abuses;

(b) to develop self-government, to take due account of the political aspirations of the peoples, and to assist them in the progressive development of their free political institutions, according to the particular circumstances of each territory and its peoples and their varying stages of advancement;

(c) to further international peace and security;

(d) to promote constructive measures of development, to encourage research, and to cooperate with one another and, when and where appropriate, with specialized international bodies with a view to the practical achievement of the social, economic, and scientific purposes set forth in this Article; and

(e) to transmit regularly to the Secretary-General for information purposes, subject to such limitation as security and constitutional considerations may require, statistical and other information of a technical nature relating to economic, social, and educational conditions in the territories for which they are respectively responsible other than those territories to which Chapters XII and XIII apply.

· · ·

Chapter XII. International Trusteeship System

ARTICLE 85

1. The functions of the United Nations with regard to trusteeship agreements for all areas not designated as strategic, including the approval of the terms of the trusteeship agreements and of their alteration or amendment, shall be exercised by the General Assembly.

2. The Trusteeship Council, operating under the authority of the General Assembly, shall assist the General Assembly in carrying out these functions.

Chapter XIII. The Trusteeship Council

ARTICLE 86

1. The Trusteeship Council shall consist of the following Members of the United Nations:

(a) those Members administering trust territories;

(b) such of those Members mentioned by name in Article 23 as are not administering trust territories; and

(c) as many other Members elected for three-year terms by the General Assembly as may be necessary to ensure that the total number of members of the Trusteeship Council is equally divided between those Members of the United Nations which administer trust territories and those which do not.

2. Each member of the Trusteeship Council shall designate one specially qualified person to represent it therein.

.　　.　　.

Chapter XIV. The International Court of Justice

ARTICLE 92

The International Court of Justice shall be the principal judicial organ of the United Nations. It shall function in accordance with the annexed Statute, which is based upon the Statute of the Permanent Court of International Justice and forms an integral part of the present Charter.

.　　.　　.

Chapter XV. The Secretariat

ARTICLE 97

The Secretariat shall comprise a Secretary-General and such staff as the Organization may require. The Secretary-General shall be appointed by the General Assembly upon the recommendation of the Security Council. He shall be the chief administrative officer of the Organization.

ARTICLE 98

The Secretary-General shall act in that capacity in all meetings of the General Assembly, of the Security Council, of the Economic and Social Council, and of the Trusteeship Council, and shall perform such other functions as are entrusted to him by these organs. The Secretary-General shall make an annual report to the General Assembly on the work of the Organization.

.   .   .

ARTICLE 100

1. In the performance of their duties the Secretary-General and the staff shall not seek or receive instructions from any government or from any other authority external to the Organization. They shall refrain from any action which might reflect on their position as international officials responsible only to the Organization.

2. Each Member of the United Nations undertakes to respect the exclusively international character of the responsibilities of the Secretary-General and the staff and not to seek to influence them in the discharge of their responsibilities.

ARTICLE 101

1. The staff shall be appointed by the Secretary-General under regulations established by the General Assembly.

2. Appropriate staffs shall be permanently assigned to the Economic and Social Council, the Trusteeship Council, and, as required, to other organs of the United Nations. These staffs shall form a part of the Secretariat.

3. The paramount consideration in the employment of the staff and in the determination of the conditions of service shall be the necessity of securing the highest standards of efficiency, competence, and integrity. Due regard shall be paid to the importance of recruiting the staff on as wide a geographical basis as possible.

.   .   .

Chapter XVIII. Amendments

ARTICLE 108

Amendments to the present Charter shall come into force for all Members of the United Nations when they have been adopted by a vote of two thirds of the members of the General Assembly and ratified in accordance with their respective constitutional processes by two thirds of the Members of the United Nations, including all the permanent members of the Security Council.

.   .   .

ARTICLES OF THE STATUTE
of the
INTERNATIONAL COURT OF JUSTICE

.   .   .

Chapter I. Organization of the Court

ARTICLE 2

The Court shall be composed of a body of independent judges, elected regardless of their nationality from among persons of high moral character, who possess the qualifications required in their respective countries for appointment to the highest judicial offices, or are juris-consults of recognized competence in international law.

ARTICLE 3

1. The Court shall consist of fifteen members, no two of whom may be nationals of the same state.

2. A person who for the purposes of membership in the Court could be regarded as a national of more than one state shall be deemed to be a national of the one in which he ordinarily exercises civil and political rights.

ARTICLE 4

1. The members of the Court shall be elected by the General Assembly and by the Security Council from a list of persons nominated by the national groups in the Permanent Court of Arbitration, in accord-ance with the following provisions.

2. In the case of Members of the United Nations not represented in the Permanent Court of Arbitration, candidates shall be nominated by national groups appointed for this purpose by their governments under the same conditions as those prescribed for members of the Permanent Court of Arbitration by Article 44 of the Convention of The Hague of 1907 for the pacific settlement of international disputes.

3. The conditions under which a state which is a party to the present Statute but is not a Member of the United Nations may participate in electing the members of the Court shall, in the absence of a special agreement, be laid down by the General Assembly upon recommendation of the Security Council.

ARTICLE 5

1. At least three months before the date of the election, the Secretary-General of the United Nations shall address a written request to the members of the Permanent Court of Arbitration belonging to the states which are parties to the present Statute, and to the members of the national groups appointed under Article 4, paragraph 2, inviting them to undertake, within a given time, by national groups, the nomination of persons in a position to accept the duties of a member of the Court,

2. No group may nominate more than four persons, not more than two of whom shall be of their own nationality. In no case may the number of candidates nominated by a group be more than double the number of seats to be filled.

ARTICLE 6

Before making these nominations, each national group is recom-mended to consult its highest court of justice, its legal faculties and schools of law, and its national academies and national sections of international academies devoted to the study of law.

ARTICLE 7

1. The Secretary-General shall prepare a list in alphabetical order of all the persons thus nominated. Save as provided in Article 12, paragraph 2, these shall be the only persons eligible.

2. The Secretary-General shall submit this list to the General Assembly and to the Security Council.

ARTICLE 8

The General Assembly and the Security Council shall proceed independently of one another to elect the members of the Court.

ARTICLE 9

At every election, the electors shall bear in mind not only that the persons to be elected should individually possess the qualifications required, but also that in the body as a whole the representation of the main forms of civilization and of the principal legal systems of the world should be assured.

ARTICLE 10

1. Those candidates who obtain an absolute majority of votes in the General Assembly and in the Security Council shall be considered as elected.

2. Any vote of the Security Council, whether for the election of judges or for the appointment of members of the conference envisaged in Article 12, shall be taken without any distinction between permanent and non-permanent members of the Security Council.

3. In the event of more than one national of the same state obtaining an absolute majority of the votes both of the General Assembly and of the Security Council, the eldest of these only shall be considered as elected.

ARTICLE 11

If, after the first meeting held for the purpose of the election, one or more seats remain to be filled, a second and, if necessary, a third meeting shall take place.

ARTICLE 12

1. If, after the third meeting, one or more seats still remain unfilled, a joint conference consisting of six members, three appointed by the General Assembly and three by the Security Council, may be formed at any time at the request of either the General Assembly or the Security Council, for the purpose of choosing by the vote of an absolute majority one name for each seat still vacant, to submit to the General Assembly and the Security Council for their respective acceptance.

2. If the joint conference is unanimously agreed upon any person who fulfils the required conditions, he may be included in its list, even though he was not included in the list of nominations referred to in Article 7.

3. If the joint conference is satisfied that it will not be successful in procuring an election, those members of the Court who have already been elected shall, within a period to be fixed by the Security Council, proceed to fill the vacant seats by selection from among those candidates who have obtained votes either in the General Assembly or in the Security Council.

4. In the event of an equality of votes among the judges, the eldest judge shall have a casting vote.

ARTICLE 13

1. The members of the Court shall be elected for nine years and may be re-elected; provided, however, that of the judges elected at the first election, the terms of five judges shall expire at the end of three years and the terms of five more judges shall expire at the end of six years.

2. The judges whose terms are to expire at the end of the above-mentioned initial periods of three and six years shall be chosen by lot to be drawn by the Secretary-General immediately after the first election has been completed.

3. The members of the Court shall continue to discharge their duties until their places have been filled. Though replaced, they shall finish any cases which they may have begun.

4. In the case of the resignation of a member of the Court, the resignation shall be addressed to the President of the Court for transmission to the Secretary-General. This last notification makes the place vacant.

ARTICLE 14

Vacancies shall be filled by the same method as that laid down for the first election, subject to the following provision: the Secretary-General shall, within one month of the occurrence of the vacancy, proceed to issue the invitations provided for in Article 5, and the date of the election shall be fixed by the Security Council.

. . .

Chapter V. Amendment

ARTICLE 69

Amendments to the present Statute shall be effected by the same procedure as is provided by the Charter of the United Nations for amendments to that Charter, subject however to any provisions which the General Assembly upon recommendation of the Security Council may adopt concerning the participation of states which are parties to the present Statute but are not Members of the United Nations.

. . .

Successive Texts of the
RULES OF PROCEDURE
OF THE GENERAL ASSEMBLY

Document symbol

1. Provisional Rules of Procedure recommended by the Executive Committee of the Preparatory Commission (12 Nov. 1945) PC/EX/113/Rev. 1, pp. 18–27

2. Provisional Rules of Procedure recommended by the Preparatory Commission (23 Dec. 1945) PC/20, pp. 8–18; A/4

3. Provisional Rules of Procedure as amended by resolutions 2, 15 and 17 during the first part of the first session (26/29 Jan. and 1, 13 Feb. 1946) A/71

4. Provisional Rules of Procedure as amended by resolutions 77, 87 and 88 during the second part of the first session (9, 19 Nov. and 7 Dec. 1946) A/71/Rev. 1

5. Rules of Procedure adopted during the second session by resolution 173 (17 Nov. 1947) A/520

6. As amended during the third session by resolution 262 (11 Dec. 1948) Inset to A/520

7. As amended during the fourth session by resolution 362 (22 Oct. 1949) A/520/Rev. 1

8. As amended during the fifth session by resolutions 377A and 475 (1, 3 Nov. 1950) A/520/Rev. 2

9. As amended during the seventh session by resolution 689B (21 Dec. 1952) A/520/Rev. 2/Corr. 2

10. As amended during the eighth session by resolution 791 (23 Oct. 1953) A/520/Rev. 3

11. As amended during the ninth session by resolution 844 (11 Oct. 1954) A/520/Rev. 4

12. As amended during the eleventh session by resolution 1104 (18 Dec. 1956) A/3660

13. As amended during the twelfth session by resolution 1192 (12 Dec. 1957) A/3660/Corr. 1

RULES OF PROCEDURE
OF THE GENERAL ASSEMBLY*

(embodying amendments and additions adopted by the
General Assembly up to and including its fourteenth session)

EXPLANATORY NOTES

*1. The Table of Contents, Introduction, Rules 51–61 relating to
languages and records and Rules 135–139 relating to the admission of
new Members, Annexes I and II, and the Index to the Rules of
Procedure, are not reproduced here.*

*2. Rules 49, 84, 85, 87, 145, 147 and 162, which reproduce textually
provisions of the Charter, are printed in heavy type and are, in addition,
provided with a footnote. A footnote has also been added in the case
of other Rules which, based directly on provisions of the Charter, do
not reproduce those provisions textually.*

*3. Rules for committee meetings which are identical or similar to Rules
for plenary meetings are not reproduced. Rules 98–105, 110, 126, 133 and
134 for committee meetings differ from the corresponding Rules for
plenary meetings and are therefore reproduced. Figures between square
brackets in sections dealing with Rules for plenary meetings refer to
identical or corresponding Rules for committee meetings, and vice versa.*

*4. Footnote 5 (to rule 31) is included in the official text of the Rules;
footnote 10 (to rule 105), which is reproduced in italics, is not included
in the official text.*

*5. Rule 163 states that "The . . . notes in italics to these rules shall be
disregarded in the interpretation of the rules."*

I. SESSIONS

REGULAR SESSIONS

Date of meeting

Rule 1 [1]

The General Assembly shall meet every year in regular session
commencing on the third Tuesday in September.

Duration of session

Rule 2

On the recommendation of the General Committee, the General
Assembly shall, at the beginning of each session, fix a closing date for
the session.

---

* United Nations Doc. A/3660 and Corr. 1, Sept. 1957.
[1] Rule based directly on a provision of the Charter (Art. 20).

Place of meeting

Rule 3

Sessions shall be held at the Headquarters of the United Nations unless convened elsewhere in pursuance of a decision of the General Assembly at a previous session or at the request of a majority of the Members of the United Nations.

Rule 4

Any Member of the United Nations may, at least one hundred and twenty days before the date fixed for the opening of a regular session, request that the session be held elsewhere than at the Headquarters of the United Nations. The Secretary-General shall immediately communicate the request, together with his recommendations, to the other Members of the United Nations. If within thirty days of the date of this communication a majority of the Members concur in the request, the session shall be held accordingly.

Notification of session

Rule 5

The Secretary-General shall notify the Members of the United Nations, at least sixty days in advance, of the opening of a regular session.

Adjournment of session

Rule 6

The General Assembly may decide at any session to adjourn temporarily and resume its meetings at a later date.

SPECIAL SESSIONS

Summoning by the General Assembly

Rule 7 [2]

The General Assembly may fix a date for a special session.

Summoning on request from the Security Council or Members

Rule 8

(a) Special sessions of the General Assembly shall be held within fifteen days of the receipt by the Secretary-General of a request for such a session from the Security Council, or of a request from a majority of the Members of the United Nations, or of the concurrence of a majority of Members as provided in rule 9.

(b) Emergency special sessions pursuant to General Assembly resolution 377 A (V) shall be convened within twenty-four hours of the receipt by the Secretary-General of a request for such a session from the Security Council, on the vote of any seven members thereof, or of a request from a majority of the Members of the United Nations

---

[2] Rule based directly on a provision of the Charter (Art. 20).

expressed by vote in the Interim Committee or otherwise, or of the concurrence of a majority of Members as provided in rule 9.

Request by Members

Rule 9

(*a*) Any Member of the United Nations may request the Secretary-General to summon a special session. The Secretary-General shall immediately inform the other Members of the United Nations of the request and inquire whether they concur in it. If within thirty days of the date of the communication of the Secretary-General a majority of the Members concur in the request, a special session of the General Assembly shall be summoned in accordance with rule 8.

(*b*) This rule shall apply also to a request by any Member for an emergency special session pursuant to resolution 377 A (V). In such a case the Secretary-General shall communicate with the other Members by the most expeditious means of communication available.

Notification of session

Rule 10

The Secretary-General shall notify the Members of the United Nations, at least fourteen days in advance, of the opening of a special session summoned at the request of the Security Council, and, at least ten days in advance, in the case of a request by a majority of the Members or the concurrence of a majority in the request of any Member. In the case of an emergency special session convened pursuant to rule 8 (*b*), the Secretary-General shall notify the Members of the United Nations at least twelve hours in advance of the opening of the session.

Notification to other bodies

Rule 11

Copies of the notice summoning each session shall be addressed to all other principal organs of the United Nations and to the specialized agencies referred to in Article 57, paragraph 2, of the Charter.

II. AGENDA

REGULAR SESSIONS

Provisional agenda

Rule 12

The provisional agenda for a regular session shall be drawn up by the Secretary-General and communicated to the Members of the United Nations at least sixty days before the opening of the session.

Rule 13

The provisional agenda of a regular session shall include:

(*a*) Report of the Secretary-General on the work of the Organization;

(*b*) Reports from the Security Council,
> the Economic and Social Council,
> the Trusteeship Council,
> the International Court of Justice,
> the subsidiary organs of the General Assembly,
> specialized agencies (where such reports are called for under agreements entered into);

(*c*) All items the inclusion of which has been ordered by the General Assembly at a previous session;

(*d*) All items proposed by the other principal organs of the United Nations;

(*e*) All items proposed by any Member of the United Nations;

(*f*) All items pertaining to the budget for the next financial year and the report on the accounts for the last financial year;

(*g*) All items which the Secretary-General deems it necessary to put before the General Assembly; and

(*h*) All items proposed under Article 35, paragraph 2, of the Charter by States not Members of the United Nations.

Supplementary items

Rule 14

Any Member or principal organ of the United Nations or the Secretary-General may, at least thirty days before the date fixed for the opening of a regular session, request the inclusion of supplementary items in the agenda. These items shall be placed on a supplementary list, which shall be communicated to the Members of the United Nations at least twenty days before the date fixed for the opening of the session.

Additional items

Rule 15

Additional items of an important and urgent character, proposed for inclusion in the agenda less than thirty days before the opening of a regular session or during a regular session, may be placed on the agenda, if the General Assembly so decides by a majority of the Members present and voting. No additional item may be considered until seven days have elapsed since it was placed on the agenda, unless the General Assembly, by a two-thirds majority of the Members present and voting, decides otherwise, and until a committee has reported upon the question concerned.

SPECIAL SESSIONS

Provisional agenda

Rule 16

The provisional agenda of a special session, summoned at the request of the Security Council, shall be communicated to the Members of the United Nations at least fourteen days before the opening of the session. The provisional agenda of a special session summoned at the request of a majority of the Members, or the concurrence of a majority in the request of any Member, shall be communicated at least ten days before the opening of the session. The provisional agenda of an emergency special session shall be communicated to the Members of the United Nations simultaneously with the communication summoning the session.

Rule 17

The provisional agenda for a special session shall consist only of those items proposed for consideration in the request for the holding of the session.

Supplementary items

Rule 18

Any Member or principal organ of the United Nations or the Secretary-General may, at least four days before the date fixed for the opening of a special session, request the inclusion of supplementary items in the agenda. Such items shall be placed on a supplementary list which shall be communicated to the Members of the United Nations as soon as possible.

Additional items

Rule 19

During a special session items on the supplementary list and additional items may be added to the agenda by a two-thirds majority of the Members present and voting. During an emergency special session additional items concerning the matters dealt with in resolution 377 A (V) may be added to the agenda by a two-thirds majority of the Members present and voting.

Explanatory memoranda

Rule 20

All items proposed for inclusion in the agenda shall be accompanied by an explanatory memorandum and, if possible, by basic documents or by a draft resolution.

Approval of the agenda

Rule 21

At each session the provisional agenda and the supplementary list, together with the report of the General Committee thereon, shall be submitted to the General Assembly for approval as soon as possible after the opening of the session.

Amendment and deletion of items

Rule 22

Items on the agenda may be amended or deleted by the General Assembly by a majority of the Members present and voting.

Debate on inclusion of items

Rule 23

Debate on the inclusion of an item in the agenda, when that item has been recommended for inclusion by the General Committee, shall be limited to three speakers in favour of and three against the inclusion. The President may limit the time to be allowed to speakers under this rule.

Modification of the allocation of expenses
Rule 24
No proposal for a modification of the allocation of expenses for the time being in force shall be placed on the agenda unless it has been communicated to the Members of the United Nations at least ninety days before the date fixed for the opening of the session.

III. DELEGATIONS
Composition
Rule 25 [3]
The delegation of a Member shall consist of not more than five representatives and five alternate representatives, and as many advisers, technical advisers, experts and persons of similar status as may be required by the delegation.

Alternates
Rule 26
An alternate representative may act as a representative upon designation by the Chairman of the delegation.

IV. CREDENTIALS
Submission of credentials
Rule 27
The credentials of representatives, and the names of members of a delegation shall be submitted to the Secretary-General if possible not less than one week before the date fixed for the opening of the session. The credentials shall be issued either by the Head of the State or Government or by the Minister for Foreign Affairs.

Credentials Committee
Rule 28
A Credentials Committee shall be appointed at the beginning of each session. It shall consist of nine members, who shall be appointed by the General Assembly on the proposal of the President. The Committee shall elect its own officers. It shall examine the credentials of representatives and report without delay.

Provisional admission to a session
Rule 29
Any representative to whose admission a Member has made objection shall be seated provisionally with the same rights as other representatives, until the Credentials Committee has reported and the General Assembly has given its decision.

[3] Rule based directly on a provision of the Charter (Art. 9, para. 2).

V. PRESIDENT AND VICE-PRESIDENTS

Temporary President

Rule 30

At the opening of each session of the General Assembly the Chairman of that delegation from which the President of the previous session was elected shall preside until the General Assembly has elected a President for the session.

Elections

Rule 31

The General Assembly shall elect a President and thirteen [4] Vice-Presidents, who shall hold office until the close of the session at which they are elected.[5] The Vice-Presidents shall be elected, after the election of the Chairmen of the seven Main Committees referred to in rule 101, on the basis of ensuring the representative character of the General Committee.

Acting President

Rule 32 [107]

If the President finds it necessary to be absent during a meeting or any part thereof, he shall appoint one of the Vice-Presidents to take his place.

Rule 33 [107]

A Vice-President acting as President shall have the same powers and duties as the President.

Replacement of the President

Rule 34 [107]

If the President is unable to perform his functions, a new President shall be elected for the unexpired term.

General powers of the President

Rule 35 [108]

In addition to exercising the powers which are conferred upon him elsewhere by these rules, the President shall declare the opening and

---

[4] Rule based directly on a provision of the Charter (Art. 21, second sentence).

[5] In the annex to resolution 1192 (XII), the General Assembly decided as follows:
1. The thirteen Vice-Presidents shall be elected according to the following pattern:
   (a) Four representatives from Asian and African States;
   (b) One representative from an Eastern European State;
   (c) Two representatives from Latin American States;
   (d) Two representatives from Western European and other States;
   (e) Five representatives from the permanent members of the Security Council.
2. The region from which the President is elected will, however, reduce by one the number of vice-presidencies allocated in paragraph 1 of the present annex.
3. At least one of the Vice-Presidents in categories (a) or (d) above, or the President or one of the Chairmen of the Main Committees, will be from a Commonwealth country, without altering the geographical distribution of seats in the General Committee, as defined in paragraphs 1 and 2 of this annex and in paragraph 1 of the resolution.

closing of each plenary meeting of the session, shall direct the discussions in plenary meeting, ensure observance of these rules, accord the right to speak, put questions and announce decisions. He shall rule on points of order, and, subject to these rules, shall have complete control of the proceedings at any meeting and over the maintenance of order thereat. The President may, in the course of the discussion of an item, propose to the General Assembly the limitation of the time to be allowed to speakers, the limitation of the number of times each representative may speak on any question, the closure of the list of speakers or the closure of the debate. He may also propose the suspension or the adjournment of the meeting or the adjournment of the debate on the item under discussion.

Rule 36 [109]

The President, in the exercise of his functions, remains under the authority of the General Assembly.

The President shall not vote

Rule 37 [106]

The President, or Vice-President acting as President, shall not vote but shall appoint another member of his delegation to vote in his place.

VI. GENERAL COMMITTEE

Composition

Rule 38

The General Committee shall comprise the President of the General Assembly, who shall preside, the thirteen Vice-Presidents and the Chairmen of the seven Main Committees. No two members of the General Committee shall be members of the same delegation, and it shall be so constituted as to ensure its representative character. Chairmen of other committees, upon which all Members have the right to be represented and which are established by the General Assembly to meet during the session, shall be entitled to attend meetings of the General Committee and may participate without vote in the discussion.

Substitute members

Rule 39

If a Vice-President of the General Assembly finds it necessary to be absent during a meeting of the General Committee he may designate a member of his delegation as his substitute. The Chairman of a Main Committee shall, in case of absence, designate the Vice-Chairman of the Committee as his substitute. A Vice-Chairman shall not have the right to vote if he is of the same delegation as another member of the Committee.

Functions

Rule 40

The General Committee shall, at the beginning of each session, consider the provisional agenda, together with the supplementary list, and shall make recommendations to the General Assembly with regard to each item proposed, concerning its inclusion in the agenda, the rejection of the request for inclusion, or the inclusion of the item in the provisional agenda of a future session. It shall, in the same manner, examine requests for the inclusion of additional items in the agenda, and shall make recommendations thereon to the General Assembly. In considering matters relating to the agenda of the General Assembly, the General Committee shall not discuss the substance of any item, except in so far as this bears upon the question whether the General Committee should recommend the inclusion of the item in the agenda, the rejection of the request for inclusion, or the inclusion of the item in the provisional agenda of a future session, and what priority should be accorded to an item the inclusion of which has been recommended.

Rule 41

The General Committee shall make recommendations to the General Assembly concerning the closing date of the session. It shall assist the President and the General Assembly in drawing up the agenda for each plenary meeting, in determining the priority of its items, and in the co-ordination of the proceedings of all committees of the General Assembly. It shall assist the President in the general conduct of the work of the General Assembly which falls within the competence of the President. It shall not, however, decide any political question.

Rule 42

The General Committee shall meet periodically throughout each session to review the progress of the General Assembly and its committees and to make recommendations for furthering such progress. It shall also meet at such other times as the President deems necessary or upon the request of any other of its members.

Participation by representatives of Members requesting the inclusion of items in the agenda

Rule 43

A Member of the General Assembly which has no representative on the General Committee, and which has requested the inclusion of an item in the agenda, shall be entitled to attend any meeting of the General Committee at which its request is discussed, and may participate, without vote, in the discussion of that item.

Formal revision of resolutions of the General Assembly

Rule 44

The General Committee may revise the resolutions adopted by the General Assembly, changing their form but not their substance. Any such changes shall be reported to the General Assembly for its consideration.

VII. SECRETARIAT

Duties of the Secretary-General

Rule 45

The Secretary-General shall act in that capacity in all meetings of the General Assembly,[6] its committees and sub-committees. He may designate a member of the staff to act in his place at these meetings.

Rule 46

The Secretary-General shall provide and direct the staff required by the General Assembly and any committees or subsidiary organs which it may establish.

Duties of the Secretariat

Rule 47

The Secretariat shall receive, translate, print and distribute documents, reports and resolutions of the General Assembly, its committees and organs; interpret speeches made at the meetings; prepare, print and circulate the summary records of the session; have the custody and proper preservation of the documents in the archives of the General Assembly; publish the reports of the meetings; distribute all documents of the General Assembly to the Members of the United Nations, and, generally, perform all other work which the General Assembly may require.

Annual report of the Secretary-General

Rule 48

The Secretary-General shall make an annual report, and such supplementary reports as are required, to the General Assembly on the work of the Organization.[6] He shall communicate the annual report to the Members of the United Nations at least forty-five days before the opening of the session.

Notification under Article 12 of the Charter

Rule 49 [7]

The Secretary-General, with the consent of the Security Council, shall notify the General Assembly at each session of any matters relative to the maintenance of international peace and security which are being dealt with by the Security Council, and shall similarly notify the General Assembly, or the Members of the United Nations if the General Assembly is not in session, immediately the Security Council ceases to deal with such matters.

Regulations concerning the Secretariat

Rule 50 [8]

The General Assembly shall establish regulations concerning the staff of the Secretariat.

$$\cdot \qquad \cdot \qquad \cdot$$

[6] Rule based directly on a provision of the Charter (Art. 98).
[7] Rule reproducing textually a provision of the Charter (Art. 12, para. 2).
[8] Rule based directly on a provision of the Charter (Art. 101, para. 1).

X. PUBLIC AND PRIVATE MEETINGS: PLENARY MEETINGS; MEETINGS OF COMMITTEES AND SUB-COMMITTEES

General principles

Rule 62

The meetings of the General Assembly and its Main Committees shall be held in public unless the body concerned decides that exceptional circumstances require that the meeting be held in private. Meetings of other committees and sub-committees shall also be held in public unless the body concerned decides otherwise.

Private meetings

Rule 63

All decisions of the General Assembly taken at a private meeting shall be announced at an early public meeting of the General Assembly. At the close of each private meeting of the Main Committees, other committees and sub-committees, the Chairman may issue a communiqué through the Secretary-General.

XI. MINUTE OF SILENT PRAYER OR MEDITATION

Invitation to silent prayer or meditation

Rule 64

Immediately after the opening of the first plenary meeting and immediately preceding the closing of the final plenary meeting of each session of the General Assembly, the President shall invite the representatives to observe one minute of silence dedicated to prayer or meditation.

XII. PLENARY MEETINGS

CONDUCT OF BUSINESS

Emergency special sessions

Rule 65

Notwithstanding the provisions of any other rule and unless the General Assembly decides otherwise, the Assembly, in case of an emergency special session, shall convene in plenary session only and proceed directly to consider the item proposed for consideration in the request for the holding of the session, without previous reference to the General Committee or to any other committee; the President and Vice-Presidents for such emergency special sessions shall be, respectively, the Chairmen of those delegations from which were elected the President and Vice-Presidents of the previous session.

Report of the Secretary-General

Rule 66

Proposals to refer any portion of the report of the Secretary-General to one of the Main Committees without debate shall be decided upon by the General Assembly without previous reference to the General Committee.

Reference to committees
Rule 67
The General Assembly shall not, unless it decides otherwise, make a final decision upon any item on the agenda until it has received the report of a committee on that item.

Discussion of committee reports
Rule 68
Discussion of a report of a Main Committee in a plenary meeting of the General Assembly shall take place if at least one-third of the Members present and voting at the plenary meeting consider such a discussion to be necessary. Any proposal to this effect shall not be debated, but shall be immediately put to the vote.

Quorum
Rule 69 [110]
A majority of the Members of the General Assembly shall constitute a quorum.

Speeches
Rule 70 [111]
No representative may address the General Assembly without having previously obtained the permission of the President. The President shall call upon speakers in the order in which they signify their desire to speak. The President may call a speaker to order if his remarks are not relevant to the subject under discussion.

Precedence
Rule 71 [112]
The Chairman and the Rapporteur of a committee may be accorded precedence for the purpose of explaining the conclusion arrived at by their committee.

Statements by the Secretariat
Rule 72 [113]
The Secretary-General, or a member of the Secretariat designated by him as his representative, may, at any time, make either oral or written statements to the General Assembly concerning any question under consideration by it.

Points of order
Rule 73 [114]
During the discussion of any matter, a representative may rise to a point of order, and the point of order shall be immediately decided by the President in accordance with the rules of procedure. A representative may appeal against the ruling of the President. The appeal shall be immediately put to the vote and the President's ruling shall stand unless overruled by a majority of the Members present and voting. A representative rising to a point of order may not speak on the substance of the matter under discussion.

Time limit on speeches
Rule 74 [115]
The General Assembly may limit the time to be allowed to each speaker and the number of times each representative may speak on any question. When debate is limited and a representative has spoken his allotted time, the President shall call him to order without delay.

Closing of list of speakers
Rule 75 [116]
During the course of a debate the President may announce the list of speakers and, with the consent of the General Assembly, declare the list closed. He may, however, accord the right of reply to any Member if a speech delivered after he has declared the list closed makes this desirable.

Adjournment of debate
Rule 76 [117]
During the discussion of any matter, a representative may move the adjournment of the debate on the item under discussion. In addition to the proposer of the motion, two representatives may speak in favour of, and two against, the motion, after which the motion shall be immediately put to the vote. The President may limit the time to be allowed to speakers under this rule.

Closure of debate
Rule 77 [118]
A representative may at any time move the closure of the debate on the item under discussion, whether or not any other representative has signified his wish to speak. Permission to speak on the closure of the debate shall be accorded only to two speakers opposing the closure, after which the motion shall be immediately put to the vote. If the General Assembly is in favour of the closure, the President shall declare the closure of the debate. The President may limit the time to be allowed to speakers under this rule.

Suspension or adjournment of the meeting
Rule 78 [119]
During the discussion of any matter, a representative may move the suspension or the adjournment of the meeting. Such motions shall not be debated, but shall be immediately put to the vote. The President may limit the time to be allowed to the speaker moving the suspension or adjournment of the meeting.

Order of procedural motions
Rule 79 [120]
Subject to rule 73, the following motions shall have precedence in the following order over all other proposals or motions before the meeting:
(a) To suspend the meeting;
(b) To adjourn the meeting;
(c) To adjourn the debate on the item under discussion;
(d) For the closure of the debate on the item under discussion.

Proposals and amendments
Rule 80 [121]
Proposals and amendments shall normally be introduced in writing and handed to the Secretary-General, who shall circulate copies to the delegations. As a general rule, no proposal shall be discussed or put to the vote at any meeting of the General Assembly unless copies of it have been circulated to all delegations not later than the day preceding the meeting. The President may, however, permit the discussion and consideration of amendments, or of motions as to procedure, even though these amendments and motions have not been circulated or have only been circulated the same day.

Decisions on competence
Rule 81 [122]
Subject to rule 79, any motion calling for a decision on the competence of the General Assembly to adopt a proposal submitted to it shall be put to the vote before a vote is taken on the proposal in question.

Withdrawal of motions
Rule 82 [123]
A motion may be withdrawn by its proposer at any time before voting on it has commenced, provided that the motion has not been amended. A motion which has thus been withdrawn may be reintroduced by any Member.

Reconsideration of proposals
Rule 83 [124]
When a proposal has been adopted or rejected it may not be reconsidered at the same session unless the General Assembly, by a two-thirds majority of the Members present and voting, so decides. Permission to speak on a motion to reconsider shall be accorded only to two speakers opposing the motion, after which it shall be immediately put to the vote.

VOTING

Voting rights
Rule 84 [9] [125]
Each Member of the General Assembly shall have one vote.

Two-thirds majority
Rule 85 [9]
Decisions of the General Assembly on important questions shall be made by a two-thirds majority of the Members present and voting. These questions shall include: recommendations with respect to the maintenance of international peace and security, the election of the non-permanent members of the Security Council, the election of the members of the Economic and Social Council, the election of members of the Trusteeship Council in accordance with paragraph 1 c of Article 86 of the Charter,

---

[9] Rules 84, 85 and 87 reproduce the three paragraphs of Art. 18 of the Charter.

the admission of new Members to the United Nations, the suspension of the rights and privileges of membership, the expulsion of Members, questions relating to the operation of the Trusteeship System, and budgetary questions.

Rule 86

Decisions of the General Assembly on amendments to proposals relating to important questions, and on parts of such proposals put to the vote separately, shall be made by a two-thirds majority of the Members present and voting.

Simple majority

Rule 87 [9] [126]

Decisions of the General Assembly on questions other than those provided for in rule 85, including the determination of additional categories of questions to be decided by a two-thirds majority, shall be made by a majority of the Members present and voting.

Meaning of the expression " Members present and voting "

Rule 88 [127]

For the purpose of these rules, the phrase " Members present and voting " means Members casting an affirmative or negative vote. Members which abstain from voting are considered as not voting.

Method of voting

Rule 89 [128]

The General Assembly shall normally vote by show of hands or by standing, but any representative may request a roll-call. The roll-call shall be taken in the English alphabetical order of the names of the Members, beginning with the Member whose name is drawn by lot by the President. The name of each Member shall be called in any roll-call and one of its representatives shall reply " Yes ", " No " or " Abstention ". The result of the voting shall be inserted in the record in the English alphabetical order of the names of the Members.

Conduct during voting

Rule 90 [129]

After the President has announced the beginning of voting, no representative shall interrupt the voting except on a point of order in connexion with the actual conduct of the voting. The President may permit Members to explain their votes, either before or after the voting, except when the vote is taken by secret ballot. The President may limit the time to be allowed for such explanations. The President shall not permit the proposer of a proposal or of an amendment to explain his vote on his own proposal or amendment.

Division of proposals and amendments

Rule 91 [130]

A representative may move that parts of a proposal or of an amendment shall be voted on separately. If objection is made to the request for division, the motion for division shall be voted upon. Permission to speak on the motion for division shall be given only to two speakers in favour and two speakers against. If the motion for division is carried, those parts of the proposal or of the amendment which are subsequently approved shall be put to the vote as a whole. If all operative parts of the proposal or of the amendment have been rejected, the proposal or the amendment shall be considered to have been rejected as a whole.

Voting on amendments

Rule 92 [131]

When an amendment is moved to a proposal, the amendment shall be voted on first. When two or more amendments are moved to a proposal, the General Assembly shall first vote on the amendment furthest removed in substance from the original proposal and then on the amendment next furthest removed therefrom, and so on, until all the amendments have been put to the vote. Where, however, the adoption of one amendment necessarily implies the rejection of another amendment, the latter amendment shall not be put to the vote. If one or more amendments are adopted, the amended proposal shall then be voted upon. A motion is considered an amendment to a proposal if it merely adds to, deletes from or revises part of that proposal.

Voting on proposals

Rule 93 [132]

If two or more proposals relate to the same question, the General Assembly shall, unless it decides otherwise, vote on the proposals in the order in which they have been submitted. The General Assembly may, after each vote on a proposal, decide whether to vote on the next proposal.

Elections

Rule 94 [105]

All elections shall be held by secret ballot. There shall be no nominations.

Rule 95 [133]

When only one person or Member is to be elected and no candidate obtains in the first ballot the majority required, a second ballot shall be taken which shall be restricted to the two candidates obtaining the largest number of votes. If in the second ballot the votes are equally divided, and a majority is required, the President shall decide between the candidates by drawing lots. If a two-thirds majority is required, the balloting shall be continued until one candidate secures two-thirds of the votes cast; provided that, after the third inconclusive ballot, votes may be cast for any eligible person or Member. If three such unrestricted ballots are inconclusive, the next three ballots shall be restricted to the two candidates who obtained the greatest number of votes in the third of the unrestricted ballots, and the following three ballots thereafter shall be unrestricted, and so on until a person or Member is elected. These provisions shall not prejudice the application of rules 144, 145, 147 and 149.

Rule 96

When two or more elective places are to be filled at one time under the same conditions, those candidates obtaining in the first ballot the majority required shall be elected. If the number of candidates obtaining such majority is less than the number of persons or Members to be elected, there shall be additional ballots to fill the remaining places, the voting being restricted to the candidates obtaining the greatest number of votes in the previous ballot, to a number not more than twice the places remaining to be filled; provided that, after the third inconclusive ballot, votes may be cast for any eligible person or Member. If three such unrestricted ballots are inconclusive, the next three ballots shall be restricted to the candidates who obtained the greatest number of votes in the third of the unrestricted ballots, to a number not more than twice the places remaining to be filled, and the following three ballots there-after shall be unrestricted, and so on until all the places have been filled. These provisions shall not prejudice the application of rules, 144, 145, 147 and 149.

Equally divided votes

Rule 97 [134]

If a vote is equally divided on matters other than elections, a second vote shall be taken at a subsequent meeting which shall be held within forty-eight hours of the first vote, and it shall be expressly mentioned in the agenda that a second vote will be taken on the matter in question. If this vote also results in equality, the proposal shall be regarded as rejected.

XIII. COMMITTEES

Creation

Rule 98

The General Assembly may set up such committees as it deems necessary for the performance of its functions.

Categories of subjects

Rule 99

Items relating to the same category of subjects shall be referred to the committee or committees dealing with that category of subjects. Committees shall not introduce new items on their own initiative.

Priorities

Rule 100

Each Main Committee, taking into account the closing date for the session fixed by the General Assembly on the recommendation of the General Committee, shall adopt its own priorities and meet as may be necessary to complete the consideration of the items referred to it.

Main Committees

Rule 101

The Main Committees of the General Assembly are:

(*a*) Political and Security Committee (including the regulation of armaments) (First Committee);

(*b*) Special Political Committee;

(*c*) Economic and Financial Committee (Second Committee);

(*d*) Social, Humanitarian and Cultural Committee (Third Committee);

(*e*) Trusteeship Committee (including Non-Self-Governing Territories) (Fourth Committee);

(*f*) Administrative and Budgetary Committee (Fifth Committee);

(*g*) Legal Committee (Sixth Committee).

Representation of Members

Rule 102

Each Member may be represented by one person on each Main Committee and on any other committee that may be constituted upon which all Members have the right to be represented. It may also assign to these committees advisers, technical advisers, experts or persons of similar status.

Rule 103

Upon designation by the Chairman of the delegation, advisers, technical advisers, experts or persons of similar status may act as members of committees. Persons of this status shall not, however, unless designated as alternate representatives, be eligible for appointment as Chairmen, Vice-Chairmen or Rapporteurs of committees or for seats in the General Assembly.

Sub-committees

Rule 104

Each committee may set up sub-committees, which shall elect their own officers.

Officers

Rule 105 [94]

Each committee shall elect its own Chairman, Vice-Chairman and Rapporteur. These officers shall be elected on the basis of equitable geographical distribution, experience and personal competence.[10] These elections shall be held by secret ballot.

The Chairman of a Main Committee shall not vote

Rule 106 [37]

---

[10] *By operative paragraph 1 of resolution 1192 (XII) the General Assembly confirmed the practice established with regard to the distribution of the chairmanships of the Main Committees, namely, two from Latin American States, two from Asian and African States, two from Western European and other States, and one from an Eastern European State.*

Absence of officers

Rule 107 [32–34]

Functions of the Chairman

Rules 108 and 109 [35 and 36]

Quorum

Rule 110 [69]

One third of the members of a committee shall constitute a quorum. The presence of a majority of the members of the committee is, however, required for a question to be put to the vote.

Speeches

Rule 111 [70]

Precedence

Rule 112 [71]

Statements by the Secretariat

Rule 113 [72]

Points of order

Rule 114 [73]

Time limit on speeches

Rule 115 [74]

Closing of list of speakers

Rule 116 [75]

Adjournment of debate

Rule 117 [76]

Closure of debate

Rule 118 [77]

Suspension or adjournment of the meeting

Rule 119 [78]

Order of procedural motions

Rule 120 [79]

Proposals and amendments

Rule 121 [80]

Decisions on competence

Rule 122 [81]

Withdrawal of motions

Rule 123 [82]

Reconsideration of proposals

Rule 124 [83]

Voting rights

Rule 125 [84]

Majority required

Rule 126 [87]

Decisions in the committees of the General Assembly shall be made by a majority of the members present and voting.

Meaning of the expression "members present and voting"

Rule 127 [88]

Method of voting

Rule 128 [89]

Conduct during voting

Rule 129 [90]

Division of proposals and amendments

Rule 130 [91]

Voting on amendments

Rule 131 [92]

Voting on proposals

Rule 132 [93]

Elections

Rule 133 [95]

When only one person or member is to be elected and no candidate obtains in the first ballot the majority required, a second ballot shall be taken, which shall be restricted to the two candidates obtaining the largest number of votes. If in the second ballot the votes are equally divided, and a majority is required, the Chairman shall decide between the candidates by drawing lots.

Equally divided votes

Rule 134 [97]

If a vote is equally divided on matters other than elections, the proposal shall be regarded as rejected.

. . .

XV. ELECTIONS TO PRINCIPAL ORGANS

GENERAL PROVISIONS

Terms of office

Rule 140

Except as provided in rule 148, the term of office of members of Councils shall begin on 1 January following their election by the General Assembly, and shall end on 31 December following the election of their successors.

By-elections

Rule 141

Should a member cease to belong to a Council before its term of office expires, a by-election shall be held separately at the next session of the General Assembly to elect a member for the unexpired term.

APPOINTMENT OF THE SECRETARY-GENERAL

Appointment of the Secretary-General

Rule 142

When the Security Council has submitted its recommendation on the appointment of the Secretary-General, the General Assembly shall consider the recommendation and vote upon it by secret ballot in private meeting.

THE SECURITY COUNCIL

Annual elections

Rule 143 [11]

The General Assembly shall each year, in the course of its regular session, elect three non-permanent members of the Security Council for a term of two years.

Qualifications for membership

Rule 144 [12]

In the election of non-permanent members of the Security Council, in accordance with Article 23, paragraph 1, of the Charter, due regard shall be specially paid, in the first instance, to the contribution of Members of the United Nations to the maintenance of international peace and security and to the other purposes of the Organization, and also to equitable geographical distribution.

Re-eligibility

Rule 145 [13]

A retiring member of the Security Council shall not be eligible for immediate re-election.

THE ECONOMIC AND SOCIAL COUNCIL

Annual elections

Rule 146 [14]

The General Assembly shall each year, in the course of its regular session, elect six members of the Economic and Social Council for a term of three years.

Re-eligibility

Rule 147 [15]

A retiring member of the Economic and Social Council shall be eligible for immediate re-election.

[11] Rule based directly on a provision of the Charter (Art. 23, para. 2).
[12] Rule based directly on a provision of the Charter (Art. 23, para. 1).
[13] Rule reproducing textually a provision of the Charter (Art. 23, para. 2, last sentence).
[14] Rule based directly on a provision of the Charter (Art. 61, para. 2).
[15] Rule reproducing textually a provision of the Charter (Art. 61, para. 2, last sentence).

The Trusteeship Council

Occasions for elections

Rule 148

When a Trusteeship Agreement has been approved and a Member of the United Nations has become an Administering Authority of a Trust Territory in accordance with Article 83 or 85 of the Charter, the General Assembly shall proceed to such election or elections to the Trusteeship Council as may be necessary, in accordance with Article 86. A Member or Members elected at any such election at a regular session shall take office immediately upon their election and shall complete their terms in accordance with the provisions of rule 140, as if they had begun their terms of office on 1 January following their election.

Term of office and re-eligibility

Rule 149 [16]

A non-administering member of the Trusteeship Council shall be elected for a term of three years and shall be eligible for immediate re-election.

Vacancies

Rule 150

At each session the General Assembly shall, in accordance with Article 86 of the Charter, elect members to fill any vacancies.

The International Court of Justice

Method of election

Rule 151

The election of the members of the International Court of Justice shall take place in accordance with the Statute of the Court.

Rule 152

Any meeting of the General Assembly held in pursuance of the Statute of the International Court of Justice for the purpose of the election of members of the Court shall continue until as many candidates as are required for all the seats to be filled have obtained in one or more ballots an absolute majority of votes.

XVI. ADMINISTRATIVE AND BUDGETARY QUESTIONS

Regulations for financial administration

Rule 153

The General Assembly shall establish regulations for the financial administration of the United Nations.

[16] Rule based directly on a provision of the Charter (Art. 86, para. 1 c).

Estimates of expenditure

Rule 154

No resolution involving expenditure shall be recommended by a committee for approval by the General Assembly unless it is accompanied by an estimate of expenditures prepared by the Secretary-General. No resolution in respect of which expenditures are anticipated by the Secretary-General shall be voted by the General Assembly until the Administrative and Budgetary Committee has had an opportunity of stating the effect of the proposal upon the budget estimates of the United Nations.

Information on the cost of resolutions

Rule 155

The Secretary-General shall keep all committees informed of the detailed estimated cost of all resolutions which have been recommended by the committees for approval by the General Assembly.

Advisory Committee on Administrative and Budgetary Questions

Rule 156

The General Assembly shall appoint an Advisory Committee on Administrative and Budgetary Questions (hereinafter called the " Advisory Committee "), with a membership of nine, including at least two financial experts of recognized standing.

Composition of the Advisory Committee

Rule 157

The members of the Advisory Committee, no two of whom shall be nationals of the same State, shall be selected on the basis of broad geographical representation, personal qualifications and experience, and shall serve for three years corresponding to three financial years, as defined in the regulations for the financial administration of the United Nations. Members shall retire by rotation and shall be eligible for reappointment. The two financial experts shall not retire simultaneously. The General Assembly shall appoint the members of the Advisory Committee at the regular session immediately preceding the expiration of the term of office of the members, or, in case of vacancies, at the next session.

Functions of the Advisory Committee

Rule 158

The Advisory Committee shall be responsible for expert examination of the budget of the United Nations, and shall assist the Administrative and Budgetary Committee of the General Assembly. At the commencement of each regular session it shall submit to the General Assembly a detailed report on the budget for the next financial year and on the accounts of the last financial year. It shall also examine on behalf of the General Assembly the administrative budgets of specialized agencies and proposals for financial and budgetary arrangements with such agencies. It shall perform such other duties as may be assigned to it under the regulations for the financial administration of the United Nations.

Committee on Contributions

Rule 159

The General Assembly shall appoint an expert Committee on Contributions, consisting of ten members.

Composition of the Committee on Contributions

Rule 160

The members of the Committee on Contributions, no two of whom shall be nationals of the same State, shall be selected on the basis of broad geographical representation, personal qualifications and experience, and shall serve for a period of three years corresponding to three financial years, as defined in the regulations for the financial administration of the United Nations. Members shall retire by rotation and shall be eligible for reappointment. The General Assembly shall appoint the members of the Committee on Contributions at the regular session immediately preceding the expiration of the term of office of the members, or, in case of vacancies, at the next session.

Functions of the Committee on Contributions

Rule 161

The Committee on Contributions shall advise the General Assembly concerning the apportionment, under Article 17, paragraph 2, of the Charter, of the expenses of the Organization among Members, broadly according to capacity to pay. The scale of assessments, when once fixed by the General Assembly, shall not be subject to a general revision for at least three years, unless it is clear that there have been substantial changes in relative capacities to pay. The Committee shall also advise the General Assembly on the assessments to be fixed for new Members, on appeals by Members for a change of assessments, and on the action to be taken with regard to the application of Article 19 of the Charter.

XVII. SUBSIDIARY ORGANS OF THE GENERAL ASSEMBLY

Creation and rules of procedure

Rule 162

The General Assembly may establish such subsidiary organs as it deems necessary for the performance of its functions.[17] The rules relating to the procedure of committees of the General Assembly, as well as rules 45 and 62, shall apply to the procedure of any subsidiary organ, unless the General Assembly or the subsidiary organ decides otherwise.

---

[17] Rule reproducing textually a provision of the Charter (Art. 22).

XVIII. INTERPRETATION AND AMENDMENTS

Notes in italics

Rule 163

The description of the rules in the table of contents and the notes in italics to these rules shall be disregarded in the interpretation of the rules.

Method of amendment

Rule 164

These rules of procedure may be amended by a decision of the General Assembly taken by a majority of the Members present and voting, after a committee has reported on the proposed amendment.

. . .

ANNEX III [18]

PROCEDURE FOR THE EXAMINATION OF REPORTS AND PETITIONS RELATING TO THE TERRITORY OF SOUTH WEST AFRICA

Special rules adopted by the General Assembly at its ninth session

PROCEDURE WITH REGARD TO REPORTS

Special rule A : The General Assembly shall receive annually from the Committee on South West Africa the report on South West Africa submitted to the Committee by the Union of South Africa (or a report on conditions in the Territory of South West Africa prepared by the Committee in accordance with paragraph 12 (*c*) of General Assembly resolution 749 A (VIII)), together with the observations of the Committee on the report as well as the comments of the duly authorized representative of the Union of South Africa, should that Government decide to follow the General Assembly's recommendation and appoint such a representative.

Special rule B : The General Assembly shall, as a rule, be guided by the observations of the Committee on South West Africa and shall base its conclusions, as far as possible, on the Committee's observations.

PROCEDURE WITH REGARD TO PETITIONS

Special rule C : The General Assembly shall receive annually from the Committee on South West Africa a report with regard to petitions submitted to it. The summary records of the meetings at which the petitions were discussed shall be attached.

Special rule D : The General Assembly shall, as a rule, be guided by the conclusions of the Committee on South West Africa and shall base its own conclusions, as far as possible, on the conclusions of the Committee.

[18] See resolution 844 (IX) of 11 October 1954.

PRIVATE MEETINGS

Special rule E : Having regard to rule 62 of the rules of procedure of the General Assembly, meetings at which decisions concerning persons are considered shall be held in private.

VOTING PROCEDURE

Special rule F : Decisions of the General Assembly on questions relating to reports and petitions concerning the Territory of South West Africa shall be regarded as important questions within the meaning of Article 18, paragraph 2, of the Charter of the United Nations.

Extracts from the
REPORT OF THE SECRETARY-GENERAL
ON MEASURES TO ECONOMIZE THE TIME
OF THE GENERAL ASSEMBLY*

1. HISTORY OF THE RESOLUTION

At the request of the Canadian Government an item was included in the agenda of the second part of the first session of the General Assembly on " Measures to economize the time of the General Assembly ". This item was referred to the General Committee for its consideration and was studied both by the Committee itself and by a special sub-committee formed for the purpose, a member of the Canadian delegation being present on each occasion to explain the views which had inspired the Canadian Government to raise the question.

The General Committee submitted its report to the General Assembly on 14 December 1946. On the recommendation of the Committee the General Assembly resolved to direct the Secretary-General to make a study of the measures to economize time and of the provisional rules of procedure, on the basis of the Canadian memoranda, the suggestions received from Members, the views expressed in the General Committee and the experience acquired and precedents established during the first session.

. . .

4. SUMMARY OF PRINCIPAL SUGGESTIONS FOR ECONOMIZING TIME OF THE GENERAL ASSEMBLY

A. AGENDA

An effort should be made to limit the Agenda of a session to those important items which can be dealt with by the General Assembly within five to seven weeks. The following suggestions would tend to restrict the agenda in this way and allow Members more time for the preliminary study of agenda items:

> 1. It is desirable that all possible items should be submitted in time for inclusion in the provisional agenda which is circulated sixty days in advance of the opening of the session, or as soon as possible thereafter for inclusion in the supplementary list. . . .
>
> 2. During the course of a session additional items should be added to the agenda only if their urgency requires it. When request is made for the inclusion of such an item, the General Committee should be informed of the circumstances which made it impossible

* United Nations Doc. A/316, 8 July 1947. Mimeographed.

to include the item in the provisional agenda or the supplementary list. The General Committee should recommend to the plenary meeting the inclusion of the item in the agenda only if it is convinced that the urgency of the matter is such as to require the Assembly to give it consideration regardless of the fact that previous notice of the item had not been given.

.   .   .

B. DEBATE

Full debate of matters before the General Assembly is necessary and desirable, and no steps should be taken that call into question this fundamental democratic right. Measures can, however, be adopted which, while protecting the rights of each Member, would accelerate the debate and avoid unnecessary repetitions. The General Assembly can, through the use of efficient procedures, allow a full expression of opinion while at the same time reducing the length of debate on many subjects. In this connection the Secretary-General suggests the following:

1. The circulation of documentation well in advance of the opening of a session will allow delegations to make the preparation necessary for the conduct of clear, concise debate. . . .

2. Adoption by the General Assembly of clear, practical rules of procedure, appropriate to the needs which are peculiar to the Assembly, will avoid procedural difficulties and much debate on the interpretation and application of the rules.

.   .   .

4. Close collaboration should be maintained between the Chairmen and secretaries of committees. The latter, through continuous service with specific committees from session to session are able to assist the Chairmen in the interpretation of the rules of procedure and in making available to committees in the most useful way the services of the Secretariat.

5. Duplication of debate can be avoided and more satisfactory schedule of meetings established by avoiding the reference of the same agenda item to two committees at the same time.

C. MATERIAL ARRANGEMENTS AND SCHEDULE

The speed with which the General Assembly progresses in its work is determined in no small degree by the material arrangements made for its meetings and by the manner in which the schedule of the Assembly is drawn up. Many of the difficulties which have been encountered will decrease or disappear when the permanent headquarters are established in Manhattan. However, the following measures would in any case tend to expedite the work of the Assembly:

1. The use of simultaneous interpretation would result in a greater economy of time than any other single measure that could be adopted. . . .

2. Changes in the announced schedule of meetings should be avoided except in unusual circumstances. Close co-operation between the Chairmen and secretaries of committees is essential whenever meetings are required in order that proper clearance is obtained from the office in the Secretariat responsible for the co-ordination of the overall schedule of the General Assembly.

3. The total time lost between the scheduled hour for beginning of meetings and the actual opening of the meetings is not inconsiderable. . . .

4. The bureaus of main committees should consider as early as possible in the committees' work the question of how the programme of the committee might be expedited through the establishment of sub-committees. It is, of course, impossible to adopt fixed rules on this matter; but the Chairman of a Main committee, together with the Vice-Chairman, Rapporteur and Secretary should not fail to give special attention to it as they plan the programme of the committee in the early stages of its work.

. . .

7. The Secretary-General recommends that Members endeavour to submit the texts of documents intended for circulation as far as possible in advance of the meeting at which they are to be discussed. Every effort will be made by the Secretariat to carry out the prompt translation, reproduction and circulation of documents.

8. The reading in plenary and committee meetings of rapporteurs' reports and other documents which had previously been circulated to Members does not appear necessary in the consideration of any matter. . . .

APPENDIX E

Extracts from the
REPORT OF THE COMMITTEE
ON PROCEDURES AND ORGANIZATION*

23 *September* 1947

INTRODUCTION

1. On 15 December 1946 the General Assembly approved resolution 102 (I) on measures to economize the time of the General Assembly.

2. The Committee on Procedures and Organization referred to in the resolution met at Lake Success on 9 September 1947 and elected as Chairman, Mr. Escott Reid (Canada), as Vice-Chairman, Mr. Holguin de Lavalle (Peru) and as Rapporteur, Mr. W. Borberg (Denmark).

3. In conformity with the General Assembly's resolution the Committee had before it a report by the Secretary-General (document A/316) based on the memoranda submitted by the delegation of Canada to the General Assembly during the second part of the first session, on the suggestions which the Secretary-General received from Members of the United Nations, on the views expressed in the Sub-Committee of the General Committee of the first session of the General Assembly during its consideration of this question, and on the experience acquired and the precedents established during the first session.

4. The Secretary-General's report to the General Assembly contains:

(*a*) A summary of principal suggestions for economizing the time of the General Assembly; proposals with respect to the agenda; suggestions with a view to accelerating the debates and avoiding unnecessary repetitions; and recommendations as to material arrangements which would tend to expedite the work of the Assembly, such as the increased use of simultaneous interpretation, the preparation and the observance of strict schedules of meetings, etc.

(*b*) Proposed re-drafts of a number of the provisional rules of procedure of the General Assembly.

(*c*) Copies of suggestions received from the Governments of the Dominican Republic, Australia, Guatemala, the Netherlands, Argentina, New Zealand, Denmark, the United Kingdom and Norway.

PART I

5. The Committee devoted its first meeting to a discussion of its terms of reference and the organization of its work. The majority of its

* G.A.O.R.: 2nd Sess., Plenary Mtgs., 1947, Vol. II, Annex 4 (A/388), pp. 1455–1461.

members considered that the terms of reference prescribed by the General Assembly made the Committee responsible for a review and study of the provisional rules of procedure for the General Assembly on the basis of the Secretary-General's report, as well as of technical and practical measures to economize the time of the General Assembly which had been proposed by Members of the United Nations, the Secretary-General and the members of the Committee themselves. Other members of the Committee, however, were of the opinion that the Committee's responsibilities were limited to a study of methods of work and internal organization of the Assembly, with a view to proposing measures which would result in an economy of time. These members felt that the Committee should examine only such rules of procedure as might be instrumental in expediting the work of the Assembly.

6. Part II of this report consists of a series of suggestions, the adoption of which would, in the opinion of the Committee, assist considerably in expediting the work of the Assembly and permit the full consideration of important problems on the agenda without requiring the representatives to stay away from their home countries for inconveniently long periods. Part III contains a proposed re-draft of the provisional rules of procedure. The Committee felt that every improvement in the rules which would make debates on procedures unnecessary would result in a definite economy of time. The draft rules prepared by the Secretary-General, and incorporated in document A/316, served as a basis for the discussions of the Committee.

7. The Secretary-General communicated to the Committee a letter from the Chairman of the Advisory Committee on Administrative and Budgetary Questions, suggesting changes in chapter VII of the provisional rules of procedure which would alter the title of the Advisory Committee and amend certain rules regarding its standing functions. The Committee took note of the proposed revisions but reviewed provisional rules 37 to 40 merely from the point of view of drafting. The opinion was expressed that the Fifth Committee should study the rules contained in chapter VII from the point of view of substance before their final adoption.

8. The Committee refrained from considering the rules contained in chapter IX (Languages) and X (Records). The Committee felt that these rules had serious political and financial aspects which should be considered by the appropriate Committees of the Assembly. The Committee was informed that a special study was being made by the Secretariat of the application of the rules on languages and records and that a full report would be made on these matters to the General Assembly.

9. Chapter XVII (Admission of new Members to the United Nations) was not examined by the Committee. A Committee entrusted with the task of preparing rules governing the admission of new Members had been established by the General Assembly on 15 December 1946 and had, after consultation with the corresponding Committee of the Security Council, presented its report directly to the General Assembly.

10. In the time allotted to it, the Committee was not able to under-take a detailed study of the probable effect of the application of each of the revised provisional rules of procedure, and would have desired more time so that it might have prepared the best possible texts.

Part II

Agenda

11. The Committee is of the opinion that wherever possible items proposed for inclusion in the agenda should be submitted in time for inclusion in the provisional agenda which is communicated to Members sixty days in advance of the opening of the session. If this is impossible, every effort should be made to ensure that they are included in the supplementary list.

12. It is recognized that no rigid rules can be established on this question, but the observance of these principles would lead to the saving of time, inasmuch as Member Governments would thus have sufficient notice of proposed agenda items to enable them to prepare more thoroughly for the debate on these items.

13. The Committee discussed the desirability of a suitable time limit for the submission of requests for the inclusion of additional items—for instance, the end of the general debate—but decided to make no specific recommendation on this subject.

Documentation

14. The circulation of essential documents well in advance of their discussion in the General Assembly or its Committees would greatly facilitate and expedite the work of the Assembly. When items are sub-mitted for inclusion in the agenda, supporting documentation should be forwarded at the same time or shortly thereafter, whenever possible. While the Committee fully realizes that this is difficult and in some cases impossible, it wishes to call the attention of the General Assembly to the desirability of this principle as an objective.

15. The Secretariat should make the best possible arrangements for a rapid and efficient distribution of documents. It is suggested that special priority be given to the *Journal* and to the *Programme of meetings,* and that when dispatched by the Secretariat they should bear some distinguishing mark so that delegations, upon the receipt of their documentation, would be able to identify these two important documents immediately. The Committee noted that the Secretariat is able to provide individual boxes for delegations at both Flushing and Lake Success where urgent documents circulated during the day may be collected, and suggests that delegations might avail themselves more fully of this service.

Organization of Committees

16. The Committee considered the desirability of suggesting that at future sessions of the General Assembly a start should be made with

the work of some at least of the Main Committees before the close of the general debate, but decided at this stage to make no recommendation on the subject.

17. While it is desirable that as many Main Committees as possible should meet simultaneously, the fact should not be overlooked that too many meetings held at one time may place too heavy a burden on the members of the General Assembly, and particularly those Member States having small delegations. If the debates are to be maintained on the high level necessary for the Assembly to conduct its business wisely and efficiently, the schedule of meetings must be so arranged as to allow the members of delegations attending them the necessary time for study and consultation. Failure to do this would be to under-estimate the importance of the deliberations of the General Assembly and of its Committees. Nevertheless, the Committee calls attention to the fact that the number of Main Committees meeting simultaneously affects materially the duration of the General Assembly. A relatively light schedule of meetings in the early weeks of the Assembly leads inevitably to an unduly heavy schedule in its later stages. The scheduling of meetings should therefore take into account: (1) the capacity of delegations to cope with the work involved; (2) the desirability of establishing a relatively uniform work-load during the entire session; and (3) the relationship of the daily schedule to the duration of the Assembly.

18. Every effort should be made by the officers of the General Assembly and by the Secretariat to announce the schedule of meetings well in advance, and to avoid as far as possible any modification therein. During the early stages of committee work, the schedule of meetings might be announced for one week in advance. However, the establishment of sub-committees, the termination of the work of some of the Main Committees, and the variable load of those still in session may require adjustments in the schedule in the later stages of the work of the General Assembly. It would seem impracticable, during this period, to establish a rigid schedule for more than two or three days in advance.

19. The time lost between the hour scheduled for the beginning of a meeting and the actual opening of the meeting is not inconsiderable. Members of the General Assembly are urged to arrive promptly, and it is suggested that the President of the Assembly and the Chairmen of Committees open the meetings as soon as a quorum is present.

Limitation of debate

20. The provisional rules of procedure provide that the General Assembly may at any time limit the time allowed to speakers. The Committee recognizes that there are occasions on which this rule can be applied in the interest of economizing time without detriment to the rights of any member of the Assembly. The Committee, however, desires to call the attention of the Assembly to the serious difficulties attendant upon any general rule limiting the length of speeches, and it did not consider it advisable to recommend such a time limit.

Establishment of sub-committees

21. The Main Committees should consider carefully at an early stage in their work how their programmes might be expedited by the establishment of sub-committees. It is, of course, impossible to adopt fixed rules on this matter. If the debate in full committee showed that there was general agreement on the question under discussion but disagreement on points of detail, it would clearly be desirable to set up a small drafting committee to prepare a resolution for submission to the Main Committee. Technical questions on which there is no substantial disagreement should be referred to sub-committees as quickly as possible. In some cases the work of sub-committees would be facilitated by working informally, and on occasion, in private.

Conduct of business

22. The Committee noted with satisfaction that the Secretary-General is preparing for the information of members a handbook containing a record of the application of the rules of procedure in this and previous sessions of the General Assembly. If this handbook is completed and placed in use, the Assembly might wish to consider whether it has served to facilitate the conduct of the business of the General Assembly.

23. Continued close collaboration between the Chairmen and the Secretariat is desirable and the assistance of the Committee secretaries and legal advisers should be available at all times.

Allocation of agenda items among Committees

24. The reference of the same agenda item to two Committees at the same time is as a general rule undesirable and often results in unnecessary duplication of debate. In addition, experience has shown that if an item is also referred to another Committee in general terms, that Committee does not always limit itself to the consideration of the aspects of the question in regard to which it is especially competent.

25. The Committee suggests that, as a general rule, one Main Committee, or one joint committee (e.g. the Joint Second and Third Committee) be given responsibility for reporting on a given agenda item and that, if the opinion of another Committee is needed, the latter be seized only of a precise and limited question. A suggestion, which received some support, was made to the effect that a small advisory committee of jurists should be established to which the first five Main Committees could submit the legal aspects of questions under consideration. Other members of the Committee felt, however, that such a committee was not necessary.

Committee reports

26. The Committee recommends that rapporteurs' reports and other documents which have been circulated to members in advance should not be read in plenary and committee meetings. This would not, of course, limit the right of members to read such documents or such passages from them as they may consider necessary.

Simultaneous interpretation

27. The Committee examined the important question of the use by the General Assembly of simultaneous interpretation, which would contribute greatly to economizing the time of the General Assembly, and was informed of certain experimental planning which had been carried out by the Secretary-General in this field. As this question is on the provisional agenda of the second regular session of the General Assembly, the Committee refrains from conclusions and limits itself to making the observations which follow.

28. It was pointed out to the Committee by several of its members that experience, not only in the United Nations but in other international bodies over a period of years, seems to have demonstrated that although the system of simultaneous interpretation has real merit, its use in all circumstances is not without serious disadvantages. Among the disadvantages mentioned are the following:

(*a*) The interpreter is obliged to follow the speaker in much the same word order as that in which the original speech is made. While in some languages this creates no insurmountable difficulties, in others it renders translation extremely difficult, especially since the rules of phrasing in certain languages differ so greatly from those in others. In following word for word in a simultaneous interpretation, the interpreter is unable, as can the interpreter in a consecutive interpretation, to follow the general line of argument and set it forth clearly for those who are listening.

(*b*) The interpreter, not knowing in advance what documents will be quoted, is unable to have at hand the official texts cited by the speaker. This creates serious difficulties when the discussion relates to draft resolutions or amendments. In consecutive interpretation, the interpreter's colleagues are able to collect the necessary documents for him during the course of the original speech.

(*c*) The representative does not hear the interpretation and is unable to control its accuracy or correct the errors of the interpreter.

(*d*) A physical and psychological barrier is created between the speaker and his colleagues, and representatives miss the opportunity of familiarizing themselves with the habits of thought and the languages spoken by the other representatives.

29. The Committee was in full agreement that the system of simultaneous interpretation can be used to advantage during a general debate in plenary or committee meetings, and that it would result in a considerable shortening of the length of the sessions of the General Assembly, but that it is not suitable when detailed negotiations or the reconciliation of various drafts are necessary.

30. It is clear that the introduction of simultaneous interpretation will make it necessary for the Secretariat to make provisions which would facilitate the passage from simultaneous to consecutive interpretation, and vice versa, during the same meeting, as well as to complement

simultaneous interpretation by the occasional use of consecutive interpretation if this should be necessary.

31. The Committee was informed by the Secretary-General that arrangements for simultaneous interpretation into all the official languages have been made for the remaining plenary meetings of the present session of the General Assembly.

Combined consecutive and telephonic interpretation

32. Several members pointed out that, in meetings where consecutive interpretation is used, the mechanism of the telephonic interpretation system can be usefully employed for interpretation into the remaining official languages during consecutive interpretation from one working language into the other.

Drafting of resolutions

33. Experience has shown that the time of the General Assembly is sometimes unnecessarily occupied by the re-drafting, during meetings of committees, of draft resolutions because of unintentional ambiguities in the text. The assistance of the Legal Department of the Secretariat which is available at any time to national delegations may usefully be asked for to avoid this as far as possible.

34. The Committee considered that the time of the General Assembly would be economized if the final texts of resolutions were drawn up simultaneously in the two working languages and the two versions kept in continuous comparison in order to avoid ambiguities in both texts.

35. The General Committee has already been given power under existing rule 36 of the provisional rules of procedure to " revise the resolutions adopted by the General Assembly, changing their form but not their substance ". The rule goes on to say: " Any such changes shall be reported to the General Assembly for its consideration." Clearly, the General Committee could not itself undertake this task. It was suggested to the Committee that the General Committee might usefully appoint a drafting committee which, with the assistance of the Secretariat, could, in the interval between the adoption of a resolution by a Main Committee and the submission of that resolution to the Assembly, examine the French and English texts of the resolution and submit it to the General Committee for transmission to the Assembly with whatever drafting changes in both texts the drafting committee might consider necessary. The recommendations for drafting changes could be submitted to the Assembly together with the report as drawn up by the Main Committee.

Extracts from the
REPORT OF THE SPECIAL COMMITTEE
ON METHODS AND PROCEDURES
OF THE GENERAL ASSEMBLY*

12 *August* 1949

I. INTRODUCTION

1. In its resolution 271 (III) of 29 April 1949, the General Assembly expressed its concern at the increasing length of General Assembly sessions and at the growing tendency towards protracted debates in its plenary meetings and committees, and established a Special Committee consisting of the representatives of fifteen Members. The Special Committee was instructed to:

(*a*) Consider methods and procedures which would enable the General Assembly and its committees to discharge their functions more effectively and expeditiously;

(*b*) Submit, if possible, a preliminary report to the General Assembly during the second part of its third session;

(*c*) Transmit a report to the Secretary-General, not later than 15 August 1949, for circulation to Members for consideration at the fourth regular session of the General Assembly.

The Secretary-General was invited to collaborate closely with the Special Committee in its work.

. . .

5. During twenty-three meetings held in June, July and August 1949, the Special Committee studied carefully the various factors affecting the duration of the General Assembly. It dealt successively with questions concerning the establishment of the agenda of sessions, the internal organization of the Assembly, the means of shortening debates in plenary meetings and committees and the clarification of rules of procedure, the application of which has given rise to difficulties in the past, thereby causing prolonged procedural debates. The conclusions which the Special Committee has the honour to bring to the General Assembly's attention in the following paragraphs consist of proposed amendments to the rules of procedure, interpretations of certain rules at present in force, and recommendations and advice to representatives to the General Assembly, especially those who are called upon as Chairmen to conduct debates in plenary meetings and committees.

---

* G.A.O.R.: 4th Sess., 1949, Suppl. No. 12 (A/937), pp. 2–12. (The footnotes in the document have not been reproduced, with the exception of one which appears on p. 322.)

6. In submitting its proposals, the Special Committee wishes to state that throughout its work its members have constantly had in mind the essential role entrusted to the General Assembly under the Charter, and the prestige and high authority that should belong to the only principal organ of the United Nations on which are represented on an equal footing all the Members of the Organization.

The Special Committee has been careful that none of its proposals should have the effect of diminishing the competence or functions of the General Assembly, or in any way hindering the natural development of that vital organ of the United Nations. The Special Committee examined only those proposals designed to save time, which, in the opinion of its members, took these fundamental principles into consideration.

The Special Committee believes that the adoption of its recommendations will fully safeguard the rights possessed by Members of the United Nations—whether on a given question they belong to the majority or the minority—to draw the General Assembly's attention to problems within its competence, to express their views and to participate fully in the adoption of resolutions on matters of which the General Assembly has been seized. The sole purpose of the Special Committee's recommendations is to adapt the organization and procedures of the General Assembly to its increasing responsibilities, as the Special Committee believes that such adaptation is indispensable in order to enable the Assembly to discharge its functions more effectively and expeditiously.

In this regard, it seemed particularly important to the Special Committee that General Assembly sessions should be planned in such a way as to facilitate the participation, as representatives of Member States, of persons holding the highest Government posts or representing the most diverse fields of national activity, whose normal functions prevent them from remaining at United Nations Headquarters for extensive periods.

7. The Special Committee does not consider that the present length of General Assembly sessions can be ascribed primarily to the rules of procedure. It is due, above all, to the number and complexity of the questions submitted to the Assembly and to the political problems raised by these questions. Nevertheless, the Special Committee thinks that the present methods and procedures of the Assembly might be usefully improved if the Assembly accepted the amendments to the rules of procedure proposed by the Special Committee and if it endorsed the interpretations and opinions suggested by the Special Committee.

8. The Special Committee is not recommending substantial modifications to the rules of procedure. It considers that, on the whole, the present rules of procedure, based as they are on the experience of other international organizations and on the relatively recent work of the Preparatory Commission of the United Nations and of several committees of the General Assembly, represent both in letter and in spirit, an adequate instrument, which can enable the General Assembly to carry out its functions effectively. Thus, the Special Committee's first conclusion is that the General Assembly's work might be considerably

accelerated if the present rules of procedure were more faithfully observed, if all their potentialities were better known to the Chairmen and members, if some of the rules were clarified, if Chairmen performed their functions more boldly and if members offered them their full co-operation and goodwill in ensuring that the rules of procedure receive their normal application.

III. RECOMMENDATIONS CONCERNING THE ESTABLISHMENT OF THE AGENDA

9. In the light of the preceding considerations, the Special Committee recommends that the General Assembly should, on the proposal of the General Committee, fix at the beginning of each session the date by which it would endeavour to complete its work.

The Special Committee did not wish to go any further in this direction or to adopt proposals which would limit the duration of the session in a more rigid manner, although it was pointed out in the course of its debates that, to enable Governments to ensure adequate representation, sessions of the General Assembly should not exceed eight weeks.

The Special Committee thought that it would be undesirable to recommend too strict a rule. The probable duration of each session can only be determined, in present circumstances, on the basis of the number and nature of the questions submitted to the Assembly and of an estimate of the length of the debates which they may occasion. The Special Committee's proposal tends thus to render permanent and to strengthen the practice, which has developed during the last two sessions, of fixing a closing date which would represent a target for the Assembly.

The General Assembly's decision on the closing date of the session might be taken either when the agenda is adopted, if the General Committee and the General Assembly consider that they have sufficient information at the time, or soon after the beginning of the session, when the general debate and the initial stages of the Committee's work have provided indications permitting a decision on the closing date with better knowledge of the facts.

. . .

10. The Special Committee considers that, in order to maintain the duration of sessions within normal limits, it is important that the provisional agenda of the General Assembly (provided for in rules 11 and 12), the supplementary list (rule 13) and requests for the inclusion of additional items (rule 14) should be scrutinized with greater care than in the past. The General Committee, in the first place, and the General Assembly itself, should examine all requests for inclusion in the agenda, not only with special attention to the importance of these questions in relation to the achievement of the purposes of the United Nations, but also in relation to the agenda as a whole and the time available for the session.

The Special Committee, therefore, deems it important to reaffirm the General Assembly's right to exclude certain questions from the agenda and also its right, under rule 14, to delete questions previously included. Such action by the General Assembly amounts, in fact, to postponement, since countries which have proposed an item for the Assembly's consideration have the right, in the event of their request being rejected, to propose its inclusion in the provisional agenda of the next session. Moreover, under rule 12, the General Assembly may itself decide to include in the provisional agenda of a future session any item that it has excluded or deleted from its agenda.

. . .

11. The Special Committee is of the opinion that the important and urgent character of additional items referred to in rule 14 should be determined with care. It believes that the inclusion of items proposed shortly before or during the session should constitute exceptions, not only because last-minute proposals may result in overloading the agenda, but also because delegations to the General Assembly find it very difficult to prepare for the examination of such proposals at short notice and to obtain adequate instructions from their Governments. The Special Committee proposes, therefore, that the inclusion of additional items in the agenda of a regular session should be decided by a two-thirds majority of the Members present and voting.

. . .

12. The Special Committee also wishes to draw the General Assembly's attention to its power to decide, at the beginning of or during the session, to refer certain items, without preliminary debate, to other organs of the United Nations, or to the author of a proposal for inclusion of an item, for further information or documentation. Such a decision would have the advantage of lightening the agenda by avoiding the discussion of questions which are not very urgent and which could usefully be studied in detail by other organs, such as one of the existing subsidiary organs of the General Assembly, an *ad hoc* committee, one of the Councils, a specialized agency, or the Secretary-General. It was emphasized, in this connexion, that questions of an exclusively economic, social or cultural nature should not as a rule be submitted to the General Assembly until they had been considered by the Economic and Social Council.

The organs to which the items would be referred might report to a future session of the General Assembly, which would thus have the advantage of dealing with questions which had been subjected beforehand to a thorough study. In this regard the Special Committee's attention was drawn to the right of the Economic and Social Council and of the Trusteeship Council to make direct recommendations to Members of the United Nations. The General Assembly would therefore have to determine in each case if it wishes reports to be submitted to it on these questions for its final approval, or if it would prefer to invite those organs to make direct recommendations to Members.

13. The Special Committee found that in the past some of the Main Committees of the General Assembly had devoted a particularly large

number of meetings to the detailed consideration, article by article, of texts of international conventions. This was even the case where the text of a convention had been drawn up by an international conference on which all Member States had been represented. It was pointed out in this connexion that experience had shown that a Main Committee, by the very fact of its size, was not particularly fitted to draft conventions, and that when it was entrusted with the detailed study of conventions, it often did not have time to deal satisfactorily with the other questions for which it was responsible.

The Special Committee recognizes the importance of the sponsorship of conventions by the General Assembly. It believes that the authority of the General Assembly and the powerful influence its debates have on public opinion should, in many cases, be used for the benefit of international legislation by means of conventions. It therefore favours the retention by the General Assembly of the necessary freedom of action.

The Special Committee therefore confines itself to recommending that, when conventions have been negotiated by international conferences in which all the Members of the United Nations have been invited to take part, and on which they have been represented, not only by experts acting in a personal capacity but by representatives of Governments, and when these conventions are subsequently submitted to the General Assembly for consideration, the Assembly should not undertake a further detailed examination, but should limit itself to discussing them in a broad manner and to giving its general views on the instruments submitted to it. After such a debate, the General Assembly could, if desirable, adopt the conclusions reached by the conferences and recommend to Members the acceptance or ratification of such conventions.

This procedure might be applied in particular to conventions submitted to the General Assembly as a result of conferences of all Member States convened by the Economic and Social Council under Article 62, paragraph 4 of the Charter.

14. Furthermore, when it is proposed that the General Assembly should consider conventions prepared by groups of experts not acting as governmental representatives, or by conferences in which all Members of the United Nations have not been invited to take part, it would be advisable for the General Committee and the General Assembly to determine whether one of the Main Committees, especially the Legal Committee, would have enough time during the session to examine these conventions in detail, or whether it would be possible to set up an *ad hoc* committee to undertake this study during the session.

If this is not possible, the Special Committee recommends that the General Assembly should decide, after or without a general debate on the fundamental principles of the proposed convention, that an *ad hoc* committee should be established to meet between sessions. Alternatively, the General Assembly might decide to convene a conference of plenipotentiaries between two of its own sessions, to study, negotiate, draft, and possibly sign, the convention. The conference of plenipotentiaries might be empowered by the General Assembly to transmit the instruments directly to Governments for acceptance or ratification. In this case too, the General Assembly might, at a subsequent session, express its general opinion on the convention resulting from the conference, and might recommend to Members its acceptance or ratification.

With regard to the drafting of legal texts, the Special Committee strongly recommends that small drafting committees should be resorted to whenever possible.

15. The Special Committee examined several proposals designed to relieve the General Committee of part of its present responsibilities by entrusting some of its functions to a special agenda committee meeting before the opening of the session. The main arguments in favour of the establishment of an agenda committee were that, at present, the General Committee performs its functions relating to the provisional agenda and the supplementary list during the first days of the session and the general debate in the plenary meetings and the work of the Committees is thereby delayed. In the opinion of the authors of the proposals, it would be advantageous to entrust the examination of the agenda to a committee which would be less pressed for time, thus making it easier for delegations to find grounds for agreement.

It was suggested that the agenda committee should consist of representatives of Members who were represented in the General Committee of the preceding session or, alternatively, that it should be composed of representatives of fifteen Members elected annually by the General Assembly.

The meetings of the agenda committee would be held during the two- to three-weeks period preceding the opening of the session and its duties would cease, at the latest, when the members of the General Committee are elected. It was proposed that, in order to avoid repetitious debate, the agenda committee's recommendations on the agenda of the session should be submitted directly to the plenary meeting of the General Assembly for approval.

Some of the proposals provided that, apart from its work on the agenda of the session, the agenda committee might prepare, with the assistance of the Secretary-General, studies and recommendations on the organization of the session, on the possible priorities to be given to items on the agenda, and on the allocation of items to the Main Committees. It was also suggested that the agenda committee might estimate, with the help of the Secretariat, the time which would have to be devoted to the consideration of each item, in committee and in plenary meetings, and might thus facilitate the adoption by the General Assembly of a target date.

Several members of the Special Committee doubted whether the establishment of an agenda committee would actually result in a shortening of the General Assembly's sessions. They also had doubts concerning the degree of authority which the agenda committee would possess and the nature of its relationship with the General Committee. Other members were not ready to express a definite opinion on the proposals which had been submitted and thought that the matter should be further studied and re-examined at a later date.

The Special Committee decided, therefore, to bring the question to the attention of the General Assembly and to transmit to the Assembly the various written proposals which it has received. It also decided to request the Secretary-General to assist the General Assembly by preparing a study on proposals previously examined, to report on such technical, legal and financial aspects of the question as he may consider pertinent, and to submit to the Assembly his views on the composition and functions of an agenda committee.

16. The Special Committee also considered proposals to set up a committee for nominations of officers of committees or to entrust this task to the agenda committee. After studying these proposals carefully, the Special Committee decided not to make a recommendation in this respect to the General Assembly.

17. Having stressed the importance of a more careful study of the agenda, the Special Committee deems it advisable to recommend that all requests for inclusion of an item in the agenda should be accompanied by a memorandum stating the reasons for the request and, if necessary, by the basic documents or by a draft resolution. Only the memorandum would be obligatory, and the advisability of annexing other documents, especially draft resolutions, would be left to the discretion of the authors of the request for inclusion. In the opinion of the Special Committee, however, this limited obligation would have not only the advantage of facilitating the task of the General Committee and the General Assembly, but also the additional advantage of enabling Member States to prepare themselves more thoroughly for the discussion of items submitted to the General Assembly for consideration.

The Special Committee wishes, however, to emphasize that the General Assembly could not refuse to include an item in the agenda on the sole grounds that the memorandum accompanying the request was inadequate.

. . . .

IV. RECOMMENDATIONS RELATING TO THE ORGANIZATION OF GENERAL ASSEMBLY SESSIONS

18. The Special Committee examined certain aspects of the internal organization of the General Assembly with a view to finding methods of accelerating the general pace of sessions. It believes that the schedule of the General Assembly must remain flexible and that the methods used for determining it must be such as will take into account the rapidly changing requirements of the Assembly and its committees. Moreover, these methods must frequently assume an informal character.

. . . .

20. In order that more frequent meetings of the General Committee should not delay the work of plenary and committee meetings, the

Special Committee wishes to mention that it would be desirable for the General Committee to be enabled to meet, whenever necessary, at the same time as the plenary or the Main Committees. (In such cases, one of the Vice-Presidents could take the chair at plenary meetings and the Vice-Chairman could replace the Chairman at Main Committee meetings.)

The Special Committee also considers that in order to save time at the beginning of the session, some of the Main Committees should not wait until the end of the general debate before starting their work.

.   .   .

22. In the past, some of the Main Committees have been allocated more items requiring prolonged consideration than have other committees. This has especially been the case with the First Committee. The Special Committee noted, however, that during the third session of the General Assembly, exception had been made to the principle laid down in rule 89, that " items relating to the same category of subjects shall be referred to the committee or committees dealing with that category of subjects ".

The Special Committee feels that the allocation of items to committees might be effected in a less rigid manner and that questions which may be considered as falling within the competence of two or more committees, should preferably be referred to the committee with the lightest agenda.

23. Another means of lightening the task of any given Main Committee would be to consider directly in plenary meeting, without preliminary reference to committee, certain questions which fall within the terms of reference of the Main Committee. This procedure would moreover have the great advantage of reducing to a notable extent repetition of debate.

It is felt that the amount of time saved by this method would be considerable, especially if the Main Committee and plenary meetings could be held concurrently.

If the Main Committee could not meet at the same time as the plenary meeting, the fact that the Committee was not meeting would enable another Main Committee to meet in its place.

The consideration of questions in plenary meetings would have the benefit of the attendance of leaders of delegations and of greater solemnity and publicity. The slightly higher cost to the United Nations of plenary meetings, due in particular to the distribution of verbatim records of the meetings, would undoubtedly be compensated by the shorter duration of the session.

The General Committee would be responsible for suggesting to the General Assembly which items on the agenda might be dealt with in this manner. The Special Committee recommends that this method should be introduced on an experimental basis at future sessions.

The Special Committee is of the opinion that this procedure would be especially appropriate for certain questions the essential aspects of which are already familiar to Members, such as items which have been considered by the General Assembly at previous sessions and which do not require either the presence of representatives of non-member States or the hearing of testimony.

24. The problem of the repetition of debate on the same item during one session of the Assembly was the cause of particular concern to the Special Committee. It was recalled in this connexion that, in the past, the same item has sometimes been the subject of full discussion in the General Committee, in plenary meeting and in the Main Committee to which it was referred. It has then been debated in a sub-committee, referred back to the Main Committee and finally considered in plenary meeting.

The Special Committee considers that the General Assembly should make every effort to see that an item reaches as rapidly as possible the committee or sub-committee which has to consider its substance in detail, without detailed discussion of the same item in the General Committee and in plenary meeting.

Once the substance of the question has been considered by the competent committee, in which all Members have had full opportunity of stating their views, all repetition in the General Assembly of the various arguments or of considerations on the technical aspects of the problem should be avoided.

.   .   .

27. The plenary meeting which examines a Main Committee's report and adopts a resolution embodying the General Assembly's decision on a problem submitted to it, is of considerable importance. In many cases it is useful to allow a general debate concerning the principles on which the Committee's recommendations were based, or even to provide opportunity for improving the proposed draft resolution by the adoption of amendments. Nevertheless, in view of the identical composition of the plenary meeting and the Main Committees, it seems to the Special Committee that the re-discussion of questions should not be encouraged, except in cases where this may be useful for the work of the General Assembly and genuinely safeguards the legitimate rights of minorities.

.   .   .

V. Recommendations Relating to the Conduct of Debates in Plenary Meetings and in Committees

28. The Special Committee recalls that much time has been lost in the past by committees and by the General Assembly itself, owing to the fact that meetings have not begun at the scheduled time. Precise calculations on this subject prove that the accumulated delays undoubtedly cause a prolongation of the session.

The Special Committee is aware that the interval between the time fixed for the opening of the meeting and its actual opening is often profitably used by certain delegations in valuable informal conversations, which in many cases serve to facilitate debates. The Special Committee considers, however, that the General Assembly should insist on greater punctuality and should take the necessary measures to remedy the present situation.

. . .

30. The Special Committee had before it several proposals to limit the time to be allowed to speakers in plenary meetings and in committees. After studying the problem, the Special Committee expresses the view that a general time-limit for statements on the substance of a question is not desirable, and that, within the limits laid down in the rules of procedure, representatives should be entitled to give full expression to their points of view.

. . .

36. The Special Committee did not examine a proposal which had been submitted to it to introduce a new rule which would define the conditions upon which the application of the rules of procedure could be suspended. The representative of Canada, who submitted this proposal, did not, in view of the shortage of time, insist on its consideration by the Special Committee, but reserved the right of his delegation to raise the question during the debate on the report of the Special Committee by the General Assembly.

37. The Special Committee also feels it desirable to clarify the meaning and application of rules 64 and 102 relating to points of order. It is the opinion of the Special Committee that a valid point of order may relate to the manner in which the debate is conducted, to the maintenance of order, to the observance of the rules of procedure, or to the manner in which Chairmen exercise the powers conferred upon them by the rules. Thus, within the scope of the General Assembly's rules of procedure, representatives are enabled to direct the attention of the presiding officer to violations or misapplications of the rules of procedure by other representatives or by the presiding officer himself. Points of order may also refer to legitimate requests for information, to material arrangements (temperature of the room, seating, interpretation system), to documents, translations and so on. On the other hand, no representative, when rising to a point of order, should be permitted to speak on the substance of the matter under discussion.

Under rules 64 and 102, presiding officers must give an immediate ruling on every point of order, and if the ruling is challenged, they must put it to the vote; no discussion may take place. Hence, there can be no question of seconding or debating a point of order. Moreover, as the presiding officer must immediately dispose of each point of order as it is raised, two or more points of order can never be before the Chair at the same time.

. . .

39. At this point the Special Committee desires to stress once more the importance of the role of the President of the General Assembly and of the Chairmen of committees. The satisfactory progress of the proceedings depends essentially on their competence, authority, tact and

impartiality, their respect for the rights both of minorities as well as majorities, and their familiarity with the rules of procedure. The General Assembly, or the Committee, as the case may be, is the master of the conduct of its own proceedings. It is, however, the special task of the Chairmen to guide the proceedings of these bodies in the best interests of all the Members.

The Special Committee considers that everything possible should be done to help Chairmen in the discharge of these important functions. The President of the General Assembly and the General Committee should assist the Chairmen of committees with their advice. The Secretary-General should place his experience and all his authority at their disposal.*

The Special Committee is happy to note the Secretariat's valuable practice of holding daily meetings of the committee secretaries, under the chairmanship of the Executive Assistant to the Secretary-General, where the procedural questions arising from day to day in the General Assembly and committees are thoroughly examined. Furthermore, the Special Committee stresses the value of having, as in the past, a legal adviser from the Secretariat in attendance at meetings to give the Chairmen or the committee such advice as they may need for the conduct of their business and the interpretation of the rules of procedure.

VI. SECRETARY-GENERAL'S PROPOSAL FOR AN INTERVAL OF PRAYER OR MEDITATION IN MEETINGS OF THE GENERAL ASSEMBLY

40. The Special Committee has examined a proposal submitted by the Secretary-General, to the effect that in the first plenary meeting of the General Assembly on a given day, the President should invite the Members of the United Nations to observe one minute of silence dedicated to prayer or meditation. The Secretary-General, in introducing this proposal, explained to the Special Committee that many hundreds of letters from private individuals and organizations have urged that the General Assembly should devote a few moments of its time to prayer.

The Special Committee recognizes the lofty motives which have inspired the authors of these communications. It is, on the other hand, aware of the fact that the Members of the United Nations represent people belonging to nearly every religion, creed and philosophical outlook in the world, and that it would not be possible to introduce a public prayer which would satisfy all tenets and give offence to none. Some of the members also felt that too frequent repetition of an act of this nature might deprive it of some of its solemnity, and were generally inclined to favour a recommendation that one minute of silence should be observed at the opening and at the closing meeting of the General Assembly.

. . .

* A suggestion was made that the Secretary-General should prepare, from time to time, commentaries on the rules of procedure, which would be placed at the disposal of Chairmen and of representatives to the General Assembly.

Extracts from the
REPORT OF THE SPECIAL COMMITTEE
ON MEASURES TO LIMIT THE DURATION
OF REGULAR SESSIONS
OF THE GENERAL ASSEMBLY*

26 *June* 1953

I. INTRODUCTION

1. At its 380th plenary meeting, held on 16 October 1952, the General Assembly decided to include in the agenda of the seventh session the item " Measures to limit the duration of regular sessions of the General Assembly ". The memorandum submitted on the subject by the Secretary-General for consideration by the governments of Member States was discussed at the 387th and 388th plenary meetings of the General Assembly, held on 23 and 24 October.

.   .   .

8. There is agreement among the members of the Special Committee that the best interests of the General Assembly, not the length of its sessions as such, must remain the overriding consideration in any study of measures designed to limit the duration of the regular sessions. It should be kept in mind that the Assembly has special characteristics which distinguish it from other more homogeneous parliamentary bodies ; its processes are largely conditioned by the wide scope of its purposes and defined by the very nature of its composition. Furthermore, the question under review cannot be judged solely on technical grounds or on grounds of efficiency. The length of the regular sessions of the Assembly has been determined mainly by the complexity and number of the international problems which have been brought to its attention as the result of differences among the Members, and by the atmosphere of deep-seated international tension in which the Assembly's discussions have taken place.

9. It follows, therefore, that if the General Assembly of the United Nations is to fulfil the high responsibilities placed upon it by the Charter and if the peoples of the world are to look with increasing respect and confidence to that body as the highest forum of the international community, all questions relating to the manner in which it functions must be considered primarily from the standpoint of their effect on the General Assembly as a whole. In the opinion of the majority of the members of the Special Committee, the unnecessary lengthening of the

* G.A.O.R.: 8th Sess., 1953, Annexes, Agenda item 54 (A/2402), pp. 2–7.

regular sessions would detract from the stature of the Assembly in the eyes of the world.

10. At the same time, it is the consensus of opinion that considerations of a practical nature must also be taken into account. The excessive length of regular sessions in itself has disadvantages for the Assembly as well as for the Organization as a whole. The past tendency to prolong the General Assembly each year has made it difficult for governments to maintain the same delegations throughout an entire session. Members of national governments and parliaments cannot be expected to be absent from their duties at home beyond a reasonable period of time. On the other hand, the work of the Assembly would benefit by the direct participation of leading statesmen, in so far as possible, at every stage of the deliberations. The majority of the members of the Special Committee believe that a greater continuity in the composition of delegations would have a favourable effect on the work of the General Assembly, and that continuity might be more easily attained if the duration of the regular sessions were more strictly limited.

11. The duration of the regular sessions has an important bearing also on questions of expense and efficiency. The necessity for every reasonable economy is the concern of all; unnecessary expenditures and unfruitful procedures must be avoided. An unduly long session is not only a burden on the United Nations budget, but it increases the expenditures incurred by the individual Members.

12. The total programme of all the organs of the United Nations cannot but be affected by the length of the regular sessions. It is essential that sufficient time should be allowed for the implementation of the Assembly's recommendations as well as for the Councils and subsidiary organs to carry out their work. Lengthy Assembly sessions shorten the period available for those purposes with possible detriment to the execution of programmes.

13. The Special Committee acknowledges that these and other difficulties related to the duration of the regular sessions should not be resolved at the expense either of the effectiveness of the General Assembly or of the right of any representative freely to explain his government's attitude on the problems before the Assembly. It is felt, however, that the Assembly, through the co-operation of its members, can initiate or strengthen certain practices so as to expedite and simplify the conduct of business.

．　　　．　　　．

III. Agenda

．　　　．　　　．

16. The Special Committee believes that economy would result should the Assembly in future indicate clearly its intentions when drafting resolutions calling for the preparation of special or annual reports. Some previous resolutions have contained specific decisions that an item or the subject of a report should be placed on the provisional agenda of a

subsequent session; others have called only for the submission of a report; yet others have requested that the question should be dealt with in a section of another report to be presented by an organ or by the Secretary-General.

17. It is evident that in some instances in the past, it was not the intention of the Assembly that the subject of a report should appear as an item in the agenda. In others, however, doubts existed on the point and an item covering such a report might have been included in the agenda when no action on the part of the Assembly was called for. The situation would be clarified if the practice were adopted of stating in the resolution whether it is intended that the report should be submitted to the General Assembly for consideration or to Members for their information. In the first case it would be included in the provisional agenda of the following session; in the second, it would not.

18. As regards, in particular, resolutions calling for the submission of annual reports, it is especially desirable to avoid any possible uncertainty as to whether or not the Secretary-General should include such reports each year in the provisional agenda.

19. Certain agenda items which recur from year to year do not necessarily require the attention of the Assembly at every session; during the seventh session, for example, with respect to at least three items it was decided that they should next appear on the agenda of the ninth session. This practice would no doubt help to relieve the agenda and it might result in an appreciable saving of time. In the view of the majority of the members of the Special Committee it would be desirable, therefore, for the Assembly to specify, whenever practicable, that an item of this character should appear only on the agenda of alternate sessions or at longer intervals.

.   .   .

21. The Special Committee further suggests that the work of the Assembly might progress more smoothly and the deliberations in the Main Committees might follow a more regular pace if the closing date of the sessions were taken into account by the Chairmen at the outset. Informal time-tables for the completion of the items on a Committee's agenda, drawn up by the Chairman for his guidance early in the session, might be helpful in maintaining an even distribution of work throughout the entire period.

IV. REPORTS OF COUNCILS

22. The majority of the members of the Special Committee believe that consideration of the reports of the Economic and Social Council and the Trusteeship Council would be facilitated if the General Assembly were to encourage the Councils to continue the practice of indicating in their annual reports those matters on which they desire that the Assembly should take action. This trend, which should be strengthened, does not prejudice the right of the Assembly to debate any aspect of the reports, and it has the advantage of providing Members in advance with more

precise information on what questions covered in the reports would be the subject of debate during a session of the General Assembly. It is, therefore, of particular interest that the reports of the Councils should be circulated to Members as much in advance of the opening of the sessions as the schedules of the Councils themselves permit.

. . .

V. Scope of proposals made in Committees

24. It is the view of the majority of the members of the Special Committee that the past tendency in Main Committees to interpret too liberally the scope of the items referred to them has, on occasions, caused the range of subjects dealt with during a session to extend beyond the limits set by the agenda items as adopted. There have been cases in which debates have taken place and draft resolutions have been proposed on matters only remotely or indirectly related to the items under discussion.

25. A reasonable interpretation of the limitations implied by the agenda of a Main Committee, as agreed upon by the Assembly, should not restrict the freedom of a Committee to give full consideration to its items; it should, however, provide a clear frame of reference for the debates, and the right and obligation of Chairmen to rule out of order extraneous remarks and proposals falling outside its bounds should be recognized.

VI. Debate in Committees

26. The Special Committee discussed several suggestions submitted in connexion with the debates in Committees. Clearly, this is one of the most important areas in the proceedings of the General Assembly and proposals touching on it should be viewed with caution. Certain practices, however, have developed over the years which, in the opinion of the Special Committee, could profitably be re-examined. The tendency has grown in the Main Committees automatically to observe independent and succeeding stages with respect to each item on the agenda—a general debate on the item, followed by debates on specific proposals, further debates on amendments and still others under the right of reply and the explanation of vote. This formal segmentation often provokes duplication of speeches and increases, as well, the risk of engaging in protracted procedural discussions.

27. The mechanics of a Main Committee cannot be simplified or altered beyond a certain point, it is true, but greater flexibility in the procedure for considering items is desirable. In general, the discussion on the broad aspects of a subject should be combined with the consideration of specific proposals. Time would be saved if Members were to introduce draft resolutions and amendments as soon as practicable in order that the Committees might direct their attention at the earliest opportunity to the examination of specific texts. The work in Committees

would also be accelerated if the items proposed for inclusion in the agenda were more frequently accompanied by a draft resolution in accordance with the provisions of rule 20 of the rules of procedure.

.   .   .

29. The Special Committee also considered the suggestion that representatives should be entitled to submit written statements instead of making oral explanations of vote. In this connexion, it was pointed out that explanations of vote frequently touch on the substance of the question under discussion and that, consequently, if these statements were made after rather than before the voting takes place, they might tend to conform more strictly to the intent of rules 88 and 127; if, in addition, they were submitted in writing, time would be gained during the sessions. The Special Committee concluded, however, that serious problems would arise regarding such questions as, for example, the relevance of remarks which had been submitted in writing and the exercise of the right of reply with respect to them; it was further felt that this procedure would entail considerable difficulties in the preparation and distribution of the records of meetings. In view of these considerations and inasmuch as some members were opposed in principle to the suggestion, the Special Committee has not formulated recommendations to this effect.

30. On the other hand, the practice in plenary meetings of imposing a limitation on the time allowed for explanations of vote has produced good results. The majority of the members of the Special Committee believe that the Main Committees could profitably follow the same procedure.

31. As was stated at the outset of the present report, the members of the Special Committee were inclined in general to suggest measures which would improve the methods and practices of the General Assembly rather than to recommend specific amendments to the rules of procedure. This approach was prompted by the conviction that the co-operation of Members in all matters relating to the work of the Assembly and the voluntary exercise of discipline and restraint in the observance of the existing rules of procedure could do more to further the aim of limiting the duration of regular sessions than the adoption of additional regulations to govern the proceedings.

.   .   .

VIII. LIST OF SPEAKERS

38. The Special Committee believes that the presiding officers of the General Assembly and of the Main Committees should urge the representatives to signify at their earliest convenience their desire to be placed on the list of speakers. Compliance with this request and readiness to speak in accordance with the order of the list would promote the orderly conduct of business in the Assembly and, particularly, in the Main Committees. This practice and the closure of the list as soon as is

reasonably possible can lead to a measurable saving of time during the sessions.

IX. Points of Order

41. A point of order is, basically, an intervention directed to the presiding officer requesting him to make use of some power inherent in his office or specifically given him under the rules of procedure. It may, for example, relate to the material conditions under which the meeting is taking place. It may be a request that the presiding officer should accord the speaker some privilege which it is in the officer's power to grant. Under a point of order, a representative may request the presiding officer to apply a certain rule of procedure or he may refer to the manner in which the presiding officer should apply a given rule, or the rules of procedure as a whole.

XII. Schedule of Meetings

49. The Special Committee wishes to draw attention to the serious loss of time that results from the lack of punctuality in the opening of meetings and from adjournments before the appointed time. On the basis of two and one-half hours per meeting, during the sixth session, for example, the total apparent loss of time amounted to fourteen working days. Allowing that these figures are of only relative value inasmuch as they reflect a mechanical computation, it can be seen, nevertheless, that the duration of regular sessions could be effectively reduced if meetings were held more closely on schedule.

50. Early adjournment of meetings, and the late cancellation of others, frequently occur owing to a lack of speakers on the item which is being considered in a Main Committee. These situations could often be avoided by the inclusion of more than one item in the Committee's daily agenda; representatives would then be in a position, when necessary, to leave one item temporarily and pass to the discussion of another without interrupting the schedule of meetings.

XIV. Continuing Review of the Question

52. The General Assembly will, no doubt, continue to adapt its methods to meet changing needs and new requirements; its procedures also will develop in the light of its own experience. The Special Committee believes that this process should be kept under review and that Member States and the Secretary-General should be encouraged to submit proposals on the matter at such times as they may deem it appropriate.

INDEX